"A significant fresh contribution to the vast litera___ ___ican II, shaped by four distinguished scholars deeply committed to the historiography and ecclesial reception of the council. Its freshness is in going beyond such concerns to ask after the lacunae in the council's focus, narration, and implementation, and what it means to bring its trajectories into conversation with the crises, concerns, and possibilities of today's Catholic Church in diverse global contexts. Its significance lies not just in the stimulating set of studies it gathers together but in the direction and character of the conversation it opens."

—Paul D. Murray, professor of systematic theology, Durham University

"This welcome collection aims to bridge the distance between Vatican II and the diverse contexts in which the council unfolded and continues to be received. The essays engage critically with the council as part of the church's living tradition, which contributes to pastoral, ethical, and ecclesiological questions while also being notably, even disastrously, silent on issues the church continues to face today. The volume insightfully highlights the need to learn from Vatican II's contributions as well as its lacunae in the hope of responding more actively to concerns such as racism, colonialism, sexual abuse, and misogyny in the church and world today."

—Amanda C. Osheim, PhD, professor of practical theology, Loras College

"Vatican II didn't quite join all the dots of its teaching; nor could it have anticipated the crises and new perspectives that have emerged during its reception. But it did give its receivers some direction on how to do so, especially by reading the signs of the times. This book acknowledges that, like every general council of the church, Vatican II's interpretation and adaptation in new contexts requires honest attention to its shortcomings and postconciliar challenges, by attending to the overall vision of the council. This book presents an important advance in Vatican II research."

—Rev. Dr. Ormond Rush, associate professor, Australian Catholic University

The Legacy and Limits of Vatican II in an Age of Crisis

Edited by

Catherine E. Clifford, Kristin M. Colberg, Massimo Faggioli,
and Edward P. Hahnenberg

**LITURGICAL PRESS
ACADEMIC**

Collegeville, Minnesota
litpress.org

Cover photo by Jeremy Bishop on Unsplash.

Scripture quotations are from New Revised Standard Version Bible: Catholic Edition © 1989, 1993 National Council of the Churches of Christ in the United States of America. Used by permission. All rights reserved worldwide.

© 2025 by Catherine E. Clifford, Kristin M. Colberg, Massimo Faggioli, and Edward P. Hahnenberg

Published by Liturgical Press, Collegeville, Minnesota. All rights reserved. No part of this book may be used or reproduced in any manner whatsoever, except brief quotations in reviews, without written permission of Liturgical Press, Saint John's Abbey, PO Box 7500, Collegeville, MN 56321-7500.

Library of Congress Cataloging-in-Publication Data

Names: Clifford, Catherine E., 1958- editor. | Colberg, Kristin, editor. | Faggioli, Massimo, editor. | Hahnenberg, Edward P., editor.
Title: The legacy and limits of Vatican II in an age of crisis / edited by Catherine E. Clifford, Kristin M. Colberg, Massimo Faggioli, and Edward P. Hahnenberg.
Description: Collegeville : Liturgical Press Academic, [2025] | Includes bibliographical references and index. | Summary: "Through historical and theological lenses, the contributors to The Legacy and Limits of Vatican II in an Age of Crisis aim to rediscover forgotten voices and overlooked moments of Vatican II. The contributors offer readers insights on the council's teaching related to the sexual abuse crisis, antiracism, politics, the Synod on Synodality, and much more. By reexamining the teaching of Vatican II from the perspective of our present ecclesial crisis, readers will have a better understanding of how its legacy and limits affect the ongoing reform of the church in a much-changed theological, ecclesial, and social landscape"— Provided by publisher.
Identifiers: LCCN 2024054396 (print) | LCCN 2024054397 (ebook) | ISBN 9780814689288 (trade paperback) | ISBN 9780814689295 (epub) | ISBN 9780814689301 (pdf)
Subjects: LCSH: Vatican Council (2nd : 1962-1965 : Basilica di San Pietro in Vaticano)
Classification: LCC BX830 1962 .L423 2025 (print) | LCC BX830 1962 (ebook) | DDC 262/.52—dc23/eng/20250110
LC record available at https://lccn.loc.gov/2024054396
LC ebook record available at https://lccn.loc.gov/2024054397

Contents

Introduction: Legacy and Limits of Vatican II in Our Present Ecclesial Crisis   ix
   Catherine E. Clifford, Kristin M. Colberg, Massimo Faggioli, Edward P. Hahnenberg

Part One: Hermeneutics of the Council in an Age of Crisis

Chapter 1: A Further Reception of Vatican II: Interim Report from the Synod on Synodality   3
   Catherine E. Clifford

Chapter 2. The "Spirit of Vatican II" and the Legacy of the Council Today   21
   Martin Madar

Chapter 3. Integralism and the Reception(s) of *Dignitatis Humanae*   37
   Daniel A. Rober

Chapter 4. *Lumen Gentium* and Doctrinal Ambivalence: Abel and the Interpretative Task of Filling the Gaps   53
   Florian Klug

Chapter 5. A Unity Beyond the Human? Legacy and Limits of Vatican II in an Age of Ecological Crisis   73
   William G. Kuncken

Part Two: Contemporary Crises and the Limits of Vatican II

Sexual Abuse

Chapter 6. Vatican II's Silence on Child Sex Abuse: Challenges and Limits of a "Pastoral" Agenda   93
   Agnès Desmazières

Chapter 7. The Limits and Legacy of Vatican II's Teaching on Priesthood: The Bishops' Responses to Clerical Sexual Abuse in Australia   109
    Josephine Laffin

Chapter 8. Jointly Committed: Examining the Sexual Abuse Scandal as a Case of Institutional Vice in Post-Vatican II Catholicism   129
    Bernard G. Prusak

Sexism

Chapter 9. Glorified and Liberated? Toward a Feminist Ecclesiology of Vatican II   147
    Mary Kate Holman

Chapter 10. The "Synodal Process" and the North American Reception of Vatican II on Women in the Church   163
    Theresa Gardner

Racism and Colonialism

Chapter 11. Disrupting the Idolatry of Blood: Catholic Antiracism as a Necessary Expression of the Council's Renewed Soteriology   181
    Jaisy A. Joseph

Chapter 12. Conciliar, Postconciliar, and Postcolonial: Vatican II, Paul VI, and the Church in South Vietnam   201
    Tuan Hoang

Chapter 13. Vatican II and Caste in Postcolonial India: Brahminization of the Catholic Church or Catholicization of Brahminical Power?   219
    Evgeniia Muzychenko

Chapter 14. Vatican II and the African Catholic Church: A Decolonial Critique   235
    William I. Orbih

Chapter 15. Becoming Antiracist: Post-Vatican II Catholicism and the "Sin of Racism"   253
    Matteo Caponi

Part Three: Ecclesial Responses

Chapter 16. Discerning Disciples: Lay Agency Sixty Years After Vatican II   275
> *Edward P. Hahnenberg*

Chapter 17. Catholic Higher Education at Our Lord's Tomb: Toward a Pedagogy of Holy Saturday in Our Age of Contempt   295
> *Timothy Hanchin*

About the Authors   313

Index of Names   317

Introduction

Legacy and Limits of Vatican II in Our Present Ecclesial Crisis

Catherine E. Clifford, Kristin M. Colberg, Massimo Faggioli, Edward P. Hahnenberg

The chapters published in this volume are an elaboration of papers presented at the conference "The Legacy and Limits of Vatican II in an Age of Crisis: Gender, Race, Abuse, and the Living Catholic Tradition," held at Villanova University from November 30 to December 2, 2023.

More than a celebration or commemoration of the Second Vatican Council, this conference intended to contribute to a new phase in the research on Vatican II, one that reflects both a broader awareness of the global dimensions of Catholicism and a deeper confrontation with the challenges facing local churches. This new phase of scholarly reception has been made possible, in part, by the "fresh eyes" Pope Francis has brought to the hermeneutics of the council. In opening the synodal process in 2021, Pope Francis reminded the church that the Second Vatican Council was itself an event of synodality *ante litteram*. Vatican II not only gathered bishops and cardinals to Rome, but it also engaged—directly and indirectly, often in an initial or hesitant way—a range of participants that would be difficult to imagine from the perspective of the council's predecessors Vatican I or Trent. Included in the worldwide event of Vatican II were parish priests and women religious, lay men and lay women, ecumenical observers, representatives from other religions, political leaders, and secular commentators—all of whom "took part" in the event, even if they did not debate in the council hall or sign the final documents. In 1965, to concretize a new awareness of collaboration between the world's episcopate and the bishop of Rome in the ongoing governance of the Catholic Church, Pope Paul VI established a new international ecclesial structure known as the Synod of Bishops. In important ways, the ongoing Synod on Synodality is a continuation of the trajectory of Vatican II into the third millennium, extending across a much-changed theological, ecclesial, and social landscape.

However, just as the synodal process reminds us of the legacy of the Second Vatican Council, it has also highlighted some of its limits. Discussions in and around the Synod on Synodality have surfaced widespread concern about the failures of the postconciliar church to embody the vision of Vatican II. These include the failure to implement structures of meaningful consultation and collaboration; to reconfigure ministries and to incorporate women into positions of leadership; to address root causes of the sexual abuse crisis; to accompany those on the peripheries and to interrogate the structures of racism, sexism, and colonialism that serve to marginalize them; to overcome polarization within the church and to overcome passivity on the part of the people of God, who are called by their baptism to be agents of the Gospel and missionary disciples in the world.

Vatican II did not anticipate our contemporary challenges, nor do its documents provide specific guidelines or step-by-step instructions for addressing them. But that does not make the council irrelevant. As a touchstone of the church's magisterial tradition, the Second Vatican Council remains foundational for the life and mission of the Catholic Church today. However, like any monument of the tradition, the council requires ongoing investigation, critical analysis, and constant reconsideration from a diversity of contemporary perspectives if it is going to contribute to the *living* tradition of the church. Until recently, the council has been studied as a pageant of great men—mostly white men—with only minor roles granted to women, who briefly stepped out from the wings or worked quietly behind the scenes. There is a richer history to be told and a richer theology to inspire our work.

The thesis of this volume is that a renewed approach to the critical study of the event and the documents of Vatican II is necessary for responding to the challenges facing the church today. There is no future that leaves the council behind. But the church cannot simply repeat the words of the council as if nothing has changed over the past sixty years. The pastoral and scholarly reception of Vatican II remains unfinished. *Historically*, we need to rediscover forgotten voices and overlooked moments that belong to the event of Vatican II and that today have something important to say. *Theologically*, we need to reexamine the teaching of Vatican II from the vantage point of our present ecclesial crisis. Indirectly, this book makes a case for the essential role of Catholic theology in advancing the ongoing reform of the church, which the council taught is "always in need of purification . . . and renewal."[1]

Three commitments drive the essays in this volume, illustrating what a renewed critical study of the council strives to do. First, in order to avoid the same conclusions that would come by simply retracing the steps of those great commentators and scholars of the council—primarily, though not exclusively, European—whose scholarship remains foundational, a new approach must build on this work in a genuinely global way, including a diversity of voices and scholarly perspectives. Second, in order to avoid offering up an uncritical encomium to the council, a new approach must attend to the limits and lacunae of Vatican II. It must point out those places where the council fell short in addressing the problems of its time or could not anticipate the problems of our day. Finally, a renewed approach to the study of the council must adopt a hermeneutical horizon that includes the reception of the council as key to understanding it. In other words, we need to attend to the development *of* the council *after* the council. On some issues, this postconciliar evolution is widely acknowledged as a faithful reception of the council's teaching. One thinks, for example, of the implementation of *Sacrosanctum Concilium* through Pope Paul VI's liturgical reforms or the development of *Nostra Aetate* through the bold interreligious initiatives of Pope John Paul II or the expansion of *Ad Gentes* through the "missionary option" of Pope Francis. However, on many other issues, the council's teaching remains frozen in amber—admired on the shelf but not brought to life in the church.

In short, this volume strives to continue the twofold dynamic of *ressourcement* and *aggiornamento* that constitutes one of the most important legacies of the Second Vatican Council. We need to return to the sources of the Christian tradition, beginning with Scripture and tradition and

---

1. Second Vatican Council, Dogmatic Constitution on the Church *Lumen Gentium*, November 21, 1964, no. 8, in Austin Flannery, ed., *Vatican Council II: Constitutions, Decrees, Declarations; A Completely Revised Translation in Inclusive Language* (Liturgical Press, 2014). See also Second Vatican Council, Decree on Ecumenism *Unitatis Redintegratio*, nos. 4, 6.

continuing through Vatican II, which is itself a classic of this tradition that needs constant recovery. At the same time, we need to continually update our theologies and structures as the people of God live out their faith in a multicultural and global church. Both dynamics are necessary. In any faithful reception of the council, they cannot be taken in isolation from one another.

The Legacy and Limits of Vatican II in an Age of Crisis is made up of three parts. Part one, "Hermeneutics of the Council in an Age of Crisis," begins with Catherine Clifford's interim report from the Synod of Synodality, where she served as an official delegate. The chapters by Madar, Rober, Klug, and Kuncken provide an assessment of the vitality of key Vatican II documents and the need to reassess them in light of our ecclesial and political context, sixty years after the council.

Part two, "Contemporary Crises and the Limits of Vatican II," consists of three sections. The chapters by Desmazières, Laffin, and Prusak address the failures of the conciliar and postconciliar church to address the scandal of sexual abuse. The chapters by Holman and Gardner examine efforts to confront sexism in the church by surveying the terrain stretching from early postconciliar feminist theology to women's participation at the Synod on Synodality. The chapters by Joseph, Hoang, Muzychenko, Orbih, and Caponi, which constitute the third section, address racism and colonialism by revisiting Vatican II from contexts other than the Euro-American.

Part three of the volume considers "Ecclesial Responses" to an age of crisis. Chapters by Hahnenberg and Hanchin develop an analysis of the possibilities for lay agency in the church's contemporary efforts at evangelization and education.

A final word of thanks to those who have supported the conference and this publication. At Villanova University, we thank the Office of the President, Rev. Fr. Peter M. Donohue, OSA; the College for Liberal Arts and Sciences; the Theology and Religious Studies Department; the Office for Mission and Ministry; the Anne Welsh McNulty Institute for Women's Leadership; the Ethics Program; and the Office for Diversity, Equity and Inclusion. Our thanks go to the Raskob Foundation and the GHR Foundation for their generous support of Vatican II research at Villanova. We are indebted to the editorial team at Liturgical Press, particularly to the excellent work of Barry Hudock and Stephanie Lancour. Hans Christoffersen accepted this project with enthusiasm, reflecting the long-standing commitment of Liturgical Press to fostering an approach to the theology of the Second Vatican Council marked by intellectual rigor and a profound *sensus ecclesiae*. For this, we are grateful.

September 15, 2024

Catherine Clifford
Kristin Colberg
Massimo Faggioli
Edward P. Hahnenberg

Part 1

Hermeneutics of the Council in an Age of Crisis

Chapter 1

A Further Reception of Vatican II

Interim Report from the Synod on Synodality

Catherine E. Clifford

I have been invited to offer a few reflections from my perspective as a delegate from North America at the first session of the 16th Ordinary General Assembly of the Synod of Bishops on the theme "For a Synodal Church: Communion, Participation, Mission." I write these lines during the "intersession," the space following the first session, which met October 4–29, 2023, and in preparation for the second and final session, which will meet in October 2024. It is quite appropriate to consider the evolving shape of the international synod and the present synodal process as we focus on "The Legacy and Limits of Vatican II in An Age of Crisis."

The Experience of the Synod on Synodality

As we gathered in Rome, synod participants were deeply aware of the multiple crises confronting the human community today and of the many hard questions facing the church. The first session of the general assembly convened just days before the outbreak of war in the Holy Land. Synod participants had come from Ukraine, Sudan, Myanmar, the Democratic Republic of the Congo, Nicaragua, and the Amazon region. We were, therefore, deeply mindful of the suffering of the peoples in these and many other contexts. During our month-long meeting, we took time to fast and pray for peace, for the millions who experience forced migration due to state-sponsored violence and the effects of the climate crisis. We gathered in the deep awareness of the crisis of confidence in the church caused by clergy sexual abuse and its cover-up by church leaders. In many contexts, the specter of a systemic abuse of power has given rise to a lack of credibility in the church's witness and has been met by a massive exodus. Thus, delegates entered the synod process with an inner attitude of humility and of ecclesial repentance.

The Synthesis Report approved by the synod, *A Synodal Church in Mission*, reflects the first session of the assembly's effort to discern the many issues and priorities that emerged from our consideration of the results of phase one of the synod—a worldwide process of listening that represents what may be the largest consultation in human history. The report frames the experience of the synodal process as "a true act of further reception of the Council, prolonging its inspiration and reinvigorating its prophetic force for today's world."[1] Synod delegates view the commitment to become a more synodal church as the product of a deepening understanding of the church that the Second Vatican Council presents as both a mystery of communion and the people of God.

It would be impossible in this short space to examine in detail the complex forty-page Synthesis Report and its eighty-one recommendations for the renewal and reform of practices, structures, and ministries in order to better express the co-responsibility of all the baptized faithful for the life and mission of the church, including their participation in the discernment of how we are called to serve the human community today, especially the poor. Because the Synod on Synodality is still underway at this writing, it would be premature to judge these early results. Instead, it is more valuable to reflect on the process, the experience, the ecclesial event of the synod. The purpose of this particular synod is to help the whole church to become more synodal—in short, to learn how to practice synodality in a manner that might engage all the baptized in a shared listening to the voice of God. The general assembly itself was styled as an experience of learning, an apprenticeship in the practice of communal discernment, more than a parliamentary debate.

I would like to underline three essential dimensions of the synodal assembly that, while deeply rooted in the tradition of the church, highlight

---

1. XVI Ordinary General Assembly of the Synod of Bishops, Synthesis Report, *A Synodal Church in Mission*, October 28, 2023, Introduction, https://www.synod.va/content/dam/synod/assembly/synthesis/english/2023.10.28-ENG-Synthesis-Report_IMP.pdf (hereafter, SR, with paragraph numbering [pages are unnumbered]).

the apparent novelty of this gathering. First, to understand fully what we have experienced, the synod must be understood as a moment of the church at prayer and as the gathering of a community nourished by the word of God. Second, the physical setting and the process of spiritual conversation were intended to help us rediscover and model the essential dignity and equality of all the baptized faithful. And third, through its broad consultative process, the delegates of the general assembly of the synod are attending to and discerning the wisdom that resides in the living faith of the local churches in a renewed experience of catholicity. The fruits of the first session are being carried into the second and are reflected especially in the July 9, 2024, *Instrumentum Laboris* for the second session of the assembly, How *to Be a Missionary Synodal Church*.[2]

An Ecclesial Event in the Context of Prayer

Christians have always understood the gathering of the church or its representatives at important moments in councils or synods to be intensive moments for receiving and reflecting on the word of God. This fact is symbolized in the presence of the Book of the Gospels that was enthroned at the center of the synod assembly. The entire month of our gathering and working together in the Synod on Synodality was framed by moments of prayer as the Book of the Gospels stood in our midst. The work of the synodal assembly was preceded by an ecumenical prayer vigil which took place on September 30, 2023, in Saint Peter's Square. Thanks to the initiative of the Taizé community, young people from many countries prepared a series of meditations and intercessions for the world in a celebration over which Pope Francis presided, together with the heads of all the Christian world communions. During the long silence that followed the proclamation of the gospel reading, we felt the weight of the moment and of the task before us. This liturgy symbolized in many respects the fact that the synodal reform of the Catholic Church today has profound implications for all Christians and for the future of Christian unity.

Pope Francis referred to synodality for the first time very early in his pontificate, most notably in the remarkable interview with Father Antonio

---

2. XVI Ordinary General Assembly of the Synod of Bishops, *Instrumentum Laboris* for the Second Session, How *to Be a Missionary Synodal Church*, July 9, 2024, https://www.synod.va/content/dam/synod/assembly2024/il/pdf/ENG---Instrumentum-laboris-2.pdf.

Spadaro in the summer of 2013 concerning the priorities of his pontificate.³ When conversation turned to the importance of ecumenism, Pope Francis indicated that he had been reading the recent work of the Joint Orthodox-Catholic Theological Commission, the "Ravenna Document" (2007), which studied the theme of conciliarity or synodality.⁴ He observed that Eastern Churches have kept alive the practice of synodality and that this is something that the Catholic Church might learn and receive from other Christians. Francis echoed this observation several months later in his apostolic exhortation on the joy of the Gospel, *Evangelii Gaudium*:

> How many important things unite us! If we really believe in the abundantly free working of the Holy Spirit, we can learn so much from one another! It is not just about being better informed about others, but rather about reaping what the Spirit has sown in them, which is also meant to be a gift for us. To give but one example, in the dialogue with our Orthodox brothers and sisters, we Catholics have the opportunity to learn more about the meaning of episcopal collegiality and their experience of synodality. Through an exchange of gifts, the Spirit can lead us ever more fully into truth and goodness.⁵

Thus, one might consider our present synodal adventure as the mature fruit of a half-century of dialogue with other Christians concerning the exercise of authority in the life of the church. Other Christian churches are also facing important challenges today. Their structures of communion, of church governance and decision-making, are under tremendous stress. They, too, are interested in and keen to learn from the Catholic

---

3. Antonio Spadaro, "A Big Heart Open to God: An Interview with Pope Francis," *America*, September 30, 2013.

4. Joint International Commission for Theological Dialogue between the Catholic Church and the Orthodox Church, "Ecclesiological and Canonical Consequences of the Sacramental Nature of the Church: Ecclesial Communion, Conciliarity and Authority," October 13, 2007, http://www.christianunity.va/content/unitacristiani/en/dialoghi/sezione-orientale/chiese-ortodosse-di-tradizione-bizantina/commissione-mista-internazionale-per-il-dialogo-teologico-tra-la/documenti-di-dialogo/testo-in-inglese.html.

5. Pope Francis, Post-synodal Apostolic Exhortation *Evangelii Gaudium*, November 24, 2013, no. 246, https://www.vatican.va/content/francesco/en/apost_exhortations/documents/papa-francesco_esortazione-ap_20131124_evangelii-gaudium.html (hereafter, EG).

experiment in synodal discernment and decision-making.⁶ Fraternal delegates from many Christian world communions were present throughout the assembly and contributed to our discussions in meaningful ways.

The ecumenical prayer vigil was followed by an intense time of prayer and shared reflection as synod delegates spent three days in a retreat center outside the city of Rome. Participants were challenged and called to task by the messages of Timothy Radcliffe, OP, who reflected with us on the Gospel message and the meaning of synodality.⁷ He helped us to see how patiently Jesus accompanied his disciples in their incomprehension and slowness to believe. We, like them, were embarking upon a long apprenticeship in what it means to listen like disciples. These messages and other biblical meditations were an encouragement and stayed with us when we were later confronted with complex issues, tensions, and divergent views, where we did not see a path forward. In the context of the retreat, delegates began to experiment and to practice the style of spiritual conversation in small groups that would characterize our work in the weeks that followed.

The month-long schedule of the synodal assembly was broken down into five stages or modules. Each began with a common eucharistic liturgy in Saint Peter's Basilica, followed by a morning of biblical reflections, spiritual exhortation, input from the theological advisors, and the witness of synod delegates from around the globe—all of which served to focus our attention on the task at hand. The liturgies were celebrated in different languages and reflected the different cultures and liturgical traditions of East and West. Each day began with an invocation of the Holy Spirit and morning prayer. Conversation in small groups and interventions in the plenary were punctuated with moments of silent reflection and prayer. This climate of prayer was a constant reminder that we had not come to debate ideas or to win others over to our point of view but to listen

---

6. For a contemporary example of a bilateral dialogue that attempts to put into practice this methodology of "receptive ecumenism," with particular attention to the structures of communion in each communion, see Anglican-Roman Catholic International Commission (ARCIC III), *Walking Together on the Way: Learning to Be the Church—Local, Regional, Universal* (SPCK, 2018), 30 (no. 80), http://www.christianunity.va/content/unitacristiani/en/dialoghi/sezione-occidentale/comunione-anglicana/dialogo/arcic-iii/arcic-iii---documents/2018-walking-together-on-the-way.html.

7. Timothy Radcliffe, *Listening Together: Meditations on Synodality* (Liturgical Press, 2024).

attentively to what the Spirit is doing in the lived reality of the diverse local churches. At each stage in the process, we asked: What is needed for the church to be more responsive to the true needs of evangelization today? How can we mobilize the gifts of all the baptized faithful and give a more effective and authentic witness to the Gospel? This style of shared discernment, which is deeply influenced by the experience of small Christian communities and the praxis-based approach of liberation theologies, is something that we hope might come to characterize the way local churches and decision-making bodies at every level of ecclesial life might operate going forward.

A Process for Sharing the Gifts of All the Faithful

In a simple but revolutionary move, synod delegates sat at round tables: patriarchs, cardinals, bishops, deacons, priests, religious and lay persons, men and women, young and old. Each participant had the same opportunity to speak in the small groups or to intervene in the plenary sessions. Interventions were limited to three minutes. Others listened without judgment, without interrupting or reacting. Participants were then invited to ponder in silence what they had heard. What was the Spirit asking as we listened together on the lived experience of local faith communities? The physical setting and the process of spiritual conversation where non-bishops acted as facilitators was a radical departure from the style of any previous synod.

The practice of spiritual conversation is, by design, one where no single voice can dominate, where all are obliged to listen. In 2015, on the fiftieth anniversary of the institution of the Synod of Bishops, Pope Francis aptly characterized a synodal church as one that listens: "It is a mutual listening," he said, "in which everyone has something to learn. The faithful people, the college of bishops, the Bishop of Rome: all listening to each other, and all listening to the Holy Spirit, the 'Spirit of Truth' (Jn 14:17), in order to know what he 'says to the churches' (Rev 2:7)."[8] The practice of conversation in the Spirit is designed to foster a climate and culture of

---

8. Pope Francis, "Ceremony Commemorating the 50th Anniversary of the Institution of the Synod of Bishops: Address of His Holiness Pope Francis," October 17, 2015, https://www.vatican.va/content/francesco/en/speeches/2015/october/documents/papa-francesco_20151017_50-anniversario-sinodo.html.

respectful listening, even to those with whom we disagree. Previous synodal gatherings were held in a synod hall where bishops were seated theater-style in order of rank and seniority. Those of higher rank were given priority when it came time to address the assembly. The dynamic was more one of speech-making or of debating ideas and principles. While the bishops worked in small language groups for a part of the time at previous synods, at this meeting, delegates remained with small language groups at every stage of the process. This dynamic fostered the nurturing of relationships. As the synod advanced from week to week, delegates grew together as a community.

Pope Francis has challenged the whole Catholic Church to recover a fundamental insight of the early church, that discernment and decision-making in matters that concern the life and mission of the church is not the sole responsibility of the bishops. In its teaching on the laity, Vatican II's Dogmatic Constitution on the Church, *Lumen Gentium*, noted that thanks to their participation in the prophetic office of Christ, the Gospel is proclaimed "not only through the hierarchy who teach in his name and by his power, but also through the laity. He accordingly both establishes them as witnesses and provides them with an appreciation of the faith (*sensus fidei*) and the grace of the word (see Acts 2:17-18; Apoc 19:10) so that the power of the Gospel may shine out in daily family and social life."[9] For this reason, the council teaches that bishops must take counsel and "willingly" follow the "prudent advice" of experienced and competent lay persons in order to arrive at sound decisions "in spiritual and in temporal matters" that will enable the church to fulfill its mission with greater effect (LG 37).

The bishops, then, cannot properly exercise their pastoral teaching office in isolation from the competencies and charisms of all the baptized faithful. Rather, they must be attentive to the voice of God speaking in and through the community of all the baptized. To serve a synodal church, a wise pastor must develop good listening skills. At the same time, lay persons, far from remaining passive recipients of clerical ministrations, have an essential responsibility to express their views in matters pertaining

---

9. Second Vatican Council, Dogmatic Constitution on the Church *Lumen Gentium*, November 21, 1964, no. 35 (hereafter, LG). All quotations of Vatican II documents are from Austin Flannery, ed., *Vatican Council II: Constitutions, Decrees, Declarations; A Completely Revised Translation in Inclusive Language* (Liturgical Press, 2014).

to the good of the church, sharing their "knowledge, competence or authority" each according to their unique gifts, for the good of all (LG 37). They must learn to speak with integrity and humility and find meaningful ways of contributing to the common search for what is good and true, as together we seek to advance the cause of the Gospel. When this pooling of many gifts and the wisdom of the whole community is realized, it becomes easier to build consensus and a shared sense of responsibility. Processes of decision-making are more effective.

In his 2018 apostolic constitution *Episcopalis Communio*, which represents an important updating of procedures for the international Synod of Bishops, Francis made the consultation of the people of God in each local church prior to any gathering of the international synod an essential feature of the synodal process. Pope Paul VI had established the synod in 1965, in response to the request of the council fathers and as a concrete expression of the collegiality of bishops in the universal church. Pope Francis has sought to improve its structures and practices to better serve the needs of the global church in our time so that it might become a more effective forum for "dialogue and cooperation among Bishops themselves and between them and the Bishop of Rome."[10] While bishops are called to service and to preside over the life of the local church, responsibility for the mission of the church resides with all the baptized—a traditional insight that the Second Vatican Council set before us in its understanding of the church as a communion of all those incorporated into Christ through the sacraments of Christian initiation.

To signify the link between the consultation of the people of God in each place and the bishops—who represent the local churches (see LG 23)—gathered in synod, Pope Francis has created the possibility for the full participation of seventy non-episcopal delegates to the synod from every continent with speaking and voting rights. Some have questioned the novelty of both the consultation process and the inclusion of non-episcopal delegates, fearing that these moves might undermine the authoritative role of the bishops. As Timothy Radcliffe put it to the delegates in their pre-synodal retreat, there are "multiple" and "mutually enhanc-

---

10. Pope Francis, Apostolic Constitution *Episcopalis Communio*, September 15, 2018, https://www.vatican.va/content/francesco/en/apost_constitutions/documents/papa-francesco_costituzione-ap_20180915_episcopalis-communio.html.

ing" authorities in the church. If we are to truly enter into the dynamics of synodality, "there need be no competition, as if the laity can only have more authority if the bishops have less, or that the so-called conservatives compete for authority with the progressives." Further, he observes, in our highly polarized world, Christians are called to model another way of exercising authority, of speaking, discerning, decision-making, and living together. "We shall speak with authority to our lost world if in the synod we transcend competitive ways of existing and talking."[11] There is no place for zero-sum games in the life of the church when we take seriously the dignity of all the baptized faithful.

The Synthesis Report of 2023 expresses the important role of non-episcopal delegates by saying, "Lay people, religious, priests and deacons were . . . witnesses of a process that intends to involve the whole church and everyone in the church" (SR Introduction). These delegates were nominated because they contributed in important ways to the consultation that took place in the local churches. In many ways, their responsibility was to ensure that the concerns of the local churches continued to be heard and to symbolize the link between the synodal assembly and the broad consultation that preceded it—the fruits of which formed the basis of the *Instrumentum Laboris* for the first session. Listening to the simple faith of ordinary Christians and relying on the competencies, gifts, and charisms of the non-ordained faithful takes nothing away from the authority that is proper to the episcopal office. All ministry exists to support the flourishing of the baptismal priesthood as the faithful following of Christ,[12] the offering of lives in service to others and proclaiming the love of God wherever they live.

Many bishops who may have had misgivings at the outset of our gathering, including concerns regarding the process or the diversity of delegates,

---

11. Radcliffe, *Listening Together*, 62.

12. "The ministerial or hierarchical priesthood of bishops and priests, and the common priesthood of all the faithful participate, 'each in its own proper way, in the one priesthood of Christ.' While being 'ordered one to another,' they differ essentially [LG 10]. In what sense? While the common priesthood of the faithful is exercised by the unfolding of baptismal grace—a life of faith, hope, and charity, a life according to the Spirit—the ministerial priesthood is at the service of the common priesthood. It is directed at the unfolding of the baptismal grace of all Christians." *Catechism of the Catholic Church*, 2nd ed., 1997, no. 1547, https://www.vatican.va/archive/ENG0015/__P4T.HTM.

were in fact changed by the process. As we entered more deeply into the work of the synod, they began to relax, to see and understand its purpose. As we moved through the respective stages, we grew together as a community—meeting not only in the synod hall, but sharing time together over coffee, at meals and liturgies, and at the many events that took place outside the synod hall. This fruit—of growing together as a community—is just as important as the report summarizing the results of our reflections. Ultimately, this experience must bear fruit in the concrete life of the local churches when the synodal process concludes and each delegate returns to their home country.

Discernment and the Sense of the Faithful

It is essential to affirm that this renewed experience of synodality is not a "one-off." This historic four-year process is to be a starting point, a launching pad for a new and more lively experience of ecclesial life, a setting of the whole church on a new trajectory for the future. The aim of the Synod on Synodality is to enable this consultative and dialogical ethos to take root and become the *modus vivendi et operandi*,[13] the way of life and of operating at every level of ecclesial life going forward. There are significant theological grounds for doing so. The first is in the synodal nature of the church itself as a community of disciples or a pilgrim people united on the way. Pope Francis has recalled the principle that characterized the governance of the early church, that all the faithful have been anointed by the Spirit in baptism and continue to be guided by this Spirit as sharers in Christ's prophetic office. Thus, the medievals held that "*quod omnes tangit ab omnibus tractari debet*," which, translated loosely, requires that "anything affecting all members of the church ought to be considered and approved by all."[14] As the consultation process of the synod has revealed, Catholics have been slow to implement the necessary structures

---

13. This expression is used by the International Theological Commission in its 2018 study, *Synodality in the Life and Mission of the Church*, to describe the synodal nature of the whole church (nos. 6, 43, 70; cf. no. 30), https://www.vatican.va/roman_curia/congregations/cfaith/cti_documents/rc_cti_20180302_sinodalita_en.html.

14. See Pope Francis, "Ceremony Commemorating the Fiftieth Anniversary." The expression is also raised up in the ITC study, *Synodality in the Life and Mission of the Church*, no. 65.

and procedures needed to support this constant dialogue and mutual exchange. A fuller recovery of structures and practices for collective listening and discernment is essential to making this principle a concrete reality in the lives of all.

Pope Francis has repeatedly exhorted the bishops to attend to the sense of the faithful, the capacity for discerning the truth of the Gospel and the wisdom of the living faith that is borne by all the baptized assisted by the Holy Spirit. It is baptism that grounds the right of all the baptized to participate in the structures of discernment and decision-making in the life of the church (pastoral councils, local synods, and so on). His comments concerning the participation of the non-ordained faithful in the synodal process in the address delivered at the outset of the four-year synodal process are worth citing at length, for they capture the crux of the challenge before us.

> Participation is a requirement of the faith received in baptism. As the Apostle Paul says, "in the one Spirit we were all baptized into one body" (1 Cor 12:13). In the Church, everything starts with baptism. Baptism, the source of our life, gives rise to the equal dignity of the children of God, albeit in the diversity of ministries and charisms. Consequently, all the baptized are called to take part in the Church's life and mission. Without real participation by the People of God, talk about communion risks remaining a devout wish. In this regard, we have taken some steps forward, but a certain difficulty remains, and we must acknowledge the frustration and impatience felt by many pastoral workers, members of diocesan and parish consultative bodies and women, who frequently remain on the fringes. Enabling everyone to participate is an essential ecclesial duty! All the baptized, for baptism is our identity card.[15]

This insight into the synodal nature of the whole church is deeply rooted in Vatican II's teaching on the people of God (see LG chapter 2). The practice of synodality invites us to rediscover what we mean by the equal dignity of the baptized Christian faithful. To take root, the synod's more collaborative vision of the life and mission of the church must lead to a more convincing model of ministry as service, a more transparent

---

15. Pope Francis, "Address of His Holiness Pope Francis for the Opening of the Synod," October 9, 2021, https://www.vatican.va/content/francesco/en/speeches/2021/october/documents/20211009-apertura-camminosinodale.html.

and accountable exercise of leadership and authority (SR 11k; 12i and 12j).[16] Indeed, it can only enhance the pastoral character of the episcopal office. The inclusion of non-episcopal participants, the setting of round tables, and the dynamics of spiritual conversation challenge us to break down the clerical culture that has dominated in the dynamics of ecclesial life. They are practices that move us from the binary of clergy and laity toward a noncompetitive culture where we welcome the complementarity of vocations and charisms.

A central issue at every stage of consultation in the synodal process and in our exchanges during the synod has been the urgent need to create avenues for women. Women are often the principal agents of the church's proclamation and ministrations, yet their contributions are not always valued or recognized. Their participation has yet to be fully integrated in a stable and consequential manner into the church's structures of discernment and decision-making (SR 9). Women on every continent have shared their experience of being marginalized and undervalued, of being excluded from centers of theological education, experiencing forms of abuse and exploitation, or being denied a just wage.[17] The Second Vatican Council recognized women as autonomous and self-determining subjects created in the image and likeness of God and enjoying the same fundamental rights as men.[18] As baptized Christians, they were recognized as full ecclesial subjects, enjoying the right to share their concerns for the good of the church, to pursue theological education and to assume eccle-

---

16. While space does not permit the development of these points in detail here, the Synthesis Report from the first session of the synod devotes considerable space to proposals for revising existing models of formation for ordained and non-ordained ministries and revisioning the configuration of diverse ministries—episcopal (SR 12), presbyteral, diaconal (SR 11), and instituted lay ministries (SR 8)—and their integration in the local church. This highly complex set of issues includes the questions of married clergy (SR 11f) and of the restoration of women to the order of the diaconate (SR 11i).

17. Notably, this was the topic that received the most extensive consideration in the document summarizing the fruits of the consultation of the local churches at the continental stage of the synodal process. See Synod of Bishops, Working Document for the Continental Stage, *"Enlarge the Space of Your Tent"* (2022), esp. the section "Rethinking Women's Participation," nos. 60–65, https://www.synod.va/content/dam/synod/common/phases/continental-stage/dcs/Documento-Tappa-Continentale-EN.pdf.

18. See Second Vatican Council, Pastoral Constitution on the Church in the Modern World *Gaudium et Spes*, December 7, 1965, no. 29.

siastical offices (see LG 33-37). It is women who represent the majority of those lay persons who serve today in the variety of new ecclesial ministries to which these insights of Vatican II have given rise. Their substantial contribution has provoked calls for the restoration of women to the permanent order of the diaconate.

While the second session of the general assembly is unlikely to resolve the particular question of diaconal ministries, it remains an open question that must be considered within the broader context of the end of the model of the *cursus honorum*, which regarded all orders as stages on the way to the order of the presbyterate. Since the Second Vatican Council, we have been witnessing a substantial reconfiguration of ministries but have not yet arrived at a point where there is either theological clarity or the broad acceptance of the existence of a stable, diverse group of collaborative ministers, ordained and non-ordained, to meet the missional needs of the local church in each place. On the other hand, the synodal assembly must reflect on the full inclusion of women and the integration of their contributions in structures of discernment and decision-making at every level of ecclesial life. This, in turn, invites renewed reflection on the participation of the baptized faithful, women and men together, in church governance as flowing from their participation in the royal office of the Servant Christ.[19]

An Experience of Catholicity in a Global Church

The diversity of participants who had come from every corner of the world placed us before the true catholicity of the church. This diversity is both enriching and challenging. Listening to the lived experience of the diverse local churches helps us to understand more deeply that we will not always find a uniform or universal solution to the issues confronting Catholics in every context. In his reflections on the role of the synod, Pope Francis has been moving us away from an understanding of a synod as an instrument of the papacy and more toward seeing it as a space where the voices of the local churches can be heard.

---

19. I have attempted to explore the state of this question in greater detail in "Power and the Exercise of Authority in the Service of the People of God," *Studia Canonica* 58 (2024): 201-23.

This experience of listening and of collective discernment has given participants a deeper sense of the creativity of local churches as they seek to live the gospel in a wide variety of cultures and social contexts. It helps us to see the need for greater autonomy and freedom of initiative for the local churches and to appreciate the challenge of maintaining the bonds of communion in faith when variously expressed. The synod is a microcosm of a truly global Catholic Church. As we listen to the experience of the living faith among the diverse local churches, each with its own challenges and each seeking to inculturate the expression of the Gospel more deeply, we have come to see that "universal" or "one-size-fits-all" solutions will not do.

Pope Francis expressed this awareness in his apostolic exhortation on the joy of the Gospel following the synod on the new evangelization, when he recalled the words of Pope Paul VI concerning the interpretation of social realities in diverse contexts: "In the face of such widely varying situations, it is difficult for us to utter a unified message and to put forward a solution which has universal validity. This is not our ambition, nor is it our mission. It is up to the communities to analyze with objectivity the situation which is proper to their own country" (EG 184).[20] Recognizing the limits of the purview of the bishop of Rome and the importance of the proximity of the local bishops to their own people and context, Francis calls for increased autonomy with the necessary diversity implied: "It is not advisable for the Pope to take the place of the local Bishops in the discernment of every issue that arises in their territory. In this sense, I am conscious of the need to promote a sound 'decentralization'" (EG 16). The "bottom-up" approach of the present synodal process might be seen as an attempt to reverse the centrifugal dynamics of the past and to move to a more centripetal model, where the whole is enriched by the wisdom of the local churches.

Among the important portents of this new catholicity, we find an important invitation in the *Instrumentum Laboris* for the second session, How *to Be a Missionary Synodal Church*, to attend, not to prescriptive solutions that might be applied in every context, but rather to the estab-

---

20. See also Pope Paul VI, Apostolic Letter *Octogesima Adveniens*, May 14, 1971, no. 4, https://www.vatican.va/content/paul-vi/en/apost_letters/documents/hf_p-vi_apl_19710514_octogesima-adveniens.html.

lishment of a set of *criteria* that might be used to guide the implementation of new structures, practices, and ministries to serve the needs of the church and its mission in various contexts.

> The synodal process has repeatedly highlighted how the discernment and promotion of charisms and ministries, as well as the identification of the needs of communities and society to which they are intended to respond, is an aspect in which the local Churches need to grow, giving themselves adequate criteria, tools and procedures. The Second Vatican Council teaches that it is the task of pastors "to acknowledge their [the faithful's] ministries and their charisms, so that all may cooperate unanimously, each in her or his own way, in the common task" (LG 30). The discernment of charisms and ministries is a properly ecclesial act: in order to recognise and promote them, the bishop is obliged to listen to the voice of all those involved: individual faithful, communities, and participative bodies. To this end, procedures suitable to the different contexts must be identified, always taking care to make possible a real consensus on the criteria and outcomes of discernment.[21]
>
> The future will be characterized by greater differentiation in the expression of one faith. For this reason, agreement on the criteria for discernment and decision-making will be essential to the living out of a church characterized by diversity in communion.

As this citation of the *Instrumentum Laboris* of 2024 suggests, one of the places that we might expect to see greater freedom and diversity is in the ministries and their configuration within the life of the diverse local churches. When the bishops of the world were consulted concerning their priorities for shared reflection in the context of the international synod, they identified two major questions. First among them was the question of the priesthood, an indication that the present model of ordained priesthood and seminary formation is not meeting contemporary needs. In its

---

21. XVI General Assembly of the Synod of Bishops, *Instrumentum Laboris* for the Second Session, How *to Be a Missionary Synodal Church*, July 9, 2024, no. 31, https://www.usccb.org/resources/ENG-INSTRUMENTUM-LABORIS-A4%20(2024).pdf (hereafter, IL2). It is also noteworthy that among the ten study groups established in response to the synodal process is one dedicated to "theological criteria and synodical methodologies for shared discernment of controversial doctrinal, pastoral and ethical issues (SR 15)." See also IL2, no. 66.

reflections on the second priority, synodality, the present synodal process has given rise to an awareness that a truly synodal church, one that takes seriously the engagement of all the baptized in the discernment and missional engagement of the church, requires an entirely different style of leadership on the part of the ordained, one that is far more consultative and collaborative, one that embodies the constant dialectic between the cultic dimension of the church at prayer and its engagement with and for the world, holding in constant and creative tension the calls to *leiturgia*, *diakonia*, and *martyria* – prayer, service, and witness. It is, therefore, not surprising that the necessity of formation in a synodal key—for all Christians, but especially for those engaged in the public ministries of the church—is a recurring theme of the Synthesis Report of the first session and has given rise to the establishment of a study group to reexamine the *Ratio Fundamentalis* for seminary formation (see IL2, p. VI, note 6).

Conclusion

The present synodal process raises important questions for the guild of theologians as we reflect together on both the legacy and the limits of Vatican II. The Second Vatican Council was a privileged moment for the collaboration of theologians and bishops in the exercise of the pastoral teaching office. The present context invites us to ask what, precisely, is the place of theology and the contribution of the theological community within a synodal church. A remarkable effort has been made by the synod office to call upon the expertise of a broadly representative group of theologians and canonists, women and men, ordained, religious, and lay persons from every continent. At each new stage of reflection, a theologian chosen for his or her competency provided important orientations to the synodal delegates. Yet the group of consultants were only invited to reflect back to the synod delegates what they were hearing and observing in our conversations on one occasion. Some were disappointed not to see a more organic interaction.

Beyond the general assembly of the international synod, theologians should be asking themselves how the task of theology might be conducted in a more synodal way. How might they engage in a more intentional way in truly listening to the living faith of the people of God? Are they reading the signs of the times in solidarity with them, being attentive especially to those who suffer and are marginalized? Might theologians learn from the practice of conversation in the Spirit, a way of proceeding that takes more seriously the lived experience of grassroots communities as a source for theology? And might the members of the guild of theologians develop these same skills for respectful conversation and dialogue among themselves when disagreements or new questions arise? Might this form of dialogue be a starting point for repairing the sometimes-frayed relationships between theologians and members of the hierarchy? Might this style of conversation help us to discover that we are all, at bottom, interested above all in serving the people of God and equipping them to give a more faithful witness to the Gospel?

The synodal process itself needs deeper theological reflection. The Synthesis Report identifies several important areas in need of new theological reflection or clarification. Among the more pressing questions is how we might understand more deeply the synodal nature of the church. There is also need for deeper reflection on the theology of ministry, especially as this pertains to the diversity of ministries (episcopal, presbyteral, diaconal, instituted, and other non-ordained ministries) and their collaboration within the life of the local church. Here we come up against some of the limits of the teaching of Vatican II and the need for fresh scholarly research. The guiding question for the synodal conversion of the church is: What structures, practices, and forms of ministry will enable the church to faithfully proclaim the Gospel in today's world? The *how* of synodality, including the much-needed concrete structures and practices for mutual listening, shared discernment, and accountability, will be the particular focus of the second session of the general assembly.

Chapter 2

The "Spirit of Vatican II" and the Legacy of the Council Today

Martin Madar

Since the mid-1980s, the "spirit of Vatican II" has been an embattled concept in discussions pertaining to the council's reception. After the council, so-called progressive Catholics invoked this term to call for developments in the church that did not have direct support in the documents of Vatican II but which they thought were consistent with its spirit.[1] With the pontificate of John Paul II (1978–2013) and its effort to counteract the centrifugal forces unleashed by the council, the "spirit of Vatican II" came under heavy criticism as a legitimate category for understanding and implementing the council. By the end of Pope Benedict XVI's pontificate, the "spirit of Vatican II" was deemed a persona non grata. Since then, however, it has been revived and—to some extent—rehabilitated.[2] This has to do with a new phase of the council's reception inaugurated by Pope Francis.

For the past six decades, the Second Vatican Council has been an indispensable point of reference for the self-understanding of the Catholic

---

1. See M. Cathleen Kaveny, "The Spirit of Vatican II and Moral Theology: *Evangelium Vitae* as a Case Study," in *After Vatican II: Trajectories and Hermeneutics*, ed. James L. Heft (Eerdmans, 2012), 43–67.

2. See Martin Madar, "Pope Francis Has Revived the 'Spirit of Vatican II,'" *La Croix International*, June 12, 2023, https://international.la-croix.com/news/religion/pope-francis-has-revived-the-spirit-of-vatican-ii/17957.

Church and for addressing its pastoral needs. The council was a momentous occurrence, impacting the church more than any other event since the Protestant Reformation. In all its undertakings, Vatican II had a pastoral concern in mind. It wished to inject more evangelical vigor into the life of the church. It also desired the church to undergo renewal so that it might better fulfill its mission. The renewal that the council set in motion has given Catholicism its present historical form. The council transformed the church in ways that those who experienced pre-Vatican II Catholicism could hardly imagine. After sixty years of implementing the council, however, the Catholic Church finds itself at a crossroads. The question that looms over it is whether Vatican II still holds some unrealized promise or whether it should be retired somewhere on a shelf as an artifact that is now of interest only to historians. Positions on this question vary.

If one turns attention to Pope Francis, one gets a strong support for the continued reception of Vatican II. Synodality is a chief example of the pope's conviction that Vatican II still has something important to offer the church today. Francis, however, has faced enormous opposition from theological conservatives. Apart from frequent criticisms that he has not maintained the tradition faithfully, creating confusion among the faithful, Francis has been subject to fraternal correction from several cardinals and even accused of heresy. This is quite unprecedented in postconciliar history. Francis's critics not only oppose changes in pastoral practice that he has authorized but also seem to be against any change in the church at all. One can infer that their view of the council, which introduced so much change, cannot be very favorable. There are also those who understand that rejecting an ecumenical council creates more problems than it solves; therefore, they formally accept it. But they see Vatican II in such continuity with the tradition that very little of significance actually happened.[3] Some of the most extreme of the pope's conservative critics have now rejected the council.

---

3. It should be noted that some in the theologically conservative camp have defended the council during this time, but one gets a sense that in their view Francis's predecessors, especially John Paul II and Benedict XVI, provided the definitive interpretation of Vatican II and there is nothing more of significance in terms of its reception that still remains. See Matthew Levering, *An Introduction to Vatican II as an Ongoing Theological Event* (The Catholic University of America Press, 2017), Matthew Levering, ed., *The Word on Fire Vatican II Collection*, 2 vols. (Word on Fire Institute, 2021, 2023), George Weigel, *To Sanctify the World: The Vital Legacy of Vatican II* (Basic Books, 2022).

The complex state of the reception of Vatican II extends beyond this binary, however. One does not always find enthusiasm for Vatican II among theological progressives either, especially in the academy. The issue is not that the council is rejected but rather that it is not seen as relevant to the practitioners of race, gender, and post/decolonial discourses. The council is not seen as a fruitful conversation partner. One can gather that the reception of Vatican II is being put to the test more than ever before.

While being its strong supporter, my focus will not be on the continued reception of Vatican II in the sense of its implementation but on the council's legacy vis-à-vis the current pastoral challenges facing the church. Many of them are markedly different from those that the council addressed. This poses a challenge for the council's legacy. I will argue that from the perspective of a continued reading of the signs of the times and addressing them in light of the Gospel, the *spirit* of Vatican II is now more important than its *letter*.

At first hearing, this claim might be perceived as an attempt to rehash the debate about the "spirit" versus the "letter" of the council, for which there may be little interest. As will become clear, however, the claim at hand is not, strictly speaking, concerned with the reception of the council or the interpretation of its documents but rather with the council's relevance for addressing the pastoral challenges pressing upon the Catholic Church today. It is also not a matter of emphasizing the spirit and ignoring the letter. Rather, it is a matter of emphasis, as the "more" intends to communicate.

Defining the "Spirit of Vatican II"

The notion of the "letter" of Vatican II is straightforward. It designates the documents the council promulgated. We know their number and titles, and there are no disputes about what they say in Latin, their original language. This does not mean, of course, that there are no disagreements about their interpretation and meaning.

The referent of the "spirit" of Vatican II does not enjoy such clarity. The basic idea is that Vatican II was more than a printing house and that it cannot be reduced to its documents.[4] To get at this "more," scholars of Vatican II employ such concepts as *experience*, *event*, and the *spirit*. In

---

4. See Ormond Rush, *The Vision of Vatican II* (Liturgical Press, 2019), 9–11.

the course of the council's reception, especially after the 1985 extraordinary assembly of the Synod of Bishops, the "spirit of Vatican II" became enveloped in a controversy. Its legitimacy as a hermeneutical category became disputed and, in some circles, completely rejected. Given this fact, constructive discussion of the "spirit of Vatican II" requires that one provides its working definition.

Among the scholars of the council, one finds various understandings of what the "spirit of Vatican II" refers to. For Ormond Rush, it designates the "mind" of the council.[5] Joseph Komonchak understands the "spirit of Vatican II" as referring to the experience of the council, which designates all that happened at the council as lived by its participants, such as their "intentions, motives, encounters, decisions, and actions during the council."[6] John O'Malley understands the "spirit of Vatican II" as the overall orientation or thrust of the council that can be discerned in the style it adopted. Based firmly on the documents, "[the spirit of the council] cuts across [them] and is recoverable through an intertextual and intratextual approach."[7] The orientation that O'Malley has in mind is an overriding vision that transcends the particulars of the documents.[8] Otto Hermann Pesch defines the "spirit of Vatican II" as "the will of the overwhelming majority of the council Fathers that emerges from the official conciliar records and from the pre-history of the council, even where it became watered down and weakened in detail by objections and at times by unfair tricks of a small minority."[9] Hermann Pottmeyer understands the "spirit of Vatican II" as "an intellectual and spiritual impulse toward renewal that animated the work of the Council itself and that emanates from it."[10]

---

5. Ormond Rush, *Still Interpreting Vatican II* (Paulist Press, 2004), 26.

6. Joseph A. Komonchak, "Vatican II as an 'Event,'" *Theology Digest* 46, no. 4 (1999): 338, 341.

7. John W. O'Malley, *What Happened at Vatican II* (Harvard University Press, 2008), 310. See also O'Malley, "The Style of Vatican II," *America* 188, no. 6 (2003): 12–15, and "Vatican II: Did Anything Happen?," *Theological Studies* 67, no. 1 (2006): 17–31.

8. O'Malley, *What Happened at Vatican II*, 11, 52.

9. Otto Hermann Pesch, *Das Zweite Vatikanische Konzil: Vorgeschichte, Verlauf—Ergebnisse, Nachgeschichte* (Echter, 1993), 160.

10. Hermann J. Pottmeyer, "A New Phase in the Reception of Vatican II," in *The Reception of Vatican II*, ed. Giuseppe Alberigo, Jean-Pierre Jossua, and Joseph A. Komonchak (The Catholic University of America Press, 1987), 41.

While not rejecting any of these ways of understanding the "spirit of Vatican II," I will adopt Pottmeyer's definition. The impulse toward renewal is what the texts of Vatican II embodied and articulated. The impetus toward reform and renewal of the church is at the core of the council's guiding vision. One can discern it by studying the deliberations among the council participants and by examining the redactional history of the council's documents from their initial drafts to their final form.[11]

Furthermore, I understand the "spirit of Vatican II" as evoking the "liberating consolation of the Gospel."[12] I belong to a generation that had no firsthand knowledge of preconciliar Catholicism. Nor did my generation live through the enthusiasm that so many older Catholics experienced after learning about what the council taught in its documents. Everything I know about Catholicism before the council and about what happened at the council, comes from learning about it, especially from my teachers. They constructed the experience of the council for me. The "spirit" of the council is enshrined in that experience as a dynamic force rooted in the gospels and inviting the church to renew itself so that it can more effectively live its mission.

Lastly, I understand the "spirit of Vatican II" as evoking a sense of courage. Courage is one of the gifts of the Holy Spirit. Given the ecclesial climate of the preceding decades, it took courage to reject two preparatory schemas and demand that more than a neoscholastic theology be incorporated in them. I see this courage also in the *ressourcement* and *aggiornamento* that the bishops promoted and especially in the commitment to dialogue with other Christians, non-Christians, and others. It took courage not only to teach that tradition develops but to develop it so boldly at the time when the episcopal motto of the head of the Holy Office was *Semper Idem* ("always the same"). The courage that I speak of refers essentially to the conviction that the Holy Spirit is present to and guides every current generation just as much as it had guided those in the past.

---

11. See Peter De Mey, "Church Renewal and Reform in the Documents of Vatican II: History, Theology, Terminology," *The Jurist* 71, no. 2 (2011): 369–400.

12. Words used by Karl Rahner to express what he hoped the preliminary schemas for Vatican II would communicate. See Declan Marmion, "Karl Rahner, Vatican II, and the Shape of the Church," *Theological Studies* 78, no. 1 (2017): 29.

The "Spirit of Vatican II" and the Legacy of the Council

At the time Pope Benedict XVI resigned the papacy in February 2013, the reception of the Second Vatican Council seemed to be at a standstill. While the church leaders acknowledged that the council was a highly consequential event in recent history, one would only rarely hear them refer to Vatican II as being relevant for addressing current pastoral challenges. Many lamented that the enormous enthusiasm that once accompanied the council's implementation was a distant memory. Then Cardinal Jorge Mario Bergoglio succeeded Pope Benedict, and within a few months it became evident that Pope Francis was inaugurating a new phase in the council's reception. In contrast to the past few decades, however, this new phase, which we continue to witness, has been marked by a positive disposition toward the "spirit of Vatican II."[13] The tide has turned. As the late Richard Gaillardetz observed early in this pope's pontificate, "Francis wishes to release the council's bold ecclesial vision and deep-seated Gospel values from decades of captivity."[14] With his program of "synodality" and other pastoral initiatives, Francis has reengaged the centrifugal forces that the council unleashed.[15] The proponents of the council commend him for having the courage to do so.

The past ten years have shown that a full reception of Vatican II is far from realized. The ignorance and distortion of the council, even among those in positions of leadership in the church, is disappointing. Moreover, opposition to the council from some theologically conservative Catholics, especially in North America and parts of Europe, is a reason for concern. Sometimes it seems that almost sixty years since the council's closing, its reception among large segments of the faithful remains at a minimal level.

There is an urgent need for a greater reception of Vatican II. In this process, both the "letter" and the "spirit" should have their rightful place. While it is valid to distinguish between them, they should not be sepa-

---

13. See Rafael Luciani, *Pope Francis and the Theology of the People* (Orbis Books, 2017), 130.

14. Richard Gaillardetz, "Francis Wishes to Release Vatican II's Bold Vision from Captivity," *National Catholic Reporter*, September 25, 2013, https://www.ncronline.org/news/vatican/francis-wishes-release-vatican-iis-bold-vision-captivity.

15. See Michael Sean Winters, "Synod Is a Milestone in the Reception of Vatican II," *National Catholic Reporter*, October 30, 2023, https://www.ncronline.org/opinion/ncr-voices/synod-milestone-reception-vatican-ii.

rated, pitted against one another, or privileged at the expense of each other. The "letter" and the "spirit" are mutually interpretive.[16] When implementing the council, it is not valid to appeal to the council's "spirit" apart from its documents nor to reduce the council to its "letter." As Ormond Rush puts it, "The documents of Vatican II must be interpreted in the light of the historical event that produced them, and the historical event must be interpreted in the light of the official documents that it promulgated."[17] In short, concerning the reception of Vatican II, neither the letter nor the spirit must have the upper hand.

Yet, I would distinguish between the issue of the council's reception in the sense of implementation of its teachings and the issue of the council's relevance for addressing current pastoral challenges. In this latter regard, I would contend that the "spirit" of the council is now more important than its "letter." Among the many challenges that the church faces today, I would emphasize the following: institutional reform, disaffiliation of a broad spectrum of the faithful from the church, clericalism and seminary formation, sexual abuse crisis, the role of women in the decision-making and their admission to the ordained ministry, the status of the LGBTQ faithful in the church, and the issue of the development of tradition.

Although the council addressed some of these challenges, they have gained new contours since its closing. Some, however, are postconciliar developments; thus, the letter of the council does not apply to them directly. There is also a sense according to which one should conceive the project of Vatican II as an "unfinished building site."[18] While affirming that the council's documents carry binding magisterial authority, it is also true that on many issues that the council addressed the theological scholarship has evolved. It is likely that if a council with a similar disposition as Vatican II were to address them today, it would not say exactly the same things as Vatican II did but would factor in the new scholarship.

While the "letter" of Vatican II holds a limited promise to address current pastoral challenges, the same is not true about the council's "spirit," which, as I see it, has lost nothing in its relevance. I will now illustrate this point on one of the contemporary challenges.

16. See Rush, *The Vision of Vatican II*, 4.
17. Rush, *The Vision of Vatican II*, 3.
18. Richard R. Gaillardetz, "Building on Vatican II: Setting the Agenda for the Church in the 21st Century," *Theoforum* 44 (2013): 68.

The status of women is one of the greatest challenges in the Catholic Church today. This has been confirmed by the workings of the Synod on Synodality, which at this writing is currently underway. One question that participants of the first session of the synod's universal global phase were prompted to reflect on is, "How can the Church of our time better fulfill its mission through greater recognition and promotion of the baptismal dignity of women?"[19] The Synthesis Report (hereafter, SR) from the synod's first session states that "it is urgent to ensure that women can participate in decision-making processes and assume roles of responsibility in pastoral care and ministry."[20] One gets a sense that, in the challenge that the status of women presents, nothing less than the truth of the Gospel is at stake. The central issue is the exclusion of women from ordained ministry and consequently from participation in church governance. For many in the church, the teaching that the church lacks authority to ordain women is poorly argued and is seen as a form of gender discrimination.

While the documents of Vatican II do not contain a sustained reflection on women, they offer a few basic statements that point toward ways forward. Catherine Clifford explains that the council "provided for several important advances and set the door ajar for more direct involvement of women in the teaching, ministry, and daily witness of the church."[21] In the Pastoral Constitution on the Church in the Modern World, we read that today "women claim parity with men in fact as well as of right, where they have not already obtained it."[22] The same document affirms the essential equality of men and women.[23] With regard to the participation of

---

19. XVI Ordinary General Assembly of the Synod of Bishops, *Instrumentum Laboris* for the First Session, *For a Synodal Church: Communion, Participation, Mission*, May 29, 2023, B 2.3, https://www.usccb.org/resources/ENG_INSTRUMENTUM-LABORIS.pdf.

20. XVI Ordinary General Assembly of the Synod of Bishops, Synthesis Report, *A Synodal Church in Mission*, October 28, 2023, 9m, https://www.synod.va/content/dam/synod/assembly/synthesis/english/2023.10.28-ENG-Synthesis-Report_IMP.pdf (hereafter, SR).

21. Catherine E. Clifford, *Decoding Vatican II: Interpretation and Ongoing Reception* (Paulist Press, 2014), 70.

22. Second Vatican Council, Pastoral Constitution on the Church in the Modern World *Gaudium et Spes*, December 7, 1965, no. 9 (hereafter, GS). All quotations of Vatican II documents are from Austin Flannery, ed., *Vatican Council II: Constitutions, Decrees, Declarations; A Completely Revised Translation in Inclusive Language* (Liturgical Press, 2014).

23. "All women and men . . . enjoy the same divine calling and destiny; there is here a basic equality between all and it must be accorded ever greater recognition" (GS 29).

women in the life of the church, the following statement in the Decree on the Apostolate on the Laity stands out: "Since in our days women are taking an increasingly active share in the entire life of society, it is very important that their participation in the various sectors of the church's apostolate should likewise develop."[24] Although common today, at the time of Vatican II such statements were novelties.[25] They "created conditions for a significant evolution in the roles of women in the life of the church in the postconciliar years."[26]

In the decades after the council, women came to play a major role in the pastoral life of the church. In some parts of the world, they now represent the majority of lay ecclesial ministers. Yet their continued exclusion from ordained ministry and consequently from participation in the church's governance remains a significant challenge.[27] Upon honest reflection, it is difficult to avoid the conclusion that women are a second class in the church simply because of their gender.

By allowing women to be lectors and acolytes and by creating an installed ministry of catechist open to women, Pope Francis augmented the ministerial status of women. While these steps can be appreciated as gestures of goodwill and signs of creative imagination within the current doctrinal and canonical constraints, they are long overdue. The exclusion of women from ordained ministry unnecessarily hurts the Catholic Church's credibility within and outside of its confines. One can argue, however, that the church possesses all the theological resources that would allow it to admit women to ordained ministry; chief among them is the

---

24. Second Vatican Council, Decree on the Apostolate of Lay People *Apostolicam Actuositatem*, November 18, 1965, no. 9.

25. See Regina Heyder, "Women and the Council: Catholic Women's Organizations and Women Theologians Prior to and During Vatican II," in *The Oxford Handbook of Vatican II*, ed. Catherine E. Clifford and Massimo Faggioli (Oxford University Press, 2023), 315–30.

26. Clifford, *Decoding Vatican II*, 75.

27. Another important point is that the exclusion of women from ordained ministry means that they are not allowed to preach a homily at Mass. One never hears an exposition on the word of God from the perspective of a woman during the event that is the source and summit of the church's life. While there are ways to bypass the stipulation of canon 767 of the Code of Canon Law, the intention is clear: only the ordained should preach a homily.

theology of baptism. Here is where the "spirit of Vatican II" could make a difference.

As I noted above, the bishops at the council showed courage when they distanced themselves on many occasions from the then-dominant neoscholastic theology and instead promoted teachings that more accurately represented the breadth and depth of the Catholic tradition. Admitting women to ordained ministry would take similar courage. While there is no historical precedence for ordaining women to the priesthood (the diaconate may be a different case), what is called for is courage to believe that the Spirit of God is with us today as in the past ages. Changes in the church's teaching have happened, and Vatican II is one of the prime examples, though by far not the only one. The "spirit of the council" is not a panacea, yet it holds a promise for us today because its impetus toward reform and renewal, and the courage it represents, align with the thrust of the Gospel.

In Defense of the "Spirit of Vatican II" as a Hermeneutical Category

When interpreting a piece of writing, it is common to distinguish between the "letter" and the "spirit." The "letter" refers to the words of the text, and the "spirit" designates the intention of the author. Because of the complex dynamics involved in human verbal communication, this distinction can be useful for understanding texts, including the documents of Vatican II, and for implementing what they ask.

Distinguishing between the "letter" and the "spirit" should not be controversial. Even Joseph Ratzinger (the future Pope Benedict XVI), who was a staunch critic of the "spirit of Vatican II," in his earlier days supported the idea that the council was more than its final documents. Reflecting on the third session of the council, especially on the change that was happening in the bishops, he wrote:

> This spiritual awakening, which the bishops accomplished in full view of the Church, or, rather, accomplished *as* the Church, was the great and irrevocable event of the Council. It was more important in many respects than the texts it passed, for these texts could only voice a part of the new life that had been awakened in this encounter of the Church with its inner self. Progress may at times have seemed difficult and slow, entangled as it

often was in the political devices and disputes, both large and small, which to a considerable degree marked the public image of the Council and often enough its daily routine. But all of this seems trivial and transitory in comparison with the true event—the awakening of the Church.[28]

It is evident that for young Ratzinger, the documents of the council did not exhaustively reflect the experience of the council and that the latter was much more than what could be inscribed in the documents. As the above quote indicates, the hermeneutical category of the "spirit of the council" has been employed as a shorthand to complement the category of the "letter of the council" in order to acknowledge this limitation of the council documents.

The fact is, however, that the "spirit of Vatican II" did become controversial. The controversy can be traced to the disagreements among the founding members of the journal *Concilium* in 1965 and the subsequent founding of the journal *Communio* in 1972, but it gained full force only in the 1980s during the pontificate of John Paul II, after Joseph Ratzinger, one of the founders of *Communio*, became the prefect of the Congregation for the Doctrine of the Faith.[29] While John Paul II was positively disposed to Vatican II, he believed that a faulty understanding and implementation of the council were in large part responsible for a fragmentation of Catholicism's global unity. To rescue the reception of the council from the wrong path on which he believed it was moving, the pope adopted the diagnosis of Joseph Ratzinger, according to which the problems with the council's implementation were due mainly to the misapplication of an otherwise valid but vague notion of the "spirit of Vatican II."[30] Ratzinger believed that progressive theologians, such as his earlier colleagues from *Concilium*, distorted the council by severing the "spirit of the council" from its documents, creating an image of the council as an agent of change that breaks with the previous theological tradition. This view of the council in turn fueled calls for further changes in the church based on the "spirit of the council" for the sake of the council. Both the pope

---

28. Joseph Ratzinger, *Theological Highlights of Vatican II* (Paulist Press, 1966), 194.

29. See Massimo Faggioli, *Vatican II: The Battle for Meaning* (Paulist Press, 2012), 50–53; Tracey Rowland, *Catholic Theology*, Doing Theology (Bloomsbury, 2017), 91–166.

30. See Joseph Ratzinger with Vittorio Messori, *The Ratzinger Report: An Exclusive Interview on the State of the Church* (Ignatius Press, 1985), 27–44.

and Cardinal Ratzinger believed, however, that further changes in the church were unwise and that justifying them based on the "spirit of Vatican II" was without merit, for they lacked support in the council's documents. They believed that the concept of the "spirit of Vatican II" actually stood in the way of an authentic reception of the council. To return the church to normalcy, they promoted a hermeneutic of the council that emphasized continuity and downplayed its discontinuity with the historical tradition. The 1985 extraordinary assembly of the Synod of Bishops was instrumental in laying the official ground for this reining in the "spirit of Vatican II" by subordinating it to the "letter" of the council and emphasizing the "continuity" of Vatican II with what preceded it. This was also the time when the debate on the hermeneutics of Vatican II took off on a large scale.[31]

John Paul II convened the synod to review, evaluate, and celebrate the achievement of the council. The debate on the reception of the council naturally led to a debate on its interpretation. The synod laid the groundwork for the interpretation and implementation of the council from the perspective of the magisterium. In their "Final Report," the synod participants spelled out several hermeneutical principles that should guide the interpretation of Vatican II. Among them were the following: "It is not legitimate to separate the spirit and the letter of the council. Moreover, the council must be understood in continuity with the great tradition of the church."[32] This became the hermeneutical lens through which John Paul II approached the reception of Vatican II. In broad terms, the "letter" of the council was correlated with continuity and the "spirit" with discontinuity. While not eliminating the "spirit of Vatican II" from discussions of the council's interpretation, its role was greatly restricted. Over time, the emphasis on continuity of the council with the tradition provided a justification for effectively halting any further implementation of Vatican II regarding most issues of the church's internal life, especially those pertaining to liturgy and ecclesiology. Appeals to the "spirit of the council" to bring out change in the church were ignored or denounced. Under Pope Benedict XVI, the "spirit of Vatican II" became a villain

---

31. See Gilles Routhier, "The Hermeneutics of Reform as a Task for Theology," *Irish Theological Quarterly* 77, no. 3 (2012): 220–35.

32. Synod of Bishops, "Final Report," *Origins* 15, no. 27 (1985): 445–46 (I.5).

whose role in the council narratives needed to be placed under tight control. Recently, some from traditionalist circles have argued that the church would be served best if the "spirit of Vatican II" were slain.[33]

Yet there is another side to the battle over the "spirit of Vatican II," which reveals a double standard in the way it was treated. As Massimo Faggioli points out, John Paul II and Benedict XVI were not consistent in their disapproval of the "spirit of the council." While they harshly criticized certain theologians and historians for appealing to the council's spirit, the popes praised the new ecclesial movements for faithfully embodying the same spirit in creative ways.[34]

One can make a case that Vatican II paved the way for the new ecclesial movements that sprang up after the council.[35] Yet it is also true that the movements find rationale and endorsement more in the council's spirit than in its letter, for the council's documents conceded the laity just a little room to play a leading role in the church. As Faggioli explains: "The movements have absorbed Vatican II not in the literal meaning of its final documents, but they have appealed to its 'spirit,' being repeatedly encouraged to do so by John Paul II's teaching and doctrinal policy toward them. . . . Historical evidence tells us that the movements as such had no role among the participants of Vatican II or in the final documents of the Council. In fact, from the 1980s on, they turned to the often repudiated 'spirit of Vatican II,' since they had little opportunity to find support in conciliar texts themselves."[36] This makes the historical picture of the controversy surrounding the "spirit of Vatican II" more complex.

While one may agree with some criticisms of how the concept of the "spirit of Vatican II" was used in the 1970s, restricting or banning it distorts the council itself. The event character of the council gets eclipsed, and the novelty of its documents goes unnoticed. For the implementation of Vatican II to make progress, due attention must be given to both the "letter" *and* the "spirit" of the council. In fact, this represents a consensus

---

33. See Robert J. Araujo and the Bellarmine Forum, *Slaying the Spirit of Vatican II with the Light of Truth* (Bellarmine Forum, 2017).

34. See Massimo Faggioli, *The Rising Laity: Ecclesial Movements since Vatican II* (Paulist Press, 2016), 105.

35. For instance, Communion and Liberation, The Community of St. Egidio, Focolare, Neocatechumenal Way, *Cursillos de Cristiandad*, and the Legionaries of Christ.

36. Faggioli, *The Rising Laity*, 104.

among most of the scholars of the council for whom "Vatican II is both a corpus of documents and an event, and that it should be known and understood both in its letter and in its spirit."[37]

There are many reasons for the tumultuous reception of the council at present. One, I would suggest, is that theology curricula in the seminaries neglect the event character of the council. What happened at the council is studied during a few class meetings in a church history course. Council documents are covered in various courses: *Dei Verbum* is taught in fundamental theology and in the introduction to Scripture; *Sacrosanctum Concilium* in courses on the liturgy and sacraments; *Lumen Gentium*, *Gaudium et Spes*, and *Unitatis Redintegratio* in ecclesiology; and *Nostra Aetate* in Christology/soteriology. The council is broken down according to how its documents fit into the curriculum framework. The result is that church leaders end up with a fragmented understanding of the council, and the "drama" of the council is passed over altogether. Unless one is exposed to the council deliberations and a redactional history of the documents, the history-making character of the council's teaching can hardly be noticed and even less appreciated. The documents of Vatican II are written in such a way that those who are not familiar with neoscholastic theology have no way of recognizing where the council was in continuity with it and where the council departed from it. Limiting the council to its documents in the seminary curriculum has resulted in forming ordained ministers whose understanding of the council leaves something to be desired. It would help the reception of the council if revisions to programs of formation included a revision of the theology curriculum in seminaries (see SR 11e). Such revision should contain a course on the history and theology of Vatican II that would give due attention to both the "letter" and the "spirit" of the council.

Conclusion

The challenges that the Catholic Church faces today require not only its "continual reformation" that the council affirmed[38] but also a reform

---

37. Faggioli, *Vatican II*, 125.
38. Second Vatican Council, Decree on Ecumenism *Unitatis Redintegratio*, November 21, 1964, 6.

and renewal that go beyond the one envisioned by the council. The notion of Vatican II as an unfinished building site suggests that "to us falls the demanding task of bringing this building project to completion by fearlessly raising new questions, concerns and insights unimagined a half century ago."[39] It further calls for relying on the council's spirit more than on its letter to guide the church in reading the signs of the times and responding to them according to the Gospel. The current pastoral challenges demand that the members of the church, both pastors and the lay faithful, act with courage, namely, that they see themselves as agents through whom the Spirit of God may bring about something new for the sake of the church's mission. As an impulse toward reform and renewal, the "spirit of Vatican II" should be invoked in all initiatives that attempt to make the church a more effective sign of God's saving love to the world. As courage to believe that God's Spirit continues to be with the church, the "spirit of Vatican II" should animate all ecclesial discernment related to addressing pastoral challenges the church faces.

The Synod on Synodality that is underway can be seen not only as an attempt to implement the poorly received aspects of the council's ecclesiology but also as an attempt to reconnect the church with the energy or the "spirit" of Vatican II. Reviving the "spirit" of the council might prove to be one of the key building blocks that are necessary to make progress toward a synodalization of the whole church as Pope Francis envisions. Lastly, only by affirming the "spirit of Vatican II" will large segments of the church be able to embrace the possibility that genuine change, innovation, and even reversal do not have to be seen as repudiation of the great tradition, but rather as signs that God's Spirit is active in the church.

---

39. Richard R. Gaillardetz, "We Have the Pillars, but the Building Is Still Unfinished," *National Catholic Reporter*, October 11, 2012, 50.

Chapter 3

Integralism and the Reception(s) of *Dignitatis Humanae*

Daniel A. Rober

Dignitatis Humanae stands as one of the most "revolutionary" of the Vatican II documents, affirming as it does a positive right to religious freedom following centuries of Catholic resistance to this idea. It indeed stands alongside *Nostra Aetate* as one of the key places where Vatican II responded to the postwar situation (and broke with much past practice), affirming religious freedom even in situations where Catholicism is the dominant religion. Much attention has been paid to the prehistory of this document, particularly the travails of its American champion, John Courtney Murray, of whom it is typically viewed as a vindication.[1] Yet its reception history is equally fascinating, with a wide variety of both pastoral implementations and theological interpretations. After years of debate about its implications, its very foundations have come under question in influential intellectual and political movements.

The last decade has witnessed the rise (or at the very least a repopularization) of an old-yet-new brand of Catholic politics—integralism—which revives ideas of Catholic political dominance seemingly ended by Vatican II. These thinkers revive ideas of the fascist era—often evoking thinkers from this period such as Carl Schmitt—in a decidedly postmodern fashion.

---

1. Barry Hudock, *Struggle, Condemnation, Vindication: John Courtney Murray's Journey Toward Vatican II* (Liturgical Press, 2015).

This paper examines the way in which these thinkers, such as Adrian Vermeule and Patrick Deneen, have revived old Catholic authoritarian ideas while attempting to avoid (by reinterpreting as favorable to them) the implications of Vatican II and subsequent papal magisterium. It situates these thinkers also with regard to the collapse of Catholic neoconservatism, for which *Dignitatis Humanae* was a key document, and with whom they share a tendency to twist the words of the document to fit their own political aims. The paper will ultimately argue that resolving the interpretive dilemmas around *Dignitatis Humanae* and the problems raised by integralism ultimately means reckoning with whether and how the church ought to engage itself with questions surrounding politics and political theology.

What Is Integralism? Why Does It Matter?

The rise of integralism within certain spheres of Catholic and more broadly Christian political discourse in the United States is perhaps surprising, but it is not unprecedented. Its most closely related antecedent came with L. Brent Bozell Jr. and *Triumph* magazine. *Triumph* emerged out of a conservative Catholic intellectual milieu that saw Francisco Franco's Spain as a model for how a modern Catholic society might function.[2] At the very moment where it seemed that Catholics had effectively assimilated into the American mainstream and attained cultural and political power, Bozell argued that they had done so in the service of the wrong kind of state. His right-wing arguments paralleled those of left-wing Catholic figures such as Dorothy Day and the Berrigan brothers in their rejection of polite postwar American society.[3] Where the latter figures did so in the name of the Gospel, Bozell did so in the name of the legacy of Christendom.

Bozell's promotion of integralism within the US context—particularly in a Cold War context, when the promotion of democracy and freedom had become central to the nation's sense of its identity and mission—was not effective. Even in a 1960s environment, when this identity and mis-

---

2. Patrick Allitt, *Catholic Intellectuals and Conservative Politics in America, 1950-1985* (Cornell University Press, 1993), 155.
3. Allitt, *Catholic Intellectuals*, 138.

sion seemed to be fraying, integralism did not have a strong appeal. His movement found itself marginalized, confined largely to institutions such as Christendom College, which were founded to carry forward its mission.[4] Its main political expression was in the "paleo-conservative" philosophy of figures such as Patrick J. Buchanan, who challenged consensus politics on social issues especially.

The contemporary revival of integralism as an intellectual construct (if not a vibrant political movement) stems from several intersecting factors. The "culture wars" over issues such as abortion and same-sex marriage in the United States have put the church's teaching and institutional apparatus at odds with huge swaths of society, putting Catholics in an uneasy relationship with each other and their fellow citizens.[5] The church's institutional influence in these areas has been weakened markedly by sexual abuse and other scandals, so its ability to form any kind of parallel order to secular society on its own, as it indeed once did quite effectively, is greatly reduced.

Patrick Deneen's thought, particularly its trajectory over a decade or so, represents this strain of integralism rather well. Deneen, who teaches political science at the University of Notre Dame and previously did the same at Georgetown, has shifted his intellectual profile from a constitutional scholar interested in the institutions and workings of democracy toward a deeply skeptical position concerning their state. This trajectory has emerged most particularly in his two most recent books, *Why Liberalism Failed* and *Regime Change*. In the latter book, with which this study is primarily concerned, Deneen argues that since liberalism in US society has culminated in a destructive tendency toward the existing (and necessary) order, it must be replaced by a different kind of polity.

Deneen entitles his alternative political theory "Aristopopulism," defined by "the full development of a distinct and new elite, attuned to the requirements of the common good."[6] For him, only such an elite can provide the necessary power base to effectively carry out the integralist

---

4. Thomas L. McFadden Jr., *Restoring All Things in Christ: A History of the Founding of Christendom College* (Christendom College, 2013), 6.

5. Stephen Schloesser, SJ, "'Dancing on the Edge of the Volcano': Biopolitics and What Happened After Vatican II," in *From Vatican II to Pope Francis*, ed. Paul Crowley, SJ (Orbis Books, 2014), lays out these issues effectively with specific reference to Vatican II.

6. Patrick J. Deneen, *Regime Change: Toward a Postliberal Future* (Sentinel, 2023), 153.

project. Drawing on conservative French political theorist Pierre Manent's argument that liberal democracy consists of a series of separations, Deneen argues for a series of reintegrations that will undo those separations (which for him have become a kind of disintegration).[7] Religion comes into this vision in several ways, most notably in the discussion of how to ensure the common good. As he argues, "a social order that is publicly *indifferent* to religious belief and practice becomes especially punitive for the 'commoners,' or those in the most economically and socially tenuous situation in today's world," drawing connection to the rise of "deaths of despair" and other social ills.[8]

Deneen has notably dealt specifically with questions about *Dignitatis Humanae*, arguing for the centrality of its argument that "the state and the citizenry as a whole cannot, in fact, be indifferent toward conceptions of the good."[9] The problems, as he sees it, come from the document's expectation that the state will affirm a true and adequate conception of liberty and that religious believers are to engage with society without coercion.[10] For Deneen, a tension arises, given that for him, state affirmation of true liberty ought to result in legal structures that coerce at least somewhat in favor of preferred moral outcomes. Essentially his interpretation of *Dignitatis Humanae* is that it presupposes a worldview that liberalism ultimately cannot affirm. He invokes Joseph Komonchak's distinction between liberal political structures (acceptable) and liberal ideology (unacceptable) to support this reading.[11] Deneen goes so far as to call for a new Declaration on Religious Liberty clarifying these points and restating traditional ideas about the freedom of the church.[12] His interpretation of *Dignitatis Humanae* and its real or interpretive drawbacks thus serves as an important support for his broadly antiliberal project.

Adrian Vermeule, a professor of constitutional law at Harvard Law School, represents a distinct strain of integralism from Deneen, focused

---

7. Deneen, *Regime Change*, 188-90.
8. Deneen, *Regime Change*, 236.
9. Patrick J. Deneen, "Religious Liberty After Liberalism: Re-Thinking *Dignitatis Humanae* in an Age of Illiberal Liberalism," *Communio* 40, nos. 2-3 (Summer-Fall 2013): 617.
10. Deneen, "Religious Liberty After Liberalism," 620-21.
11. Deneen, "Religious Liberty After Liberalism," 625.
12. Deneen, "Religious Liberty After Liberalism," 629.

sharply upon issues concerning the administrative state. A disciple of Carl Schmitt, Vermeule situates his arguments within the framework of a legal theory he calls "common-good constitutionalism."[13] As the name indicates, this legal theory has direct connections to Catholic social thought concerning the common good. It is no accident that Vermeule uses this language in the process of writing otherwise "secular" legal theory. In so doing, he echoes earlier Catholic corporatist thought going back to the 1920s and 1930s.[14] He is concerned especially to refute the idea of originalism in US jurisprudence, arguing instead for what he calls "developing constitutionalism" which "celebrates continuity with the enduring principles of the past" and recognizes changes to the civil order "as necessary in order for those principles to unfold in accordance with their true natures."[15]

Vermeule's theory of integralism develops in conjunction with his constitutional theory and in response to Deneen's diagnosis of liberalism's failure. For Vermeule, Deneen correctly diagnoses the problem but fails—at least in his earlier book—to go far enough in laying out what is to replace it. As he argues, "It takes a comprehensive theory to beat a comprehensive theory."[16] Vermeule proposes models drawn from the Hebrew Scriptures—particularly Joseph, Mordecai, Esther, and Daniel—as programmatic for how to replace liberalism by taking control of the levers of the state. In the same vein, and particularly evocative for his Christian integralist project, he invokes St. Cecilia's conversion of her husband and St. Paul's preaching of "the advent of a new order from within the very urban heart of the imperium." They evince what he calls a "determination to co-opt and transform the decaying regime from within its own core."[17] Decaying liberal regimes, for Vermeule, should be objects not of teardown but of co-optation.

For Vermeule, then, the task for those concerned by the decline of liberal democracy is not to form communities of resistance but rather to

---

13. Adrian Vermeule, *Common Good Constitutionalism* (Polity Press, 2022), 28.

14. James Chappel, *Catholic Modern: The Challenge of Totalitarianism and the Remaking of the Church* (Harvard University Press, 2018), 79.

15. Chappel, *Catholic Modern*, 118.

16. Adrian Vermeule, "Integration from Within," *American Affairs Journal* 2, no. 1 (February 2018): 202-13, https://americanaffairsjournal.org/2018/02/integration-from-within/.

17. Vermeule, "Integration from Within," 202-13.

take advantage of this for their own ends—a positive task rather than a negative one. The common good, as he argues, is the "structure of justification" for various activities pursued by what he views as a large and complex enterprise of government.[18] For Vermeule, relying on studies of the Code of Justinian among other sources, administrative law occupies a central place.[19] Subsidiarity also figures prominently, though with the proviso of the "state of exception" in which subsidiary institutions malfunction and higher authority must step in.[20] For the purposes of this study, the key takeaways for Vermeule's constitutional thought is that he allows for authoritarian forms and levels of government power to be put to use (in part) in pursuit of a confessional state.

Deneen and Vermeule, then, represent two sides of integralism as a project. Deneen brings forward the postliberal sense that the political status quo has failed irrevocably and that drastic action must be taken to repair it. He thus provides the diagnosis that something has gone seriously wrong and that a new order must be instantiated. Vermeule, meanwhile, provides the intellectual structure for thinking about what such a new order might look like. Moreso than prior integralist thinkers in the American context, such as Bozell, Vermeule articulates a theory for how to take and hold power on behalf of Catholicism.

Integralism is a marginal political project in terms of overall impact; it is unlikely that this exact kind of project—with the Catholic Church in particular as the primary driving ethos and beneficiary—could be enacted in the United States. Its danger arises as a revival of a version of Catholic social thought that had seemingly been discredited by the events of World War II and left in the past by Vatican II. Integralism as a reality is unlikely, but integralism as an ideal is almost as dangerous due to the political agenda it authorizes. The next section of this essay will contextualize this discussion by examining *Dignitatis Humanae* in relation to previous traditions and ideologies of integralism in Europe.

---

18. Vermeule, *Common Good Constitutionalism*, 135.
19. Vermeule, *Common Good Constitutionalism*, 138; and Vermeule, "Rules, Commands, and Principles in the Administrative State," *Yale Law Journal* 130 (2020-21), https://www.yalelawjournal.org/forum/rules-commands-and-principles-in-the-administrative-state.
20. Vermeule, *Common Good Constitutionalism*, 154-55.

Yves Congar, John Courtney Murray, and the Shadow of European Integralism

Dignitatis Humanae along with *Nostra Aetate* is one of the unlikeliest Vatican II documents in the sense that it ran up against a strong opposition consensus, which held sway during the pontificate of Pius XII.[21] John Courtney Murray's attempts to advise the Vatican on issues relating to church-state relations in the United States in the face of rising secularism among intellectuals came under particular scrutiny.[22] At Vatican II, it originated in connection with the schema on ecumenism and became controversial with bishops from "integralist" societies such as Spain.[23] In many aspects it reflected a meeting of the theological visions of Yves Congar and Murray.[24] These thinkers, coming as they did from very different political experiences and climates, encompassed two schools of thought that influenced the document in different ways.[25] The tension between their priorities has also influenced the reception of *Dignitatis Humanae*.

The document itself emerged out of several strands of thought and practical realities that had come to the fore in the postwar era. The atrocities of World War II gave new impetus to "Christian humanist" strains of thought, such as that of Jacques Maritain, which opened out onto questions about human rights.[26] Simultaneously, new movements emerged for

---

21. Silvia Scatena, "Religious Liberty at Vatican II," in *The Oxford Handbook of Vatican II*, ed. Catherine E. Clifford and Massimo Faggioli (Oxford University Press, 2023), 267-68, describes the condemnation procedures against authors such as Murray who had attempted to explore this issue.

22. Joseph Komonchak, "'The Crisis in Church-State Relations in the U.S.A.': A Recently Rediscovered Text by John Courtney Murray," *Review of Politics* 61, no. 4 (1999): 677-78.

23. Nicholas J. Healy Jr. "The Drafting of *Dignitatis Humanae*," in *Freedom, Truth, and Human Dignity*, ed. David L. Schindler and Nicholas J. Healy Jr. (Eerdmans, 2015), 218.

24. Agnes de Dreuzy, "'Dignitatis Humanae' as an Encounter Between Two 'Towering Theologians': John Courtney Murray, S.J., and Yves Congar, O.P.," *U.S. Catholic Historian* 24, no. 1 (Winter 2006): 36: "Because he was always dealing with a pragmatic situation, Murray focused on the juridical and political effects of religious freedom instead of its theological grounding, favored by Congar."

25. Scatena, "Religious Liberty at Vatican II," 275-76.

26. Samuel Moyn, *Christian Human Rights*, Intellectual History of the Modern Age (University of Pennsylvania Press, 2015), 67: "The spiritual and often explicitly religious philosophy of the human person was the conceptual means through which continental Europe initially incorporated human rights."

ecumenical dialogue with other Christian groups as well as rethinking the relationship between Catholics and Jews.[27] Repression of religion within communist Eastern Bloc nations as compared to Western democracies also highlighted the practices around religious freedom in the latter.

For Yves Congar, the affirmation of religious liberty flows from a theological account of the mission of the church. The disagreement between integralism and pluralism is thus not a question of the theological substance of this mission but rather how to enact it. Integralism and a more positive approach to religious liberty are thus a response to the same fundamental evangelical call.[28] He thus seeks to return the church to its originating mission: "The church serves her own interests best . . . the more purely she is a Church."[29] Congar goes so far as to argue that there is a "totalitarianism of the Faith," based in truth, which cannot be given up in principle even as a pluralistic political situation is accepted.[30] Like the broader theological renewal movement of which he was a part, Congar sought renewal in this and other areas for the sake of being truer to the core theological commitments of the institution.

Murray's thought on religious freedom developed in dialogue particularly with Jacques Maritain, whose work had increasingly turned to questions of political philosophy.[31] Maritain practiced a very different version of Thomism than did Congar, much more comfortable with philosophies of "pure nature" that were being discredited by Henri de Lubac and others. Even within the "American" side of the debate on what became of *Dignitatis Humanae*, there can be seen traces of these French debates.

The document, as its title indicates, roots its account of religious freedom in human dignity, following in the French trajectory of philosophies of the human person that had emerged in the previous decades. It quickly connects this dignity to the question of human rights and to the papal

---

27. John Connelly, *From Enemy to Brother: The Revolution in Catholic Teaching on the Jews, 1933–1965* (Harvard University Press, 2012).

28. Yves M. J. Congar, OP, "The Theological Conditions of Any Pluralism," in *Tolerance and the Catholic: A Symposium*, ed. George Lamb (Sheed and Ward, 1955), 172.

29. Congar, "The Theological Conditions of Any Pluralism," 174.

30. Congar, "The Theological Conditions of Any Pluralism," 197.

31. Florian Michel, *La pensée catholique en Amérique du Nord: Réseaux intellectuels et échanges culturels entre l'Europe, le Canada et les États-Unis (années 1920–1960)* (Desclée de Brouwer, 2010), 497.

encyclical tradition of social teaching dating back to Leo XIII.[32] Following a discourse on the political dimensions of religious freedom, the text returns to its philosophical foundations. This section reasserts traditional teaching about the "rights of the church" in the context of the church as a free association within society (see DH 13). The multivalence of its argumentation gave rise to varying schools of interpretation, especially in the US context.

Dignitatis Humanae's American Catholic Trajectories

Dignitatis Humanae has gained a reputation (despite its at least equal French origins) as the American contribution to Vatican II, and it is thus unsurprising that the United States has been a center for competing interpretations of this document and of Murray's broader legacy. These interpretations have encompassed three main strands that I will summarize here, following an overview of the document's origins. These existing positions, which can be roughly described as the neoconservative, *Communio,* and liberal positions, provide the crucial intellectual backdrop to the rise of the new integralism in the US

For neoconservative Catholic thinkers such as George Weigel and Michael Novak, *Dignitatis Humanae* provided an opening for a new kind of political understanding in the US context.[33] Weigel's analysis of the "Murray project" makes this quite clear. For Weigel, *Dignitatis Humanae* "vindicated the American experience of Catholicism, and the Catholic experience of America."[34] It responded to the facts on the ground, namely, that "religious plurality or difference was the new normal throughout the world" and thus required an adjustment on the part of the church.[35]

---

32. Second Vatican Council, Declaration on Religious Liberty *Dignitatis Humanae*, December 7, 1965, no. 1 (hereafter, DH). All quotations of Vatican II documents are from Austin Flannery, ed., *Vatican Council II: Constitutions, Decrees, Declarations; A Completely Revised Translation in Inclusive Language* (Liturgical Press, 2014).

33. Jesse Russell, "'Whig Thomism' and the Making of the Catholic Neoconservative Movement," *Politics and Religion* 14 (2021): 289-99.

34. George Weigel, *Tranquilitas Ordinis: The Present Failure and Future Promise of American Catholic Thought on War and Peace* (Oxford University Press, 1987), 105.

35. George Weigel, *To Sanctify the World: The Vital Legacy of Vatican II* (Basic Books, 2022), 183.

For Weigel and fellow travelers such as Michael Novak, *Dignitatis Humanae* provided a path for the American political economy to influence Catholicism more broadly. As Weigel puts it, *Dignitatis Humanae* affirmed that "the deepest roots of limited government lay in the Gospel's revolutionary distinction between spiritual and political authority, not in Enlightenment political theory."[36] He thus interprets the affirmation of religious freedom in terms of a broader affirmation of a certain kind of "limited state that acknowledged constitutionally its incompetence in certain matters."[37] This is in keeping with a classical liberal vision of the state in which economic regulation ought to be kept minimal.[38]

This neoconservative vision coheres well with rational choice theory as laid out by Roger Finke and Rodney Stark in *The Churching of America, 1776-2005*. Under this theory, separation of church and state creates a "free market" in religion in which certain forms of faith—particularly those that make demands on their followers—will tend to win out over those more willing to make compromises.[39] For Catholic neoconservatives, *Dignitatis Humanae* thus situates Catholicism more thoroughly as a competitor in this "market." Weigel's vision of "evangelical Catholicism" runs according to these ideas and tracks with other influential voices such as Robert Barron.[40]

An alternative vision to that of Weigel, though still fitting into a broadly conservative cultural-political space, comes from American *Communio* thinkers such as David L. Schindler. Schindler was particularly concerned to push back against the neoconservative vision in terms of its attempts to square Catholic social teaching with capitalism, but the interpretation of *Dignitatis Humanae* also figured into these arguments. For Schindler, interpretation of *Dignitatis Humane* ought to focus on the relationship

---

36. Weigel, *To Sanctify the World*, 192.

37. Weigel, *To Sanctify the World*, 191.

38. Weigel, *To Sanctify the World*, 173. Weigel's harsh treatment of *Gaudium et Spes* makes clear his contempt for critiques of economic inequality, in particular.

39. Roger Finke and Rodney Stark, *The Churching of America, 1776-2005: Winners and Losers in Our Religious Economy* (Rutgers University Press, 2005), 249-51.

40. George Weigel, *Evangelical Catholicism: Deep Reform in the 21st-Century Church* (Basic Books, 2013), 50, contrasts "institutional-maintenance Catholicism" with an evangelical approach centered on truth and conversion.

between truth and person.⁴¹ This interpretation, like much of Schindler's work, centers on a reading of Pope John Paul II's thought.

Schindler's theology project more broadly focuses on a vision of the world in which the church, as the instrument of salvation of the world, must be central to any politics: "To cure the world, to liberate any human or nonhuman entity or any aspect thereof to be what it truly is, we must look to the Church."⁴² As such, Schindler challenges approaches that would tend to give too much credence to liberalism, particularly when present as a kind of neutral theory.⁴³ The challenge, however, is that to acknowledge the non-neutrality of the liberal state would seem to cohere with integralism. This is not the case, since, as Schindler puts it, "the order of grace is not first a juridical order."⁴⁴ Thus, it would be inappropriate and indeed idolatrous to assume that a confessional state could effectively mix these orders.

Schindler's interpretation coheres with the *Communio* school's broader critique of political theology. This can be found implicitly and explicitly in many *Communio* thinkers, particularly in Henri de Lubac's late work on Joachim of Fiore.⁴⁵ For de Lubac and Joseph Ratzinger especially, political theology risks a compromise of the church's witness in the world through an overly irenic relationship with political authority. As Schindler himself puts it, "the liberationist opens the Church to the world, but in a way that appears now to import the structures of the world into the Church."⁴⁶ This concern has been echoed by Michael Baxter and other Catholic Hauerwasians, as well as *Communio* thinkers from elsewhere in the world such as Tracey Rowland.⁴⁷

---

41. David L. Schindler, "Freedom, Truth, and Human Dignity: An Interpretation of *Dignitatis Humanae* and the Right to Religious Liberty," *Communio* 40, nos. 2–3 (Summer–Fall 2013): 209.

42. David L. Schindler, *Heart of the World, Center of the Church*: Communio *Ecclesiology, Liberalism, and Liberation* (Eerdmans, 1996), 29.

43. Schindler, *Heart of the World*, 44.

44. Schindler, *Heart of the World*, 84.

45. Henri de Lubac, *La postérité spirituelle de Joachim de Flore* (Cerf, 2014), in its last chapter describes a series of ideas he views as "neo-Joachimite" with a clear emphasis on political and liberation theologies.

46. Schindler, *Heart of the World*, 4.

47. Tracey Rowland, *Culture and the Thomist Tradition: After Vatican II* (Routledge, 2003), 168: "Plain persons fall into the pit of nihilistic despair and/or search for transcendence in

The debate between Schindler's school of thought and that of the neoconservatives represents a clear fault line within what one might call the center-right of American Catholicism in the late twentieth century. It contrasts usefully with the "center-left approach" exemplified by David Hollenbach. Hollenbach's approach, grounded in human-rights language, dovetails in certain respects with Weigel's while coming to different conclusions. For Hollenbach, *Dignitatis Humanae* had as its chief purpose "to bring Catholic teaching abreast of modern Western thought on the right to religious liberty" and thus "brought Catholic social thought into a new relationship with the entire Western liberal tradition."[48]

For Hollenbach, the legacy of *Dignitatis Humanae* should be placed in a global context, setting the tone for thinking about the public role of religion as a force in the world.[49] On this construal, the document sets the tone for the church as a good-faith dialogue partner on the contemporary global stage and within democratic states. As Vincent J. Miller argues, politics on this construal becomes "an essentially moral undertaking in service to the common good."[50] Like any moral undertaking this involves tradeoffs in pursuit of shared goods.

The US bishops began to emphasize religious freedom as an issue in response to the Obama administration's contraception mandate. Weigel defines this as an ironic unintended consequence of *Dignitatis Humanae*.[51] In this context, religious freedom as an emphasis took on a different visage than it had in the era of John Courtney Murray and largely thereafter. In that context, religious freedom emerged in a form centered on protection of individual consciences from state coercion on moral matters indirectly related to religious practice. Nancy Dallavalle has argued that

---

the secular liturgies of the global economy, whereas the more highly educated pursue strategies of stoic withdrawal and individual self-cultivation which are destined to end in despair, and even madness."

48. David Hollenbach, *Claims in Conflict: Retrieving and Renewing the Catholic Human Rights Tradition* (Paulist Press, 1979), 75.

49. David Hollenbach, "Religious Freedom in Global Context Today," in *The Legacy of Vatican II*, ed. Massimo Faggioli and Andrea Vicini, SJ (Paulist Press, 2015), 249.

50. Vincent J. Miller, "The Disappearing Common Good," in *Voting and Holiness: Catholic Perspectives on Political Participation*, ed. Nicholas Cafardi (Paulist Press, 2012), 194.

51. George Weigel, "*Dignitatis Humanae*: Origins and Unexpected Consequences," *Communio* 40, nos. 2-3 (Summer–Fall 2013): 382.

this approach seeks to place teaching about sexuality at the center of Catholic faith.[52] This neoconservative approach has continued to undergird the US bishops' approach to political matters.[53]

Of the above interpretations of *Dignitatis Humanae*, Weigel and Hollenbach share a commitment to engaging the church with the liberal polity in a constructive manner that involves some degree of back-and-forth. The differences largely center on to what end this engagement takes place and what kinds of compromises must be made to achieve it. Schindler, meanwhile, questions the liberal presuppositions of these other approaches while seeking persuasion and evangelization rather than domination. As such, Schindler's "post-liberal" approach coheres with integralism on a formal, intellectual level but departs from it on a tactical one. Indeed, the instrumentalization of religion inherent to Deneen and Vermeule's project is particularly noxious for Schindler's version of post-liberalism. It is notable that the interpretations represented by Schindler and Hollenbach have been influential in different parts of the theological academy, while that proffered by Weigel has been more influential with the bishops and church institutions.

Resisting Integralism's Subversion of *Dignitatis Humanae*

The return of integralism represents, on the one hand, a non-reception or highly contrarian reception of *Dignitatis Humanae* and, at the same time, an attempt to address emerging issues, particularly secularization. In classic postmodern fashion, it takes advantage of the plurality of interpretations to advance an extreme agenda. In the face of an increasingly secular West, now including the United States, integralism seeks to recapture its institutions for Christianity. In stark contrast to the neoconservative embrace of

---

52. Nancy A. Dallavalle, "Our 'First Freedom'? Sex, Gender, and Sexuality in Religious Freedom Claims," in *Voting and Faithfulness: Catholic Perspectives on Politics*, ed. Nicholas P. Cafardi (Paulist Press, 2020), 83.

53. Steven P. Millies, *Good Intentions: A History of Catholic Voters' Road from* Roe *to* Trump (Liturgical Press, 2018), 138: "The bishops spent those years following the scandal in Boston . . . deepening their commitment to the culture war and the divisions it affirms in American social and political life."

the free market in religion as well as economics, for the integralists the law must lead toward a specific vision of the common good.

Integralist reception of *Dignitatis Humanae* thus seeks to take advantage of the plural reception described above to articulate a way around it. Thomas Pink, one of integralism's key figures, does so by interpreting the document as acknowledging but not endorsing the existence of religious liberty within civil societies around the world.[54] On this reading, which seeks to reconcile *Dignitatis Humanae* with a static vision of Catholic political engagement, the kind of religious liberty envisioned by Vatican II is best realized in a confessional state. In the face of the failures of liberal democracies to sustain the postwar project, then, integralism takes on the appeal of a new direction despite overall trends toward secularization.

Franco's Spain loomed larger over the 1960s version of integralism, and its end is worth considering for purposes of analyzing the contemporary movement. The church as an institution had been closely tied up with the Franco regime for much of its duration, yet it was the church that was one of the first to start distancing itself from it.[55] This came about both through self-preservation on the part of the institutional body in the face of an increasingly unpopular government and through the influence of priests and others influenced by Catholic social teaching to push back against the authoritarian state.[56] Vatican II played a strong role in this, although perhaps came too late to prevent some worker priests in particular from thinking, "You do not stop being a worker, but you stop being a member of the Church."[57] Thus even in the "integralist" state of Franco's Spain that inspired Bozell and others, dissent rose not just from the anticlerical left but from within the church itself.

The Latin American church has experienced a similar reckoning with its political legacy, particularly the way in which the church has been complicit with authoritarian regimes and antidemocratic movements. In Argentina, the "Dirty War" revealed a church whose bishops were willing

---

54. Thomas Pink, "In Defense of Catholic Integralism," *Public Discourse*, August 12, 2018, https://www.thepublicdiscourse.com/2018/08/39362/.

55. Alan Woods, *Spain's Revolution Against Franco: The Great Betrayal* (Wellred Books, 2019), 90.

56. Woods, *Spain's Revolution Against Franco*, 92.

57. Woods, *Spain's Revolution Against Franco*, 93, 95.

to cooperate with evil to serve their own ends, even as some priests and religious risked their lives to oppose it.[58] Similar situations arose in other Latin American countries, with bishops working closely with authoritarian regimes.[59] Some of these bishop-collaborators later worked in notable Vatican roles under John Paul II. Such examples of "integralist" cooperation are reprehensible and scandalous, yet it is what confessional or quasi-confessional states produce.

Ireland and Quebec also provide cautionary tales for the direction of an intentional confessional state in the contemporary world. Both featured a very strong relationship between the church and the government, and both fell apart rapidly through mass rejection on the part of the people coupled with rebellion on the part of political elites. In Quebec, this took the form of the "Quiet Revolution," a largely peaceful but thorough shift toward secularization with roots in the active Catholic Action groups that began in the 1930s.[60] For Ireland, the process has involved a more public and rhetorically violent rejection of Catholicism, with the sexual abuse crisis looming large.[61] In this case, the close relationships between church and state has devolved almost overnight into a thoroughgoing rejection of the church by the state.

In recent decades, antidemocratic movements have again gained steam precisely in those places where the postwar consensus was formulated and seemed most secure. In that context, *Dignitatis Humanae* stands as a prophetic document articulating a vision of freedom from repression. Hollenbach's reading thus stands as the most adequate of those sketched out above, but it needs to be updated in light of emerging circumstances.

---

58. Gustavo Morello, SJ, *The Catholic Church and Argentina's Dirty War* (Oxford University Press, 2015), 4–5: The Argentine bishops showed notably less energy for fighting the regime or standing up for the poor than their counterparts in other Latin American nations during this period. As Morello describes, the reestablishment of Catholicism as a national church was a reward for this behavior.

59. Theresa Kelley, *Reagan's Gun-Toting Nuns: The Catholic Conflict over Cold War Human Rights Policy in Central America* (Cornell University Press, 2020), 73–74.

60. Michael Gauvreau, *The Catholic Origins of Quebec's Quiet Revolution, 1931–1970*, McGill-Queen's Studies in the History of Religion (McGill-Queen's University Press, 2005), 12–13.

61. Hugh Turpin, *Unholy Catholic Ireland: Religious Hypocrisy, Secular Morality, and Irish Irreligion* (Stanford University Press, 2022).

The most important takeaway from this analysis should be that the key work of *Dignitatis Humanae* was raising the question about how the church should engage with politics—to protect the rights of the church or the human rights owed to all through their inherent dignity? And if the latter, on what ground? Pope Francis, having seen himself the contradictions created in Argentina by a version of integralism, has placed his emphasis squarely there. In this sense, the rise of integralism and of movement that integralists see as potentially useful is frightening yet clarifying. Given its stark reminder of the logic of Vatican II on religious freedom, it demonstrates the wisdom of ideas and movements such as the "Pact of the Catacombs" that were inspired by its "spirit" to divest the church of the trappings of wealth and power.

Chapter 4

Lumen Gentium and Doctrinal Ambivalence

Abel and the Interpretative Task of Filling the Gaps

Florian Klug

In contrast to all previous councils, the convening of the Second Vatican Council was not prompted by a specific threat of heresy. Instead, the council's reconsideration of the church's nature followed a prominent current of early- and mid-twentieth-century Catholic theology. How to understand the church and its role in salvation history were not questions from the theological margins; they arose from within, as we can see in the famous opening words of a 1922 book by Romano Guardini: "A religious process of incalculable importance has begun—the Church is coming to life in the souls of men."[1] Guardini's perception is a paradigm of Catholicism in the early twentieth century. Furthermore, this reconsideration of the church did not emerge as an elitist approach; rather, the common faithful themselves began to rethink the church as an institution and question their role within it. Ecclesiology became a focal point of theological debate. Thus, it is not an exaggeration to state that in Catholic

---

1. Romano Guardini, *The Church and the Catholic, and The Spirit of the Liturgy*, trans. Ada Lane (Sheed & Ward, 1953), 11. For the original publication, see Romano Guardini, *Vom Sinn der Kirche: Fünf Vorträge* (Matthias Grünewald, 1922), 1.

theology, the twentieth century was the century of the church.² In opposition to a previous understanding of catholicity in apologetical terms, the Catholic Church surpassed the denominational limitations and static ecclesiology of the nineteenth century and focused, in the twentieth century, on its fundamentals.

Vatican II shared this outlook and participated in this momentum. In that regard, *Lumen Gentium* did not refute any particular heresy. Taking a fundamental approach, it sought to fathom the church's nature and illustrate its mystery to all the faithful as well as to the world.³ To engage in this endeavor, *Lumen Gentium* took a twofold approach to illustrating the Catholic Church. Firstly, the document states its continuity with previous councils of the Catholic Church, highlighting its apostolicity and implicitly intending to resume the incomplete work of Vatican I. However, Vatican II does not declare how to understand this continuation of the previous councils. This ambiguous gap will lead to several debates about the council's interpretation.⁴ Secondly, *Lumen Gentium* addresses not only the Catholic faithful but also the whole world, as a means to elaborate on the church's catholicity.

This catholicity goes beyond a geographical understanding, insofar as the Catholic Church is an *analogous sacrament* to mediate God's grace to the contemporary world. The church's catholicity is further embedded in salvation history and highlights its encompassing scope in time. Since the beginning of creation, the church has existed because God's will for salvation has always accompanied humanity. As a paradigm for the temporal universality and exceeding a denominational limitation of catholicity, *Lumen Gentium* refers to the traditional motif of "Abel the Just"

---

2. See Gabriel Flynn, "Theological Renewal in the First Half of the Twentieth Century," in *The Cambridge Companion to Vatican II*, ed. Richard R. Gaillardetz (Cambridge University Press, 2020), 19.

3. See Second Vatican Council, Dogmatic Constitution on the Church *Lumen Gentium*, November 21, 1964, chap. 1 (hereafter, LG). All quotations of Vatican II documents are from Austin Flannery, ed., *Vatican Council II: Constitutions, Decrees, Declarations; A Completely Revised Translation in Inclusive Language* (Liturgical Press, 2014).

4. This issue is most apparent in Joseph Ratzinger's emphasis on continuity between Vatican I and Vatican II, against interpretations of Vatican II favoring a reformist framework of discontinuity. See Erich Garhammer, *Genie und Gendarm: Wenn eine Theologie amtlich wird am Beispiel von Benedikt XVI* (Echter, 2023).

(see LG 2). However, it does not develop the idea or declare how to understand it within Catholic ecclesiology or as a motif of catholicity.[5] Even more important, the document does not explain the relation between the Abel motif and other apparently conflicting passages, such as the less grim variation of *nulla salus extra ecclesiam* (see LG 14). Yet these explanations are necessary for a sound Catholic ecclesiology when there is a dangerous potential for deeply contradictory interpretations of and dealings with Vatican II, as we can see in contemporary ecclesiological debates in North America.

Therefore, this paper aims to give insight into the historical foundation of catholicity as an ecclesiological conception. Then, the paper illustrates the role of dogma within the church for social cohesion. Further, it elaborates the motif of Abel and its ecclesiological contexts in Augustine; by this, the paper can consider the ecclesiological implications that Vatican II (implicitly or explicitly) adheres to by utilizing this motif. The paper closes with remarks on the gaps and ambivalences in *Lumen Gentium*, their impact on the reception of Vatican II, and the subsequent debates in Catholic ecclesiology.

The Catholicity of the Church

In its founding period, the church could not rely on any given definition of itself that was already at hand. Due to its separation from Judaism and its development into a genuine institution, the church faced major issues relating to its own identity, such as circumcision, obedience to the Mosaic law, and the offering of temple sacrifices; also, the question of the canonization of the Old Testament was pressing. Besides those matters of practical self-expression, the church needed to clarify its self-understanding. To do so, it utilized several biblical motifs, such as the people of God, a pilgrim, and the new covenant. As part of this self-understanding, it also needed to illustrate its relation to Jesus Christ and the relation of local churches to one another; here the biblical motif of the body of Christ was important. But in these dynamics of conceptional development, it was

---

5. The sentence in LG that refers to Abel offers a footnote that links this motif to Augustine, Gregory the Great, and John Damascene, but it states nothing further about its specific meaning or intentions.

necessary to go beyond biblical motifs and continue the unfolding process of self-becoming.

Therefore, the church went beyond the array of biblical motifs to fathom itself and its relation to God and the world. We find a prime example of this ongoing ecclesial development in reference to catholicity: καθολικός (*katholikós*) is not a biblical term, and yet catholicity can illustrate that, in Christ's salvific works, he gave all peoples access to himself as the wellspring of salvation and made the church responsible for administering this access in terms of sacramentality. For illustrating the vertical relation of the local church to Christ himself, the church referred to πλήρωμα (*pléroma*). In the Eucharist, with the local bishop presiding over it and acting as a sacramental representative of Christ, Christ is fully present in this sacramental encounter. Here, the sacramental plethora translates the notion of πλήρωμα (*pléroma*). Shortly after, καθολικός (*katholikós*) became a synonym for πλήρωμα (*pléroma*);[6] it illustrates that the church lacks nothing in its personal relation to Christ, that is, in the Eucharist with her local bishop. After establishing catholicity as sacramental fullness, the church was to illustrate the horizontal relation of the local churches to one another; for that matter, the church was able to expand the semantical range of πλήρωμα (*pléroma*) to signify universal spatiality by the community of bishops and their relation to Christ. In consequence, the sacramental foundation of πλήρωμα (*pléroma*) in the Eucharist (with the local bishop representing Christ and presiding over the Eucharist), the sacramental bond of the bishops to each other and to Christ were the very factors so that catholicity could become a key notion of the church's self-conception. In regard to καθολικός (*katholikós*), the church illustrates its sacramental fullness and spatial universality that makes it an *inclusive institution*.[7] In her notion of catholicity, it highlights that the encounter with Christ is accessible to the whole world and does not have any exclusive limitations to certain people, gender, social class, intellect, or morality.[8]

---

6. See Dominik Schultheis, *Die Katholizität der Kirche: Versuchung einer Bestimmung der dritten nota ecclesiae in der deutschsprachigen Systematischen Theologie seit dem Zweiten Vatikanum*, Bonner Dogmatische Studien, vol. 55 (Echter, 2015), 20.

7. See Schultheis, *Katholizität*, 25-26.

8. In this understanding of inclusiveness, the church picks up Paul's understanding of universalism, as we can see in Galatians 3:26-29.

However, in this foundational period of the early church, threats from outside and especially from the Roman government were common because the church, in her monotheistic faith, appeared as a hazard to the political stability of the empire.[9] To foster internal solidarity in times of state persecution and general suspicion from outside, Cyprian of Carthage asked his fellow Christians not to engage in divisive debates of moral purity, restrictive church belonging, and proper worship that would end in schism and heresy. Highlighting this need for internal solidarity in times of persecution, Cyprian used rather harsh rhetoric and tried to avoid any schismatic attempts by stating that outside the Catholic Church no salvation is possible (*nulla salus extra ecclesiam*). In this origin, Cyprian did not have any groups of nonbelievers in mind; in his use of the axiom, he opted for an intra-ecclesial sense of cohesion and solidarity against threats from outside.[10] Hence, for an adequate understanding of Catholicism, it is utterly important to contextualize these notions of sacramentality, universality, and necessity for church belonging in their origins and to balance certain notional aspects that come along with it.

The Aim of the Dogma

After Jesus' ascension into heaven (see Luke 24:51), it was not clear how his disciples should continue his mission and, especially, how to understand and structure this group, because Jesus did not instruct his disciples with specific rules about how the church was to function.[11]

Since then, the church has engaged in the endeavor to find a common ground of belief for establishing itself as a social enterprise in solidarity and shared faith. As one of the first steps, it decided against the compulsory

---

9. The Roman Empire saw in the benevolence of the Roman deities that asked for offerings and devotion a guarantee of its stability. In the Christian adoration of God alone, such adoration of the Roman deities was unacceptable, and therefore the Christians refused to offer anything to them. This refusal appeared to the Roman authorities and ordinary Romans as profoundly dangerous, because it put the Roman deities' benevolence at stake.

10. See Joyce E. Salisbury, "'The Bond of a Common Mind': A Study of Collective Salvation from Cyprian to Augustine," *Journal of Religious History* 13, no. 3 (1985): 240. See also Cyprian of Carthage, *Epistles*, 72:20-21 (ANF 5:384-85).

11. For the absence of clear instructions, see John 15:12-17.

status of the Jewish law (see Acts 15) without rejecting the salvific role of Israel. Further, against the dualistic reduction of the church's sacred Scriptures by Marcion of Sinope, the church established its canon and made sure that a multifaceted approach to understanding Jesus and his bond to the Jewish people persisted.[12]

As paradigms of ecclesial consensus, elucidation of faith, and solidarity, we can refer to the Councils of Nicaea and Chalcedon in their dogmatic function. Prompted by heretical teachings that were incompatible with the church's teaching due to their extreme and irreconcilable perspectives, the church developed the *safeguarding institutions of council and dogma* to establish a common ground of shared faith and belief.[13] These doctrinal symbols (after the Greek σύμβολον [*sýmbolon*], as a means of mutual recognition and acknowledgment) served to reject extreme and untenable positions for the church as a social entity.[14]

It is a truism that dogma and God are not identical. Instead, doctrinal promulgations are stepping stones into the mystery of faith,[15] insofar as the faithful acknowledge their lack of sovereignty to define God's mystery. In that regard, we can recognize heresy as an inappropriate attempt to have intellectual control of defining God. Accordingly, dogma of the church cannot surpass the limitations of human language, as Lateran IV pointed out.[16]

Moving on in the history of Catholic doctrine, we find a similar stance even in the Council of Trent. Facing the questions of the Protestant Refor-

---

12. See Martin Ebner, "Der christliche Kanon," in *Einleitung in das Neue Testament*, ed. Martin Ebner and Stefan Schreiber, Kohlhammer Studienbücher Theologie, vol. 6 (Kohlhammer, 2008), 25-28.

13. See Florian Klug, *The Fragility of Language and the Encounter with God: On the Contingency and Legitimacy of Doctrine* (Fortress, 2021), 110-11.

14. See Klug, *Fragility of Language*, 99-109, 116-19.

15. See Bonaventure, *III Sent*, d. 24 a. 3 q. 2 (*Opera Omnia* 3, 527): "An article [of faith] provides a glimpse at Divine truth, tending toward it" ("Articulus [fidei] est perceptio divinae Veritatis tendens in ipsam"; my translation).

16. See Heinrich Denzinger, ed., *Enchiridion symbolorum, definitionum et declarationum de rebus fidei et morum: Compendium of Creeds, Definitions, and Declarations on Matters of Faith and Morals*, revised, enlarged, and, in collaboration with Helmut Hoping, ed. Peter Hünermann for the original bilingual edition, ed. Robert Fastiggi and Anne Englund Nash for the English edition, 43rd ed. (Ignatius Press, 2012), 806 (hereafter, DH): "For between Creator and creature no similitude can be expressed without implying a greater dissimilitude."

mation, Trent refrains from promulgating a definitive ecclesiology or sacramental theology of the Catholic Church; this stance stems from the fact that intra-Catholic disputes and theological plurality also influenced Trent.[17] Especially in matters of the church's liturgy, Trent promoted Catholic plurality and the continuation of liturgical traditions against the assumed Protestant abandonment of traditions, as a matter of discontinuity.[18] In that regard, Trent understands the Protestant Reformation as an unsound approach of discontinuity and promotion of untenable positions to the rest of the church. Hence, Trent regards Protestantism as stepping out of the realm of catholicity. But at the same time, as an example of ongoing ambivalences within Catholicism, *after* Trent we have a Romanization of the liturgy in the sense of abolition of local Catholic rites, such as, for example, the rite of the Patriarchate of Aquileia, abolished in 1597.

In continuation of Trent, Robert Bellarmine experiences the Protestant conception of the spiritual church and the subsequent invisible belonging as matters of great uncertainty.[19] To promote a stable foundation of certain church belonging, he searches for a reliable tenet. In his conception of church belonging, Bellarmine refers to the church as the body of Christ. Since the body of Christ consists of both a divine and a human nature, humanity and especially the church have no direct insight into the divine nature and, therefore, cannot make definitive statements about it.[20] As

---

17. See Hubert Jedin, *Geschichte des Konzils von Trient*, vol. 4:2 (Herder, 1975), 244–45. See also Klaus Ganzer, "Trient. 3) Konzil," in *Lexikon für Theologie und Kirche*, ed. Walter Kasper et al., vol. 10, 3rd ed. (Herder, 2006), 231.

18. See Hubert Wolf, *Der Unfehlbare: Pius IX. und die Erfindung des Katholizismus im 19. Jahrhundert*, 3rd ed. (C. H. Beck, 2020), 142–45. We can see this promotion of liturgical plurality in the acknowledgment of local traditions of liturgy which are at least two hundred years old. Thus, Trent aims at stopping liturgical fashions that have no roots in the church's tradition.

19. Bellarmine is afraid that by distinguishing between an invisible, spiritual side and a corporeal, visible side of the church, and declaring that belonging to the church as a visible institution to be an unnecessary matter while belonging to the spiritual church is necessary matter to experience God's saving grace, Protestant ecclesiology might double the church and thus tear apart the body of Christ. See Robert Bellarmine, *De conciliis*, lib. 3, cap. 2 (*Opera Omnia* 2, 317).

20. Also, Bellarmine refers to Abel's belonging to the church as an analogy to the catechumens and their belonging to the church. They do not share the visible belonging via baptism and the profession of faith, two of the three *vincula*. The third *vinculum* is the recognition of the hierarchy of the Catholic Church with the pope as the supreme

a matter of certainty about church belonging and God's saving grace through church membership, Bellarmine develops the concept of the *tria vincula* (the triple bonds of shared faith, sacraments, and hierarchy) as core criteria to belong to the human side of the body of Christ.[21] For Bellarmine, Christ's incarnation guarantees that the divine and human side of the church will never fall apart.[22]

Narrowing and Widening of the Church's Scope

However, the aftermath of Trent and Bellarmine's theology displays that there is no guarantee of paying close attention to the historical contexts and engaging in a process of differentiated and balanced reception. Contrary to a balanced view, both Trent and Bellarmine become part of a reductive understanding of Catholicism, insofar as catholicity becomes solely a denominational matter. This notion of Catholicism tries to cope with the existential dangers from outside the church through a unified yet simplistic understanding of it. However, without room for multiple perspectives, the notion of the Catholic Church collapsed into a monolithic conception and eliminated large parts of the church's tradition for an apologetic agenda.[23] This approach to Catholic unity and uniformity reaches its pinnacle in the late nineteenth and early twentieth centuries, in the promulgation of Vatican I's dogmatic constitution *Pastor Aeternus* and the subsequent *Syllabus Errorum*.[24] As a result, the Catholic Church ended up with a *static ecclesiology* with little to no room for hermeneutical differences and theological development for the sake of doctrinal clarity.[25]

---

pontiff. In analogy to Abel, the catechumens are part of the church, and yet they do not belong explicitly to the visible institution. See Bellarmine, *De conciliis*, lib. 3, cap. 3 (*Opera Omnia* 2, 319).

21. See Bellarmine, *De conciliis*, lib. 3, cap. 2 (*Opera Omnia* 2, 318).

22. See also Florian Klug, *Beyond the Visible Church: The Motif of the* ecclesia ab Abel *from Augustine to James Alison* (Liturgical Press, 2024), 278-82.

23. See Wolf, *Der Unfehlbare*, 148-51.

24. See Patrick Granfield, "The Church as Societas Perfecta in the Schemata of Vatican I," *Church History* 48, no. 4 (1979): 433-37.

25. See Peter Hünermann, "Theologischer Kommentar zur dogmatischen Konstitution über die Kirche *Lumen Gentium*," in *Herders Theologischer Kommentar zum Zweiten Vatikanischen Konzil*, ed. Peter Hünermann and Bernd Jochen Hilberath, vol. 2 (Herder, 2009), 273.

In the early twentieth century, this static ecclesiology left numerous theologians, such as Romano Guardini, Yves Congar, and Henri de Lubac, unsatisfied with the conceptional depiction of the Catholic Church. By going beyond the contemporary Catholic ecclesiologies, they engaged in the theological enterprise of *ressourcement* by rediscovering the richness of the Catholic tradition. Therein, they unearthed the inner plurality of Catholic theology and let the dynamic nature of the church resurface. They illustrated that the church is embedded in the dynamics of salvation history and, subsequently, shaped by the historical interactions in its self-understanding.[26]

Due to Congar's involvement in Vatican II, he was able to include his insights into *ressourcement* theology for ecclesiological matters. In that regard, it is fair to state that the general outline of Vatican II's ecclesiology is shaped by *ressourcement* theology, focusing on the dynamics of the church within salvation history. Hence, the most prominent metaphor for the church is the people of God (*populus Dei*) on its pilgrimage toward the eschatological consummation.[27] As a part of this reconsideration of the church's embeddedness in salvation history and its encompassing scope throughout time, *Lumen Gentium* refers to Abel as the first (besides Adam) member of the church, due to his righteousness.[28] This reference to Abel stems from Congar's studies in *ressourcement* theology;[29] and yet, besides the general reference to the church's encompassing scope in salvation history, *Lumen Gentium* does not clarify how to understand the Abel motif, concerning specific ecclesiological matters. Regarding a notion of ecclesiological connectivity, *Lumen Gentium* expresses profound solidarity with all who are poor and who suffer.[30] In this, we can see an

---

26. For one prime example, see Henri de Lubac, *Corpus Mysticum: The Eucharist and the Church in the Middle Ages*, trans. Gemma Simmons with Richard Price and Christopher Stephens (University of Notre Dame Press, 2006).

27. See LG 9–16.

28. For the discussion at Vatican II about Adam as a member of the church before Abel, see Klug, *Beyond the Visible Church*, 329-31.

29. See Yves Congar, *My Journal of the Council*, trans. Mary John Ronayne and Mary Cecily Boulding (Liturgical Press, 2012), 871. For Congar's investigation into the motif of Abel, see Yves Congar, "Ecclesia ab Abel," in *Abhandlungen über Theologie und Kirche: Festschrift für Karl Adam*, ed. Marcel Reding (Patmos, 1952), 79-108.

30. See LG 8.

implicit relation to Abel as the first martyr, insofar as *Lumen Gentium* affiliates those who suffer with the church.

For a better understanding of the Abel motif and its implications for the ecclesiology of Vatican II, it is crucial to go back to Augustine and his elaboration on this motif for ecclesiological matters. Afterward, we can illustrate how the reference to Abel in *Lumen Gentium* does not appear to be a mere coincidence; rather, we can see that this motif serves as a paradigm for the ecclesiological approach of Vatican II.

Abel in Augustine as a Means for Rectifying Ecclesiological Imbalances

After becoming bishop, Augustine's prime concern was no longer his own existential concerns. Instead, he saw himself responsible for moderating and rectifying current debates within the Catholic Church and on the outskirts of Christianity.

In principle, Augustine sees Christ as the final bringer of salvation, and a sound relation to Christ only takes place within the church. This is the reason that Augustine adheres to the notion of *nulla salus extra ecclesiam* in general. However, in Christ's incarnation and salvific work out of divine love, it is impossible, according to Augustine, to be in a salvific relation to Christ without engaging in a loving relationship to each neighbor and fellow Christians.[31] In an ongoing approach of promoting an open conception of catholicity and "keeping the Church in the middle,"[32] Augustine seeks to deconstruct several schismatic, heretical, and exclusivist conceptions of divisive Christian groups and alter their ecclesiological imbalances. For that reason, Augustine engages with the Manicheans, Donatists, and Pelagians to promote the church's universality regarding time, membership, and moral capacity.

---

31. See Michael Root, "Augustine on the Church," in *T&T Clark Companion to Augustine and Modern Theology*, ed. C. C. Pecknold and Tarmo Toom (T&T Clark, 2013), 64.

32. See Anthony Dupont, "Keeping the Church in the Middle: Augustine of Hippo's Practical-Theoretical Ecclesiology," in *'Nos Sumus Tempora': Studies on Augustine and His Reception Offered to Mathijs Lamberigts*, Bibliotheca Ephemeridum Theologicarum Lovaniensium 316, ed. Anthony Dupont, Wim François, and Johan Leemans (Peeters, 2020), 78–80.

In each debate with the Manicheans, Donatists, and Pelagians, Augustine refers to Abel as the first righteous or the church beginning with Abel. Although, the motif of the *ecclesia ab Abel* is not a central figure in Augustine's works, we can nevertheless highlight it as an important theme in his time as bishop. For his ecclesiology, it has its main value in providing balance against the threats of schismatic, heretical, and exclusivist ecclesiologies.

In more detail, Augustine uses the motif of Abel for the following matters. Firstly, in his debate with the Manicheans, Augustine refers to Abel as the first member of the church to dodge their rejection of the Old Testament. In Christianity's continuity with Judaism's monotheistic faith, God is not only the creator of the universe but also its savior. This is the reason the Old Testament is part of the Christian canon.[33] Further, in Jesus' incarnation, God redeems humanity and makes salvation accessible to everyone. Yet even before the incarnation established deep solidarity with humanity as bodily creatures, salvation was possible. Augustine illustrates this salvific transgression of the incarnation date by referring to Abel, his faith, and offerings. Abel stands in a salvific relation to Christ through his implicit hope for Christ's eschatological coming.[34]

Secondly, in his debate with the Donatists, Augustine can illustrate that not only the vertical relation to Christ is essential for salvation, but further the horizontal relation to one's neighbor is equally important. By their separation as the holy remnant from the Catholic Church and the ongoing violent behavior against the Christian community,[35] Augustine shows that the Donatists follow the example of Cain that does not lead to salvation. In contrast, Augustine uses Abel not only to illustrate the rejection of the Donatists' violence as faithful behavior and a practical expression of faith but also to present him as a prototypical forerunner to Christ in his martyrdom. Further, Abel had an implicit hope for the coming of God and his eschatological reign, while the Donatists saw themselves in an apocalyptical contraction of time, sharing the identical

---

33. See Michael Cameron, "Augustine and Scripture," in *A Companion to Augustine*, ed. Mark Vessey (Wiley-Blackwell, 2012), 204.

34. See Augustine, *Letters 100–155*, The Works of Saint Augustine: A Translation for the 21st Century, vol. 2:2, trans. Roland Teske, SJ (New City Press, 2003), 102:12 (26-27).

35. See Maureen A. Tilley, *The Bible in Christian North Africa: The Donatist World* (Fortress, 1997), 155-62.

fate of the Old Testament's martyrs, such as the Maccabees.[36] Like certain martyrs of the Old Testament, the Donatists saw a strict necessity for complete obedience to the Mosaic law, especially in ritual purity, and could not recognize any development since the incarnation of Christ. For them, in their static ecclesiology, the revocation of the Mosaic law or the eschatological completion of time were untenable.[37] The Donatists focused heavily on moral and ritual purity, while Catholic Christians dismissed Donatists as simulators of piety. Countering their elitist stance, Augustine elaborates on the church as a complex entity (*ecclesia permixta*) that includes good and bad Christians in the time of the church's pilgrimage toward the heavenly Jerusalem.[38] In his debate with the Donatists, Augustine used Abel in multiple ways to show the necessity for the love of neighbor and understanding solidarity with those who cannot fulfil the moral standards of an elite, especially within the church. In the grand scheme of salvation history, Augustine could illustrate the linearity of time toward the eschatological completion via Abel's hope,[39] in contrast to an apocalyptical stasis.

Thirdly, in the debate with the Pelagians, Augustine showed in regard to Abel that no one is exempt from the necessity of God's grace for faithful behavior, because after Adam's transgression, humanity's capacity for good deeds is deeply flawed. The Pelagians themselves, especially Julian of Eclanum, saw in Abel an example that shows that Adam's transgression did not lead to a fundamental corruption of human will and nature.[40] While Julian could point at systemic inconsistencies in Augustine's conception of grace and original sin, the underlying issue of the Pelagian debate was their moral pride, insofar as they had no awareness for implicit privileges and looked down upon everyone who could not follow their elitist stance

36. See Jesse A. Hoover, *The Donatist Church in an Apocalyptic Age* (Oxford University Press, 2008), 80-82.

37. See Augustine, *Breviculus conlationis cum Donatistis: libri tres*, 3:10 (CCL 149A: 277-79), 3:20 (CCL 149A: 285-87).

38. See Dupont, "Keeping the Church in the Middle," 76.

39. See Augustine, *Exposition of the Psalms: 121-150*, The Works of Saint Augustine: A Translation for the 21st Century, vol. 3:20, trans. Maria Boulding, OSB (New City Press, 2004), 142:3 (345).

40. See Augustine, *Answer to the Pelagians III: Unfinished Work in Answer to Julian*, The Works of Saint Augustine: A Translation for the 21st Century, vol. 1:25, trans. Roland J. Teske, SJ (New City Press, 1999), 2:67 (1:25:192).

of moral capability.⁴¹ They lack a sense of communal solidarity, and further, in their conception of freedom and morality, there was hardly any theological space for Christ dying on the cross to redeem humanity and bestow grace through the sacraments. Their ecclesiological conceptions opt for individualism instead of belonging to a community of shared redemption. In opposition to a rather elitist stance of morality and capability, Augustine strongly favors the church as a complex community (*corpus permixtum*) that is moderate in its demands and tries to avoid any form of extremism.⁴² Further, Augustine sees the church as a community of shared faith and solidarity, in contrast to a collection of mere individuals.

In general, in Augustine's theology, the Abel motif is neither a prominent element that runs continuously through his whole theological development nor is it an aspect with a cogent definition. Instead, the Abel motif is a sidenote that occurs on several occasions and has the *function of a rhetorical topos* that is more shaped by the argumentative surroundings than having a defined and stable content.⁴³ However, for ecclesiological matters, the Abel motif is deeply interesting because Augustine uses it as a means for *deconstructing ecclesiological imbalances*. In Abel, he can show the necessity of humility, nonviolence, and the salvific relation to Christ.⁴⁴ This relation is not only important for each Christian vertically, but it also entails a collective belonging to a group, as a horizontal relation that rests on divine charity and calls for practicing charity personally.

In his time as bishop, Augustine tried to counter ecclesiological imbalances that stemmed from elitist, separatist, or heretical conceptions. In his Christological ecclesiology, he saw the inseparable connection between vertical and horizontal solidarity. In following Christ's example, practical

---

41. See Nozomu Yamada, "Rhetorical, Political, and Ecclesiastical Perspectives of Augustine's and Julian of Eclanum's Theological Response in the Pelagian Controversy," *Scrinium* 14 (2018): 186.

42. See James K. Lee, *Augustine and the Mystery of the Church* (Fortress, 2017), xxvi.

43. See Oliver Primavesi, "Topik; Topos: I," in *Historisches Wörterbuch der Philosophie*, ed. Joachim Ritter and Karlfried Gründer, vol. 10 (Schwabe, 1998), 1266.

44. See Augustine, *Answer to Faustus, a Manichean*, The Works of Saint Augustine: A Translation for the 21st Century, vol. 1:20, trans. Roland J. Teske, SJ (New City Press, 2007), 12:9 (131). For a similar passage, arguing even more succinctly, see Augustine, "Miscellany of in Response to Simplician," in *Responses to Miscellaneous Questions*, The Works of Saint Augustine: A Translation for the 21st Century, vol. 1:12, trans. Boniface Ramsey (New City Press, 2008), 58:2 (77).

charity holds a key role for a sound ecclesiology. Thinking ecclesiologically with Abel, this motif serves as a means for a balanced yet incomplete conception of the church. Consequently, the Abel motif is for Augustine a leverage to promote relationality and eschatological openness against reductionist or overly narrow conceptions of the church. Hence, Augustine is embedded in the (early) church's attempt to express a sound self-conception while being aware of her historical development as a pilgrim. In this ecclesiological modesty, Augustine lets God be in charge of the church's course within history and its way to the eschatological completion.[45]

For the subsequent generations of theologians in the West, Augustine's conceptional approach and theological imaginary provided a general roadmap and served quite often as an authoritative starting point for theological trajectories. In Augustine's role as a prime authority, the following generations also picked up the motif of Abel, as the first member of the church and the first righteous person after Adam's transgression. Since Augustine did not refer to the Abel motif identically each time and gave it a specific ecclesiological function, the subsequent uses of the Abel motif in ecclesiological matters show a lot of variety. However, from early medieval times (e.g., Gregory the Great), through high medieval times (e.g., Thomas Aquinas or Bonaventure), late medieval times (e.g., Jan Hus), or early modern times (e.g., Francisco Suárez, Martin Luther, or even Robert Bellarmine),[46] all these uses share a common feature: The Abel motif opens the ecclesiological perspective, avoids unsound theological limitations, and rectifies ecclesiological imbalances. In its context, definitions of the necessary conditions for belonging to the church become less absolute, since Abel did not confess his faith explicitly. Even further, ecclesiological considerations surpass the reality of the church in the present stage of history and its contemporary limitations, and the theological notion of time opens onto the entirety of salvation history. In reference to the Abel motif, a profound recontextualization of theology and Christianity takes place: Because of Abel's status as the first of the righteous, the very beginning of humanity is at hand and puts Christianity in the context of the history of humanity. Regarding Abel, it is untenable

---

45. See Lee, *Augustine and the Mystery*, 44–48.
46. For a listing of these passages and other theologians, see Congar, "Ecclesia ab Abel," 79–108.

to look at Christianity or even Catholicism as a matter of a faithful elite or even a holy remnant; the Abel motif suggests an ecclesiological universalism. In other words, the motif of the *ecclesia ab Abel* shows that the monotheistic God of Judaism and Christianity is a God of history; God accompanies creation and guides humanity from the very beginning to the consummation of time.

Unsurprisingly, in continuation of Augustine's heritage, the Abel motif points not only to the beginning of creation, time, and humanity; eschatology and the completion of time are likewise matters that are enmeshed in this motif. The matter of justice is especially important in regard to eschatology and redemption from violence:[47] Abel shows that from the very beginning of humanity, crime and injustice are present. Yet crime and injustice are also accompanied by the call for justice and the compensation of suffering and torment. Throughout almost all references to Abel, he appears as a prefiguration of Jesus Christ and his violent death on the cross. Therefore, in its ecclesiological function, the Abel motif has a specific Christological focus. Further, this relation of Abel's death, Christ's suffering, and God as a companion of humanity broadens the theological and, especially, ecclesiological horizon. Moreover, it illustrates profoundly that the matter of justice cannot be absent from ecclesiology. Hence, an exclusivist approach of detachment from the world and reducing the church to matters of the right form of Catholic piety or even becoming a holy remnant is incompatible with the ecclesiological trajectories of the Abel motif, as a prime figure regarding the church's catholicity.

The Irresolvable Task of Bridging the Gaps

Coming back to the matters of Vatican II, *Lumen Gentium* states at the very beginning that this council continues the task of the previous councils in elaborating on the mystery of the church. However, it does not clarify how we can understand this continuity. This gap is crucial and leaves a certain ambiguity and even ambivalence.

Looking back at nineteenth-century Catholicism as the context of the First Vatican Council, we see that this period features a stark separation

---

47. See Bonaventure, *Hexaemeron*, 14:17-18 (*Opera Omnia* 5, 396).

of the church from the secular realm. Here, the church was understood to provide access to a detached realm of grace that was exempt from the dangers of Enlightenment, philosophical skepticism, and modernity in general. One pinnacle of this separative stance surfaces in Catholic romanticism, a movement that imagined an alternative world that is exempt from the dangers of the present.[48] In a similar stance, Vatican I's constitution on the church *Pastor Aeternus* (1870) presents the papal office as a visible and personal guarantee for the existence of the church and safeguard of the revealed truths of faith, saving the faithful from contemporary errors and the gates of hell.[49] In sum, Catholicism of the nineteenth century takes a stance of defending the church against the dangers of the modern world. Resulting in a detachment of the church from the common world and its dynamics, the main ecclesiology of that period becomes blind to the dynamics of salvation history; in other words, it becomes static. Due to the apologetic approach, Catholicism of that period was unable to acknowledge the richness and complexity of the Catholic tradition.

Looking from Vatican I to Vatican II, the idea of continuity is hard to unfold. Thus, after its statement of continuity, *Lumen Gentium* takes a different approach in illustrating the church's relation to the world. Instead of highlighting the separation of the church's realm of grace from the secular realm, it presents the church's entanglement in human history and her temporal universality.[50] One key motif for illustrating this entanglement and the church's encompassing nature is Abel, as the first member of the church.

Lumen Gentium does not delineate a fully developed and systematically coherent ecclesiology. Instead, in serving the genuine aim of dogma, it provides an ecclesiological common ground with connectivity to multifaceted approaches, by relying on traditional motifs.[51] Its approach is

---

48. See Wolf, *Der Unfehlbare*, 102–3.
49. See *Pastor Aeternus*, Prologue (DH 3051–52).
50. *Nostra Aetate* even augments this entanglement in human history. Further, this document also illustrates the encompassing nature of grace, insofar as other religions cannot be seen in complete separation from God, as the source of truth and insight. See Second Vatican Council, Declaration on the Relation of the Church with Non-Christian Religions *Nostra Aetate*, October 28, 1965, no. 2.
51. See Walter Kasper, "Volk Gottes—Leib Christi—Communio im Hl. Geist: Zur Ekklesiologie im Ausgang vom Zweiten Vatikanischen Konzil," in *Erinnerung an die Zukunft: Das Zweite Vatikanische Konzil*, ed. Jan-Heiner Tück (Herder, 2012), 225.

both inclusive and traditional in the best possible meaning. Its prominent reference to Abel is therefore not a mere coincidence; the Abel motif highlights the far-reaching continuity in tradition. Therein, *Lumen Gentium* goes beyond the defensive stance of Catholicism of the nineteenth century, along with its rather narrow and static ecclesiology that stems from the urge for denominational uniformity and theological clarity.

Due to its underlying ambivalence between which form of continuity and between inclusivist and exclusivist ecclesiological matters, *Lumen Gentium* enables multiple perspectives in Catholic ecclesiology, without contradicting each other.[52] Further, in its focus on salvation history and the pilgrimage of the people of God, it provides doctrinal space for developments in ecclesiology; thus, there is no need for it to adopt a definitive and systematically coherent ecclesiology. To engage with the specific demands of the times, Vatican II, especially *Lumen Gentium*, passes the theological responsibility onto the faithful themselves. They ought to develop appropriate ecclesiologies that are sensible to timely demands.

In this ambiguity, *Lumen Gentium* takes an indirect path to the genuine aim of doctrinal statements, in providing a common ground of shared faith and solidarity.[53] Therein, it promotes the key concern of ecumenical councils against heretical and schismatic movements that threaten the social and faithful cohesion of the church.

In its ecclesiological openness toward the course of salvation history and its solidarity with humanity, starting with Abel as the first among the faithful, *Lumen Gentium* presents itself as a document of hope and the church as an institution of hope and solidarity.[54] These aspects of hope and solidarity become even more apparent by the fact that Vatican II did not produce a single document offering the traditional anathemas for reinforcing ecclesial cohesion.

However, while this theological framework of openness represents a welcoming, noncompetitive gesture on the one hand, it also introduces a certain vulnerability on the other hand. In its theological gaps as well as spaces for development and constructive interpretation, Vatican II is

---

52. This is also a feature that runs from Augustine to Bellarmine in their uses of the Abel motif.

53. This inclusive aim of Vatican II of solidarity and inclusivity surfaces in the fact that it does not include anathemas. From a stance of hope and in a welcoming gesture, Vatican II does not see a need to do so.

54. See LG 5, 8.

rather unable to defend itself against misinterpretations, especially due to the absence of anathemas. This weakness is apparent in demanding times that lack a perspective of hope and include multiple crises (climate change, ecology, clergy abuse crisis, politics, wars, and so on).

One way of escapism is the revival of nineteenth-century Catholicism and its separation of the church from the world, as a realm of grace and security.[55] Due to *Lumen Gentium*'s ambiguous or even conflictive relation between inclusivist and exclusivist passages, it is easy to engage in a selective reading of it, take up the romanticism of the nineteenth century, and present again Catholicism as a counterculture to the modern world. For this endeavor, we find in section 14 of *Lumen Gentium* the definitive necessity of belonging to the Catholic Church and the rather simplistic reiteration of Bellarmine's *tria vincula*, which are athwart to the otherwise welcoming and inclusive nature of Vatican II. Yet the complexities and crises of the contemporary world are demanding, and they affect humanity in general. By a stance of escapism and return to the Catholic ghetto of the nineteenth century,[56] the neoconservative revival in Catholicism becomes blind to the inescapable challenges of the future that concern

---

55. In an interview, Pope Francis takes up this stance of spiritual courage and advises the faithful to become creative when engaging the world and its demanding nature. He sees escapism not as a feasible approach for the faithful:

> The creativity of the Christian needs to show forth in opening up new horizons, opening windows, opening transcendence toward God and toward people, and in creating new ways of being at home. . . . What comes to my mind is a verse from the Aeneid in the midst of defeat: the counsel is not to give up, but save yourself for better times, for in those times remembering what has happened will help us. Take care of yourselves for a future that will come. And remembering in that future what has happened will do you good. Take care of the *now*, for the sake of tomorrow. . . . But don't run away, don't take refuge in escapism, which in this time is of no use to you. (Austen Ivereigh, "*The Tablet* Interview with Pope Francis on COVID-19, April 2020," in *Maynooth College Reflects on COVID-19: New Realities in Uncertain Times*, ed. Jeremy Corley, Neil Xavier O'Donoghue, and Salvador Ryan [Messenger Publications, 2021], 23; also available as Austen Ivereigh, "An Interview with Pope Francis: 'A Time of Great Uncertainty,'" *Commonweal*, March 12, 2023, https://www.commonwealmagazine.org/time-great-uncertainty.)

56. For the notion of the Catholic ghetto, see Hugh McLeod, "Building the 'Catholic Ghetto': Catholic Organisations, 1870–1914," in *Voluntary Religion*, Studies in Church History, vol. 23, ed. W. J. Sheils and Diana Wood (Oxford University Press, 1986), 411–44.

humanity as a whole.[57] Further, all theological efforts of Vatican II and *ressourcement* theology are at stake if extreme neoconservative tendencies gain more momentum and start to prevail in theological debates.

It is a task for contemporary and future theologians to find ways to bridge the gaps between universalism and ambivalence. The Abel motif is a barely tapped resource to continue the Catholic tradition and enable multifaceted approaches without contradicting each other. The main issue is how to develop a robust and welcoming form of theology that does not fall prey to unsound temptations of simplistic answers.

---

57. It is a good sign that Pope Francis engages in this task to cope with the ecological and climate crises in his pontificate. His encyclical *Laudato Si'* highlights the grave responsibility of the Catholic Church to care for humanity and creation.

Chapter 5

A Unity Beyond the Human?

Legacy and Limits of Vatican II in an Age of Ecological Crisis

William G. Kuncken

Recent international reporting[1] has continued to confirm what countless scientific studies have suggested for decades: If the global population is to reduce the harmful effects of anthropogenic ecological destruction, substantive actions to mitigate the cataclysmic effects of climate change are indispensable. Such a task necessitates the collective commitment of the international community to move beyond current political discord and social estrangement and toward the realization of an ecologically inclusive future.[2] In a Catholic theological context, the grounding for this vision of unity is in the transformative events and documents of the Second Vatican Council. Through the council's advancement of "social and exterior union,"[3] its texts paved a pathway to a deeper appreciation

---

1. See the Intergovernmental Panel on Climate Change, *Climate Change 2022: Impacts, Adaptation, and Vulnerability* (2022), https://www.ipcc.ch/report/ar6/wg2/.

2. This chapter will include a number of references to twentieth-century Jesuit theologian Pierre Teilhard de Chardin. Although the Second Vatican Council convened following Teilhard's death in 1955, the influence of his ecologically inclusive thoughts on the future is observable throughout the documents of council.

3. Second Vatican Council, Pastoral Constitution on the Church in the Modern World *Gaudium et Spes*, December 7, 1965, no. 42 (hereafter, GS). Except where indicated, all quotations of Vatican II documents are from Austin Flannery, ed., *Vatican Council II:*

for biodiversity and wider ecological consideration. This chapter seeks to highlight how the Second Vatican Council provided the church with a foundation for its subsequent ecological statements, initiatives, and advocacy through a reflection on the major conciliar themes of ecumenism, interreligious dialogue, and global engagement. Subsequently, we will also focus on the interplay of the metaphysical claim of relational oneness/holism[4] with the ecclesiological position of the church as a mystical *Body of Christ*, with each member and each branch distinct yet part of an irreducible whole. While this examination will highlight points of continuity between conciliar theology, its ecumenical/unitive focus, and the ecologically conscious thought of relational holism, to illustrate the connection effectively in an age of ecological crisis, it must also discuss some of the fundamental limits of the theology of the Second Vatican Council in the present situation. Although prescient in many ways concerning the signs of the times, the council fell short of providing the church with a framework to receive an ecologically inclusive sense of unity beyond the human, a holistic grounding that might enable the church to embrace critical doctrinal shifts from its accustomed/traditional anthropocentrism.

We will begin with a reflection on John XXIII's aspiration for a unified global community at the commencement of the Second Vatican Council, encapsulated within the pope's *Gaudet Mater Ecclesia*[5] and the council's *Message to Humanity*.[6] Proceeding from these opening messages of worldwide unity, we will turn our attention to instances where the council embraced this vision, first with the Decree on Ecumenism, *Unitatis*

Constitutions, Decrees, Declarations; A Completely Revised Translation in Inclusive Language (Liturgical Press, 2014).

4. Although ultimately a claim of theological significance, the metaphysical concept of relational holism will be identified in this chapter as "ecologically conscious" due to its consonance with systems biology. See Edward O. Wilson, "Biophilia and the Conservation Ethic," in *The Biophilia Hypothesis*, ed. Stephen R. Kellert and Edward O. Wilson (Island Press/Shearwater Books, 1993), 31–41.

5. Pope John XXIII, "Gaudet Mater Ecclesia—Pope John XXIII's Address on the Occasion of the Solemn Opening of the Most Holy Council," in *The Documents of Vatican II*, ed. Walter M. Abbott, SJ (America Press, 1966), 710–19.

6. Second Vatican Council, "Message to Humanity from the Council Fathers," in Abbott, *The Documents of Vatican II*, 3–7.

Redintegratio,[7] and its explicit call for interdenominational reunification, followed by the pivotal Declaration on the Relation of the Church to Non-Christian Religions, *Nostra Aetate*,[8] and its acknowledgment of the "ray of that truth which enlightens all men and women" (NA 2). Lastly, we will unpack the resonant message of relational holism found in *Gaudium et Spes*, which explicitly outlines a new era of engagement and reconciliation with the tantamount scientific discoveries of the modern world. Evidenced by conciliar adaptations in approach and amendments in language, the Second Vatican Council ushered in a new era of the global Catholic Church. In this liminal period, the church began to recognize its pivotal role in guiding the planet toward a union that transcends overt religious affiliation, social distinction, and even the separation of the human condition/experience from that of other members of the wider ecological community. Nevertheless, the council's confidence in human development and growth ultimately failed to consider the relation of this development and growth to widespread ecological harm. Without this treatment, any conciliar grounding for a robust environmental ethic remains inhibited by the conventional restraints of its time.

John XXIII on Global Unity

Often written off initially as an interim or transitional pope, John XXIII shocked the ecclesiastical hierarchy and global media alike by announcing his intention to convene the Second Vatican Council.[9] In the wake of

---

7. Second Vatican Council, Declaration on the Relation of the Church to Non-Christian Religions *Nostra Aetate*, October 28, 1965 (hereafter, NA).

8. Second Vatican Council, Decree on Ecumenism *Unitatis Redintegratio*, November 21, 1964 (hereafter, UR).

9. James M. Childs writes, "John XXIII is perhaps best remembered by the world at large as the pope who called Vatican II into session. This was a surprise if not a shock to many church leaders since it had been only ninety years since Vatican I (1869–1870), which was not convened until three hundred years after the Council of Trent. Pope John XXIII however expressed the need for *aggiornamento* (literally, 'up to date') for the church. *Aggiornamento* then became a paramount theme of the Vatican Council, which enacted far-reaching changes in liturgy, ecumenism, and the church's relation to the world." James M. Childs, "Pope John XXIII and Vatican II," in *Christian Social Teaching: A Reader in Christian Social Ethics from the Bible to Present*, 2nd ed., ed. George W. Forell and James M. Childs Jr. (Fortress Press, 2013), 224.

an increasingly interconnected world population, John XXIII insisted that the church adapt to an often-volatile reality. An ever-hopeful thinker, he witnessed the tumultuous terrain of rapid human development and technological innovation and saw an unprecedented opportunity to communicate a call for global cooperation. In *Gaudet Mater Ecclesia*, his opening address to the assembly of bishops and clerics before him but also to the whole ecclesial community, under the auspicious guidance of the Holy Spirit, John XXIII contended that the church was being called to embrace "a new order of human relations," which he asserted was "directed toward the fulfillment of God's superior and inscrutable designs."[10] Indeed, John XXIII's unitive vision came at a pivotal moment of discovery and subsequent social change. Acknowledging this occasion, he remarked of the church: "She must ever look to the present, to the new conditions and new forms of life introduced into the modern world which have opened new avenues to the Catholic apostolate."[11] With an openness to growth and the emergence of novelty, under John XXIII's direction, the church began a process of reimagining itself in a modern world, a necessary step for a global population facing unprecedented devastation by its own hands.[12]

Nine days following his October 11, 1962, address opening the council, the bishops gathered at Vatican II echoed this commitment to global engagement in their October 20 *Message to Humanity*. They asserted that like Christ, "the Church too was not born to dominate but serve,"[13] thus cementing the church's role as a dialogue partner with modernity as opposed to a tenacious adversary. The message proceeded with a broad acknowledgment of the influence of the natural sciences on the collective human sense of place in observable reality, going so far as to state, "While we hope that the light of faith will shine more clearly and more vigorously as a result of this Council's efforts, we look forward to a spiritual renewal

---

10. John XXIII, "Gaudet Mater Ecclesia," 713.
11. John XXIII, "Gaudet Mater Ecclesia," 714.
12. Although the ecological crisis was already well underway, it did not preoccupy the papacy of John XXIII in the way it captured the attention of his successors in the decades to come. Nevertheless, John XXIII's immersion in world affairs made him well aware of the human capacity for destruction since, as Childs notes, "the arms race and the cold war were in full swing." Childs, "Pope John XXIII and Vatican II," 224.
13. Second Vatican Council, "Message to Humanity," 5.

from which will also flow a happy impulse on behalf of human values such as scientific discoveries, technological advances, and a wider diffusion of knowledge."[14] With this bold and ambitious stance, they laid the foundation and guiding principles for the council. Although Pope John XXIII, who died on June 3, 1963, did not live to see the further articulation of a dynamic and pastorally-oriented church, the emphasis of these texts on unity, service, and openness to growth set the tone for the conciliar documents that would emerge from a renewed ecclesial consciousness reflected in an understanding of a people of God on the move and as participants called to discern a properly oriented relationship with the wider ecological community in their shared terrestrial biosphere.

Unitatis Redintegratio: A Relational Call for Wholeness in Ecumenism

With an ardent appeal to the communal dimension of faith, *Unitatis Redintegratio* insists upon the overriding urgency of Christian unity. In the opening lines, the decree stated that "division openly contradicts the will of Christ, scandalizes the world, and damages the sacred cause of the preaching of the Gospel to every creature" (UR 1). *Unitatis Redintegratio* contended that it is building on the commitments reflected in previous papal statements made seventy years prior, at the turn of the century, by Leo XIII.[15] Nevertheless, there is a profound ecclesiological shift on display in this opening line. The decree claimed that Christian division exposed a deeper rift beyond institutional dysfunction.[16] The effort to restore Christian unity needed to incorporate the "eschatological dimension of the

---

14. Second Vatican Council, "Message to Humanity," 5.

15. The decree later mentions that "this sacred council confirms what previous councils and Roman pontiffs have proclaimed" (UR 18). I am referring to Pope Leo XIII, Encyclical *Praeclara Gratulationis Publica*, June 20, 1894, https://www.papalencyclicals.net/leo13/l13praec.htm (hereafter, PGP).

16. Speaking on the refocus, Cardinal Walter Kasper remarks, "The Council was able to embrace the ecumenical movement because it understood the church as a whole as movement, namely as the people of God on the move." Cardinal Walter Kasper, "Lasting Significance of *Unitatis Redintegratio*—Read Anew After Forty Years" (intervention at the Conference on the 40th Anniversary of the Promulgation of the Conciliar Decree *Unitatis Redintegratio*, November 11, 2004), 2, https://cadeio.org/blog/wp-content/uploads/2022/03/3B.-Kasper-Lasting-Significance-of-UR-Read-Anew-2004.pdf.

church," and thus the council "described the church not as a static but as a dynamic entity, as the people of God undertaking a pilgrimage."[17] One can witness this reinterpreted eschatological dimension in the decree's emphasis on the emergence of novelty beyond the constructed borders of denominational classification. The decree stated, "Moreover, some, even very many, of the most significant elements and endowments which together go to build up and give life to the church itself, can exist outside the visible boundaries of the Catholic Church" (UR 3). Thus, *Unitatis Redintegratio* broke out of the limited perspective of a territorialized, geographically restricted church and the subsequent enclosure of revelation within a framework of centralized religious authority.

Rather than seeking to reestablish the safeguards of the past, when the imaginative project of Christian unity was envisioned as an enactment through the coercive practices of political force,[18] *Unitatis Redintegratio* opened the church up to the wider Christian community. The decree advanced a mutually affirming ecumenism: "Such actions [of renewal and reform through ecumenical dialogue], when they are carried out by the catholic faithful prudently patiently and under the attentive guidance of their bishops, promote justice and truth, concord and collaboration, as well as the spirit of love and unity" (UR 4). With this articulation, *Unitatis Redintegratio* highlighted the radical creativity of a world moving toward greater unity. Although the document addresses a fractured Christian population mired in doctrinal and dogmatic divergences, it expresses confidence that division has not deterred the greater emergence of a providential and constructive novelty across theological fault lines.[19]

---

17. Kasper, "Lasting Significance of *Unitatis Redintegratio*," 3.

18. Against the tide of scholarship concentrated on the decline of organized participation throughout the West, missiologist and religious studies scholar Lamin Sanneh wrote of a modern Christian unity, which echoed the theological imagination of Christendom, insomuch as the Christian witnesses every aspect of creation as a manifestation of divine life. Nevertheless, Sanneh establishes an important distinction between the ordering principles of the past and the boundless, uncontained vision of a worldwide Christianity, clarifying, "under Christendom the basis and rationale for transmitting the gospel were colonial annexation and subjugation, with the church as an afterthought." Lamin Sanneh, *Whose Religion Is Christianity? The Gospel Beyond the West* (Eerdmans, 2003), 54.

19. While division and scriptural obscurity may be pneumatic realities of our present, historical theologian and commentator on Christian division in the West Ephraim Radner argues that there is a codependency between the severed parts of the Christian body.

Unitatis Redintegratio maintained: "We must become familiar with the outlook of the separated churches and communities. Study is absolutely required for this, and it should be pursued in fidelity to the truth and with a spirit of good will" (UR 9). While the fissures of Christianity remain a tragic dismemberment of the mystical body of Christ, from the perspective of *Unitatis Redintegratio*, alternative remedies beyond "obedience in all things to the teaching and Authority of the Church" (PGP 22) were taken into serious consideration with the conciliar aim of ecumenism. Significantly, *Unitatis Redintegratio* proposed a careful evaluation of the fragmented remains of the once-united church and the acknowledgment of the dynamic activity of the Spirit outside of the Roman Catholic tradition.

In the decree's treatment of the Eastern churches separated from Rome, *Unitatis Redintegratio* stated, "Far from being an obstacle to the church's unity, such diversity of customs and observances only adds to the beauty of the church and contributes greatly to carrying out her mission" (UR 16). Here, the decree continued to build on a relationally holistic ecclesiology that marks a profound shift in the church's position toward theological trajectories outside of the Roman Catholic tradition. The East-West divide ceased to be seen exclusively as a necessary point of divergence, but the diversity of practices between the distinct traditions was to be considered as a unique expression of an irreducible whole. *Unitatis Redintegratio* continued: "To remove all shadow of doubt, then, this holy synod solemnly declares that the churches of the east, while keeping in mind the necessary unity of the whole church, have the power to govern themselves according to their own disciplines, since these are better suited to the character of their faithful and better adapted to foster the good of souls. The perfect observance of this traditional principle—which however has not always been observed—is a prerequisite for any restoration of union" (UR 16).

With this development, the decree paved the way for both sacred traditions to envision themselves as united within the indivisible mystical

---

In all the bewildering disputation between those who profess belief in the one triune God, he contends that one must keep one's mind fixated on the active engagement of the Spirit. Piercing through the voices across time, he states that "any discussion of Christian division, implies the scrutiny of a providential history, whose descriptive limits depend only on the breadth or contraction of human capacity." Ephraim Radner, *The End of the Church: A Pneumatology of Christian Division in the West* (Eerdmans, 1998), 2.

body of Christ, itself the underlying foundation for what some Christian thinkers would begin to regard as the cosmic whole encapsulated within the very heart of materiality.[20]

At the close of *Unitatis Redintegratio*, the decree's relational call for unity pivoted toward Christian communities fully separated from the church since the disintegration of Western Christianity in the sixteenth century.[21] *Unitatis Redintegratio* continued, "Although the ecumenical movement and the desire for peace with the Catholic Church have not yet taken hold everywhere, it is nevertheless our hope that an ecumenical spirit and mutual esteem will gradually increase among all Christians" (UR 19). While the plethora of theological and doctrinal differences present a particularly onerous obstacle to reunification, the decree underscored the common grounding of Christ's teachings and the sacramental bond of our baptism (see UR 2) through which we are at once incorporated into Christ and his church. *Unitatis Redintegratio* contended, "If in moral matters there are many Christians who do not always understand the Gospel in the same way as Catholics, and do not admit the same solutions for the more difficult problems of modern society, they nevertheless want to cling to Christ's word as the source of Christian virtue" (UR 23).

Here, the document argued for the importance of the figure of Christ in uncovering the interconnectivity of the universe. The decree advanced the common association with the figure of Christ and his sacraments as a bridge that connects our love of each other with other things in our created reality. *Unitatis Redintegratio* realized the transformative and radically unitive nature of Christ and expressed a desire for unity, ultimately welcoming diversity in interpretations of Christ. While still decades, if not centuries, away from binding the wounds of fractured Christian identity, the conciliar aim of ecumenism enabled the church to "confidently look

---

20. In his writings in the decades leading up to the council, Teilhard described the Christic holism at the heart of materiality, writing, "In one great surge, Cosmogenesis becomes personalized, both in the things it adds, which *centrify us for Christ*, and in the things, it subtracts, which *draw us out of our own centres onto him*." Pierre Teilhard de Chardin, *The Heart of Matter*, ed. and trans. Rene Hague (Houghton, 1979), 51.

21. Earlier in the decree, *Unitatis Redintegratio* states, "Other divisions arose in the West more than four centuries later. These stemmed from the events which are commonly referred to as the Reformation. As a result, many communions, national or confessional, were separated from the Roman See" (UR 13).

to the future" (UR 24) so that it may realize the fiery heart of Jesus that impelled Catholics and other Christians to articulate a dynamic and "active feeling of communion with God, through the Universe."[22]

Nostra Aetate: Recognizing the Rays of Truth in the Earth's Religious Energies

In its discussion of religious systems outside of Christianity, the council's Declaration on the Relations of the Church to Non-Christian Religions, *Nostra Aetate*, upholds the holistic vision of relationships found in *Unitatis Redintegratio*. In its opening lines, *Nostra Aetate* acknowledged: "In our day . . . people are drawing more closely together and the bonds of friendship between different peoples are being strengthened" (NA 1). In an increasingly interconnected world, the declaration further stressed the need for the church to adapt and change its traditional approach. The foundation for the church's postconciliar global aspiration for creative interreligious dialogue, *Nostra Aetate* saw that the very future of Christianity rests on the church's ability to "enter with prudence and charity into discussion and collaboration with members of other religions" and on the ability of Christians, "while witnessing to their own faith and way of life, [to] acknowledge, preserve and encourage the spiritual and moral truths found among non-Christians, together with their social life and culture" (NA 2). Correspondingly, *Nostra Aetate* affirms the idea of Christ's universalization when it asserts that belief in the incarnate God reveals a "hidden power, which lies behind the course of nature and the events of human life" (NA 2). In corroboration with the notion of the unifying and evolutive energy of Christ, *Nostra Aetate* encouraged believers to open their minds and hearts to the teeming presence of God in their surroundings, an acknowledgment of God's presence so wide that it transcends defined religious barriers.

Nostra Aetate notably embraced the possibility of truth in other religious systems through a profound commitment to "overcome the restlessness of people's hearts by outlining a program of life covering doctrine, moral precepts, and sacred rites" (NA 2). The declaration paved the way for the church to encounter complexity as it extends its consideration

---

22. Teilhard, *The Heart of Matter*, 47.

beyond a closed system of revelation, thus enabling the church to promote cooperation with the wider global community. Such an encounter is crucial, especially in confronting the concurrent environmental crises plaguing the biosphere and propelled by human activity. *Nostra Aetate* exhorts the reader to preserve and promote the spiritual and moral goods found in other religions. These sociocultural values encapsulated within distinct religious communities alongside the church's teachings can be seen as guiding lights[23] for the troubled global population of human systems hurtling toward a destructive end.

Gaudium et Spes: A New Era of Relational Holism for a Modern Church

The last of the final documents approved by Vatican II, the Pastoral Constitution on the Church in the Modern World, *Gaudium et Spes*, aimed to reinvigorate the institutional church through the lens of relational holism. In its decisive preface, the document declared, "Now that the Second Vatican Council has studied the mystery of the church more deeply, it addresses not only the daughters and sons of the church and all who call upon the name of Christ, but the whole of humanity as well, and it wishes to set down how it understands the presence and function of the church in the world of today" (GS 2).

Gaudium et Spes encouraged the church to turn its attention toward the new horizons now consciously discernible in the lived reality of human experience and humanity's encounters with the wider ecological community in our shared biosphere. The church's embrace of its "responsibility of reading the signs of the times and of interpreting them in the light of the Gospel" (GS 4) charts a path toward extending the ecumenical/

---

23. Francis later builds on this precedent in his encyclical on the environment: "Care for nature is part of a lifestyle, which includes the capacity for living together and communion. Jesus reminded us that we have God as our common Father and that this makes us brothers and sisters. Fraternal love can only be gratuitous; it can never be a means of repaying others for what they have done or will do for us. That is why it is possible to love our enemies. This same gratuitousness inspires us to love and accept the wind, the sun, and the clouds, even though we cannot control them. In this sense, we can speak of a *universal fraternity*." Pope Francis, Encyclical *Laudato Si'*, May 24, 2015, no. 228, https://www.vatican.va/content/francesco/en/encyclicals/documents/papa-francesco_20150524_enciclica-laudato-si.html (hereafter, LS).

unitive mission expressed within *Unitatis Redintegratio* and *Nostra Aetate* well beyond classical human-centered considerations. In acknowledging that there are "profound and rapid changes spreading gradually to all corners of the earth" (GS 4), the church opened itself up to a process of totalization, a realization[24] that the global human community is part of an emergent and irreducible whole.

In a larger reflection on human dignity, *Gaudium et Spes* contended, "Human dignity rests above all on the fact that humanity is called to communion with God. The invitation to converse with God is addressed to men and women as soon as they are born" (GS 19). *Gaudium et Spes*, therefore, emphasized that our emergent consciousness has led us to a deeper awareness of an interconnected reality. From this heightened realization, we can begin to appreciate that our capacity for self-reflection is not what separates us from nature but what binds us to our created world. As consciousness enables us to commune with other-than-human life, it is intimately part of what makes humans relational creatures. Describing a collective movement forward through the complexification of consciousness and interconnectivity of the modern world, *Gaudium et Spes* observed, "Because of the increasingly close interdependence which is gradually extending to the entire world, we are today witnessing an extension of the role of the common good, which is the sum total of social conditions which allow people, either as groups or as individuals, to reach their fulfillment more fully and more easily. The resulting rights and obligations are consequently the concern of the entire human race. Every group must take into account the needs and legitimate aspirations of every other group, and even those of the human family as a whole" (GS 26).

The Second Vatican Council envisioned a church that promotes a wider, holistic network of social relationships. Therefore, while the document does not contradict the early attestation in *Unitatis Redintegratio* and *Nostra Aetate* that Christianity personalizes the emergence of complex life, beginning with the creation of our universe[25] so that it can be

---

24. Evolutionary Catholic systematic theologian John Haught writes, "It is true that evolution is not just about competition and wasteful struggle. Evolution is also, as we are now beginning to realize more clearly, a story of cooperation among many diverse layers of organisms." John F. Haught, *God After Darwin: A Theology of Evolution* (Westview Press, 2000), 21.

25. What Teilhard de Chardin and other evolutionary thinkers referred to as the cosmogenic unfolding of life.

consciously witnessed by humanity, the movement toward increasing interconnectivity and interdependency is purported by *Gaudium et Spes* to be fluid and alive in the evolutionary process. Therefore, if the church is to fully accept this dynamic flow, which has caused the creatures of the universe to move into deeper relationships with each other,[26] it must recognize the voice of God in the evolutionary process and our intensified interactions with other-than-human life. In other words, who we *are* must be conceptualized within a wider framework, as *part* of a larger emerging wholeness.[27] *Gaudium et Spes* paved the way for a dynamic reorientation of the church. The pastoral constitution affirms that the church "acknowledges and holds in high esteem the dynamic approach of today" (GS 41). Thus, this conciliar notion of the church in *Gaudium et Spes* serves as a crucial point of departure for a pilgrim church, journeying toward a relationally holistic future.[28]

The Limits of the Council's Teaching and Obstacles to Wider Ecological Unity

The Second Vatican Council charted a path forward that embraced a church outside of its traditional, visible, sociological, and institutional confinements, a mystical communion of members in dynamic discernment of the future. It was an innovative moment of hope and promise

---

26. *Gaudium et Spes* explains that "we are witnessing the birth of a new humanism, where people are defined before all else by his responsibility to their sisters and brothers and at the court of history" (GS 55).

27. Remarking on this reconstructed anthropology, Thomas Berry writes, "We misconceive our role if we consider that our historical mission is to 'civilize' or 'domesticate' the planet, as though wildness is something destructive rather than the ultimate creative modality of any form of earthly being. We are not here to control. We are here to become integral with the larger Earth community." Thomas Berry, *The Great Work: Our Way into the Future* (Bell Tower, 1999), 48.

28. In his commentary on a future of relational holism, Teilhard writes, "Faith is no longer merely an escape route from the world [i.e., a transient/soteriological assurance of deliverance]—but the ferment and co-principle of the actual fulfillment of the world." Pierre Teilhard de Chardin, "The Contingence of the Universe and Man's Zest for Survival or How Can One Rethink the Christian Notion of Creation to Conform with the Laws of Energetics," in Teilhard, *Christianity and Evolution: Reflections on Science and Religion*, ed. and trans. Rene Hague (Harcourt, 1974), 222.

for a world that was just beginning to realize the deleterious effects of its living and growth on the wider ecological community to which it belongs. Yet the conciliar vision followed existing conventions in its prioritization of human life, clinging to the anthropocentrism of the past over the ecologically inclusive horizon.[29] Despite its call to embrace the world holistically, when *Gaudium et Spes* advances that God desired for humans to form one family as they are "destined to the very same end, namely God himself" (GS 24), the document maintains a lens of human-centered progress and social kinship. Thus, when the document acknowledges that "human beings are social by nature" and that "the betterment of the person and the improvement of society depend on each other" (GS 25), there remains a constructed barrier between the human and the wider ecologically community.[30] Rather than asserting that all creatures are good by the fact that they exist, the conciliar aim of human progress limits this vision of growth to human innovation and development, carried out often at the expense of other-than-human life. Although there is more scientific knowledge of the natural world today than at any other point in human history, this is not the kind of understanding that has led human civilization into an intimate biophilic relationship with the natural world. While the conciliar church widened its horizons and embraced a necessary global perspective that advanced rather than marginalized human observations of the natural world, the Second Vatican Council did not

---

29. In her critical assessment of the anthropocentric leanings of the Second Vatican Council, Carmody Grey writes, "[*Gaudium et Spes*] 24.3 appears to deny an intrinsic value to nonhuman creatures, and so to corroborate a sentiment of disregard for nonhuman life, and the belief in human superiority over nature that has been widely deplored as the cause of the ecological crisis." Carmody Grey, "'The Only Creature God Willed for Its Own Sake': Anthropocentrism in *Laudato Si'* and *Gaudium et Spes*," *Modern Theology* 36, no. 4 (2020): 865–83.

30. Intriguingly some scholars have pointed out that this anthropocentrism can even be contrasted with instances within Sacred Scripture when the authors portray all creatures moving toward a similar end, when together they give praise to God. For one notable example, see Basil of Caesarea's commentary on Psalm 148's "chorus of creation" in his third homily on the Hexaemeron. Basil of Caesarea, "On the Hexaemeron," in *Exegetic Homilies*, trans. Sister Agnes Clare Way (The Catholic University of America Press, 1963), 3–150, esp. homily 3.9, at 52–53. Basil exclaimed that even the waters above the heavens (waters that yield rain, snow, sleet, and hail) are "sometimes invited to praise the common Master of the universe."

attend to the domineering human-centered orientation at the heart of the ecological crisis.[31]

Now more than two decades into the new millennium, the human society at the forefront of the Second Vatican Council's focus is witnessing an unprecedented break with the natural process of geological cycles. In 2023, the world population experienced the warmest year on record.[32] Wildfires raged across Canada, burning more than 45.7 million acres—shattering previous records. Twenty-five billion metric tons of fertile topsoil were lost to erosion, and the overexploitation of the fishing industry and plastics continued on the path toward the eradication of marine life. With this apocalyptic scenario in mind, it is reasonable to cast doubt upon John XXIII's confidence in our collective tenacity. John XXIII said, "We must quite disagree with those prophets of doom who are always forecasting disaster as if the end of the world were at hand."[33] It is necessary that the dynamic and globally-oriented church assist[34] the world in a transition from a period of human devastation to an age when humans exist within the biosphere in a mutually beneficial manner with all non-human life forms—even if such a transition requires us to jettison the

---

31. Concurrently with the proceedings of the council, American Lutheran theologian Joseph Sittler expressed in his 1962 address of the World Council of Church in New Delhi, "A doctrine of redemption is meaningful only when it swings with the larger orbit of a doctrine of creation. For God's creation of earth cannot be redeemed in any intelligible sense of the word apart from a doctrine of the cosmos which is his home, his definite place, the theater of his selfhood under God, in cooperation with his neighbor, and in caring relationship with nature, his sister." Joseph Sittler, "Called to Unity," in Forell and Childs, *Christian Social Teaching*, 411.

32. According to the National Oceanic and Atmospheric Administration's 2023 Annual Climate Report, https://www.ncei.noaa.gov/access/monitoring/monthly-report/global/202313.

33. Pope John XXIII, "Gaudet Mater Ecclesia," 712.

34. In his time, Teilhard argued that the current frame of institutional religion had to embrace a transformation, writing in a 1953 essay that "it is physically necessary that [humanity] believe, as vigorously as possible, in some absolute value possessed by the movement [through] which it is [their] duty to forward." Moreover, Teilhard encourages his readers to move away from reductive anthropocentric perspectives, contending that "[Humanity] used to be regarded as an anomaly in the universe; from now on, he is tending to be seen as the extreme point attained at this moment, in the field of our experience, by the combined process of corpuscular arrangement and physical interiorization." Teilhard, "The Contingence of the Universe," 221–22.

celebrated claims of human existence made by the council in the middle of the last century.

Conclusion

Through an analysis of *Unitatis Redintegratio*, *Nostra Aetate*, and *Gaudium et Spes*, one can observe a relationally holistic vision of Christianity encapsulated within the revolutionary ecclesiological shifts of the Second Vatican Council building a new unity through global solidarity. The council articulated a creative union that embraces pluralism, opens itself up to an intimate companionship with the wider ecological community, and orients itself toward a future of hope. Thus, the shift toward a church beyond the limited concerns of the human was born in the middle of the last century and continues to unfold in the present. Nevertheless, we must continue this pilgrimage in our time, moving beyond the confinements and narrow scope of the Second Vatican Council and toward a true embrace of an ecologically inclusive church. We believe the church [*credo Ecclesiam*], a mystical/holistic vision of a globally interconnected world on the move, informs us, challenges us, and inspires us to recognize a "God of love" who shows "us our place in this world as channels of [God's] love for all the creatures of this earth" (LS 246). May we heed this pressing vision of unity. May we recognize the direction of the Holy Spirit guiding us in our enactment of ecological inclusion. And may we be more attuned to the dynamism of divine love ever-emergent in our shared space and time.

Part 2

Contemporary Crises and the Limits of Vatican II

Sexual Abuse

Chapter 6

Vatican II's Silence on Child Sex Abuse

Challenges and Limits of a "Pastoral" Agenda

Agnès Desmazières

During the preparation of the Second Vatican Council, eighty bishops from all over the globe discussed the opportunity of revising the Catholic Church's legislation on child sex abuse to penalize it more strongly. This debate reveals a growing concern over child sex abuse perpetrated by priests and religious at the dawn of the 1960s. However, the failure of the project and its subsequent oversight show the limits of the council's "pastoral" agenda and its incapacity to tackle a major problem that would provoke an unprecedented crisis in the contemporary Catholic Church some decades later.

The silence of Vatican II's historiography on this episode is especially striking.[1] It invites one to envisage not only how the debate on child sex abuse was muted at the council but also how an optimistic and overly positive understanding of Vatican II, inspired by the accounts of its participants, contributed to the concealing of the child sex abuse phenomenon. The council's emphasis on "pastorality," relayed by the historiography, became criticized as the crisis of child sex abuse in the Catholic Church sparked off; it was perceived by some as the main reason for a presumed expansion of child sex abuse in the postconciliar Catholic Church.

---

1. It was, for instance, not mentioned in the five-volume *History of Vatican II* directed by Giuseppe Alberigo and published in seven languages (originally in Italian, 1995–2001).

I will argue that if Vatican II's failure to address the child sex abuse issue indeed resulted primarily from a discredit of canon law in the name of "pastorality," such a pastoral approach was already present—in a minor way—in the decades preceding the council. Vatican II continued to depend on a preconciliar logic of the dissimulation of the "scandal," recustomized in a "pastoral" perspective. It is thus no wonder that the Holy Office's instruction *De modo procedendi in causis sollicitationis* (1922), defining the manner of proceeding in child sex abuse cases, had also been concealed until the American lawyers Daniel J. Shea and Carmen Curso, in the context of Boston's child sex abuse crisis, made the document public in 2002.[2]

Additionally, I will show that the child abuse phenomenon should be examined within the frame of a longer history, beginning years before Vatican II. I will underline how the ecclesial authorities were already aware of the extent of child sex abuse by priests and religious in the late 1930s. In that respect, the novelty of Vatican II's project consisted not so much in putting the spotlight on child sex abuse but rather on considering the possibility of a public debate, involving bishops of the entire world, on the matter. The discussions had been confined, up to that point, to the Holy Office (now called the Dicastery for the Doctrine of the Faith), which was (and remains) in charge of addressing these crimes. Moreover, child sex abuse was no longer addressed separately but rather in relation with other clerical delicts, financial delicts especially. In this sense, the systemic nature of the child sex abuse phenomenon was already perceived by some—however in a minority—ecclesial actors.

---

2. Alan Cooperman, "Vatican Memo Cited in Sex Abuse Cases," *The Washington Post*, August 25, 2003, https://www.washingtonpost.com/archive/politics/2003/08/25/vatican-memo-cited-in-sex-abuse-cases/de496188-bc95-4c7d-913e-b7845f6cc2db/. See Supreme Congregation of the Holy Office, Instruction On the Manner of Proceeding in Causes Involving the Crime of Solicitation, March 16, 1962, https://www.vatican.va/resources/resources_crimen-sollicitationis-1962_en.html. This is the 1962 revised version of the original 1922 document, in its official English translation. For the original, in Latin, see Supremae S. Congregationis S. Officii, Instructio *De modo procedendi in causis sollititationis*, June 9, 1922, http://www.bishop-accountability.org/archives/Wall/1922_06_09_Solicitation_Instruction_Latin.pdf.

A Rising Concern for Child Sex Abuse

At the end of the nineteenth century, a new concern for child sex abuse perpetrated by priests emerged as societies increasingly condemned sexual violence against children. Clerical scandals were increasingly publicized by the press in general and by anticlerical pamphlets in particular. Anticlerical campaigns arose first in France, before reaching Spain and Italy in 1907, urging the Holy See to discipline child sex abusers effectively.

A Secret Instruction

The 1922 Instruction *De modo procedendi in causis sollicitationis* represented an important step in a better consideration of child sex abuse. For the first time, a detailed procedure was established to prosecute these crimes universally. Furthermore, the Holy Office's competence in addressing the crime was officially specified. The reference in the 1917 Code of Canon Law to the "delict against the sixth commandment with minors under sixteen" contributed to this evolution. In fact, the Holy Office's instruction was designed as a practical guide for the bishops, helping them to address cases of child sex abuse in their dioceses.

However, the Holy Office, in the process of writing the instruction, took some distance from the Code of Canon Law and favored a praxis that gave more weight to dispensations, accommodations, and decisions on a case-by-case basis. Avoiding the categorization of the "delict against the sixth commandment with minors under sixteen," it chose to invent a new crime, the "*crimen pessimum*" ("the gravest crime"). While the *crimen pessimum* properly regarded homosexual facts, the treatment of sexual violence against children in the paragraphs of the instruction on the *crimen pessimum* conflated child sex abuse with homosexuality. Furthermore, the Holy Office chose not to handle all the cases of sexual violence against minors under sixteen, but only abuses involving prepubescent minors: girls under twelve and boys under fourteen, creating a gendered disparity. As a matter of fact, boys older than fourteen could still make accusations of sexual aggression, based on the ambiguous definition of the *crimen pessimum*.

The secrecy that surrounded the diffusion of the 1922 instruction—unlike the official publication of the Holy Office's nineteenth-century instructions on sexual solicitation in confession—impeded its full enforcement. The instruction was reserved to bishops and delivered by hand by the nuncios. It did not even reach some faraway countries, such as Colombia or the Philippines. At the death of the bishops who had received the document, memory of the instruction in the dioceses was frequently lost, as attested in Germany in the 1930s.

The Nazi Trials: A First International Crisis

The Nazi campaign against pedophile priests and religious, which began in 1936, can be viewed as the first international child sex abuse crisis in the Catholic Church because of the considerable number of priests and religious—rightly—targeted and the international media coverage of their trials. The extent of the child sex abuse phenomenon in Germany was an electroshock for the Holy Office. As one of its officials stated, the notice of the events made the Holy Office "suspect that such a delict [was] more frequent that what [it] imagined."[3]

The scandal nevertheless was rapidly stifled by Catholic counterpropaganda, denouncing the Nazi exploitation of the trials. Cardinal George Mundelein of Chicago was especially active in denying the reality of the phenomenon.[4] The Holy Office's initial determination to discipline more efficiently child sex abusers eroded as the veracity of the cases exposed by the Nazi propaganda was put under suspicion internationally. The success of the cover-up strategy employed by some German bishops and their Vatican and North American allies prompted the Holy Office to temper its initial ambitions of a vast reform of the procedure.

The German affair, however, compelled the congregation to leak information on the 1922 instruction during a reunion of Roman professors of theology and canon law, so that the procedure would be better known. This partial and unofficial diffusion of the Holy Office's procedure, however, proved to be insufficient, the ethics and canon law textbooks being often misleading.

---

3. Annotation of Giuseppe Latini to the letter from Karl Schulte, archbishop of Cologne, to Pope Pius XI of April 29, 1936 (Archives of the Congregation for the Doctrine of Faith, Priv. S.O. 1936, 24).

4. See Thomas M. Keefe, "The Mundelein Affair: A Reappraisal," *Records of the American Catholic Historical Society of Philadelphia* 89 (1978): 74–84.

The "Parallel" Justice of Religious Communities, or the Failure of the Holy Office's Case-by-Case Policy [5]

From the 1940s, particularly as a result of the Nazi trials, the Holy Office became also more preoccupied by religious pedophilia, a phenomenon that has been underinvestigated and, thus, underestimated to the present time. Religious superiors, to whom the 1922 instruction had not been addressed, were often taking sanctions against their subordinates, avoiding the intervention of the bishops or the Holy Office. Moreover, non-ordained religious escaped from the control of the Holy Office, as the instruction only dealt with cleric perpetrators. For this reason, the congregation decided in 1940 to expand the *crimen pessimum* to include non-ordained religious but failed to amend the procedure on that note. In particular, the penalties foreseen by the Code of Canon Law and the instruction referred to the crimes of clerics.

Additionally, the debate around the *crimen pessimum* of the religious increasingly focused on the prevalence of homosexuality in the religious convents. This contributed to strengthening the perceived relationship between child sex abuse and homosexuality. While the Holy Office pointed out the deficiencies of the "parallel" justice of religious communities, whose penalty system of transfers or dismissals facilitated the cover-up of crimes, it never succeeded in overcoming the religious orders' resistance to the Roman congregation's control. Their resistance, organized by the religious who were consultors at the Holy Office, found support in the congregation's case-by-case policy.

The difficulties with religious communities encountered by the Holy Office highlight the way the Roman congregation was losing influence at the eve of Vatican II. It was struggling to impose the celibacy discipline on the Latin clergy and reacted with great difficulty to the rapid changes brought on by the "sexual revolution": priests departing in large numbers, growing objections to clerical celibacy, and clerical sexual liberation more broadly. Child sex abuse was still considered more as an infringement of the law of celibacy (among others) than as a despicable sexual violence perpetrated against the most vulnerable persons. The extreme scandalous

---

5. See Roberto Morozzo della Rocca, "Le chiese parallele: I religiosi," in *Le chiese di Pio XII*, ed. Andrea Riccardi (Laterza, 1986), 119–34.

potential of child sex abuse was nevertheless perceived by ecclesiastical authorities at that time.

Toward a New Appraisal of Child Sex Abuse?

The discussions at the Holy Office regarding the religious communities reveal the inadequacy of Catholic Church's response to child sex abuse and its penalty system more broadly, which would be soon criticized in the context of the preparation of the council. The announcement of the revision of the Code of Canon Law by Pope John XXIII pushed bishops, religious superiors, universities, and Roman congregations to present their own propositions of reform of the Catholic penal law. Bishops notably endorsed the concerns expressed by their priests who requested a more transparent and impartial justice. The contribution of the Salesian Pontifical Athenaeum in Rome stands out, for it is the only recommendation to the council that specifically addressed the issue of child sex abuse, offering a new insight on the phenomenon.

The Challenge of a New "Social Sensitivity"

In its intervention, the Salesian Pontifical Athenaeum—a pontifical university in Rome run by the Salesians of Don Bosco, known more informally as the Salesianum—referred to child sex abuse in a section on the "Accommodation of the penal system to the present exigences."[6] In line with many other petitions, the professors of the Salesianum demanded a revision of the penalties defined by the Code of Canon Law in accordance with the "new conditions of life."[7] However, the athenaeum characterized in an unprecedented way this changing context by referring to the emergence of a new "social sensitivity."[8] This distinct "social sensitivity" made the faithful more offended by two classes of clerical and religious delicts: child sex abuse and the "violations of social justice."[9] Regarding the latter,

---

6. Pontificium Athenaeum Salesianum, "De delictis et poenis. Votum 48: De systemate poenali Codicis hodiernis exigentiis accommodando," *Acta et documenta Concilio oecumenico Vaticano II apparando. Series I, Volumen IV, Pars I, 2* (Typis polyglottis vaticanis, 1971), 215–20.
7. Pontificium Athenaeum Salesianum, "De delictis et poenis," 216.
8. Pontificium Athenaeum Salesianum, "De delictis et poenis," 217.
9. Pontificium Athenaeum Salesianum, "De delictis et poenis," 217.

the Salesianum insisted more specifically on the financial and "administrative frauds."[10] This apparently odd association highlights a new preoccupation for human dignity and, consecutively, the appearance of new moral standards expected of priests and religious.

The athenaeum justified its treatment of the issue by the fact that sexual assaults against children and adolescents were "not rare."[11] To address adolescent sex abuse, the Salesianum suggested that the church's penal law punish all sexual offences against minors under sixteen perpetrated by priests and religious. Its recommendation reflects a new distinction of child and adolescent sex abuse from homosexuality. The penalty it proposed for child offenders—the excommunication *latae sententiae*, that is, automatically—had been used against ephebophile priests in the first centuries of the church, before vanishing during the early modern and modern periods. It was primarily meant to be pronounced against non-ordained religious who could not be punished with the traditional penalties reserved to priests, such as the prohibition from performing the sacraments. For its severity and its symbolic value, excommunication was also especially effective in extinguishing scandal among the faithful. Excommunications could, however, be easily and quickly lifted by the Holy See. Finally, the suggestion to impose the excommunication *latae sententiae*—automatically rather than after a trial—was based on the consideration that the delict often remained "occult."[12] On the brink of Vatican II, some ecclesial leaders became more conscious that quite often instances of child sex abuse were not reported to church authorities.

The Preparatory Commission for the Discipline of Clergy Embraced the Salesianum's Claim

The reform of the penalty system did not appear on the agenda defined by Pope John XXIII for the various preparatory commissions. However, the Preparatory Commission for the Discipline of Clergy decided to prepare a schema to be discussed at the council, where the penalization of child sex abuse was considered. The endorsement of the Salesianum's proposal by the commission signals a wider concern for child sex abuse,

10. Pontificium Athenaeum Salesianum, "De delictis et poenis," 217.
11. Pontificium Athenaeum Salesianum, "De delictis et poenis," 218.
12. Pontificium Athenaeum Salesianum, "De delictis et poenis," 218. "Occult" here means hidden/secret.

shared by curial officials, bishops, theologians, and canon lawyers. At that stage of the discussions, the addition of a new penalty encountered only some minor opposition, coming notably from the Jesuit canonist Eduardo Regatillo, who had notably contributed to the diffusion of the Holy Office's procedure in his publications and preferred to stick to the Holy Office's instruction.[13]

The assessment expressed by Charles Lefebvre, the main writer of the commission's schema, that child sex abuse was "not sufficiently punished,"[14] seems to have reached a consensus. While the commission tended to reduce the number of delicts in which the excommunication *latae sententia* could apply, for it typified the arbitrariness of ecclesiastical law, its members decided to impose the penalty for a delict to which it was not usually prescribed. It appears then that excommunication should not disappear completely from the church's arsenal but should be reserved for the gravest crimes.

The debate in the commission also manifests that the discipline of clergy had become a disputed field between the Holy Office, which no longer had the monopoly over it, and the Congregation of the Council, supervising the Preparatory Commission for the Discipline of Clergy. Unable to impose its procedure, especially among religious, or to adapt it to the new "social sensitivity," the Holy Office was losing control over child sex abuse. The commission's schema represented, in that regard, a certain return to the 1917 Code of Canon Law at the expense of the Holy Office's blurred and insufficient praxis.

A Missed Opportunity

A Predictable Rejection of the Schema

The Holy Office did not remain inactive, and it is arguable that the publication of a revised version of the 1922 instruction in March 1962 was related to the debates at the Preparatory Commission for the Discipline of Clergy. This publication occurred in the period of time between

---

13. Eduardo Regatillo, "Ad relationem de censuris notanda," Vatican Apostolic Archives, Fondo Concilio Vaticano II, *busta* 1329.

14. Charles Lefebvre, "De censuris earumve reservationibus: Relatio Il.mi et Rev.mi Caroli Lefebvre," December 11, 1961, Vatican Apostolic Archives, Fondo Concilio Vaticano II, *busta* 1329.

the vote in favor of the schema at the Commission for the Discipline of Clergy and the discussion at the Central Commission, which selected the schemas to be discussed at the council. Not surprisingly, the few modifications made dealt with the inextricable problem of the prosecution of religious, which the Salesianum's proposal had contributed to bringing anew to the forefront. The revisions manifest the Holy Office's loss of influence at the verge of the council: The congregation surrendered to the demands of autonomy expressed by the religious superiors and legitimized their "parallel" justice.

The terms of the debate were, therefore, unexpectedly changed with the Holy Office's intervention. Even if none of the participants in the Central Commission referred to the revised instruction, the communication of the document might have had some impact on the discussions. In fact, it might have alerted them to the topicality of the child sex abuse issue. It might have also weighed on the decision not to proceed on a reform path, since the Holy Office had just reaffirmed the approach of the 1922 instruction.

A Debate Behind Closed Doors

The Central Commission's debate, while held behind closed doors, can be retraced thanks to Pope Paul VI's wish that all the acts of the council would be published. In early May 1962, the Central Commission met to debate on the schema prepared by the Commission for the Discipline of Clergy. The new penalty of excommunication for sex perpetrators was only one of many recommendations presented to reform the church's canonical system. Therefore, it did not arouse so much attention. The convenience of discussing such a legal reform at the council constituted the core of the debate.

Only a few members of the Central Commission—eight—expressed their opinion on the penalization of child sex abuse. Alfredo Ottaviani, the secretary of the Holy Office, kept silent. Three cardinals supported the Commission for the Discipline of Clergy's proposition, making some recommendations to improve it. Significantly, the positions on child sex abuse of the various participants in the debate did not reflect the usual distinction between conservative and progressive. The rather conservative Cardinal Paul Richaud, archbishop of Bordeaux in France, was the most ardent proponent of a hardline policy toward sex abusers, asking that the

Code of Canon Law be revised to raise the age of the victims considered in the delict up to twenty-one—the age of majority in France at that time.

Cardinal Josef Frings, archbishop of Cologne, who would soon become a prominent figure of the reformist wing at Vatican II, also endorsed the Commission for the Discipline of Clergy's project, with the support of Cardinal Bernard Alfrink of Utrecht. He, however, contested the decision that the excommunication would be *latae sententiae*, preferring that the penalty would be pronounced *ferendae sententiae*, that is, after an ecclesiastical trial. Frings's contribution reflects the criticisms expressed by many bishops in their *vota* regarding the arbitrariness of current policies regarding the discipline of the clergy. It should nevertheless be noted that some years before, in 1956, he had questionably requested—and obtained—from the Holy Office that his vicar general could intervene in secular trials involving pedophile priests to obtain an expurgation of the acts to avoid scandals.

Similarly, the five opponents to the Commission for the Discipline of Clergy's recommendation came from both the reformist and the most conservative sides of the church. Three of them—Clemente Micara of Rome, Paul-Émile Léger of Montreal, and Maximos IV Saigh of Antioch—objected to discussion of the topic at the council. Both Micara and Maximos employed the classic rhetoric about the preservation of the "honor" of the clergy and the church. Though Micara acknowledged that child sex abuse was an "abomination," he said the disclosure of a new penalty would cause "a great dishonor for the clerical order and the ecclesiastical celibate."[15] For his part, Maximos defended that "the utterance of this delict in the acts of an ecumenical council [was] not suitable for the honor the Church and the dignity of the clergy."[16] Léger, meanwhile, stressed that such a mention at Vatican II would reveal the extent of child sex abuse and would cause "an odious surprise."[17]

---

15. "De censuris earumque reservatione: De modo procedendi in poenis in via administrativa infligendis (Tertia et quarta Congregatio: 5 et 7 maii 1962)," *Acta et documenta Concilio oecumenico Vaticano II apparando. Series II, Volumen II, Pars III* (Typis polyglottis vaticanis, 1968), 880.

16. "Vota sodalium qui sextae sessioni non interfuerunt. VI Beat. mi P. D. Maximi IV Saigh, Patriarchae Antiocheni Melchitarum," *Acta et documenta Concilio oecumenico Vaticano II apparando. Series II, Volumen II, Pars III*, 1335.

17. "De censuris earumque reservatione, " 885.

Maximos IV Saigh and two American cardinals—Albert Meyer of Chicago and Joseph Ritter of St. Louis—also argued for the bishops' autonomy. Maximos's harsh reaction was typical of the long-time rivalry between the Eastern patriarchs and Rome regarding control of the discipline of clergy. His written intervention offered a virulent charge against the Holy Office's administration of justice. The patriarch of Antioch identified the project of reform as a "subterfuge" to "dominate consciences," and denounced the risk that the Holy See would be transformed in a "police bureau of investigation."[18] Moreover, Maximos questioned the need to define penalties for child sex abuse since the "malice of the sin . . . should suffice for diverting [clerics] from such a shameful delict."[19] His strong denial of the priest-pedophile phenomenon suggests that the new "social sensitivity" pointed out by the Salesianum did not yet extend all over the world. It did not yet prevail even in Rome, as Micara's remarks made clear.

Using a softer line of argumentation, Meyer and Ritter argued that the responsibility for determining penalties for the crime should be passed to the bishops. The Commission for the Discipline of Clergy's project had indeed confirmed the reservation of child sex abuse to the Holy See, and, thus, concretely, to the Holy Office. The two American cardinals contended that the bishops were better suited to handle these cases. For Meyer, the crime was supposedly "better treated"[20] by the bishops. Ritter added that this was because they had a deeper knowledge of the "particular circumstances of the places and persons."[21] Meyer's and Ritter's arguments convinced the Commission for the Discipline of Clergy to revise the schema in such a way that the penalty of excommunication would be reserved to the bishops.

The silence of most cardinals and bishops signals at least that the issue of child sex abuse was not their top priority. It is highly significant that the future Pope Paul VI, as other bishops, supported concurrently Richaud's

---

18. "Vota sodalium qui sextae sessioni non interfuerunt. VI Beat. mi P. D. Maximi IV Saigh, Patriarchae Antiocheni Melchitarum," *Acta et documenta Concilio oecumenico Vaticano II apparando. Series II, Volumen II, Pars III*, 1335.

19. "Vota sodalium qui sextae sessioni non interfuerunt. VI Beat. mi P. D. Maximi IV Saigh," 1335.

20. "De censuris earumque reservatione," 887.

21. "De censuris earumque reservatione," 887.

and Léger's interventions on the schema without noticing that their positions were antithetical regarding child sex abuse. This silence also suggests a certain embarrassment, which could be confirmed by the fact that none of the participants leaked information on that discussion.

Exclusion from the Conciliar Agenda

Many bishops, in fact, objected to discussion of the schema at Vatican II since it regarded the revision of the Code of Canon Law, a project that John XXIII had announced in January 1959 together with the convocation of the council. For them, child sex abuse was a strictly canonical and disciplinary question and did not fit into Vatican II's pastoral program. This option, which ultimately led to the burying of the schema, manifests some weaknesses in the conciliar program, partly caused by a restricted understanding of the church's reform, which put aside its juridical dimension.

The debate among the Central Commission reveals that prejudices against a canonical approach were already present during the preparatory phase. Indeed, this bias had greatly obstructed the Holy Office's efforts to implement its sex abuse policy in the past decades. Despite an increasing Roman centralism, the sphere of the discipline of clergy largely slipped out of the control of the Holy See. The growing protests against the Holy Office's inquisitorial practices regarding the doctrinal discipline also contributed to discrediting its fight against clerical sexual violence on the eve of the council. Moreover, its difficulty in distinguishing child sex abuse from other violations of priestly celibacy resulted in a tendency to minimize the crime in the new context of sexual liberation. With the Holy Office's decline in influence, bishops and religious superiors were more prone to relax their vigilance and turn a blind eye to the cases of sexual assaults reported to them.

Their permissiveness was intrinsically related to a pastoral—or paternal—approach to priest perpetrators of child sex abuse, understood as a sin rather than as a crime punishable by the church's law. Bishops and religious superiors were, therefore, much more concerned about their subordinates' repentance than about the damage done to their victims. They manifested a consideration for the faithful insomuch as the crime could lead to scandals, threatening the "honor" of their diocese or religious congregation. Consequently, they tended to treat the accusations they received "paternally,"[22] that is, by avoiding trials. Despite its intentions to address the issue effectively, the Holy Office's approach was marked by this tendency also; the 1922 instruction added a new step to the previous procedure: the judge was supposed to "exhort paternally" the accused to confess his crime before being officially questioned.[23]

This reference highlights how the relationships between priests and the canonical authority—bishops or their delegated judges—were marked by an inherent ambiguity. The use of a paternal vocabulary emphasizes the affective nature of this relationship, a clear obstacle to an objective judgment. Moreover, this vocabulary was not employed to define the relationship between bishops and lay faithful, reinforcing the idea of a disparate—and unequal—treatment of the various parties involved in a case. Ritter's call for attention to the "particular circumstances of the places and persons" supports this thesis. The specific relationship between bishops and their priests was a crucial element of these circumstances. Vatican II's characterization of the bishop's mission as a pastoral office reinforced this already-present tendency to avoid assuming judicial duties. Even if the paternal vocabulary was increasingly used to describe the nature of the "relationship" (LG 37; original Latin: "*familiari commercio*") between the bishops and the lay faithful, the latter continued to endure prejudices and a denial of justice while denouncing child sex abuse.

In the case of child sex abuse, Vatican II's pastoral character remained, in fact, disconnected from the need of justice and reparation for the victims of abuse and for the wounded ecclesial communities. The conciliar discussion highlights a difficulty of overcoming the common opposition between pastorality and law, secular law being especially despised even concerning penal matters. At the same time, the implications of Vatican II's acknowledgment of the fundamental equality of all faithful in the practice of ecclesiastical justice were not completely perceived. Additionally, the debate within Vatican II's preparatory Central Commission reveals that cultural diversity—when absolutized—can constitute a serious impediment to a common resolution of the crisis, questioning

---

22. Letter from Ismael Perdomo, coadjutor bishop of Bogotá, to Rafael Merry Del Val of July 23, 1928 (Archives of the Congregation for the Doctrine of Faith, R. V. 1928, 8).

23. Supremae S. Congregationis S. Officii, Instructio *De modo procedendi*, no. 48.

the very foundations of the Catholic Church and the authenticity of the Christian message it proclaims.

Conclusion

Vatican II's silence on child sex abuse results from the combined effect of a fear of a media scandal and a disdain of law. It highlights some limits of the council's pastoral agenda, which favored a discourse style consistent with the use of an "art of persuasion," a "panegyric-epideictic genre [that] looks to reconciliation," aimed at encouraging internal conversion through the promotion of a positive image of the church.[24] There was, therefore, no room for a public acknowledgment of its weaknesses. In that respect, theologian and conciliar peritus Yves Congar failed in his efforts to include in the "pastoral" constitution *Gaudium et Spes* an expression of the church's penance for its past faults.[25] The conciliar fathers were also probably too optimistic regarding the effectiveness of persuasion, especially in criminal matters. By renouncing the legal language of past councils—identified as legalism—Vatican II avoided facing some juridical aspects of church reform, and, more specifically, the reform of its penal system. The Salesianum's call for a stronger penalization of child sex abuse remained isolated at a time in which clerical corporatism prevailed and the voice of the lay faithful still struggled to be heard. Sexual abuse by priests was, however, quite frequently denounced in the ever-increasing petitions to the popes, asking for the abolition of priestly celibacy. If the new "social sensitivity," pointed out by the Salesianum, was spreading, few ecclesial officials, at the Holy Office especially, understood the full measure of child sex abuse and its pastoral impact on the faithful as well as nonbelievers. The Salesianum's concern for sexual violence also stands out, for it emanates from a religious institution. In fact, such concern was rarely shared then by the religious orders, which were more prone to lobby against any strengthening of the legislation in the Vatican.

The failure to resolve this already pressing issue at Vatican II proved to be more damaging as the revision of the Code of Canon Law suffered

---

24. John W. O'Malley, *What Happened at Vatican II* (Harvard University Press, 2008), 48.
25. See Agnès Desmazières, "A Conversion to Dialogue: The Church's Dialogical Reform in the Light of *Gaudium et Spes*," in *Reforming the Church: Global Perspectives*, ed. Declan Marmion and Salvador Ryan (Liturgical Press, 2023), 159-60.

delays and did not occur until 1983. The new Code did not follow the Salesianum's proposition to reinstate the penalty of excommunication for child molesters. Distancing itself from the 1917 Code, it nevertheless reinforced the penalization of child sex abuse by authorizing the laicization of perpetrator priests.[26] This penalty was already—infrequently—used by the Holy Office to punish child sex abuse in the gravest cases or when the priests were recidivists. The 1983 Code, however, did not face the problem of religious pedophilia; it did not contemplate, for instance, the possibility of dismissing religious for child sex abuse. It was only in 2001 that the Congregation for the Doctrine of Faith promulgated new norms to prosecute child sex abuse in the motu proprio *Sacramentorum Sanctitatis Tutela*. Distancing from its twentieth-century policy of secrecy, it officially published the document in the *Acta Apostolicae Sedis*.[27]

Vatican II represented a missed opportunity for a public debate around child sex abuse, debate which continues to be needed today and should involve not only bishops but also religious superiors, theologians, and canonists, as well as the lay faithful. The major role played by the press in the disclosure of child sex abuse in the Catholic Church highlights how, far from being an enemy, the media can contribute to an authentic reform of its structures and culture. The preconciliar discussions suggest several avenues of reflection for the future. How could the various abuses of power and "violations of social justice," which fuel sexual violence, be addressed more strongly and effectively? The prominence of child sex abuse in religious congregations, rightly pointed out by the Salesianum, is still underestimated. The reasons for this prevalence in both ancient and more recently established institutes, as well as in the new ecclesial movements, should be investigated more in depth. Additionally, the 1962 debate invites us to rethink a penal system that focuses on clerical delinquency. The old dual justice system of the church—in which the crimes of the lay faithful are addressed in secular courts, while those of the

---

26. *The Code of Canon Law* (Canon Law Society of America, 1999), 1395.2; also at https://www.vatican.va/archive/cod-iuris-canonici/cic_index_en.html.

27. These norms were first revised by Pope Benedict XVI in 2010, before being replaced by a new procedure defined by Pope Francis's motu proprio *Vos Estis Lux Mundi* (2019), following Chile's child sex abuse crisis. In 2021, Pope Francis promulgated the apostolic constitution *Pascite Gregem Dei*, which updated book VI of the Code of Canon Law, on penal sanctions.

"privileged" priests are prosecuted by ecclesial authorities—has not completely disappeared. Since, in the 1960s, the Catholic Church did not contemplate the possibility that clerics could be taken to secular courts, it seems especially necessary to redefine the church's penal system in relation with the various national and state laws to which all the faithful are subjected.

Chapter 7

The Limits and Legacy of Vatican II's Teaching on Priesthood

The Bishops' Responses to Clerical Sexual Abuse in Australia

Josephine Laffin

The Second Vatican Council did not directly address two related issues that, from the late twentieth century, emerged in scandal after scandal around the world: clerical sexual abuse and episcopal efforts to conceal it. Nor did the council fathers envisage the decline from the late 1960s in the number of men willing to commit themselves to priestly ministry or the number who would leave after ordination in the years after the council. It is inconceivable, however, that the council's teaching on priesthood did not have some impact. This paper traces the subtle influence of Vatican II on the way two Australian bishops responded to these serious problems. Both men were deeply committed to implementing conciliar decrees and strove to develop, in accordance with *Presbyterorum Ordinis*, Vatican II's Decree on the Ministry and Life of Priests, a more paternal/ pastoral relationship with their priests than had often been the case with their "prince bishop" predecessors. Both, however, struggled to articulate a healthy theology of priesthood and to discipline clergy when necessary. The consequences were disastrous.

"In Spite of Our Inadequacy"

On a wintery day in June 1978, four Catholic bishops and over one hundred priests gathered in Timboon, in the Diocese of Ballarat in southeastern Australia, to bid farewell to the small, rural town's parish priest, Msgr. John Day (1904–78).[1] The principal celebrant was Ronald Mulkearns (1930–2016), the bishop of Ballarat from 1971 until his retirement in 1997. In his homily during the funeral service, Mulkearns quoted from Pope Paul VI's apostolic exhortation *Evangelii Nuntiandi*, which was issued on December 8, 1975, the tenth anniversary of the close of the Second Vatican Council: "As pastors, we have been chosen by the mercy of the Supreme Pastor, in spite of our inadequacy, to proclaim with authority the Word of God, to assemble the scattered People of God, to feed this people with the signs of the actions of Christ which are the sacraments, to set this people on the road to salvation." Msgr. Day, Mulkearns claimed, had done all this with "unresting zeal."[2] He did not mention that the senior priest had also been accused of sexually molesting children and that in 1973 he had transferred him from the parish of Mildura to Timboon, at the opposite end of the diocese, after reports were made to the police.[3]

By the time Mulkearns himself died in 2016, the Royal Commission into Institutional Responses to Child Sexual Abuse was underway in Australia.[4] This federal government inquiry ran from 2013 to 2017. It did not

---

1. "The Death of Mgr John Day," *Light* (magazine of the Diocese of Ballarat), September 1978, 8.

2. Homily of Bishop Mulkearns at the Requiem Mass for John Day at Timboon, June 28, 1978. A copy of this homily was tabled as an exhibit at the Royal Commission into Institutional Responses to Child Sexual Abuse in 2015, https://www.childabuseroyalcommission.gov.au/sites/default/files/CTJH.120.01093.0015.pdf.

3. The Royal Commission found that fifteen people had made allegations against Day between 1954 and 1973. The average age of the children at the time of the abuse was ten years old. Royal Commission into Institutional Responses to Child Sexual Abuse, *Report of Case Study No. 28: Catholic Church Authorities in Ballarat* (2017), 459, https://www.childabuseroyalcommission.gov.au/sites/default/files/file-list/un-redacted_report_of_case_study_28_-_catholic_church_authorities_in_ballarat.pdf.

4. See the website: https://www.childabuseroyalcommission.gov.au/. For the implications for the Catholic Church, see Neil Ormerod, "Sexual Abuse, a Royal Commission, and the Australian Church," *Theological Studies* 80, no. 4 (2019): 950–66.

concentrate exclusively on the Catholic Church, but over half of the 4,029 men and women who testified that they had experienced abuse as children (2,489, or 61.8 percent) had accounts that involved the church. In its final report in 2017, the commission concluded that, of 9,025 Catholic priests identified as being in ministry in Australia from 1950 to 2010, 507 (5.6 percent) faced accusations of child sexual abuse. Almost three-quarters of the victims were male; the average age at the time of the first alleged incident of sexual abuse was 10.4 years. Between 1980 and 2015, Catholic authorities throughout Australia paid a total $250.7 million in monetary compensation to victims, at an average of $88,000 per claim.[5]

In 2016, with the spotlight of the commission focused on the Ballarat diocese and Ronald Mulkearns's history of concealing abuse by priests, the retired bishop's death from cancer took place amidst a barrage of negative news reports. "One should never speak ill of the dead as the saying goes," a columnist wrote in the national newspaper, *The Australian*. "I think we can rule this out in the case of the former bishop of Ballarat."[6] There was no grand farewell. A private funeral service was held in the chapel of the aged-care facility where Mulkearns died. Diocesan priests were not invited. Their emeritus bishop was buried in a simple grave in the Ballarat cemetery instead of with his predecessors in the cathedral crypt, and a planned memorial service was cancelled after vocal protests from survivors of abuse and their supporters.[7]

---

5. Royal Commission into Institutional Responses to Child Sex Abuse, *Final Report: Religious Institutions*, vol. 16, book 2 (2017), 75–85, https://www.childabuseroyal commission.gov.au/sites/default/files/final_report_-_volume_16_religious_institutions _book_2.pdf. The findings of the commission are similar to those of a report for the United States Conference of Catholic Bishops, which calculated that about 4 percent of Catholic priests and deacons in active ministry between 1950 and 2002 had been accused of the sexual abuse of a youth under the age of eighteen, with the percentage for individual dioceses ranging from 3 to 6 percent. John Jay College of Criminal Justice, *The Nature and Scope of Sexual Abuse of Minors by Catholic Priests and Deacons in the United States 1950–2002* (USCCB, 2004), 27.

6. "Jack the Insider" [Peter Hoysted], "The Disgraceful Life of Bishop Ronald Mulkearns," *The Australian*, April 5, 2016.

7. "Diocese of Ballarat Cancels Memorial Service for Disgraced Bishop: Petitions, Planned Protests and 'High Levels of Stress,'" *La Croix International*, May 13, 2016, https://

This chapter does not challenge the verdict of the Royal Commission that there were "catastrophic failures of leadership over many decades" in the Catholic Church in Australia.[8] It will not exonerate Mulkearns or Francis Little (1925–2008), archbishop of Melbourne from 1974 to 1996. They are the two Australian bishops who, more than any others, now bear the brunt of anger directed at "paedophile enablers." Instead, this chapter seeks to understand why they acted the way they did. The obvious conclusion to draw from various legal proceedings and investigations by journalists is that they were motivated by loyalty to the institutional church and a determination to avoid scandal. However, other explanations have been put forward. Peter Connors, Mulkearns's successor in Ballarat, opined that his predecessor was "terribly naïve" and "didn't know how to deal with it."[9] With less sympathy, Cardinal George Pell, a former priest of the Ballarat diocese and Little's successor in Melbourne, accused Mulkearns of "errors of judgement" that were "grave and inexplicable."[10]

In contrast to Pell's attempt to portray Mulkearns as simply a "bad apple" in the hierarchy—an argument that became increasingly unsustainable as more Catholic leaders, including Pell himself, were implicated in scandalous behavior[11]—retired barrister (and former seminarian) Kieran Tapsell insists that Mulkearns, who had a doctorate in canon law and was one of the founders of the Canon Law Society in Australia, duti-

---

international.la-croix.com/news/religion/diocese-of-ballarat-cancels-memorial-service-for-disgraced-bishop/3165.

8. Royal Commission into Institutional Responses to Child Sex Abuse, *Final Report*, 278.

9. Quoted by Kieran Tapsell, *Potiphar's Wife: The Vatican's Secret and Child Sexual Abuse* (ATF Press, 2014), 296. Bishop Connors made the comment at the Victorian Parliamentary Inquiry into Handling of Sexual Abuse by Religious and Other Organisations in 2012.

10. Cardinal George Pell, transcript of public hearing on March 1, 2016, Royal Commission into Institutional Responses to Child Sexual Abuse. "Do you think Bishop Mulkearns is just one bad apple, as it were, within the Catholic Church as a bishop?" Pell was asked. He responded: "Unfortunately, I would have to say that I can't nominate another bishop whose actions are so grave and inexplicable." https://www.childabuseroyal commission.gov.au/sites/default/files/file-list/Case%20Study%2028%20-%20Transcript%20-%20Catholic%20Church%20authorities%20in%20Ballarat%20-%20Day%20160%20-%2001032016.pdf.

11. Pell was convicted of sexual offences in 2018 but later acquitted on appeal.

fully adhered to the church's legal system in his response to allegations of abuse.[12] Tapsell points out that Pope Pius XI's 1922 decree *Crimen Sollicitationis*, reissued with minor revisions by Pope John XXIII in 1962, and Pope Paul VI's *Secreta Continere* (1974) imposed strict confidentially on accusations and investigations of sexual abuse by clerics. To these can be added the 1983 Code of Canon Law, which made it very difficult for a diocesan bishop to dismiss a priest.[13]

While other attempts have been made to shift the focus from the failings of individual bishops to the culture in which they operated (often labelled clericalism or, more recently, "vicious hierarchicalism"[14]), little attention has so far been paid to the most transformative ecclesial event which took place during Mulkearns's and Little's priestly ministry—the Second Vatican Council—and the impact that it might have had on their responses to child sexual abuse by priests. Although Mulkearns and Little did not personally attend the council, both men came to be regarded as

---

12. Tapsell, *Potiphar's Wife*, 286–87.

13. A notorious case in Australia concerned John Nestor, a priest of the Diocese of Wollongong in New South Wales who challenged attempts by Bishop Philip Wilson to ban him from public ministry. Nestor successfully appealed to the Congregation for Clergy in Rome, whereupon the diocese took the case to the Supreme Tribunal of the Apostolic Signatura. The process eventually resulted in Nestor's dismissal from the priesthood by Pope Benedict XVI in 2008, ten years after Wilson's initial attempt to remove him from ministry. Case Study 14 of the Royal Commission, "The Response of the Catholic Diocese of Wollongong to Allegations of Child Sexual Abuse, and Related Criminal Proceedings, against John Gerard Nestor, a Priest of the Diocese" (2014) highlights the complexity of the procedures in canon law for the removal of clergy. https://www.childabuseroyalcommission.gov.au/sites/default/files/file-list/Case%20Study%2014%20-%20Findings%20Report%20-%20Catholic%20Diocese%20of%20Wollongong.pdf.

14. James F. Keenan, "Hierarchicalism," *Theological Studies* 83, no. 1 (2022): 84–108. See also Marie Keenan, *Child Sexual Abuse and the Catholic Church: Gender, Power and Organizational Culture* (Oxford University Press, 2013). In Australia, the literature includes Geoffrey Robinson, *Confronting Power and Sex in the Catholic Church: Reclaiming the Spirit of Jesus* (John Garratt Publishing, 2007); Chris Geraghty, "Sexuality and the Clerical Life," in *Child Sexual Abuse, Society and the Future of the Church*, ed. Hilary Regan (ATF Theology, 2013), 59–73; Kevin Peoples, *Trapped in a Closed World: Catholic Culture and Sexual Abuse* (Garratt Publishing, 2017); and John E. Ryan, *A Priesthood Imprisoned: A Crisis for the Church* (Coventry Press, 2017). Notably, Robinson was a bishop, Ryan is a priest, Geraghty a former priest, and Peoples, like Tapsell, a former seminarian who did not go on to ordination.

leaders in the implementation of Vatican II in Australia. "We thought Ron Mulkearns was one of the best bishops in Australia," a priest ordained in 1966 for the Archdiocese of Adelaide commented sadly after he heard of Mulkearns's death.[15] In tributes after Little died, Sir Frank (he was knighted in 1977) was described as "mild-mannered" and "a gentle guide for rough times."[16] A retired priest of the Melbourne archdiocese was quoted saying "The priests liked him. He understood Vatican II and its spirit."[17]

The council did not specifically address the issue of clerical sexual abuse. As Agnès Desmazières relates, a draft schema was prepared by the Commission for the Discipline of Clergy and Christian People, which recommended reforms to the 1917 Code of Canon Law's penalty system. The proposed changes included the provision that a cleric who sexually abused a child should incur automatic excommunication. The Preparatory Central Commission decided not to add the schema to the council's agenda, in part because a focus on canon law was thought to be inappropriate for the council's "pastoral agenda."[18] The existence of the draft demonstrates, however, that there was awareness of this terrible problem well before scandals erupted with ferocious intensity in the late twentieth and early twenty-first centuries.

It is important to make this point because, for some Catholics, Vatican II is indirectly to blame for the sexual abuse crisis. Pope Emeritus Benedict XVI provided support for this view when, in an essay published in 2019, he attributed a growing moral relativism in the years after the council to progressive theological thinking that converged with increasing permissiveness in society and homosexual cliques infiltrated seminaries.[19] Yet, while the evidence is not as prolific, there are examples of clerical sexual

---

15. The late Rev. Dr. Denis Edwards in conversation with the author in 2016.

16. Barney Zwartz, "Mild-Mannered Archbishop Little Dead at 82," *Age*, April 9, 2008, https://www.theage.com.au/national/mild-mannered-archbishop-little-dead-at-82-2008 0409-ge6y0d.html; Mark Brolly, "A Gentle Guide for Tough Times," *Sydney Morning Herald*, April 10, 2008, https://www.smh.com.au/national/a-gentle-guide-for-tough-times -20080410-gds8uk.html.

17. Eric Hodgens, quoted in Zwartz, "Mild-Mannered Archbishop."

18. Agnès Desmazières, "Vatican II's Silence on Child Sex Abuse: Challenges and Limits of a 'Pastoral' Agenda," chapter 6 of this volume.

19. Pope Emeritus Benedict XVI, "The Church and the Scandal of Abuse," April 10, 2019, trans. Anian Christoph Wimmer, https://www.catholicnewsagency.com/news /41013/full-text-of-benedict-xvi-essay-the-church-and-the-scandal-of-sexual-abuse.

abuse that predate Vatican II, and most of the perpetrators in the 1960s and 1970s had been ordained before the council or at least undergone most of their seminary formation before changes were introduced in its wake. An example is the aforementioned John Day, who was born in 1904. He was not a product of the 1960s sexual revolution. Thus, a caricature of the 1960s does not do justice to the interwoven threads of continuity and change in the recent history of clerical sexual abuse.

Threads of Traditional Piety and Conciliar Reform

It can be difficult now to comprehend the elevated status of priests in Catholic piety before Vatican II. Ronald Mulkearns and Frank Little both began their priestly ministry in the 1950s.[20] One of Little's fellow students and close friends at the Collegio Urbano in Rome was John Molony, ordained for the Diocese of Ballarat in 1950. Looking back on his time as a priest before Vatican II, Molony reflected in his autobiography: "As well as his own understanding, and humble acceptance, of the holy mystery of his priesthood, the main thing that sustained a young priest was the great faith of the Catholic people in that same mystery and their almost fierce loyalty to and pride in him. The priest was accepted as the *alter Christus,* the other Christ who celebrated the Mass, dispensed the sacraments and gave his life for the people. In short, the priest did 'the Father's work' as Jesus himself had done. He could ask for no more from man or God."[21]

While remaining a committed Catholic, Molony left the priesthood in the mid-1960s to marry and pursue an academic career. Another man who wrote an account of his time as a priest is retired judge Christopher Geraghty. Ordained a priest for the Archdiocese of Sydney in 1962, Geraghty alludes to the dark side of the traditional exaltation of priesthood:

> In those distant days the priest was seen by himself and his flock as a special messenger from God and the dispenser of divine mysteries. He was the representative of Christ on earth—God's interpreter and ambassador. Since he was invested with divine powers (to forgive sins, to make Christ present and to lay down the law), he was entitled to the utmost deference and

---

20. Little was ordained in Rome in 1950 for the Diocese of Melbourne; Mulkearns in Melbourne in 1956.

21. John Molony, *By Wendouree* (Connor Court, 2010), 241.

respect. It was incomprehensible that a priest could be avaricious and greedy, jealous, unreasonable, lazy, self-indulgent, a thief or a sexual predator. We believed, and the people believed, that we enjoyed a status above the angels, forever cloaked in a graced aura of supernatural powers.[22]

It is not possible to explore here all the cultural and ecclesial factors that helped bring priests down from this lofty pedestal in the second half of the twentieth century. However, *Lumen Gentium*, Vatican II's Dogmatic Constitution on the Church, undoubtedly contributed to the process by encouraging lay Catholics to see themselves (with the clerical hierarchy) as the "people of God," members of a community of disciples of Christ, equipped through baptism with various gifts for ministry and service.

Unlike *Lumen Gentium*, *Presbyterorum Ordinis*, the Decree on the Ministry and Life of Priests, is not regarded as one of the great achievements of the council. Dubbed "a half-hearted reform" and "one of the Council's stepchildren" by Peter Hünermann,[23] it appeared in 1965 almost as an afterthought, a belated attempt to consider the ministerial priesthood after all the attention paid to the episcopate, on the one hand, and the laity, on the other. Understandably, as the council drew to a close, "general weariness" afflicted participants.[24] This was certainly the experience of theologian Yves Congar, who complained bitterly in his journal about his fatigue, the tight deadline he was given to revise sections of *Presbyterorum Ordinis*, and the challenge of incorporating the viewpoints of bishops with different understandings of ordained ministry.[25]

As Congar also had a major role in the drafting of *Lumen Gentium*, it is not surprising that *Presbyterorum Ordinis* acknowledges the common priesthood of the baptized. However, it does not distinguish this from the priesthood of the ordained with the clarity of the 1992 *Catechism of the Catholic Church*: "The ministerial priesthood is at the service of the

---

22. Christopher Geraghty, *Dancing with the Devil: A Journey from the Pulpit to the Bench* (Spectrum, 2012), 9–10.
23. Peter Hünermann, "The Final Weeks of the Council," in *History of Vatican II*, vol. 5, ed. Giuseppe Alberigo (Orbis Books, 2006), 457.
24. John W. O'Malley, *What Happened at Vatican II* (Belknap Press, 2008), 274.
25. Yves Congar, *My Journal of the Council* (Liturgical Press, 2012), 817–51.

common priesthood."²⁶ In keeping with the best contemporary biblical and ecclesial scholarship, the decree stresses the pastoral and relational nature of ordained ministry, but it does not break away completely from the cultic model of priesthood that had dominated Catholic piety for most of the second millennium. Priests were to live with the people of God "as with brothers and sisters" but "set apart in some way."²⁷

Another point of tension is that *Presbyterorum Ordinis* strongly affirms the hierarchical nature of the church while assuring priests that they "share with the bishops the one identical priesthood and ministry of Christ" and that bishops should "regard their priests as brothers and friends" (PO 7). Not surprisingly, as Pope Paul VI excluded it from the agenda of the council, the treatment of clerical celibacy is also inadequate. In a nod to the Eastern churches and ancient Christian practice, *Presbyterorum Ordinis* admits that celibacy "is not demanded of the priesthood by its nature," but it praises it as a "gift . . . liberally granted by the Father" to Latin-rite priests (PO 16). A pious exhortation to priests to lead lives of holiness and perfection is accompanied by a realistic acknowledgment of human weakness. Priests (and presumably bishops as well) are urged "always to treat with fraternal charity and compassion those [brother priests] who have failed in certain ways" (PO 8).²⁸ The "certain ways" are not specified.

Australian archbishop Guilford Young of Hobart was invited to write the introduction to *Presbyterorum Ordinis* for Walter Abbott's English translation.²⁹ In 1986 he remembered how he "wrote on the run, still scribbling on stray paper as I tossed clothes into the suitcase to come home after the Council's end."³⁰ He emphasized in 1965 both the close relationship

---

26. *Catechism of the Catholic Church* (Libreria Editrice Vaticana, 1993), no. 1547, https://www.vatican.va/archive/ENG0015/_INDEX.HTM#fonte.

27. Second Vatican Council, Decree on the Ministry and Life of Priests, *Presbyterorum Ordinis*, December 7, 1965 (hereafter, PO), no. 3. All quotations of Vatican II documents are from Austin Flannery, ed., *Vatican Council II: Constitutions, Decrees, Declarations; A Completely Revised Translation in Inclusive Language* (Liturgical Press, 2014).

28. The Flannery translation reads ". . . in any way." Here I have offered a more literal translation of the document's original Latin: *in quibusdam* = "in certain ways" or "in some cases."

29. Walter M. Abbott, SJ, ed., *The Documents of Vatican II* (Geoffrey Chapman, 1966), 526–31.

30. Guilford Young, "The Priested Man's Sacramental Reality," *Advocate*, October 23, 1986, 9.

that should exist between a diocesan bishop and his priests and the fact that "this brotherhood is not a mere communion of mind and heart but is a sacramental reality."[31] Looking back in 1986, he reiterated the significance of what is sometimes referred to in the language of Thomist philosophy as an "ontological change": "I assert the decree does teach, and so do other documents of the Council, that the sacrament [of ordination] effects a new intrinsic change, new in kind, within the baptised man, and makes over his whole being. It consecrates his whole self *really* to God." Young added that "my focus is not on the priest's moral living out of his transformation and consecration."[32] The sexual abuse crisis has highlighted how appallingly some priests failed the "moral living out."

Responding to Sexual Abuse

At a hearing of the Royal Commission into Institutional Responses to Child Sexual Abuse in November 2015, Msgr. Thomas Doyle, director of the Catholic Education Office in the Archdiocese of Melbourne from 1979 to 2010, testified that he had reported to Archbishop Little serious incidents involving Peter Searson (1923–2009), the parish priest of Doveton from 1984 to 1997, and children and staff at the parish primary school.[33] Only Little had the power to remove Searson from the parish and control of the school, which he refused to do. Asked why he thought Little took this approach, Doyle, who knew Little well, responded, "I'd put it down to two things actually: I think he had an exaggerated respect for the priesthood, and I think he really didn't think these things were happening." "Do you mean he wanted to protect the reputation of the priesthood?" the counsel assisting the commissioner queried. "No," Doyle

---

31. Abbott, *Documents of Vatican II*, 527.
32. Young, "The Priested Man's," 9.
33. The Royal Commission found that three people made a claim of child sexual abuse that was substantiated against Peter Searson, but he was also accused of other forms of aberrant behavior that amounted to psychological abuse. He features prominently in *Report of Case Study No. 35: Catholic Archdiocese of Melbourne* (2017), https://www.childabuseroyalcommission.gov.au/sites/default/files/file-list/un-redacted_report_of_case_study_no._35_-_catholic_archdiocese_of_melbourne_-.pdf.

clarified, "I think he just had a great respect for priesthood in itself. . . . He found it hard to believe that a priest would do these sorts of things."[34]

Little's former secretary (1974–76), vicar general (1976–87) and then auxiliary bishop (1987–97), Peter Connors (who succeeded Mulkearns as bishop of Ballarat), also gave evidence at the Royal Commission. Interviewed in 2008, after Little's death, he commented, "I had thirteen lovely years sitting opposite him [Little] at breakfast every morning. He was a holy man. He loved God and God's people." Significantly, however, Connors added, "He was always fearful of hurting priests and found it hard to correct or reprimand a priest."[35] At the Royal Commission, when questioned on this disastrous failing, he recalled that Little once told him, "'My best friend left the priesthood, and he left the priesthood because of the way he was treated by the Bishop and the Vicar-General of the diocese.' I thought to myself, now I have a clue as to what is your major problem; you're finding it very hard to correct or to chastise or even to reprimand a priest."[36]

The friend who left was John Molony. His bishop was James O'Collins (1892-1983), Mulkearns's predecessor at Ballarat. "Bishop O'Collins dealt with his priests as if we were his servants," Molony recalled in his memoir.[37] "On not a single occasion did he ever ask me about the state of my health, whether I was happy, or even whether I wished to serve the diocese as a curate in another parish. In truth, he never asked me anything. He simply told me what I was to do and even then not to my face. Bill McCunnie [O'Collins's secretary] relayed his commands."[38] In contrast to this impersonal approach, and in accordance with *Presbyterorum Ordinis*,

---

34. Royal Commission into Institutional Responses to Child Sexual Abuse, Public Hearing—Case Study 35 (Day C127), November 26, 2015, 13432–33, https://www.childabuseroyalcommission.gov.au/sites/default/files/file-list/Case%20Study%2035%20-%20Transcript%20-%20Catholic%20Archdiocese%20of%20Melbourne%20-%20Day%20C127%20-%2026112015.pdf.

35. Zwartz, "Mild-Mannered Archbishop."

36. Royal Commission into Institutional Responses to Child Sexual Abuse, Public Hearing—Case Study 35 (Day C131), December 2, 2015, C13930, https://www.childabuseroyalcommission.gov.au/sites/default/files/file-list/Case%20Study%2035%20-%20Transcript%20-%20Catholic%20Archdiocese%20of%20Melbourne%20-%20Day%20C131%20-%2002122015.pdf.

37. Molony, *By Wendouree*, 232.

38. Molony, *By Wendouree*, 329.

both Frank Little and Ronald Mulkearns tried to develop closer relationships with their priests.

Mulkearns began a three-page, newsy letter on December 27, 1978: "Dear Paul, I am sorry I did not get around to writing before Christmas, as I had hoped to do."[39] The recipient, Paul David Ryan, was in Washington, DC, where Mulkearns had sent him shortly after his ordination to undergo counselling and spiritual direction under the watchful eye of John Francis Harvey, OSFS, who was running a program to help same-sex attracted Catholics remain abstinent from sexual activities.[40] Harvey, who read some of the correspondence between the bishop and the young priest, commented to the former that while it was good that Ryan had such "great trust" in him, there was a danger that it could develop into a "a kind of father-son relationship, thereby restricting your freedom as the bishop of the diocese."[41] Despite Harvey's warning, Gerard Ridsdale, arguably Australia's worst pedophile priest,[42] was also the recipient of friendly letters from Mulkearns while overseas on a treatment program run by the Servants of the Paraclete in New Mexico ("I will be in touch again as soon as I can and, in the meantime will of course welcome any

39. Ronald Mulkearns to Paul David Ryan, December 27, 1978, https://www.childabuseroyalcommission.gov.au/sites/default/files/WAL.0001.002.0107_R.pdf.

40. The Royal Commission noted that four people had made complaints against Paul David Ryan (b. 1948). Two of the claims concerned alleged incidents in parishes in the Ballarat diocese and two concerned the Star of the Sea Parish in Virginia Beach in the Diocese of Richmond in the United States, where Ryan undertook parish work in 1978-79. Royal Commission into Institutional Responses to Child Sexual Abuse, *Report of Case No. Study 28: Catholic Church Authorities in Ballarat* (2017), https://www.childabuseroyalcommission.gov.au/sites/default/files/file-list/un-redacted_report_of_case_study_28_-_catholic_church_authorities_in_ballarat.pdf. In 2006 Ryan pleaded guilty to sexually abusing three youths and was sentenced to eighteen months imprisonment. He was convicted of further offences in 2019 and sentenced to seventeen months jail.

41. John Harvey to Ronald Mulkearns, January 14, 1978, https://www.childabuseroyalcommission.gov.au/sites/default/files/CTJH.120.60019.0028.pdf.

42. Convicted of child sexual offences in multiple parishes, Ridsdale has spent most of the last thirty years in jail. The Royal Commission concluded that seventy-eight people made a claim of child sexual abuse against him. The complaints dated between 1961 and 1988; 88 percent of victims were male and 12 percent female. Their average age at the time was ten years for females and eleven years of age for males. Royal Commission into Institutional Responses to Child Sexual Abuse, *Report of Case Study No. 28*, 462.

communication from yourself as to how things are going. Be assured of my prayers. I ask you for yours").[43]

Mulkearns visited Ryan in Washington in 1978 and travelled to Jemez Springs in New Mexico in 1990 for the "discharge meeting" with Ridsdale's therapists at Villa Louis Martin. Ridsdale received a glowing report card: "Feedback from staff was very positive and affirming of Gerald's progress in treatment, and the gifts he brings to the priesthood."[44] Mulkearns was so impressed by his experiences at Jemez Springs that he tried to get the Australian bishops to invite the Servants of the Paraclete to run a similar center in Australia. "A facility established by the Servants would not be a punitive centre," Mulkearns stressed. It "would have a theological, pastoral and therapeutic emphasis."[45]

In his ultimately unsuccessful proposal, Mulkearns pointed out that a center in Australia could be less costly than sending priests overseas—he had spent over $70,000 on Ridsdale's treatment in New Mexico. By 1993 he was also lending Ridsdale money to pay his legal bills. When questioned on this in an interview with Catholic Church Insurance, Mulkearns admitted that he felt uncomfortable giving Ridsdale more financial help than his victims. But he added that, although he had a "pastoral concern" for the victims, he could not accept responsibility for them in the same way that he had to do for Ridsdale.[46]

Caring for the Carer

While Mulkearns's prioritizing of support for priests guilty of child sexual abuse over their victims is indefensible, his commitment to ensuring they received counselling and treatment is consistent not with toxic

---

43. Mulkearns to Ridsdale, January 12, 1990, https://www.childabuseroyalcommission.gov.au/sites/default/files/CCI.0001.00632.0067.pdf.

44. Planning/Discharge Meeting, Villa Louis Martin, September 13, 1990, https://www.childabuseroyalcommission.gov.au/sites/default/files/CCI.0001.00632.0099.pdf.

45. Ronald Mulkearns, "Possibility of a Facility for Treatment of Priests in Need of Therapy," December 1990, https://www.childabuseroyalcommission.gov.au/sites/default/files/CTJH.301.02002.0016.pdf. In 1995, facing increasing lawsuits for failed treatment, the Servants of the Paraclete closed the center at Jemez Springs.

46. Transcript of Interview Between Catholic Church Insurance Limited and Bishop Mulkearns, April 14, 1993, https://www.childabuseroyalcommission.gov.au/sites/default/files/CCI.0001.00644.0208_R.pdf.

clericalism or "hierarchicalism," but with his broader efforts to help priests cope with the challenges they faced. These multiplied in the aftermath of the Second Vatican Council. In the early 1970s, Francis Carroll, recently appointed bishop of the Diocese of Wagga Wagga in New South Wales, hosted a series of week-long meetings for priests near the Hume Weir on the border between New South Wales and Victoria. Priests from other dioceses were welcomed, with up to two hundred attending. Carroll later reflected, "These were exciting and turbulent times. People had unreal expectations of Vatican II and thought everything espoused would be embraced wholeheartedly. The truth is that change takes far longer. The clergy suffered greatly. They had the responsibility of organising the changes but had not been formed in the substance of the changes."[47] Mulkearns was one of three Australian bishops present at the gathering in December 1973, which focused on the theme "Priest—Wounded Healer." The National Council of Priests' Newsletter reported that "Archbishop Gleeson [Adelaide] and Bishops Frank Carroll and Ron Mulkearns were not conspicuous by their attire but were noticeable by their close involvement in the groups that formed and reformed continually around the dining tables. . . . Priests began to feel (some for the first time) the truth of the ordination rite that declares them to be trusted partners of the bishop."[48]

Providing support for priests, the men who were expected to provide pastoral care for their parishioners, was one of Mulkearns's main concerns: "Who cares for the carers? That has been a real worry to me. . . . Priests need help and support. I know I had the impression when I was through the seminary, 'Okay. You've done the course. You ought to be able to cope with anything now on your own.' That just doesn't work."[49] As chairman of the Australian Bishops' Committee for Priests and Religious in the 1980s, Mulkearns was the driving force behind the establishment of the St. Peter's Centre, which opened in Canberra in 1982 to provide continuing education for priests. It offered a three-month, residential sabbatical

---

47. Quoted by Frank Devoy in Paul Casey, ed., *Where Did All the Young Men Go? Life Stories from 1960's Student Catholic Priests* (FeedARead.com Publishing, 2015), 502.

48. "Success Again at Hume Weir," in National Council of Priests' Newsletter, January 1974.

49. Nicholas Kerr, "The Church and Her Priests," *Southern Cross*, December 6, 1984, 6.

program "designed to provide pastorally-focused theology in the spirit of Vatican II as well as spiritual guidance and renewal with the foremost aim being to reaffirm and revitalise priests in their ministerial commitment."[50] Between 1982 and 1990, when the St. Peter's Centre closed, over three hundred men participated in this program; however, they comprised less than 10 percent of Australian priests at the time.[51]

Keen for more opportunities for ongoing formation at the diocesan level, Mulkearns arranged for the Center for Human Development, based on the campus of The Catholic University of America in Washington, DC, to establish an outpost in Canberra. Between 1985 and 1988, sixteen Australian dioceses took up the center's "Ministry for Priests Program." The center's founder and director, Trappist priest Vincent Dwyer, made numerous trips across the Pacific to lead motivational retreats for priests to promote personal growth and mutual support.[52] "Something really marvellous is happening in our midst," exclaimed Archbishop Little after 260 Melbourne priests attended a pre-retreat preparation day in 1985.[53]

One of Dwyer's catch phrases was "God doesn't choose junk." He encouraged priests to remember "their dream" when they first became a priest and to strive to reignite their youthful enthusiasm. This, however, presupposed that their original motives were pure, a dangerous assumption given the inadequacy of vetting processes for entry into a seminary at the time most men joined. In retrospect, Paul David Ryan recognized that he had "an underlying need for security and that's one of the things I think why I entered the seminary was to find security. I didn't realise at the time but I think I had a real deep sense of insecurity, certainly immaturity."[54] When asked at the Royal Commission why he became a priest, Gerard Ridsdale could not provide a clear answer, but he acknowledged the influence of

---

50. National Council of Priests' Newsletter, June 1981.
51. Frank Devoy, in Paul Casey, ed., *Where Did All the Young Men Go?*, 502.
52. Dwyer himself would face accusations in the 1990s for sexual abuse. Jason Berry, "Survivors Connect to Heal, Raise Voices," *National Catholic Reporter*, November 8, 2002, https://www.natcath.org/crisis/110802j.htm.
53. "Archbishop Little Writes," *Advocate*, October 10, 1985, 7.
54. Royal Commission into Institutional Responses to Child Sexual Abuse, Private Hearing of Paul David Ryan, February 25, 2015, 827, https://www.childabuseroyalcommission.gov.au/sites/default/files/TRAN.5002.001.0001_E_R.pdf.

parish priest Dan Boylen, who was a friend of his family. In the late 1950s, Boylen was also the vocations director for the Ballarat diocese. Ridsdale divulged, "The only thing I can remember about any conversation with Dan Boylen with regard to the priesthood was, he was talking about spiritual books that I was reading, and I remember him saying, 'Always remember, when you're reading books like that, that that's not necessarily how people like that lived, but that's how they would like to have lived,' and I don't know why that stuck in my mind, but that's something that I've always remembered."[55] Obviously, "this was an unfortunate thing to take notice of, given that Ridsdale would go on to represent the extreme in the disjunction between priestly appearance and reality."[56]

In an address to the Australian Bishops Conference in 1984, the first director of the St. Peter's Centre, John Ryan, quoted a report by Dutch-American psychologist Conrad Baars that was based on a study of over a thousand priests in the late 1960s and early 1970s. Baars concluded: "In general we estimate 10-15% of all priests in western Europe and North America are mature; 20-25% have serious psychiatric difficulties, especially in the form of neuroses and chronic alcoholism or a combination of both and 60-70% suffer from a degree of emotional immaturity which does not prevent them from exercising their priestly function but precludes their being happy men and effective priests whose fundamental role it is to bring people the joy of Christ's love."[57]

Ryan told the Australian Bishops Conference that, from his own experience and observations, he thought Baars's assessment was "a fairly accurate description of the Australian priesthood."[58] More than 1,300 Australian priests participated in psychological surveys that were part of

---

55. Royal Commission into Institutional Responses to Child Sexual Abuse, Transcript of Public Hearing—Case Study 28 (Day C083), May 27, 2015, https://www.childabuse royalcommission.gov.au/sites/default/files/file-list/Case%20Study%2028%20-%20 Transcript%20-%20Catholic%20Church%20authorities%20in%20Ballarat%20-%20 Day%20C083%20-%2027052015.pdf.

56. James Franklin, "Gerard Ridsdale, Paedophile Priest, In His Own Words," *Journal of the Australian Catholic Historical Society* 36 (2015): 220.

57. Conrad Baars, "The Role of the Church in the Causation, Treatment and Prevention of the Crisis in the Priesthood," *Linacre Quarterly* 39, no. 1 (1972): 50.

58. Ryan, *A Priesthood Imprisoned*, 113.

the Ministry to Priests Program. The collated results indicated that Ryan's judgment was not awry. As a cohort, Australian priests were found to be above average in traditional theological and spiritual concepts, but they were functioning "below average in areas of personal emotion, maturity, expression of self through interpersonal relationships, and moral integrative achievement."[59] Only one in ten seemed to have reached a high level of maturity, one in five suffered from low self-esteem, and around two-thirds were experiencing some level of anxiety with regard to loneliness, sexuality, and celibacy.[60]

What Does It Mean to Be a Priest?

At an international symposium in Rome in 1995 to mark the thirtieth anniversary of *Presbyterorum Ordinis*, Ronald Mulkearns admitted that there was "a real crisis of vocations to the priesthood in the Australian Church" and that "the morale of priests has been deeply affected by the disclosure of scandalous behaviour on the part of some of their number and the departure of many others." He declared bluntly, "Important questions urgently need answers. These concern not only how a priest can best function in the Church today and relate to others, but also what is the identity of the priest as an ordained leader in the Church and how can that identity be affirmed."[61]

Mulkearns and Little did not become part of the solution. Overwhelmed by the growing crisis over clerical abuse, both men opted for early retirement. "I was not doing the job as well as I felt I should be

---

59. Center for Human Development, *The Profile of the Priests of Australia* (Center for Human Development, 1989), 1. See also John McKinnon, *A Closer Look at Australian Priests: A Reflection on the Report "The Profile of the Priests of Australia"* (Catholic Institute for Ministry, 1990).

60. One in five reported no anxiety over loneliness, 44 percent "slight," and 32 percent "much." For sexuality, 22 percent identified no anxiety, 47 percent "slight," and 28 percent "much." With regard to celibacy, 33 percent said they felt no anxiety, 40 percent "slight" and 25 percent "much." McKinnon, *A Closer Look*, 12.

61. Ronald Mulkearns, "Some Australian Initiatives for the Continuing Education of Clergy," in Congregation for the Clergy, *Priesthood: A Greater Love* (Congregation for the Clergy, 1997), https://www.vatican.va/roman_curia/congregations/cclergy/documents/rc_con_cclergy_doc_28101995_intsy_en.html.

doing," Mulkearns admitted to the Royal Commission shortly before his death in 2016.[62] In his evidence to the commission, Cardinal Pell denied rumors that he had instigated Little's resignation but conceded that his predecessor as archbishop of Melbourne might have been under pressure from the apostolic nuncio to leave office.[63]

In the last two decades, theologians have made progress in the development of theologies of priesthood that build on *Presbyterorum Ordinis*'s emphasis on ministry as service and highlight the change in ecclesial relationships following ordination rather than the acquisition of sacred powers.[64] However, the reception of renewed theologies remains patchy. This was evident at the Australian Royal Commission when bishops were invited to attend sessions to provide information to help the commission prepare its final report. Theologian Neil Ormerod found it "disconcerting to watch church leaders struggle to explain the rationale behind celibacy, or the seal of the confessional, or to give a coherent explanation of the notion of 'ontological change' in relation to priestly ordination . . . to an uncomprehending and largely secular panel of commissioners."[65]

For some Catholics, a radical overhaul of ordained ministry is needed to purge it of clericalism. This would include expanding the pool of eli-

---

62. Royal Commission into Institutional Responses to Child Sexual Abuse, Public Hearing—Case Study 28 (Day C153), February 25, 2016, C16136, https://www.child abuseroyalcommission.gov.au/sites/default/files/file-list/Case%20Study%2028%20-%20 Transcript%20-%20Catholic%20Church%20authorities%20in%20Ballarat%20-%20 Day%20C153%20-%2025022016.pdf.

63. Royal Commission into Institutional Responses to Child Sexual Abuse, Public Hearing—Case Studies 28 and 35 (day 161), March 2, 2016, 16349, https://www.child abuseroyalcommission.gov.au/sites/default/files/file-list/Case%20Study%2028%20-%20 Transcript%20-%20Catholic%20Church%20authorities%20in%20Ballarat%20-%20 Day%20161%20-%2002032016.pdf.

64. Two notable projects were the Collegeville Ministry Seminar, which resulted in Susan K. Wood, ed., *Ordering the Baptismal Priesthood: Theologies of Lay and Ordained Ministry* (Liturgical Press, 2003), and more recently Boston College's Seminar on Priesthood and Ministry for the Contemporary Church, which led to Richard R. Gaillardetz, Thomas H. Groome, and Richard Lennan, eds., *Priestly Ministry and the People of God: Hopes and Horizons* (Orbis Books, 2022). The late Richard Gaillardetz was involved in both. Susan Wood pays tribute to his work in "Ordered Ministries for a Missionary and Global Church: The Contribution of Richard R. Gaillardetz," *Ecclesiology* 19 (2023): 285.

65. Ormerod, "Sexual Abuse, a Royal Commission," 954.

gible candidates to include women and married men.[66] At the other end of the spectrum are Catholics who seek a resacralizing of ordained ministry. Notably, an increasing number of Catholic seminarians seem attracted by a high theology of ordination that confers on male clergy a special ontological status.[67] Pope Francis has lamented this development, expressing dismay "at the scandal of young priests [in ecclesiastical tailors' shops in Rome] trying on cassocks and hats or albs and lace-covered robes" rather than striving to be shepherds who "smell like their sheep."[68] As Massimo Faggioli has pointed out, this upsurge in clericalism is being exacerbated not only by vocal opposition to Pope Francis and Vatican II but also by a "de-historicization of theological studies."[69]

At the opening of the Second Vatican Council on October 11, 1962, Pope John XXIII quoted one of his favorite aphorisms: "History is the teacher of life." Lessons must be learnt from the terrible mistakes and suffering of the past. Some of these are obvious, such as the need for greater care in the selection of candidates for priesthood and better supervision and accountability after ordination. Others are less evident. It is, for example, easy to dismiss bishops who mishandled the sexual abuse crisis as "bad apples" or products of a toxic clerical culture. The reality, in the case of men like Ronald Mulkearns and Frank Little is more complex. Aside from their grave errors of judgment when dealing with priests

---

66. See, for example, Jennifer Slater, "The Catholic Church in Need of De-clericalisation and Moral Doctrinal Agency: Towards an Ethically Accountable Hierarchical Leadership," *HTS Teologiese Studies/Theological Studies* 75, no. 4 (2019): 709–19.

67. See, for example, Brad Vermurlen, Mark Regnerus, and Stephen Cranney, "The Ongoing Conservative Turn in the American Catholic Priesthood," *Sociological Spectrum* 43, no. 2 (2023): 72–88.

68. Francis has referred a number of times to the importance of priests being shepherds, with the "odour of the sheep." See, for example, his homily at the Chrism Mass on March 28, 2013, https://www.vatican.va/content/francesco/en/homilies/2013/documents/papa-francesco_20130328_messa-crismale.html. Similarly, he has made recurrent attacks on clericalism, including in his intervention at the Eighteenth General Congregation of the Synod of Bishops on October 25, 2023, when he castigated young clergy for their interest in ecclesiastical vestments, https://www.vatican.va/content/francesco/en/speeches/2023/october/documents/20231025-intervento-sinodo.html.

69. Massimo Faggioli, "The Catholic Sexual Abuse Crisis as a Theological Crisis: Emerging Issues," *Theological Studies* 80, no. 3 (2019): 576.

guilty of sexual abuse, Mulkearns and Little were exemplary "Vatican II bishops," outstanding in their pastoral care and support for priests. The fact that they were constrained by canon law and the remnants of the cultic model of priesthood was also part of the legacy and limitations of the Second Vatican Council.

As we have seen, toward the end of his time as a working bishop, Mulkearns identified an urgent need to clarify the identity and role of ordained ministers. Thirty years on, that challenge remains a pressing concern. *Presbyterorum Ordinis* provides a good starting point for renewed theologies of priesthood but not the final word on the subject.

Chapter 8

Jointly Committed

Examining the Sexual Abuse Scandal as a Case of Institutional Vice in Post-Vatican II Catholicism

Bernard G. Prusak

The Unfinished Work of Vatican II

The late great historian John O'Malley dated what he termed the Roman Catholic Church's "long nineteenth century" from the French Revolution in 1789 to the death of Pope Pius XII in 1958.[1] Arguably, however, that counterrevolutionary, intensely clerical, ultramontane period in the church's life extended beyond Vatican II and met its final end only within the last twenty years—with the revelations of the scale of the church's sexual abuse scandal. As John McGreevy remarks in his recent history of the church from the French Revolution to the present, while the bishops at the council changed much about the church, they did not "assess [its] structures," with the result that the "evolution toward transparency and shared governance" in many other institutions largely passed the church by.[2] Until . . . now. With report after report documenting

---

1. John W. O'Malley, *What Happened at Vatican II* (Harvard University Press, 2008), 4; see also 53–92.

2. John McGreevy, *Catholicism: A Global History from the French Revolution to Pope Francis* (W. W. Norton, 2022), 303–4.

violence, secrecy, complicity, and complacency, a kind of transparency has come with a vengeance, though shared governance still lags.

The historian Thomas Albert Howard makes a similar observation to McGreevy's with respect to the unfinished work of Vatican II. "On a host of issues, such as religious liberty and ecumenism," Howard writes, "change has taken place. Other issues, however—the nature of church authority, priestly celibacy, the role of the Curia, the place of women—sometimes appear, in the words of Matthew Arnold, '[w]andering between two worlds, one dead, the other powerless to be born.'"[3] A legacy of the council's failure to take on such issues is that its agenda of *aggiornamento* is now in peril. Disgusted that an institution charged by its founder to care preferentially for children and other "little ones" should have been so slow, even relative to other institutions, to recognize and respond to sexual abuse as the scourge that it is,[4] growing numbers of Catholics are exercising a peculiar form of "lay ecclesial agency" by leaving the church altogether.[5]

In this paper, I propose to examine the church's sexual abuse scandal as a case of institutional vice—a moral failing of the institution and not merely of some number of its members who went astray. When there are repeated instances of much the same bad behavior by multiple actors dispersed across an organization, the refrain that there are bad apples in every barrel—that the problem is merely one of individual pathology that just happens, who knows why, to be widespread—ought quickly to lose its plausibility and be seen, instead, as an excuse to maintain the status quo. Repeated instances of such bad behavior also ought to kindle skepticism about the adequacy of procedural fixes, which is to say, new rules

---

3. Thomas Albert Howard, "A Question of Conscience: The Excommunication of Ignaz von Döllinger," *Commonweal*, October 10, 2014, 14. The poem is Arnold's "Stanzas from the Grande Chartreuse" (1855).

4. Rapport de la Commission indépendante sur les abus sexuels dans l'Église, *Les violences sexuelles dans l'Église catholique France 1950–2020* (October 2021), 367, https://www.ciase.fr/medias/Ciase-Rapport-5-octobre-2021-Les-violences-sexuelles-dans-l-Eglise-catholique-France-1950-2020.pdf. See Matthew 18:1-14.

5. See Edward Hahnenberg, "Discerning Disciples: Lay Agency Sixty Years After Vatican II," in this volume. I think it should be considered whether Catholics are paradoxically leaving the church *as* Catholics—in other words, reneging on this identity on account of this identity.

and reporting mechanisms designed to prevent the bad behavior or at least to detect it and cut it off. New rules and reporting mechanisms are no doubt necessary, but they are unlikely to be sufficient to root out bad behavior that reaches down into an organization's settled ways of seeing things and doing things—in a word, its "culture."

Those are basic points of organizational ethics: on one construction, the discipline of ethics that takes as its object an organization's ethos, analogous to the character of an individual person. An organization's ethos is constituted by the values, dispositions, and attitudes embodied and enacted by the individuals who belong to it and represent it in official capacities, some more powerfully than others according to the organization's structure. Just as we may ascribe moral excellences and deficiencies to an individual in view of her actions over time, so may we ascribe virtues and vices to an organization in view of behaviors that recur across it.

There are several advantages to using the language of organizational or, as it is often called, institutional vice to describe such patterns of culpable bad behavior. First, to speak of institutional vice focuses attention on the organization or institution as a whole. In other words, attention is redirected from alleged bad apples who failed to follow the rules or supposedly violated norms. That red herring is thereby set aside. Second, using the language of institutional vice suggests that remedies must go beyond procedural fixes, important and necessary though they are. A vice—habitually missing the mark, repeatedly failing with respect to some good—is not eradicated by the implementation of a few further, precisely targeted rules. Granted, the rules, if followed, may reduce particular manifestations of the vice in question: It may no longer manifest, at least with the same frequency, in the behaviors that the rules target. That would obviously be for the better, but it is a mistake to think that a vice has only one form of expression. The medievals depicted vices as trees for a reason: vices ramify both into other vices and into a multitude of behaviors with the same root.

Finally, using the language of institutional vice allows for the possibility that an institution may have a vice that many, most, or perhaps even all of the individuals who belong to it do not "personally" have, which is to say, do not exhibit other than in their official capacities representing the institution ("qua" member of it). That may sound strange and unlikely, but it is true to the experience that, in colloquial terms, people may not be "like that" across the board, from one context to the next. Instead, even the morally monstrous may surprise us by turning out to speak with a human voice.[6] Yet there is a flip side. The possibility that an institution may have a vice that cannot be explained by saying that all, most, or many of the individuals who belong to it "personally" have it and brought it to work, so to speak, also suggests that joining an institution or assuming an office may degrade a person's moral character. In colloquial terms again, the person may become "like that," when he or she never had been or wasn't so much. The person may become damaged and damaging by virtue of coming to belong to a whole greater than, as well as, in this case, worse than, the sum of its parts.

Three Reasons to Examine the Scandal as a Case of Institutional Vice

There are several reasons to undertake this study. First, both abusers and the bishops who oversaw them popularly figure as moral monsters through and through.[7] From the testimony of survivors, some may well have been, but this popular depiction of the scandal casts it in terms of individual pathology and accordingly deflects attention from the scandal's organizational dimensions, which beg for understanding. As Marie Keenan has remarked, there is an "unusually consistent pattern . . . in the handling of abuse complaints by Catholic leaders across jurisdictions and continents."[8] That surely is not just an unhappy coincidence. Examining the abuse scandal as a case of institutional vice enables us to make sense of such recurring patterns of behavior.

---

6. I paraphrase Marie Keenan, *Child Sexual Abuse and the Catholic Church: Gender, Power, and Organizational Culture* (Oxford University Press, 2012), 275. Helen Prejean's *Dead Man Walking* (Random House, 1993) provides striking examples.

7. Consider, for example, John Boyne, *A History of Loneliness* (Doubleday, 2014), which I acknowledge is richer than its invocation here might suggest.

8. Keenan, *Child Sexual Abuse and the Catholic Church*, xxiv–xxv; see also 24, "fairly consistent response patterns of individual bishops, not just across individual countries but across entire continents," and 180, "remarkable consistency . . . in the Church response." McGreevy comments, "The global nature of the ultramontane revival and the parallel church structures built up in almost every country made national variations on sexual abuse less striking than similarities." McGreevy, *Catholicism*, 406.

Second, while it is clear that, as Peter Steinfels has underscored with respect to the US church,[9] much has changed for the better in its handling of sexual abuse since the early 1990s, when lurid cases prompted many bishops to introduce new procedures for investigating allegations, and all the more since 2002, when the United States Conference of Catholic Bishops approved the Charter for the Protection of Children and Young People (the "Dallas Charter"), it is much less clear that these necessary procedural fixes, in the United States and elsewhere, have gotten to the root of the problem. The church's sexual scandal abuse is twofold: There is the scandal of priests abusing children and other vulnerable people,[10] and there is the scandal of how the knowledge of that scandal was managed by bishops and other church authorities. The focus of this paper is the latter scandal, though the former also has organizational dimensions.[11] Examining the abuse scandal as a case of institutional vice enables us to consider whether "fixes" need to target more than procedures.

Although this paper is not a work of theology, a third reason to examine the scandal as a case of institutional vice is to advance both the church's mission and the agenda of Vatican II. As Father Ken Lasch, a priest of the Diocese of Paterson, New Jersey, and a vocal advocate for abuse survivors, observed nearly twenty years ago, sexual abuse is a pro-life issue.[12] To the point, the report of the French Independent Commission

9. Peter Steinfels, *A People Adrift: The Crisis of the Roman Catholic Church in America* (Simon & Schuster, 2003), 48–49.

10. As Carolina Montero Orphanopoulos remarks, "Vulnerability is an inherent, universal, and anthropological attribute that is . . . individualized in concrete women and men in different ways." It follows that, in situations of abuse, "the problem is not the vulnerability of the victim" but instead the asymmetry of power in a social structure. It also follows that the term "vulnerable people" may include not only, for example, adults with intellectual or physical disabilities, but young men and women above the age of eighteen (so no longer minors) who are sexually naïve. See Orphanopoulos, "Vulnerability, Ecclesial Abuse, and 'Vulnerable Adults,'" in *Doing Theology and Theological Ethics in the Face of the Abuse Crisis*, ed. Daniel J. Fleming, James F. Keenan, SJ, and Hans Zollner, SJ (Pickwick, 2023), 30, 34.

11. See Keenan, *Child Sexual Abuse and the Catholic Church*, especially chap. 8 (169: "the men attempted to live by the rules until the life became impossible to live") and chap. 10 (257: "the sexual abuse of children in the private realm functioned to preserve the priesthood in the public sphere").

12. Father Lasch made this observation in his "Harvey Interviews," published periodically over 2005 and 2006 on his website, https://fatherlasch.com.

on Sexual Abuses in the Church describes sexual abuse as "a work of death" and recommends that it be classified as a sin not against the Sixth Commandment (all things sex), but against the Fifth (all things killing), given how shattering it can be psychologically and spiritually.[13] The church can hardly hope to lead on this issue, however, unless and until it has learned from its own failings and limitations—in a words, its vices. Coming to terms with those vices is also part of the unfinished work of Vatican II. Ironically, as Agnès Desmazières has suggested, it may be because the council intended to be "pastoral" that it failed to take on the disciplinary problem of child sexual abuse, which had been recognized from the 1930s.[14]

The paper proceeds in three steps. First, it describes, to quote Keenan again, the "unusually consistent pattern . . . in the handling of abuse complaints by Catholic leaders." Second, it lays out a framework for understanding institutional vice and then applies that framework to the case at hand. Third, the paper names some of the institutional vices in evidence and considers just why those particular vices took hold in the church.

See Little, Say Nothing: The McCarrick Case

The Vatican's so-called McCarrick report, published in November 2020, provides ample material to work with.[15] For background, Theodore McCarrick, ordained a priest in 1958, was "elevated" to the role of auxiliary bishop in New York in 1977, going on to serve as bishop of Metuchen, New Jersey (1981–86), archbishop of Newark (1986–2000), and finally archbishop of Washington (2001–06), in which position he was made a cardinal by Pope John Paul II. When McCarrick turned seventy-five in 2005, the age at which bishops must resign, Pope Benedict XVI initially gave him a two-year extension, only to request that he step down in 2006, amid allegations about his conduct. McCarrick was defrocked in 2019, after being found guilty of what the Vatican termed "solicitation in the

---

13. Rapport de la Commission indépendante, *Les violences sexuelles*, 26 ("œuvre de mort"), 62–63, and 341 (Fifth Commandment rather than Sixth).

14. See Agnès Desmazières, "Vatican II's Silence on Child Sex Abuse: Challenges and Limits of a 'Pastoral' Agenda," in this volume.

15. I draw for this section from my article, "Who Knew? The Sexual Abuse Crisis and 'Epistemic Injustice,'" *Commonweal*, October 2022, 36–39.

sacrament of confession, and sins against the Sixth Commandment with minors and adults, with the aggravating factor of the abuse of power."[16] The McCarrick report notes that the Vatican began "an active search" for victims and witnesses in 2017, after the "first known allegation of sexual abuse by McCarrick of a victim under 18 years of age."[17] Seventeen people abused as boys or young men came forward.

McCarrick's is a case where "everyone knew" that something was not right, and more than a few people had known that and more for years. In the words of the report, before his appointment to Washington, "McCarrick was known to have shared a bed with young adult men in Metuchen and Newark."[18] It was "known and a source of joking among the clergy" that McCarrick often would invite seven seminarians to join him at his beach house in New Jersey, though the house had only seven beds, which led to McCarrick's having one of the seminarians share a bed with him.[19] Sexual overtures followed. Father Boniface Ramsey, a Dominican priest who taught seminarians at Seton Hall University in the 1980s and '90s, attested in a 2000 memo to the papal nuncio that "the archbishop's behavior seemed to be quite well known to the clergy of the Newark archdiocese, and also to many others."[20] Anonymous letters sent to New York's Cardinal John O'Connor assert, in 1992, that McCarrick's "misconduct has been common knowledge in clerical and religious circles for years" and, in 1993, that "authorities here and in Rome have known for decades of McCarrick's proclivity for young boys."[21]

McCarrick's successor as bishop of Metuchen, Edward Hughes, knew of McCarrick's sexual assaults on seminarians: at least two told him, both recalling that Hughes had reacted in a way suggesting that he had already heard similar accusations and was loath to hear more.[22] The McCarrick

---

16. Secretariat of State of the Holy See, *Report on the Holy See's Institutional Knowledge and Decision-Making Related to Former Cardinal Theodore Edgar McCarrick (1930 to 2017)*, November 10, 2020, 437, https://www.vatican.va/resources/resources_rapporto-card-mccarrick_20201110_en.pdf.
17. Secretariat of State of the Holy See, *Cardinal Theodore Edgar McCarrick*, 439, 14.
18. Secretariat of State of the Holy See, *Cardinal Theodore Edgar McCarrick*, 6.
19. Secretariat of State of the Holy See, *Cardinal Theodore Edgar McCarrick*, 133.
20. Secretariat of State of the Holy See, *Cardinal Theodore Edgar McCarrick*, 188.
21. Secretariat of State of the Holy See, *Cardinal Theodore Edgar McCarrick*, 95, 97.
22. Secretariat of State of the Holy See, *Cardinal Theodore Edgar McCarrick*, 75, 86–87.

report also narrates a stunning incident at a Newark catering hall in 1990. Three men—a priest of the diocese of Camden, Camden's Bishop James McHugh, and a Newark auxiliary bishop—all witnessed McCarrick fingering the crotch of a young cleric, described as "terrified" and "paralyzed."[23] But they didn't confront McCarrick, who was drunk, or intervene to help the cleric. Instead, they abruptly got up from the table and left the hall. In the car on the way back to Camden, McHugh told the diocesan priest, "Well, you know, sometimes the Archbishop says things and does things that are very 'different.'"[24] The priest told his spiritual advisor about the incident but then no one else until 2018, having figured that "no one . . . would take his account seriously."[25] The excess of credibility accorded to McCarrick as a priest and prelate, together with his charm and more than likely his prowess as a fundraiser, shielded him from scrutiny. "Everyone knew," but the knowledge circulated only so far, and people in power declined to know too much.

To choose one more example, basic elements of this story recur across the so-called Murphy report on the Archdiocese of Dublin, Ireland, from 2009. Dublin "bishops heard suspicions and concerns but they did not take the obvious steps of asking precisely what was involved or challenging the priest concerned."[26] They accepted denials but failed to interview victims and witnesses and declined to "carry out further investigations."[27] They sought to "ensure that as few people as possible knew" of allegations

---

23. Secretariat of State of the Holy See, *Cardinal Theodore Edgar McCarrick*, 91.
24. Secretariat of State of the Holy See, *Cardinal Theodore Edgar McCarrick*, 93.
25. Secretariat of State of the Holy See, *Cardinal Theodore Edgar McCarrick*, 93.
26. Commission of Investigation, *Report into the Catholic Archdiocese of Dublin*, July 2009, 8, §1.29, https://www.gov.ie/en/publication/13804-report-by-commission-of-investigation-into-catholic-archdiocese-of-dublin/. The commission was chaired by Judge Yvonne Murphy. See for critical discussion Fergal Sweeney, "Commissions of Investigation and Procedural Fairness," *Studies: An Irish Quarterly Review* 102, no. 408 (2013): 377–88, which takes the Murphy report to task for having "looked at the events of twenty to thirty years ago through the prism of today's glasses" (384). Marie Keenan concurs that Dublin's priests and bishops were not "out of step with the state of knowledge" at that time, but she comments further that, if "the Irish bishops were on a steep learning curve . . . , they still are" with respect to the systemic dimensions of the problem. See Keenan, *Child Sexual Abuse and the Catholic Church*, 207, 208.
27. Commission of Investigation, *Catholic Archdiocese of Dublin*, 182, §12.25; 185, §12.43; 290, §20.20; 467, §29.54.

and problems,[28] sometimes not even giving full information to treatment facilities for abusing priests.[29] Standard procedure with respect to a complainant was to "*gain his knowledge/tell him nothing*."[30]

Let us return, however, to the story of McCarrick fingering the crotch of the young cleric. How did that incident *not* lead to McCarrick's immediate exposure and downfall? Why did the three men who witnessed McCarrick's behavior—two bishops among them!—not confront him and come to the cleric's aid? How does it make sense that they would let McCarrick's behavior pass? From the fact that they left the hall so abruptly, it seems clear that they did not individually regard his behavior as acceptable. But it also seems clear that they conformed themselves to what was apparently the default uptake: quickly look away and say or do next to nothing. It follows that we must look beyond individual failures to understand the pathologies of the sexual abuse scandal. If the three men acted in those circumstances as members of the church understood themselves as *supposed* to act, we are dealing with institutional vice.

One of Us

Two questions must now be considered. First, how do individuals come to act qua members of an institution? And second, how does individual judgment come to be pushed aside?

Here it is helpful to consider the work of the philosopher Margaret Gilbert on the formation of so-called *plural subjects*—subjects that can speak in the first-person plural. On her account, persons form a plural subject by jointly committing themselves to some activity, cause, or other undertaking. More fully, persons "A and B form a plural subject of X-ing if and only if A and B are jointly committed to X-ing as a body."[31] The X in question might be, say, teaching piano, as for an association of piano teachers A and B and C, and so on. For a commitment to count as "joint," not only must each person in the would-be body commit herself or himself

---

28. Commission of Investigation, *Catholic Archdiocese of Dublin*, 10, §1.35.
29. Commission of Investigation, *Catholic Archdiocese of Dublin*, 19, §1.71.
30. Commission of Investigation, *Catholic Archdiocese of Dublin*, 77, §4.85.
31. Margaret Gilbert, "Remarks on Collective Belief," in *Socializing Epistemology: The Social Dimensions of Knowledge*, ed. Frederick F. Schmitt (Rowman & Littlefield, 1994), 244.

to it, but it must be common knowledge that each person is likewise committed. Up to that point, each person's commitment is conditional on others' likewise committing, and the body is not yet constituted.[32] Once the body is constituted, however, members can speak for it in the first-person plural in a distinctive way. "We hold this or that view," they might say, even if some members privately hold a different view. Or "We don't do things that way," even if some members privately think that way of doing things might be the better way to go. Members who bluntly, publicly break from the group, without the caveat that they are speaking merely "personally" or some similar preamble, open themselves to censure, rebuke, or expulsion. At the least, they owe the group an account of why they went against it, after having committed to act as "one of us."[33] This is because, on the joint commitment theory, groups may be ascribed views or beliefs even if not all members—indeed, logically, even if no members—"personally" accept the view or belief in question.[34] What matters is whether they *jointly* accept a view with others. If they do, they are committed to "granting [it] the status of an assumption in their public reasoning, their discussions, arguments, and conversations."[35] In other words, they knowingly subject themselves to its constraint.

It is also key for purposes of understanding institutional vice to consider how views or beliefs come to be those of a group, which is to say what conditions need to be satisfied for views or beliefs to be ascribed to it. A formal vote would certainly suffice—say, a vote of the piano teachers' association in favor of the proposition that teachers should not charge less than $35 per half-hour lesson. But nothing so formal is necessary. Instead, it is enough "that all or most members of the group have expressed willingness to let a certain view 'stand' as the view of the group."[36] In other words, it suffices for members effectively to go along with a view,

---

32. See Margaret Gilbert, *On Social Facts* (Princeton University Press, 1989), 205.
33. Gilbert, *On Social Facts*, 305.
34. Gilbert, *On Social Facts*, 289. In other words, Gilbert defends a *non-summative* account of group belief. At the same time, she is not committed to postulating a "group mind" or the like. For her, picking out beliefs is less about "pick[ing] out a special state of mind" than it is about picking out propositions that have "an explanatory role to play in an account of the behavior" of individuals or sets of individuals (313).
35. Gilbert, *On Social Facts*, 309.
36. Gilbert, *On Social Facts*, 289.

accommodating it rather than seeking to block it or contest it in some other way.[37] Further, the view may be explicitly stated, such as the view of the piano teachers' association about the proper cost of a lesson, or it may be unstated and tacit—say, about the proper course of conduct in a given set of circumstances.

Crucially, as Miranda Fricker has observed, every time members go along with some view or corresponding practice, "letting it stand and thereby accommodating it, they raise the level of pressure—genuine normative pressure—to conserve the status quo" and conform.[38] Moreover, as Gilbert observes, "once formed, a jointly accepted view is likely to have an influence on the views of individuals."[39] In particular, "collective beliefs . . . are likely to suppress the development of contrary ideas at both the individual and collective level."[40] This is because it is potentially costly to think differently qua individual than qua member of the group, not only for one's integrity but also for one's belonging to the group. The more one's self-understanding is tied to belonging to that group, the more painful disidentification from the group becomes.[41]

Against that background, a vice can be called *institutional* when it arises from individuals' joint commitment, deepened and hardened over time, to go along with or let pass morally blameworthy views, beliefs, attitudes, practices, and other behaviors, whether the individuals "personally" accept or approve of them or not. There is room in this account for some members of the organization or institution to refuse to go along and to raise objections, but they can be expected to meet resistance and criticism themselves, since after all they are supposed to act as "one of us." This account also allows for the possibility that some members who went along but initially did not "personally" concur might eventually be corrupted, perhaps

---

37. See Rae Langton, "Blocking as Counter-Speech," in *New Work on Speech Acts*, ed. Daniel Fogal, Daniel W. Harris, and Matt Moss (Oxford University Press, 2018), 144–64.

38. Miranda Fricker, "Institutional Epistemic Vices: The Case of Inferential Inertia," in *Vice Epistemology*, ed. Ian James Kidd, Heather Battaly, and Quassim Cassam (Routledge, 2021), 97.

39. Gilbert, *On Social Facts*, 304.

40. Gilbert, "Collective Epistemology," *Episteme* 1, no. 2 (2004): 102.

41. See further Miranda Fricker, "Silence and Institutional Prejudice," in *Out from the Shadows: Analytical Feminist Contributions to Traditional Philosophy*, ed. Sharon L. Crenshaw and Anita M. Superson (Oxford University Press, 2012), 299–300.

without realizing it. It is further conceivable that, motivated by camaraderie or bonds of affection and loyalty, some members might fail to see misdeeds by others that really should be plain to sight.[42]

As noted above, this paper is focused on the scandal of how the knowledge of priests abusing children and other vulnerable people was managed. In philosophers' terminology, the focus is on the scandal's "epistemic" dimension. Specifically epistemic institutional vices will show, as Fricker writes, "inadequate commitment to good epistemic ends," either "the ultimate end of cognitive contact with reality" or mediate ends such as "looking carefully at the evidence, fact checking, being open to counterarguments, realizing when one's evidence base is too narrow, and so on."[43] It seems to be a fair description of the church during at least its so-called dark ages of sexual abuse that many of its members showed "inadequate commitment to good epistemic ends." The Murphy report, for example, underscores the Dublin bishops' regular failures to look carefully at the evidence, fact check, and seek out voices that would counter priests' denials of allegations. For another example, "winking" at McCarrick's behavior was apparently the norm among clerics of all ranks.[44] McCarrick's "different" ways of doing things, as Camden's Bishop James McHugh absurdly termed his abuses, did not go unnoticed, but it was rare that anyone objected, and when someone did, she or he was ignored.

Father Ken Lasch's experiences as an advocate for abuse survivors are especially revealing of how epistemic vices had been institutionalized in the church or, in other words, made part of its organizational culture. Although, as he surmises, some of his priestly colleagues had more than likely learned of abuses under the sacramental seal of confession, "98 percent . . . walked away" from Lasch once he began speaking out in the mid-1980s, and "at priest meetings, very few would come near me."[45] Lasch was called a Judas by his bishop, and another priest warned Lasch that he had been "overcome with Satan."[46] All that was for his having

---

42. That seems to me a fair, though incomplete, description of the narrator of John Boyne's *A History of Loneliness*, Father Odran Yates.

43. Fricker, "Institutional Epistemic Vices," 99.

44. See Michael L. Papesh, "Farewell to the Club," *America*, May 13, 2002, https://www.americamagazine.org/issue/372/article/farewell-club. He writes, "Before I was 19, I learned that when it came to sexual matters, the clerical culture winked."

45. Father Ken Lasch, in discussion with the author, April 13, 2023.

46. Lasch, "Harvey Interviews."

violated what he calls the "clerical code of 'courteous' silence" by speaking out and insisting on accountability.⁴⁷ As "one of us," he was supposed to go along. His refusal put him under great pressure.

Marie Keenan has observed that "many [priests] live their lives always and constantly in the priestly role," to the point that there is "no functional distinction between their work and their personal lives."⁴⁸ In the words of one of the priests in her studies, "many clergy seldom have a strong sense of personal identity apart from being a priest."⁴⁹ In that context, it can be understood (though not justified) why there was such intense pressure on Lasch to "keep [his] mouth shut."⁵⁰ What he calls the "clerical code of 'courteous' silence" was not only or perhaps even primarily about protecting the institution. According to Keenan, it was often about "salvag[ing] the priesthood of the offending cleric," which often was equivalent to saving him as a person given the frequent "over-identification with the priestly role."⁵¹ Fraternal bonds of affection between priests and a kind of father-son relationship between bishops and priests thus contributed to engendering a culture of pervasive epistemic vice.⁵²

Vices, Structures, and Mentalities: The Role of Bishop and the Legacy of Vatican II

I propose that we can discern three admittedly overlapping institutional epistemic vices common among bishops, clergy, and even lay people who came to know of the scandal of priests abusing children and other vulnerable people:⁵³

---

47. Lasch, "Harvey Interviews."
48. Keenan, *Child Sexual Abuse and the Catholic Church*, 42, 239.
49. Keenan, *Child Sexual Abuse and the Catholic Church*, 176.
50. Lasch, "Harvey Interviews."
51. Keenan, *Child Sexual Abuse and the Catholic Church*, 205, 239.
52. See Papesh, "Farewell to the Club": "Why did we wink? Our affective bonds, the connecting tissue of the clerical culture, affirmed by what we understood to be the Gospel call, were the primary reason. . . . At some level, I suppose, we sought, too, to protect the institution we loved and served, but that was not the heart of our behavior." See also the Rapport de la Commission indépendante, *Les violences sexuelles*, 256, on bishops' relationship with priests ("de type filial," "protection paternelle").
53. As Massimo Faggioli has remarked, it is important to understand the scandal as "ecclesial and not just clerical." See Faggioli, "The Need for the Historiographical Approach to Understand and Address the Sex Abuse Crisis in the Catholic Church," in Fleming,

1) willful ignorance, which is to say, not wanting to know or, more fully, not wanting to know so much that it would be unthinkable not to act;

2) inferential inertia, which is to say, not following through, not taking the logical next steps, instead "winking" and letting pass;

3) accommodation of untruths, which is to say, settling for convenient fictions instead of squarely reckoning with what one has seen or heard.

Each of these vices was aided and abetted by two structural obstacles to the circulation of information.[54] First, until the turn of the millennium if not later, each bishop managed cases of abuse largely on his own, without accountability either to other bishops or to clergy, religious, and lay people. Dioceses often lacked anything "resembling a management structure" with clear job descriptions and responsibilities.[55] This "concentration of responsibilities on the person of the bishop" was in fact a legacy of Vatican II, where the role of the bishop as overseer was stressed rather than reassessed.[56] Not only, then, was there no advantage in this system to communicating bad news up the hierarchy, but there also was no urgency to do so, since who, after all, was to hold the bishop accountable for not rendering himself accountable?[57] The upshot is that the church

---

Keenan, and Zollner, *Doing Theology and Theological Ethics*, 278. By way of example, the Murphy report notes that, during the period it investigated, "A number of very senior members of the Gardaí . . . clearly regarded priests as being outside their remit," and the Gardaí occasionally even reported complaints of abuse to the Dublin archdiocese "instead of investigating them" (Commission of Investigation, *Catholic Archdiocese of Dublin*, 24). Meanwhile, in Boston, before the *Globe*'s explosive investigation in the early 2000s, the paper had in fact buried coverage of clergy sexual abuse.

54. I do not term structural obstacles themselves institutional vices but only because of how I have explicated institutional vices in this paper: roughly put, as the bad habits of plural subjects. Structural obstacles are more vices in organizational design than in organizational ethos.

55. Commission of Investigation, *Catholic Archdiocese of Dublin*, 15.

56. Rapport de la Commission indépendante, *Les violences sexuelles*, 430.

57. James F. Keenan speaks in this regard of "a hierarchicalism, capable of rising with impunity above any sense of accountability." See Keenan, "Hierarchicalism," *Theological Studies* 83, no. 1 (2022): 95.

became a "well of secrets and secret-keeping."⁵⁸ Second, there was, in fact, one place in which clerical sexual abuse was discussed, but it was the confessional, which, Keenan notes from her research, "allowed . . . men to resolve the issues of guilt resulting from their abusing" yet "contained the problem of clergy sexual abuse" under the sacramental seal. The problem was that "no pathway existed for this important information . . . to flow back into the system."⁵⁹ Instead, it languished for all too long as "inferentially inert epistemic particles dispersed in the organization."⁶⁰

Each of the three vices was also keyed to a false virtue in service of a counterfeit good, themselves grounded in longstanding mentalities and corresponding practices. Assume a basic, Ignatian-style commitment to thinking, judging, and feeling with the church, even if not to the extent of holding that the white we see is black if the hierarchy say so.⁶¹ Against this background, the vice of willful ignorance might appear to be the virtue of maintaining the good reputation of one's brothers or sisters in Christ; the vice of inferential inertia might appear to be the virtue of giving one's brothers or sisters the benefit of the doubt; and the vice of accommodating untruths might appear to be the virtue of charity.⁶² (Recall McHugh on McCarrick: "Well, you know, sometimes the Archbishop says things and does things that are very 'different.'") In the context of the sexual abuse scandal, these false virtues served not genuine goods but subtle and deceptive imitations that masked profound and revolting distortions.⁶³

In the end, the letter of Vatican II may have little to say to help heal the anguish of the church's sexual abuse scandal. What the scandal does present the church is an opportunity to draw close to suffering humanity. If nothing else, in the sexual abuse scandal, the church has a new grief

---

58. Keenan, *Child Sexual Abuse and the Catholic Church*, 38.

59. Keenan, *Child Sexual Abuse and the Catholic Church*, 178.

60. The phrase is Fricker's, applied to a different case. See Fricker, "Institutional Epistemic Vices," 104.

61. See Ignatius of Loyola, *Spiritual Exercises and Selected Works*, ed. George E. Ganss, SJ (Paulist Press, 1991), 213 (rule 13).

62. I am indebted to Sister Theresa Aletheia Noble for these insights. As she would be the first to say, there is more to say here, though for a different paper.

63. I follow for this analysis of vices Rebecca Konyndyk DeYoung, *Glittering Vices*, 2nd ed. (Brazos, 2020), 36.

from which it can cry out in lamentation.[64] It can also thereby seek to demonstrate what *Gaudium et Spes* claims: "The joys and hopes, the grief and anguish of the people of our time, especially of those who are poor or afflicted, are the joys and hopes, the grief and anguish of the followers of Christ as well."[65]

---

64. See M. Cathleen Kaveny, "Anger, Lamentation, and Common Ground," *Theological Studies* 82, no. 4 (2021): 663–85.

65. Second Vatican Council, Pastoral Constitution on the Church in the Modern World *Gaudium et Spes*, December 7, 1965, no. 1, in Austin Flannery, ed., *Vatican Council II: Constitutions, Decrees, Declarations; A Completely Revised Translation in Inclusive Language* (Liturgical Press, 2014).

Sexism

Chapter 9

Glorified and Liberated?

Toward a Feminist Ecclesiology of Vatican II[1]

Mary Kate Holman

At the closing Mass of the Second Vatican Council on December 8, 1965, Pope Paul VI offered a series of short addresses to "categories" of people in the church. For each category, a few representative individuals processed up St. Peter's Square to symbolically receive their address, among them "rulers," "men of thought and science," "artists," and "women." Three women approached to receive their exhortation, including Luz-Marie Alvarez-Icaza, the only wife and mother invited to the council as an auditor. From a bleacher in the square, her fellow auditor Mary Luke Tobin whispered with dissatisfaction to a neighbor, "But women are not a *category* in the church. They should not be honored as women more than men should be honored as men. Men *and* women are the church, aren't they?"[2]

The content of the pope's address was not likely to assuage Tobin's concern. Deploying the familiar trope of female domesticity ("You women

---

[1]. The author would like to thank members of the Women Shaping Theology Workshop, sponsored by the Center for the Study of Spirituality at Saint Mary's College, who provided generous feedback on a draft of this piece: Jessica Coblentz, Kathy Lilla Cox, Julia Feder, Donna Freitas, Rita George-Tvrtkovic, Shannon McAlister, Meg Stapleton Smith, and Rachel Wheeler.

[2]. Mary Luke Tobin, *Hope Is an Open Door: Journeys in Faith*, ed. Robert A. Raines (Abingdon, 1981), 30–31.

have always had as your lot the protection of the home, the love of beginnings and an understanding of cradles . . ."), the pope extended a staggering injunction, "Reconcile men with life and above all, we beseech you, watch carefully over the future of our race. Hold back the hand of man who, in a moment of folly, might attempt to destroy human civilization." Simultaneously overestimating women's geopolitical power while underestimating the diversity of their life experience and expertise, Paul VI affirmed women's dignity by placing them on pedestals and structured the document by subcategorizing women into wives, mothers, and consecrated virgins. The text reduces women to an archetype, what Susan Bigelow Reynolds calls "a monolithic, quasi-theoretical body with an articulable essence, singular vocation, and narrow set of essentialized gifts."[3]

Yet the address also boldly proclaimed that "the Church is proud to have glorified and liberated woman, and in the course of the centuries . . . to have brought into relief her basic equality with man."[4] Given the benevolent sexism infusing the rest of the document, we might assess this statement as exaggerated, or at best premature, in its celebration of women's liberation and equality in or by the church. That disconnect clarifies the profound cognitive dissonance of most postconciliar papal statements about women. There is an affirmation not only of women's dignity but also of women's fundamental equality with men. Yet this equality is simply not reflected in the rest of the document nor in the ecclesial structures out of which it emerges.

The story of women and Vatican II is richer than this papal address suggests. But in considering the legacy and limits of the council from a feminist perspective, its central claims serve as helpful orienting questions. Sixty years later, in the wake of the Second Vatican Council, has the church brought, or is it bringing, into relief the basic equality of men and women? Has the church glorified and liberated "woman"? (One might also ask whether liberation and glorification can coexist.) Have we arrived at a closer proximity to Mary Luke Tobin's whispered theology at that closing Mass: "Men *and* women are the church, aren't they?"

---

3. Susan Bigelow Reynolds, "Are We Protagonists Yet?," *Commonweal*, December 9, 2022, https://www.commonwealmagazine.org/women-church-synod-francis-catholic.

4. Pope Paul VI, "Address of Pope Paul VI to Women," December 8, 1965, https://www.vatican.va/content/paul-vi/en/speeches/1965/documents/hf_p-vi_spe_19651208_epilogo-concilio-donne.html.

Feminist Ecclesiology: Criterion, Method, and Challenge

The central problem with Paul VI's address to women is the disconnect between what it said *about* women and what women were actually experiencing. A feminist analysis redresses this disconnect by privileging the experiences of women. I borrow the "critical principle" for feminist theology proposed by Rosemary Radford Ruether: "the promotion of the full humanity of women." She explains: "Theologically speaking, whatever diminishes or denies the full humanity of women must be presumed not to reflect the divine or an authentic relation to the divine, or to reflect the authentic nature of things, or to be the message or work of an authentic redeemer or a community of redemption. This negative principle also implies the positive principle: what does promote the full humanity of women is of the Holy, it does reflect true relation to the divine, it is the true nature of things, the authentic message of redemption and the mission of redemptive community."[5] Drawing on Ruether's principle, feminist theology judges that any structures, be they secular or ecclesial, that impinge upon women's full humanity and dignity need reform and re-imagination not only as a matter of justice, but of truth.

Here I join the broader conversation of feminist ecclesiology. As the theological study of the church, ecclesiology is always situated in the tension between the church as it is and the church as it could be, the institution and the eschaton, the status quo and the hoped-for. In other words, ecclesiology has both a descriptive and a prescriptive function. While recognizing that the church will always fall short of its creedal aspiration to be truly one, holy, catholic, and apostolic, its members must always strive toward this vision in their theology and praxis. A sound ecclesiology maintains that eschatological vision while honestly reckoning with the temporal church's failures to realize that vision. A feminist ecclesiology analyzes both this vision and its failures by centering the perspective and experience of women.

Women's narratives become a crucial theological source for evaluating ecclesial structures' promotion (or not) of the full humanity of women. A deductive model of ecclesiology, reliant on metaphors like "Mystical Body" or "Mother Church" as a starting point, can conflate the prescriptive with

---

5. Rosemary Radford Ruether, *Sexism and God-Talk: Toward a Feminist Theology*, 2nd ed. (Beacon Press, 1993), 18–19.

the descriptive and, in so doing, efface the concrete reality of experience in the church in favor of an unrealized ideal. Recognizing the shortcomings of such an approach, Natalia Imperatori-Lee proposes a shift in methodology: "Rather than deduct ecclesiology from principles, the time has come to attempt an inductive approach, beginning with praxis."[6] Beginning with individual and communal narratives, ecclesiologists can "tell a truer story about the church," one that leaves fewer people out.[7] And because women have so often been written out of the ecclesial narrative, privileging their stories becomes essential to a feminist ecclesiology.

In that spirit, I approach Vatican II via the narratives of women who themselves attended and contributed to the council. Their undercelebrated contributions and, even more significantly, their experiences in Rome illuminate the strides the council took toward recognizing the full humanity and dignity of women, as well as how far there is left to go. This method allows us to "tell a truer story," to go beyond the mainstream scholarly narrative of Vatican II, which is almost entirely male-dominated.

What Happened at Vatican II?

Things didn't look promising for women's inclusion during the first two sessions of the council. Women were present, especially as journalists, but were persistently marginalized. Two examples illustrate the point. At the first conciliar press conference for German speakers in 1962, Josefa Münch asked a straightforward question: "Have women also been invited to the Council?" Laughter abounded, and Bishop Walter Kampe responded, "Perhaps to the Third Vatican Council!"[8] During the second session of the council, American journalist Eva Fleischner attended a Mass at St. Peter's

---

6. Natalia Imperatori-Lee, *Cuéntame: Narrative in the Ecclesial Present* (Orbis Books, 2018), xv.

7. Imperatori-Lee, *Cuéntame*, xx.

8. Regina Heyder, "Women and the Council: Catholic Women's Organizations and Women Theologians Prior to and During Vatican II," in *The Oxford Handbook of Vatican II*, ed. Catherine E. Clifford and Massimo Faggioli (Oxford University Press, 2023), 320. Münch had been writing to the pope since 1954, expressing her vocation to the priesthood, and would go on to obtain a degree in theology so she could be ready for the moment for ordination, should it arrive during her lifetime. See Josefa Theresia Münch, "Letters to the Pope," *The Catholic Citizen* 72, no. 1 (1991): 18–29, https://womenpriests.org/vocation/munch-josefa-theresia-munch/.

open to journalists as well as council fathers. Fleischner happened to be the only female journalist in attendance, and as she approached the altar in the Communion line, a Swiss Guard appeared before her and put up his hands. As she recounted, "I didn't know what he meant, so I kept coming toward him. He pushed me back and physically prevented me from going to communion."[9] Because the confrontation occurred quite literally in front of the press corps, it was widely reported. Rather than apologizing, the Vatican changed its practices for the second session and stopped inviting journalists to Mass. But at the beginning of the third session, quite suddenly, several women received invitations to attend the council as auditors.

Contemporary readers might be understandably surprised to learn that women were present at the council in this capacity, given the current state of scholarship on the topic. The most accessible and authoritative monograph on the history of the Second Vatican Council is *What Happened at Vatican II* (2008), by my late beloved mentor John O'Malley. In researching this piece, I revisited my well-worn copy of the book, scanning its index for mention of the women who attended the council. I found that the entry "women, position in society" has a single entry: a mention of two (obviously male) bishops who made interventions on the floor supporting the church's promotion of women's position in society.[10] The rest of the index contains a total of three women: the eighth-century Empress Irene, Raïssa Maritain (mentioned in relation to her husband, Jacques), and, unsurprisingly, the Virgin Mary. Far from having attended the council, none of these women were even alive and physically present during its four sessions.

One could come away from this excellent book by an accomplished scholar, himself a great promoter of female scholars, and have no idea that women attended the Second Vatican Council. The predominant narrative of Vatican II, what O'Malley calls "the most important religious event of the twentieth century,"[11] is that it was entirely a men's affair. The recent and more encyclopedic *Oxford Handbook of Vatican II* makes strides to include more female perspectives, with two strong essays

---

9. Carmel McEnroy, *Guests in Their Own House: The Women of Vatican II* (Crossroad, 1996), 99; Heyder, "Women and the Council," 320.

10. John W. O'Malley, *What Happened at Vatican II* (Harvard University Press, 2008), 235.

11. O'Malley, *What Happened at Vatican II*, 1.

concerning women's contributions to, and their influence on the reception of, the council.[12] Yet women's narratives have yet to permeate the mainstream scholarly history of Vatican II. Women are sometimes included but almost never privileged as sources. A major exception to this is Carmel McEnroy's 1996 *Guests in Their Own House*[13] (unmentioned in O'Malley's tome), a history of the twenty-three women auditors at the council. McEnroy's commitment to tracking down these women across the globe and her attempt to interview as many as possible before they died was a feminist labor of love and a great service to the history of the council. In terms of primary sources, the same androcentrism persists. While the council notebooks of male bishops and periti are translated and reprinted in the twenty-first century, women's experiences of the council appear in memoirs now largely out of print and ignored. In what follows, I draw on these understudied sources for narratives that might help us better understand what really happened at Vatican II.

It was nearly impossible to choose which women to feature, because there were so many present at the council with such rich stories. I've chosen to examine more closely three who have received little attention in the historical and ecclesial record: two auditors who appeared in the opening anecdote and another influential woman whose status was more marginal. Each came from a different country, spoke a different language, and were in very different life states at the time of the council. Taken together, their narratives offer us a fuller picture of women's experiences of the council. For every woman mentioned here, there are countless others: secretaries, journalists, housekeepers, and students whose presence contributed in large and small ways to the council. At press conferences, liturgies, and dining tables throughout Rome, women were the church at Vatican II.

Mary Luke Tobin

Mary Luke Tobin was an American Sister of Loretto who, in August 1964, had been elected chair of the Conference of Major Superiors of Women Religious (now the Leadership Conference of Women Religious).

---

12. See Heyder, "Women and the Council," 315–30, and Serena Noceti, "Theologians, Theologies, Church: Feminist Theologies in the Process of the Reception of Vatican II," in Clifford and Faggioli, *The Oxford Handbook of Vatican II*, 449–71.

13. See note 8, above.

Tasked by her fellow sisters to hang around the Vatican and learn what she could about the conciliar goings-on "on the periphery of the action,"[14] Tobin set sail for Rome. While on the boat crossing the Atlantic, she received a call from a journalist asking how it felt to be named one of the first female auditors of the council. Tobin was stunned to learn of the invitation. Upon arrival to Rome, she was informed that women had been invited to participate in sessions "which would be of interest to them," implying that perhaps there were particular issues to which women would be drawn. Tobin resolved to attend *every* session, since whatever was going on in the life of the church was of profound interest to her.

While auditors had a chiefly passive role in council plenaries, Tobin was invited to serve actively on the drafting commissions of Schema XIII, which would become *Gaudium et Spes*. She and the other commission members were able to steer the drafts, which would then receive an audience on the council floor. Tobin remembers a meeting in which Yves Congar read aloud a draft passage about women that he had prepared for the document, and his disappointment that she and the other women on the commission were not thrilled with it. He asked Australian auditor Rosemary Goldie, "You don't like it?" Tobin remembers her responding, "No, you can cut out all the references to women as flowers and light, etc. We don't need any of that grandiose stuff that has no basis in women's reality. All we want is to be treated as full human beings, accorded the same equality as men."[15] The resistance of these women to language that placed women on a pedestal averted the inclusion of such platitudes in *Gaudium et Spes*.

Tobin was deeply involved with the movement for a reform of religious life, placing her in frequent conflict with Cardinal Ildebrando Antoniutti, the prefect of the Congregation for Religious and Secular Institutes (known today as the Dicastery for Institutes of Consecrated Life and Societies of Apostolic Life). Her memories of their arguments over changes to women religious habits reveal a great deal:

> He gave me instructions, while never looking me straight in the eye. He kept saying, 'Now, now, now, you know . . . we don't want to have anything contrary to the church.' I had to have some battles royal with him. . . .

---

14. Tobin, *Hope Is an Open Door*, 19. Many women did something similar during the extraordinary meeting of the Synod on Synodality in 2023—among others, the Discerning Deacons pilgrimage group.

15. Tobin, *Hope Is an Open Door*, 24–25.

> All we were asking for in those days was a simple veil and suit with a skirt a bit below the knee. I think I still have a photograph I took to him of how the sister was going to look. There she was in her little dark suit and white shirt. He took his pen and pulled her sleeve down to her wrist—drawing with the pen—and her skirt all the way down to the floor. Then the veil had to be pulled out so that the hair didn't show.[16]

This scene of a religious sister and bishop arguing over the habit captures well the tension of Vatican II from a feminist perspective. The fact that Tobin was able to advocate for her community in this way was indeed a breakthrough, unthinkable prior to 1964. The cardinal's inability to look her in the eye and his insistence that he knew better what women religious should be wearing capture his struggle to see her as a true equal. Ultimately, the council allowed for a two-year period where congregations could experiment with their own attire, so this conflict never came to blows, but as an anecdote it is instructive.

In a later interview, Tobin described the complexity of the bishops' treatment of women auditors: "There was none of the 'pedestal' mentality. I would say there was something else—either we were ignored or trivialized. . . . There were three categories: (1) A minority of 'good guys' really appreciated our being there . . . and displayed a respectful sense of support. (2) The majority acted indifferently. Some appeared scared and shied away from even meeting us. (3) Then some clearly disapproved of our being there and avoided us totally."[17] Such experiences reveal the women auditors' struggles to be recognized as equals, treatment they received from only a minority of bishops.

Tobin went on to a life of leadership in the reform of religious life, anti-war activism, and social justice movements. Clear-eyed about the council's limits, she also maintained hope in the agency of Catholics to strive toward an increasingly just church. Her 1981 memoir acknowledges, "To translate the ideal of collegiality into the practice of participation will require years of commitment."[18] Seeing seeds of promise planted during the council, she recognized that its legacy was still in its infancy and committed her life to its reception in her own context.

---

16. McEnroy, *Guests in Their Own House*, 167.
17. McEnroy, *Guests in Their Own House*, 97.
18. Tobin, *Hope Is an Open Door*, 23.

Luz-Marie Alvarez-Icaza

While Tobin was one of several women religious, only one married woman and mother was invited as an auditor: Luz-Marie Alvarez-Icaza from Mexico. She and her husband José were leaders in the international Christian Family Movement. Initially only José was invited as an auditor, but he suggested to the papal nuncio extending the invitation that Luz-Marie might also come. The nuncio responded, "But what would she do? She doesn't represent anything international. She hasn't written a book. She hasn't high standing in church or society." José responded, "That's precisely why she must go. She's the mother of a family. She has the biggest job of passing on the faith to the family." And the nuncio replied, "Right, how could we have forgotten that? How wonderful! The first married couple is going to the council because of me!"[19]

The Icazas' experience in Rome brought into stark relief the gendered discrepancies at play during the council. For example, women were restricted to their own coffee bar—a distinction made not by ordination status but by gender. While José was free to rub elbows with the bishops during their frequent refreshment breaks, his wife and all other women were relegated to a separate area, a space they pithily dubbed "Bar None." Evidently the bishops were uncomfortable crowding in small spaces where women might brush up against them. Luz-Marie and José decided that such separation was absurd and attempted to desegregate the coffee bars. When a Swiss Guard tried to physically restrain José from joining his wife, the couple asked Archbishop Felici to deal with the matter. Felici was confused as to why he was being drawn away from important matters for something trivial like coffee. But, José argued, it wasn't trivial: "You are discussing at this moment the changing front of the world today—the theme of the church in the modern world . . . while it is being played out here in front of your eyes."[20] He later analyzed the experience this way in an interview with Carmel McEnroy: "Never would it have occurred to the council fathers that in a restaurant, at work, etc. I would never have to be alone with the men and Luz-Ma with the women. This shows how archaic the actual mentality of the church was. It was a protection for

---

19. McEnroy, *Guests in Their Own House*, 90.
20. McEnroy, *Guests in Their Own House*, 103.

priestly celibacy, and they were imposing it on the laity."[21] Through a feminist lens, we can see how structures that fearfully enforce celibacy by segregating the sexes inhibit a recognition of the full humanity of women. Physically barred from these informal conversations, women auditors were excluded from the all-boys' club where much of the conciliar work occurred. This was not an instance of clericalism, since lay men were welcomed into these spaces.

The Icazas' most substantial contribution to the council occurred during a plenary session of the mixed commission charged with the redaction of *Gaudium et Spes*. In response to Bishop Michael Browne's forceful intervention opposing any potential change in the church's teaching on marriage or birth control, Luz-Marie volunteered her own intervention. She opened her remarks, "I'm just imagining the face Catholic couples of the world are going to make when they find out what you think about family life." Suggesting that the legalistic way the bishops were describing marriage was entirely abstracted from experiences of love, she volunteered her own experience: "Since I am the only married woman here, I feel I have the responsibility of saying that when we have had intercourse, giving life to our children, it wasn't an act of concupiscence but an act of love, and I believe this is true of most Christian mothers who conceive a child. With all respect, I tell you that when your mothers conceived you, it was also in love." Recounting the story later to McEnroy, she remembered many wide-eyed responses from the bishops: "First they turned red, and then they laughed." After the fact, Bishop Sergio Méndez Arceo "came running to our house shouting, 'Luz-Ma, you have just created motherhood for the bishops!'"[22] While the council famously punted on the issue of birth control, *Gaudium et Spes* did introduce the language of conjugal love into its description of the ends of marriage and family life.[23] The witness of the Icazas, especially of Luz, helped to bring about this change.[24]

---

21. McEnroy, *Guests in Their Own House*, 104.

22. McEnroy, *Guests in Their Own House*, 143–44.

23. See Second Vatican Council, Pastoral Constitution on the Church in the Modern World *Gaudium et Spes*, December 7, 1965 (hereafter, GS), nos. 45–51. All quotations of Vatican II documents are from Austin Flannery, ed., *Vatican Council II: Constitutions, Decrees, Declarations; A Completely Revised Translation in Inclusive Language* (Liturgical Press, 2014).

24. So argues Adriana Valerio in "The Legacy of the 23 Conciliar Mothers," *L'Osservatore Romano*, November 4, 2023, https://www.osservatoreromano.va/en/news/2023-11/dcm-010/the-legacy-of-the-23-conciliar-mothers.html.

While this anecdote reveals the breakthrough made possible by having a woman in spaces of ecclesial decision-making attesting to her lived experience, it also highlights a profound limitation of the council. Luz was the only mother and wife among the auditors. While her testimony was powerful, it was taken as universal when, of course, it was particular to her own experience. A woman happily married to an equally devout husband who had enough local community and material support to leave eleven of their twelve children behind for an extended voyage to Rome presented a rather idyllic picture of marriage and motherhood. This points to a deeper need for a plurality of voices to be heard, a need for the church to consider the lived experiences of women whose lives and relationships do not correspond to this narrow ideal. It is to be hoped that six decades later, our burgeoning processes of synodality might mitigate this limitation of the Second Vatican Council, offering a listening model attuned to a wider array of life experiences.

Marie-Thérèse Lacaze

Tobin and Icaza both followed ecclesiastically sanctioned paths to the council: both invited as auditors, inhabiting the two states of life for women most intelligible to bishops—woman religious on the one hand, wife and mother on the other. Our third figure was more radical in her expressions of faith, more transgressive in her chosen state of life, and is thus even lesser known to scholars of the council. Finding her name in one footnote sparked my initial realization that women were often invisible, though present, at Vatican II. She adds an important dimension to this study.

The French lay woman Marie-Thérèse Lacaze came to the council by way of the Holy Land, where she and the worker-priest Paul Gauthier had cofounded an intentional community called the Companions of Jesus the Carpenter in 1958. These men and women lived among the poor, seeking closeness to Christ through geographic proximity to the land where Jesus himself had lived, prayed, and worked. While maintaining a ministry of communal presence with workers in factories and construction jobs, Lacaze and Gauthier also became outspoken advocates for Palestinian rights in particular and the rights of workers and the poor on a global scale.

Their activism and solidarity led them to the Second Vatican Council in the hopes of drawing the attention of the wider church to the plight of the poor and oppressed, to which they could personally testify. Invited by Melkite bishop George Hakim, Lacaze and Gauthier found a group of sympathetic bishops and theologians, from which the Church of the Poor Working Group was born. Most sources refer to Paul as the "secretary" of this unofficial but well-organized group, but Desmond O'Grady identifies Paul as the founder and Marie-Thérèse as the group's secretary.[25] Because he was a priest and because he was a man, it is unsurprising that Paul's work at the council is much better documented than Marie-Thérèse's.[26]

Paul and Marie-Thérèse had a romantic relationship, which they publicly acknowledged when Paul left the priesthood in 1971 and they married. In the meantime, while this relationship gave Marie-Thérèse more intimate access to the council than most women, it also rendered her invisible to the bigwigs of the council and to historians of the council as well. For example, Henri de Lubac's council notebooks describe lunching at a trattoria with "Father Paul Gauthier and two young, consecrated women who were accompanying him."[27] Their names, it seems, are not important.

Lacaze's memories of the council reflect firsthand this experience of being overlooked. While she was frequently at Paul's side, because, as she put it, "our work was effectively the work of a couple," it became clear that "the number of theologians or bishops who could simply speak with a woman, who were daring enough to risk the thought, was small."[28] The norms and taboos of an all-male celibate priesthood rendered Marie-Thérèse doubly invisible: while clerics unaccustomed to female presence created a culture of discomfort around women, her role as Paul's partner would be unmentionable and therefore unrecognized, no matter how open they were about their relationship.

Brazilian bishop Hélder Câmara is a notable exception to Lacaze's experience of being ignored: he mentions Lacaze frequently in his conciliar

---

25. Desmond O'Grady, *Eat from God's Hand: Paul Gauthier and the Church of the Poor* (Geoffrey Chapman, 1965), 138–39.

26. I initially made this argument in "Marie-Thérèse Lacaze and 'The End of Promised Lands,'" *Catholic Re-Visions*, Political Theology Network, February 10, 2023, https://politicaltheology.com/marie-therese-lacaze-and-the-end-of-promised-lands/.

27. Henri de Lubac, *Vatican Council Notebooks*, vol. 1, trans. Andrew Stefanelli and Anne Englund Nash (Ignatius Press, 2015), 434.

28. Marie-Thérèse Lacaze, *La fin des terres promises* (Éditions Syros, 1979), 41.

letters, identifying her as the host of most gatherings of the Church of the Poor Group, in a small apartment in Rome rented with her friend Bernadette with the wages from their factory work in Nazareth. Extraordinarily, he repeatedly calls Lacaze a "deaconess" (*diaconisa*),[29] and his notebook documents an anecdote that illuminates this reference. Lacaze shared with him that after four years in Bethlehem among the workers and the poor, a bishop (unnamed, but perhaps Hakim) laid his hands on her in a blessing of her ministry. A sacramental experience of grace, she called it. During this laying on of hands, the unnamed bishop cited the Acts of the Apostles and, as Lacaze recounted, "I know that I received the Holy Spirit and that this memory is decisive in difficult times."[30] Fascinated by this story, Câmara considered proposing a discussion of women's ordination to the diaconate during the council, although he ultimately determined that the time was not yet right for such a conversation. Yet he notes after this experience that he saw no reason why women should not be ordained not just to the diaconate but to the priesthood as well. This powerful encounter between a lay woman and bishop reveals the transformative possibilities of genuine relationship, listening, and narration of experience. Bishop Câmara respected and listened to the experience of Lacaze, and it opened a new possibility for ministry in his imagination.

But for Lacaze, that encounter with Câmara was an exception to the rule. Her experiences of ecclesiastical marginalization so bruised her that these moments of hope and beauty are largely absent from her own memoir; we only know Câmara's side of this story. In fact, Lacaze's main takeaway from the council in her memoir is this damning line: "The masculine structure of the council went hand in hand with the disdain for women and thus their absence from the council."[31] After years of such experiences, she and Paul publicly left the Catholic Church in the 1970s. For Lacaze, the tension between the reality and the eschatological vision of church was too acute; the utter lack of equality she experienced as a woman in the church drove her out of its doors.

---

29. Dom Hélder Câmara, *Circulares Conciliares*, vol. 1, tomo II (Companhia Editora de Pernambuco, 2015), 75, 77, 478.

30. Maria Cecilia Domezi, *Mulheres do Concílio Vaticano II* (Paulus, 2016), 39, Kindle.

31. Lacaze, *La fin des terres promises*, 41.

Conclusion

These stories of women at the council invite a reassessment of Paul VI's proclamation at its closing that "the Church is proud to have glorified and liberated woman, and in the course of the centuries . . . to have brought into relief her basic equality with man." For a framework for this final analysis, I turn to ecclesiologist Joseph Komonchak's 2008 lecture "Who Are the Church?" Komonchak exhorts scholars to be precise when using the term *church*, and to know to whom we are referring when we use the term. While expressing appreciation for the various images, metaphors, and models historically invoked to describe the church, Komonchak suggests that any true statement about the church must find that truth in the concrete, "in individual Christians and in their local communities and Churches, in the varied circumstances of time and place, before the differing challenges of their historical moments."[32]

So, did the church glorify and liberate women? Did it bring into relief her basic equality with man? Is it true? Did the church do that? A feminist adaptation of Komonchak's principle must interrogate the truth of ecclesiological statements from the concrete experiences of women.

If we apply Ruether's principle, that "whatever diminishes or denies the full humanity of women" does not reflect the divine, the conciliar texts and the ecclesial praxis tell two different stories. Notably the only text to have women on the initial drafting commission, *Gaudium et Spes* affirmed unequivocally, "Any type of social or cultural discrimination in basic personal rights on the grounds of sex, race, color, social condition, language or religion, must be curbed and eradicated as incompatible with God's design" (GS 29). This is the prescriptive language of ecclesiology, the hope of what the church might be. We see in the narratives above that the praxis at Vatican II fell radically short of this vision, as each aforementioned woman experienced overt sexual discrimination during their time at the council. The fact that their presence and influence has evaded much scholarly attention also points to ecclesial structures and intellectual frameworks that prevent the full humanity of women from being recognized.

Their contributions to Vatican II did, however, lay the groundwork for the Catholic Church's ongoing recognition of the full humanity and dig-

---

32. Joseph A. Komonchak, *Who Are the Church?*, The Père Marquette Lecture in Theology 2008 (Marquette University Press, 2008), 78.

nity of women. The women who bore witness in Rome for any or all those four years, as well as the bishops who invited them, who listened to them, and voted on the documents they helped to draft, contributed to this process. So much more could be said about those who received the council's directives, from the diocesan to local levels, whose work lay foundations for future women to carry on this struggle for genuine equality.[33] The legacy of the council opened the study of Catholic theology to women; this very project of feminist ecclesiology would not exist without it.[34] The postconciliar years also brought periods of great disappointment for women, where women's full humanity and equality seemed much further away than it had during the council. We are still in this ongoing process of receiving the council and have a very long way to go toward recognizing the full humanity and dignity of women.

At the time this essay is being written, the ongoing Synod on Synodality seems to be making strides toward a fuller recognition of the humanity of women, both in its history-making procedural inclusion of women as voting members of the synod and its more honest assessment of women's experiences of ecclesial marginalization. The listening sessions during the consultative stage captured recurring narratives across the globe of women's lack of equality in the church, summarized in the Working Document for the Continental Stage published in October 2022: "Those who were most committed to the synod process were women, who seem to have realized not only that they had more to gain, but also more to offer by being relegated to a prophetic edge, from which they observe what happens in the life of the Church."[35] Rather than rehearsing papal tropes of "feminine genius," genuine listening to women's voices led to the recognition that far from being glorified and liberated, Catholic women are almost universally excluded from leadership and ministry. This was a necessary step of descriptive ecclesiology to lay the foundations for a prescriptive vision, toward which the first session of the general assembly made strides in October 2023. The Synthesis Report from this

---

33. See, for just one of many examples, Mary J. Henold, *The Laywoman Project: Remaking Catholic Womanhood in the Vatican II Era* (University of North Carolina Press, 2020).

34. See Noceti, "Theologians, Theologies, Church," 452–55.

35. Synod of Bishops, Working Document for the Continental Stage, *"Enlarge the Space of Your Tent,"* October 2022, no. 61, https://www.synod.va/content/dam/synod/common/phases/continental-stage/dcs/Documento-Tappa-Continentale-EN.pdf.

period explicitly recognized, "It is urgent to ensure that women can participate in decision-making processes and assume roles of responsibility in pastoral care and ministry," at every level of ecclesial life, and goes on to enumerate seven concrete proposals to meet this urgent need.[36] This synodal process builds upon the imperfect but important groundwork laid at Vatican II, offering a more realistic assessment of present shortcomings and articulating a vision (albeit an incomplete one) to change ecclesial structures to better recognize women's full humanity.

Even if all seven proposals come to fruition, women are and will still be marginalized by the institutional church in terms of canon law, teaching authority, and "licit" sacramental ministry. This is a descriptive fact but need not be a prescriptive principle. This, I think, is a distinction that can honor the prophetic place from which women exist ecclesially and recognize it as locus for theological truth and praxis, without sacralizing this marginality. A descriptive feminist ecclesiology recognizes that women are marginalized to "the prophetic edge." A prescriptive feminist ecclesiology brings us beyond this marginalization, envisioning a church that does not create margins in the first place.

If Tobin was right, that "men and women are the church," then the church is bringing into relief women's basic equality, because women (and some men) in the church have done and are doing that, both during the council and in its present reception. Women have striven and are striving to narrow the gap between a descriptive and prescriptive ecclesiology—the church as it is and the church as it ought to be. As we have always done, Catholic women's lives of discipleship continue to overflow the limits of what ecclesiastical documents are able to say about us. The more that theologians and ecclesial leaders pay attention to that overflow, the closer we will come to a church in which women's basic equality with men is honored not just in word but in deed.

---

36. XVI Ordinary General Assembly of the Synod of Bishops, Synthesis Report, *A Synodal Church in Mission*, October 28, 2023, 9m, https://www.synod.va/content/dam/synod/assembly/synthesis/english/2023.10.28-ENG-Synthesis-Report.pdf.

Chapter 10

The "Synodal Process" and the North American Reception of Vatican II on Women in the Church

Theresa Gardner

Halfway through the Second Vatican Council, in an address delivered on October 22, 1963, during the second session, Cardinal Leo Jozef Suenens of Mechelen–Brussels suggested the appointment of women auditors to the council while reminding his fellow bishops that women constituted half of humanity.[1] Following this provocative statement, twenty-three women were invited to attend the third (1964) and fourth (1965) sessions of the Second Vatican Council as auditors. Now, at this writing, sixty years later, the Catholic Church finds itself in the midst of a synod—the Synod on Synodality.

In an attempt to better understand the role of women in the church and how the church has responded, this paper will conduct a comparative analysis between what women were asking for at Vatican II and what they continue to ask for today through the synodal process. This comparative study will reveal several key discoveries. The first is what exactly has changed for women at and since Vatican II by looking at the proposals

---

1. Cardinal Leo Jozef Suenens, intervention in aula, October 22, 1963, in *Acta Synodalia Sacrosancti Concilii Oecumenici Vaticani II*, vol. 2/III (Typis Polyglottis Vaticanis, 1972), 177: "inventur ut auditores etiam *mulieres* quae, ni fallor, dimidiam partem humanitatis constituent" (emphasis in the original).

of the women auditors present at the council. Secondly, it will highlight the concerns and desires that women raised after the council and specifically in the last five years. Finally, it will look directly at the synodal documents, specifically the Working Document for the Continental Stage, to see what the listening related to the synod reveals about current trajectories in the debate over the role of women in the Catholic Church.

Women and/at Vatican II

In the recently published *Oxford Handbook of Vatican II*, the chapter by German theologian Regina Heyder provides a rich historical context to situate the women, events, and climate at the time leading up to and during the Second Vatican Council. During the preparation of the council in 1960, the World Union of Catholic Women's Organizations (WUCWO) submitted several requests to the council on behalf of the more than 36 million women from every continent. One of the blunter requests from the WUCWO was that "the personal and not sexual value of women" be acknowledged by the council, as well as their positions not only in the family but in society, the workplace, and the universal apostolic call of women and men alike. With regard to pastoral concerns, the WUCWO called for a better "psychological, pedagogical and theological training of priests," as many women during this time felt uncomfortable with the pastoral approaches that male priests showed toward women.[2] Along this same vein, the WUCWO called for an overall end to misogyny, a sentiment that can still be heard loud and clear today from women all over the world.

Another international organization that sent suggestions to the preparatory commissions for Vatican II was the St. Joan's International Alliance (SJI), founded originally in 1911 as the Catholic Women's Suffrage Society. The SJI shared suggestions similar to those of the WUCWO, but it also advocated for an expansion of the diaconate to women, arguing that the diaconate was an independent ministry and should, therefore, be open to women and men alike. Additionally, the SJI called for a revi-

---

2. See Regina Heyder, "Women and the Council: Catholic Women's Organizations and Women Theologians Prior to and During Vatican II," in *The Oxford Handbook of Vatican II*, ed. Catherine Clifford and Massimo Faggioli (Oxford University Press, 2023), 315–30, esp. 316.

sion of the rite of marriage and of canon law, and it "pleaded for the participation of women in the council." A top priority request of the WUCWO was a plea to "end all expressions of misogyny."[3]

It is important to clarify that women's issues were just as diverse during the time of the Second Vatican Council as they are today. Depending on perspective and regionality, there is a vast range of women's issues and concerns that the WUCWO was cognizant of and attentive to, realizing that grouping women's issues together would lead to a detrimental view of women around the globe as a homogenous group without any differences when, of course, this is not true. Such sensitivity and attention to regional diversity of concerns can be seen during the synodal process of 2021–24 as well. This attention to diversity, both during the council and the synod, is in response to the homogenization of women that has often been done by church leaders, bishops, and priests.[4]

---

3. Heyder, "Women and the Council," 317.

4. At the inauguration of the presence of women as auditors at the council in 1964, Pope Paul VI made it clear that the women present were meant to be a *symbolic* and more passive representation, and indeed, lay auditors were not allowed to speak and certainly not allowed to vote. Their main role then was networking (Heyder, "Women and the Council," 323). Additionally, some of the women kept meticulous records of what was said, the documents that were written, and insider details of how they were treated, as women and as auditors, during the council. Australian theologian Rosemary Goldie and the president of the Conference of Major Superiors of Women at the time of the council, Sr. Mary Luke Tobin, two of the original women auditors, were determined not to be mere symbols with passive roles, as they believed that "*all* aspects of the Church's life were important to women" (Heyder, "Women and the Council," 321). In a 1986 *America* magazine article, Mary Luke Tobin recalled an encounter between Rosemarie Goldie and one of the authors of commission documents. When the author read aloud a "flowery and innocuous" statement about women, the author then asked Goldie condescendingly, "Why don't you respond happily to my praise of women and what they have contributed to the church?" Goldie replied solemnly, "All women ask for is that they are recognized as the full human persons they are, and treated accordingly." Mary Luke Tobin, "Women in the Church Since Vatican II," *America*, November 1, 1986, https://www.americamagazine.org/issue/100/women-church-vatican-ii. Out of the twenty-three women auditors, only one, Luz-Marie Alvarez-Icaza, was married, and she was invited only in the final year of the council. Though she was only one, Alvarez-Icaza was mighty, as she and her husband conducted a survey of more than forty thousand people from thirty-five countries to extract what people were thinking. Responses ranged from suggestions concerning birth control to encouraging the lay apostolate (Heyder, "Women and the Council," 322).

Mary Luke Tobin, Rosemary Goldie, and Luz-Marie Alvarez-Icaza were auditors at Vatican II and are just a few examples of the incredible strength and impact women had leading up to and during the Second Vatican Council. Another example was Sr. Carmel McEnroy, a member of the congregation of the Sisters of Mercy of Ireland and South Africa who later became best known for the book, *Guests in Their Own House: The Women of Vatican II,* which gives one of the most in-depth accounts of the twenty-three women auditors present at Vatican II.[5] Sr. McEnroy not only documented the proceedings and people who were involved in the Second Vatican Council, but she also shed light on the ideas and proposals that were *not* passed by the council. One of these changes, proposed by German and Canadian bishops, was to start using more inclusive language when speaking about God and God's people. But this request was not reflected in the Vatican's official English translation of the conciliar documents.[6] Though the women present at the council faced setbacks and many moments of discrimination, there were also changes that marked important moments of progress. Sr. Mary Luke Tobin lists many of these moments that she witnessed as having a positive impact on women and, more broadly, on the laity and religious. One of these changes was an increased focus on the individual person and their participation in the context of faith and the world. Furthermore, following Vatican II, there was an increase in women theologians and biblical scholars who began uncovering new layers of theology, Christology, anthropology, and many other disciplines by considering these areas of study through a feminist theological lens. Women could now not only be a part of the theological and ecclesiological conversation, but they also could claim this theology as their own in and through their perspective

---

5. Sarah MacDonald, "Sr. Carmel McEnroy, Author Who Captured Women's Role in Vatican II, Dies," *Global Sisters Report*, December 3, 2019, https://www.globalsistersreport.org/sr-carmel-mcenroy-author-who-captured-womens-role-vatican-ii-dies.

6. The different English translations of Vatican II documents (Abbott, Tanner, and Flannery) have adopted different choices for gender-inclusive language. On the proposals coming from women auditors at the council (women's ordination to the diaconate and priesthood, women's leadership roles within the church, birth control, the lay apostolate), see McEnroy, "Guests in Their Own House: The Women of Vatican II," April 1, 2013, News, Congregation of the Sisters of Mercy, https://sistersofmercy.ie/2013/01/guests-in-their-own-house-the-women-of-vatican-ii/.

as women and through a feminist theological approach.⁷ Tobin quotes Rosemary Ruether, one of the pioneers of Catholic feminist theology: "Whatever diminishes, denies or distorts the full humanity of women does not reflect the divine and therefore is not redemptive; by the same token, whatever promotes the full humanity of women is 'of the Holy.'"⁸

Following Vatican II, in the 1980s, a process was undertaken by the US bishops' conference to draft a pastoral letter on women. In the extensive listening sessions that were a part of the drafting process, which was headed by Bishop Joseph Imesch of the Diocese of Joliet, women spoke freely in their criticisms of the church, calling out the "sin of sexism" and broaching topics such as women's ordination to the priesthood. But Pope John Paul II and then Cardinal Joseph Ratzinger both criticized the early drafts, stressing the importance of recognizing the complementarity between genders and warning against using overly-inclusive language, such as using the word *person* instead of *man* for human beings.⁹ The last draft was finally rejected in a vote of the bishops' conference in 1992.

There was quite a chill of expectations among feminist theologians following Pope John Paul II's publication of the apostolic letter *Ordinatio Sacerdotalis* in 1994, which rejects women's ordination to the priesthood, stating that "the constant practice of the Church, which has imitated Christ in choosing only men . . . has consistently held that the exclusion of women from the priesthood is in accordance with God's plan for his Church."¹⁰ The document then goes on to say that the church shows honor and gratitude toward women as they are the irreplaceable "martyrs, virgins, and mothers of families . . . who bring up their children in the spirit of the Gospel" (OS 1). Such statements imply that, firstly, women are not a true imitation of Christ and, secondly, women are confined to stereotypical gender roles that render them subservient to men and confined to a sexist and patriarchal system. *Ordinatio Sacerdotalis* was a

---

7. Tobin, "Women in the Church Since Vatican II."

8. Rosemary Radford Ruether, *Sexism and God Talk: Toward a Feminist Theology* (Beacon Press, 1993), 41.

9. See Ruth A. Wallace, "Catholic Women and the Creation of a New Social Reality," *Gender and Society* 2, no. 1 (1988): 24–38, https://www.jstor.org/stable/190467.

10. Pope John Paul II, Apostolic Letter *Ordinatio Sacerdotalis*, May 22, 1994, no. 1, https://www.vatican.va/content/john-paul-ii/en/apost_letters/1994/documents/hf_jp-ii_apl_19940522_ordinatio-sacerdotalis.html (hereafter, OS).

twofold blow: it undermined all of the work that had been done so far in support of women, and it revealed a magisterium that was still shaped by a traditional view of gender roles.

American Women's Input for the Synod on Synodality

Fifty-six years after the end of the Second Vatican Council, in 2021, the Catholic Church undertook, under the leadership of Pope Francis, a global Synod on Synodality. The purpose behind this synod is multifaceted. One facet is to create a space for healing across the board of the wounds within and *caused* by the church as an institution, as well as within the hearts of all the people who make up the Body of Christ. Another facet is discerning how the church can hold itself accountable to the *sensus fidelium*, or the living voice of the people of God. The synod calls all the baptized to engage in deep listening to one another, beginning with the church and its hierarchy listening to the baptized. Beginning at the diocesan level and going to the universal level, the goal is that the church will become better equipped to overcome clericalism, leave behind prejudices and stereotypes, and be open to conversion and dialogue with humility and an openness to newness.

On the official synod website, there is a paragraph devoted to a warning to pay special attention to those groups of people that have a history of being excluded: women, people with disabilities, migrants, minorities, those living in poverty, and more. My focus will be on the role of women in the "synodal process" between 2021 and early 2024, with particular consideration of whether the aforementioned warning has been heeded. I will do this by specifically looking at the role of women as presented in the documents for the preparation for the synod, such as proposals for the synod, what they hope will come from the synod regarding women's leadership, as well as the ways in which women are viewed and treated by the church today.

To begin, the most revolutionary change that has occurred in favor of women in this synod is their ability to vote. For the first time in the history of the Synod of Bishops, fifty-four women have been chosen as voting members, making up 15 percent of the total number in the two assemblies (2023 and 2024) of the synod. In 2023, 21 percent of the 370 participants were non-bishops and half of those were women—all will be granted the right to vote on the final document that will then be sent to Pope Francis.[11] This decision aligns with Pope Francis's desire for the synod to be based on a culture of active listening to *all* Catholics and their individual and unique experiences of faith in order to get a broader and more diverse spectrum of faith. Comparing this to the recent past, we recall that during the 2018 assembly of the synod on youth, as women fought for their right to vote, two lay brothers and eight priests were granted the right to vote, while three representatives of the International Union of Superior Generals, who were all appointed by Francis, were not admitted to vote. It was not until 2021, when Nathalie Becquart of France, a member of the Xavière sisters, became the first woman able to vote at a synod due to her new appointment as undersecretary of the Synod of Bishops. Women religious and laity getting the vote can serve as a potential catalyst for the changes they've been asking for since Vatican II and more recently in anticipation of the synod.

Out of the ten delegates chosen to represent North America, six of those delegates are women, with many of those women representing marginalized groups of people within the North American church. Though these delegates represent many of the changes that women have been advocating, there are different views among American and global Catholic women on the role of women in the church. Though Phyllis Zagano, a member of the first pontifical commission for the study of ordaining women to the diaconate (2016-18), advocates for women's ordination to the diaconate, while Kate McElwee, executive director of the Women's Ordination Conference, supports women's ordination to the diaconate and to the priesthood, both share the belief that the synod must reconsider the role of women within the church's leadership, decision-making, and overall structure. Without such a conversation, the two believe the synod will be incomplete. Such a statement reflects just how removed women have and continue to feel from church leadership and participation, not only from the hierarchy but also from the Eucharist.

One of the women representing the United States at the synod is Cynthia Bailey Manns, director of adult faith formation at St. Joan's Parish in

---

11. See Sebastian Gomes, "Synodality Is Working: Women Getting a Vote at the Vatican Is the Latest Proof," *America*, May 3, 2023, https://www.americamagazine.org/faith/2023/05/03/pope-francis-synod-women-vote-245214.

Minneapolis, Minnesota, and adjunct faculty member at United Theological Seminary of the Twin Cities. As a black Catholic woman, Bailey Manns represents two marginalized groups. In a 2023 *America* magazine interview, she said, "I'm an African American woman in a space that is doing the kind of work that . . . Christ is calling us to do. To reach out, through the profound love of God, to our neighbor, without distinction." As someone who was "born during the height of segregation," Bailey Manns knows intimately the importance of process as well as the impact that patience can have within a process. Seeing herself as someone "to plant seeds and create processes that may move things forward" within the church, she says she will rely on hope and patience as she works as an official delegate of the synod.[12]

Another lay woman representing North America as a delegate is Canadian theologian Catherine Clifford. Clifford echoes much of what feminist theologians have been calling for since Vatican II, specifically that lay women be integrated on all levels of church participation, management, and leadership. She also calls for an honest confrontation with past traditions and structures to see if they are serving their original purpose in today's church or if that original purpose engages with the diversity of the Body of Christ. As a theologian focused on the church in the modern world, Clifford calls for an adaptation of church structures and ministries, as it has historically always done, because the church cannot deny its inability to meet baseline responsibilities to welcome those on the margins and incorporate women into more leadership positions. In light of the paralyzing fear that deters such renewal and progress, Clifford's goal as a delegate will be to listen and face those issues *together*: "The process is as important as whatever decisions might be taken."[13]

One cannot overlook the progress and reforms that have been made within the realm of women's leadership especially. Lay women such as Tania Tetlow, the president of Fordham University; Colleen Hanycz, presi-

---

12. Michael J. O'Laughlin, "Meet the Black Catholic Lay Woman Representing the U.S. at the Synod," *America*, August 8, 2023, https://www.americamagazine.org/faith/2023/08/08/cynthia-bailey-mann-245808.

13. Brian Fraga, "Lay Synod Member Catherine Clifford Praises Pope Francis' Method of Dialogue, Participation," *National Catholic Reporter*, July 13, 2023, https://www.ncronline.org/news/lay-synod-member-catherine-clifford-praises-pope-francis-method-dialogue-participation.

dent of Xavier University; Musa Dube, president of the Society of Biblical Literature; Mary Pat Donaghue, executive director of the US bishops' conference's Secretariat of Catholic Education; Nathalie Becquart, XMCJ, the first female undersecretary of the Synod of Bishops; theologians such as M. Shawn Copeland, Kathryn Tanner, and Elisabeth Schüssler Fiorenza; and social justice advocates such as Sr. Helen Prejean and Mary Novak. These are just a few of the hundreds of women who serve as leaders within the church, academy, and nonprofit/NGO and social justice advocacy sectors.[14]

Pope Francis has led a papacy of reform, and though his relationship with women is complicated, there can be no doubt that he has made room for women at the Vatican and given them a platform, where there had previously been none, to at least be heard. In an article about the evolution of the relationship between Pope Francis and women, Kate McElwee acknowledges Pope Francis's shortcomings, stating that women are still novelties in the eyes of the magisterium as he continues to use the arguably outdated concept of the Marian (femininity) and Petrine (ministry) principles within the church, which support stereotypical gender roles of men and women through the guise of theological jargon and labels.[15] But she also acknowledges Francis's victories, because after opening two papal commissions to further investigate the female diaconate and by giving women the ability to vote, he has certainly paved a path for women to become more than just novelties within the church as an institution. Though the concept of synodality can at times be perceived as a paradoxical concept, with some women seeing it as a stifling of women's equality while others see it as a calling forth of those on the margins, McElwee states that because there are now "opportunities for women's voices to be heard, at least we have a pope who has shown he knows how to listen every now and again."[16]

---

14. Jill Rice, "What Convinced Me that We Need More Women Leading at the Vatican," *America*, May 5, 2023, https://www.americamagazine.org/faith/2023/05/05/women-leadership-church-245226.

15. See, for example, The Editors, "Exclusive: Pope Francis Discusses Ukraine, U.S. Bishops and More," *America*, November 28, 2022, https://www.americamagazine.org/faith/2022/11/28/pope-francis-interview-america-244225.

16. Kate McElwee, "The Evolution of Pope Francis on Women: Some Movement, but More Needed," *National Catholic Reporter*, March 7, 2023, https://www.ncronline.org/opinion/guest-voices/evolution-pope-francis-women-some-movement-more-needed.

Reception of the Inputs by the Synodal Process

The six paragraphs dedicated to "Rethinking Women Participation" in the Working Document for the Continental Stage, *"Enlarge the Space of Your Tent"* (2022), start off by stating, "The call for a conversion of the Church's culture, for the salvation of the world, is linked in concrete terms to the possibility of establishing a new culture, with new practices and structures."[17] This call for a new culture regarding the role of women challenges not only the status quo of women in the church but, more fundamentally, the mission of the church itself.[18] Following this initial statement, the section continues, going through the synod reports based on listening sessions conducted in several regions around the world, including South Korea, New Zealand, South America, and the Holy Land, spelling out how women are calling for similar changes: greater inclusivity of women in decision-making, more opportunity for leadership roles and active participation, addressing sexism, fair wages for ministry jobs, better training of priests in parish settings, the ability for women to preach during Mass, and women's diaconate (see WD 60–65).

Zagano suggests that clericalism is the root cause of many of the issues raised by women: "The seven continental responses to the Document for the Continental Stage were clear that women are ill-treated, even ignored, by 'the Church.' Each noted that clericalism in all its forms contributed to or in fact was the direct cause of so much difficulty. High on the list of antidotes is the improvement of seminary formation. And, both directly and indirectly, the responses pointed to the restoration of women to the diaconate." Furthermore, Zagano states that the church's reasoning for excluding women from the diaconate is "because they cannot image Christ. . . . This is the root cause of the denigration and disrespect for women on every continent."[19] Even if one disagrees with Zagano's cor-

---

17. Synod of Bishops, Working Document for the Continental Stage, *"Enlarge the Space of Your Tent,"* October 2022, no. 60, https://www.synod.va/content/dam/synod/common/phases/continental-stage/dcs/Documento-Tappa-Continentale-EN.pdf (hereafter, WD).

18. See Susan Bigelow Reynolds, "Are We Protagonists Yet?," *Commonweal*, December 9, 2022, https://www.commonwealmagazine.org/women-church-synod-francis-catholic.

19. Phyllis Zagano, "Women Deacons? The Synodal Process and Women's Ordination," *Commonweal*, July 23, 2023, https://www.commonwealmagazine.org/synodality-francis-diaconate-women-clericalism-grech.

relation or conclusion, one must seriously ponder the words "because they cannot image Christ."

The Working Document for the Continental Stage stated that Catholic women all around the world are asking that the church be their ally by addressing the violence, impoverishment, exclusion, and marginalization that is the reality for many women (WD 62). Such a statement suggests that a baseline of support and solidarity has not yet been felt by women and that misogyny and sexism, which were being discussed by women before, during, and after Vatican II, are still prevalent. Susan Bigelow Reynolds describes the synodal document's global vision. Up until this point, she writes, women were grouped together as a monolithic group of "women," without any distinction or diversity. Such a description is not only incorrect, but it also reveals a blatant misconception of the many needs and gifts that women could bring to the table. Referring to a statement from the synodal report from the Holy Land, that "those who were most committed to the Synod process were women, who seem to have realized not only that they had more to gain, but also more to offer by being relegated to a prophetic edge, from which they observe what happens in the life of the Church" (WD 61), Reynolds affirms that the church has offered sentimental glorifications of the nature of the roles women play in it, seeing that it is only on the ground of "prophetic edges" from which they have been allowed to speak. Reynolds praises the document because it holds the history of the church, adopting the blunt language in many of the national and regional reports it drew from, such as "sexism in decision-making," "cheap labor," and "lack of equality for women."[20]

The *Instrumentum Laboris* of the first (2023) session of the synod, was created to help the participants discern and discuss key points gathered from the first two stages (the diocesan phase and the continental phase). That document includes a section (B.23) on how the church can better fulfill its mission through greater recognition and promotion of the baptismal dignity of women. It emphasizes the need to recognize the plurality of women's experiences, stating that they can no longer be spoken about as a homogenous group, as experiences and contexts amongst women vary greatly. Another point is the need to end discrimination toward women and to recognize mutually supportive relationships between men

---

20. Zagano, "Women Deacons?"

and women in the church, reflected through their participation in church leadership roles. Furthermore, the document states that there must be a realization within the life of the church of the mutuality, reciprocity, and complementarity of men and women. It then lists several questions for reflecting on how women and men can better cooperate within a pastoral setting, how women can better contribute to the church's governance and leadership, and how to recognize and support the contributions of women in the church in a way that validates and protects such work.[21]

How the First Session of the Synod on Synodality Was Received by Women

Following the first session of the Synod of Synodality, which took place October 4–29, 2023, the Synthesis Report titled *A Synodal Church in Mission* was released, first in Italian and then in other languages. The report is comprised of three main sections, with subsections that were voted upon for inclusion and specific wording by the full assembly (363 eligible voters total). These sections represent the convergences and proposals that came about through dialogue.

In Part II, titled "All Disciples, All Missionaries," subsection nine is devoted to "Women in the Life and Mission of the Church."[22] Here we find paragraphs regarding the ordination of female deacons, which are also the paragraphs that received the most "no" votes from synod participants of all the paragraphs in the forty-one-page document. Such an outcome was predicted by Zagano, who sees such a dismissal of women as an insult to the baptismal equality that both men and women share. As Australian Jesuit Frank Brennan wrote, "A synodal Church must address these questions together, seeking responses that offer greater recognition of women's baptismal dignity and rejection of all forms of discrimination and exclu-

---

21. XVI Ordinary General Assembly of the Synod of Bishops, *Instrumentum Laboris* for the First Session, *For a Synodal Church: Communion, Participation, Mission*, May 29, 2023, https://press.vatican.va/content/salastampa/en/bollettino/pubblico/2023/06/20/230620e.html.

22. XVI Ordinary General Assembly of the Synod of Bishops, Synthesis Report, *A Synodal Church in Mission*, October 28, 2023, https://www.synod.va/content/dam/synod/assembly/synthesis/english/2023.10.28-ENG-Synthesis-Report.pdf (hereafter, SR, with paragraph numbering [pages are unnumbered]).

sion faced by women in the Church and society." The members of the synod had mixed feelings about a female diaconate, Brennan wrote, with some seeing it as a threat to and discontinuity of the tradition, as well as something that would "marry the Church to the spirit of the age."[23] But what exactly is the institutional church afraid of when thinking about marrying itself to the spirit of the age? Is it really the fear that the church would be "widowed in the next [generation]" or is it a more fundamental fear of the loss of power? This is worth reflection, because this idea is the catalyst for the fear that is stunting progress for women.

For others, the female diaconate was seen as something that would restore the practices of the early church. The issue of clericalism was mentioned as supportive of chauvinistic attitudes within the church and disruptive of the communion between men and women. The document also suggested there must be an acknowledgment of both sexual abuse and abuse of authority as evidence so that structural changes and relational renewal can take place (SR 9g). More inclusive language within church documents and teachings, as well as more input from women on the process of forming seminarians, were also requested. There was also a call for the continuation of theological, exegetical, and pastoral research on the possibility of a female diaconate, and "if possible, the results of this research should be presented to the next session of the assembly" (SR 9n). Considering that a plethora of research has already been done on this topic by biblical scholars, theologians, and historians, many wonder why such research was *not* present at such a historic gathering as the synod.

Many of these requests mirror what women have been saying since Vatican II. Furthermore, research on the historical and theological issues related to the possibility of a female diaconate has already been done through two Vatican commissions and many theologians and biblical scholars. One wonders why such research was not present at the synod or if such theological exploration and biblical scholarship was not welcome, given the tenor of the synod as a time for synodal dialogue. Indeed, journalist Christopher Lamb offered the comment of one source who said, "The progressives got the process, and the conservatives got the content."[24]

---

23. Frank Brennan, "A Good Start for the Synod . . . ," *Commonweal*, November 8, 2023, https://www.commonwealmagazine.org/good-start-synod.

24. Quoted in Brennan, "A Good Start."

Upon hearing so many echoes of the voices of women at Vatican II in the current synod, the overall tenor of women's responses to the Synthesis Report of 2023 was disappointment. There were simply not enough concrete changes or initiatives to move women's ministry and roles forward in the church, and it is still unclear how the institutional church views women; it is not completely clear whether women are acknowledged as true equals within the church. Frank Brennan notes that the synod was certainly a good start in acknowledging the rawness of the wounds many women have felt due to the church, but it has not been enough, and the accouterments of the clerical office are still at the forefront of the church.[25]

In their response to the synod, the Women's Ordination Conference celebrated the significance of the role that women played in the process and the event, which stands as a hopeful contrast to the role that women had at Vatican II. But the WOC also shared its disappointment in "the failure of the synod to take seriously the overwhelming calls to open all ordained ministries to women. The indication that the conversation on women in ordained ministries should be limited to the permanent diaconate or undefined 'new ministries,' simply does not reflect the needs of the church today, nor the fullness of women's vocations."[26]

But on a more hopeful note, women such as Sister Maria de los Dolores Palencia Gomez, a Sister of St. Joseph of Lyon and one of ten president-delegates named by Pope Francis, saw the synod as the beginning of gradual change and the "setting of the stage for what's to come." Gomez also describes the synod as a new "*modus vivendi*," in which the church is engaged in a "permanent and ongoing dialogue."[27] Though the synod does not have the same amount of authority as the Second Vatican Council, it has set a new precedent for what it means to engage the church on a global level, with regard to who should be represented and how dialogue

---

25. See Brennan, "A Good Start."

26. Women's Ordination Conference press release, "Women's Ordination Conference Responds to Final Document of Pope Francis' October 2023 Synod on Synodality," October 28, 2023, https://www.womensordination.org/2023/10/womens-ordination-conference-responds-to-final-document-of-pope-francis-october-2023-synod-on-synodality/.

27. Jonathan Liedl, "Synod 'Setting the Stages for Future Changes' on Role of Women; First Woman Presides over Assembly," Catholic News Agency, October 14, 2023, https://www.catholicnewsagency.com/news/255690/synod-setting-the-stages-for-future-changes-on-role-of-women-first-woman-presides-over-assembly.

should occur. The church is not stagnant, and the processes and formation of the church and its people must not remain stagnant. It continues to grow in tandem with the realities of people's lives and the constant evolution of all of creation.

Conclusions

In considering the role of women at the Second Vatican Council and at the Synod on Synodality, one can see that there has been a continuation, reiteration, and parallelism in the topics of concern by women at both events. Women at Vatican II worked to make their voices heard, even if they weren't actually allowed to speak during its formal sessions. But women's voices have been heard loud and clear through the synodal process, as they carry with them the legacy of those women of Vatican II. Issues of seminary formation, misogyny, clericalism, women's ordination to the diaconate and priesthood, women's representation in church leadership, and inclusive language are all topics raised at Vatican II and the synod. Though there is much work still to be done, especially regarding the implementation of the female diaconate, immense progress has been made for women since the time of Vatican II, beginning with women serving as voting members. As Mónica Santamarina, president general of the World Union of Catholic Women's Organizations, commented, "Being heard and being involved are important signs of change."[28]

Pope Francis set a new precedent when he picked fifty-four women to be voting members at the Synod on Synodality, creating an atmosphere where everyone present could speak freely and openly about their experiences and hopes for the church, without the pressures of public opinion and the press. Women are divided between feelings of disappointment at how little it actually does for their role in the church and feelings of satisfaction at having women present, voting, and sharing their voices on behalf of women around the world. When looking especially at the proposal for a female diaconate, the synod has shown that there remain deep divisions and instabilities regarding women and their full inclusion in the church.

---

28. Catherine Hadro and Rachel Thomas, "Synod on Synodality: Role of Women in the Synodal Spotlight," *National Catholic Register*, October 2, 2023, https://www.ncregister.com/news/synod-on-synodality-role-of-women.

The synod has been a time to practice mutual listening, calling *all* members of the church to open their hearts and minds so that there may be space for humility, conversion, and renewal. This spirit of the synod bears witness to the voices of those women at Vatican II, all of whom desired to be listened to with authenticity and given a seat at the table. As we contemplate the stories and experiences of one another, if we choose to encounter one another, we may come to realize that we are being called to an ever-deeper wholeness and belonging to one another and to God, as equal members of one body.

Racism and Colonialism

Chapter 11

Disrupting the Idolatry of Blood

Catholic Antiracism as a Necessary Expression of the Council's Renewed Soteriology

Jaisy A. Joseph

Willie James Jennings begins his classic text *The Christian Imagination: Theology and the Origins of Race* by describing a scene that took place at dawn on August 8, 1444. As Prince Henry the Navigator sat on horseback on the southern beaches of Portugal, crowds lined the streets of Lagos to catch a glimpse of the cargo that would mark their country's arrival as a world power. Two hundred thirty-five individuals from different parts of Africa were escorted off the boat and herded to a field for auction and distribution. Standing alongside Muslims, Valencians, Catalans, and the Genoese, Catholic Portugal now possessed "power over black flesh. They now emerged as bearers of black gold, slave traders."[1] A decade later, Pope Nicholas V blessed the actions of the Portuguese crown by insisting on the soteriological significance of these commercial exploits. In his 1455 bull *Romanus Pontifex*, the pope stated that it was now possible for all sheep to enter a single divine fold.[2] Unfortunately, before the enslaved

---

1. Willie James Jennings, *The Christian Imagination: Theology and the Origins of Race* (Yale University Press, 2011), 15.
2. Nicholas V, *Romanus Pontifex*, January 8, 1455, https://www.papalencyclicals.net/nichol05/romanus-pontifex.htm. The bull granted the Portuguese a perpetual monopoly in trade with Africa.

were sent across the Atlantic Ocean, they entered this divine fold through a distorted baptism performed *en masse* at one of the slave fortresses that lined the western coast of Africa. Through this Christian ritual of initiation, they were forced "to die to their former, chosen life and rise to life in a state of unchosen social death."[3]

Jennings argues that the term *European expansion* does not fully capture the weight of spatial disruption and human consumption that occurred during the era of colonial discovery. Four simultaneous actions led to this reconfiguration of both land and identity, resulting in generational wounds that continue to harm the possibility of communion between different peoples today: "First, people are being seized (stolen); second, land is being seized (stolen); third, people are being stripped from their space, their place; and fourth, Europeans are describing themselves and these Africans at the same time."[4] To justify this expansion that resulted in the theft of land and the abduction and subsequent displacement of various peoples, European colonizers had to convince themselves of their own superiority in relation to the perceived inferiority of Africans. Reflecting on Jennings's argument, Anne Carpenter claims that "theology is intimately involved in every one of those movements, and that theology is transformed, deformed by that support."[5] The first part of this essay will examine this theological deformation by considering how blood-purity logics in the Western hemisphere distorted theologies of salvation in the aftermath of African enslavement and Indigenous captivity.

It is not, however, until this idolatry of blood returns to European soil in the form of Nazi ideology that theologians of *ressourcement* begin to reflect on this deformed soteriology. In doing so, they turned to the early church to retrieve a renewed soteriology that disrupts racial hierarchies in light of Christian revelation. Thus part two will explore how Henri de Lubac's 1938 work *Catholicism* retrieved this early soteriology—offering a framework to help us assess the legacy and limits of the Second Vatican Council. In many ways, the post-Holocaust theologians of the council took responsibility for the church's contributions to the death-dealing

---

3. Katie Walker Grimes, *Christ Divided: Antiblackness as Corporate Vice* (Fortress Press, 2017), 190.

4. Jennings, *The Christian Imagination*, 24.

5. Anne M. Carpenter, *Nothing Gained Is Eternal: A Theology of Tradition* (Fortress Press, 2022), 68.

outcomes of anti-Semitism. Yet, just as this legacy was being discussed at the council, many of the theological distortions that undergirded racist colonialism were also being challenged in the sociopolitical sphere through movements for independence. Attentive to the ways in which the sin of racism damaged the church's relationship with Jews, the council paid little attention to how the legacies of racist colonialism wounded relationships within the church.

Considering the council's willingness to take responsibility for the past theological distortions of anti-Semitism and repent for their death-dealing consequences for the lives of millions, we must consider, as Jeannine Hill Fletcher asks, whether our contemporary theologies will continue to "leave undisturbed the unjust status quo of White supremacy."[6]

The final part of this essay will consider how the soteriological renewal of *nouvelle théologie* and the impact of this movement on the Second Vatican Council form the basis for contemporary Catholic antiracism, particularly as the church gathers the wounded descendants of the colonizer and the colonized around the same eucharistic table.

Racist Colonialism and Blood-Purity Logics

In *Chronicle of the Deeds of Arms Involved in the Conquest of Guinea* (1457), Prince Henry's official royal chronicler, Gomes Eanes de Zurara (or Azurara), recorded the founding events of Christendom's colonialism. He also recorded his own emotional response to the events as they unfolded. Zurara writes in this often-quoted passage:

> O, Thou heavenly Father . . . I pray Thee that my tears may not wrong my conscience; for it is not their religion but their humanity that maketh mine to weep in pity for their sufferings. . . . And these, placed all together in that field, were a marvelous sight; for amongst them were some white enough, fair to look upon, and well proportioned; others were less white like mulattoes; others again were as black as Ethiops [Ethiopians]. . . . But what heart could be so hard as not to be pierced with piteous feeling to see that company? For some kept their heads low and their faces bathed in tears, looking upon another; others kept groaning very dolorously, looking

---

6. Jeannine Hill Fletcher, *The Sin of White Supremacy: Christianity, Racism, and Religious Diversity in America* (Orbis Books, 2017), 105–6.

up to the height of heaven, fixing their eyes upon it, crying out loudly, as if asking help of the Father of Nature; others struck their faces with the palms of their hands, throwing themselves at full length upon the ground; others made their lamentations in the manner of a dirge, after the custom of their country. And though we could not understand the words of their language, the sound of it right well accorded with the measure of their sadness. . . . The Infante was there, mounted upon a powerful steed, and accompanied by his retinue, making distribution of his favours, as a man who sought to gain but small treasure from his share . . . for he reflected with great pleasure upon the salvation of those souls that before were lost.[7]

Analyzing this passage, Jennings makes two important points. First, Zurara's penitent tears reveal fissures in the triumphant story of Catholic Portugal's rise to world power. Zurara is unable to deny the humanity of those held captive before him. The intense suffering of enslavement haunts any victorious claim and hints at a profound contradiction in the Christian tradition. Yet, Jennings argues, the affective recognition of this contradiction is mitigated by a grave theological error that rationalizes away the intensity of human suffering. Rather than see the parallel between these faces bathed in tears and the face of Christ crucified, these Catholics rhetorically contained such brutality with the false soteriological claim that "African captivity leads to African salvation."[8] Just as Zurara records the enslaved crying aloud to the heavens outside the city and throwing themselves to the ground in lamentation, the Scriptures note the cry of Jesus on the cross, "My God, my God, why have you forsaken me?" (Mark 15:34). Both the captives and Jesus suffered at the hands of state power—Iberian and Roman—in a public display of domination over human flesh.

At the beginning of European colonialism, at the beginning of the so-called modern age, there exists a soteriological deformation that contains a reversal of the reversal. Jesus freely chose to suffer and overcome death so that we might not turn again against our own. This horrific colonial scene, however, reveals that the telos of these captured bodies is not redemption but only continued consumption of human flesh. The horror lies hidden under false soteriological promises that suffering in this life will lead to eternal salvation in the next.

---

7. Quoted in Jennings, *The Christian Imagination*, 18–19.
8. Jennings, *The Christian Imagination*, 20.

This soteriological distortion reaches a crisis point in Latin America, after the so-called Columbian discovery of the Americas.[9] As Michael Prior writes in his book *The Bible and Colonialism: A Moral Critique*, "12 October 1492 marks the beginning of a long and bloody Good Friday in Latin America and the Caribbean, which continues to this day, with little sign of Easter Day. The original sin of colonial exploitation is summed up as follows: 'In 1492 death came to this continent: the deaths of human beings, the death of the environment, death of the spirit, of indigenous religion and culture.'"[10] Not only did the Iberian colonizers conquer and decimate the Indigenous populations with war and disease, but they also displaced Africans from their original land, stripping them of all former identity and reducing them to constructed categories of black and slave. They were brought to Latin America to model for the Indigenous populations their common destiny—service to empire.[11]

After nearly a century, the ideology of racialized skin color developed into an Iberian obsession with *limpieza de sangre,* or purity of blood. Originally, this concept was first deployed against Jewish converts after the *Reconquista*, wanting only those who had pure "Old Christian" ancestry to have access to certain institutions and ecclesiastical offices. However, as María Elena Martínez argues in her book *Genealogical Fictions*, this ideology of blood purity created a Spanish society obsessed with genealogy and the idea that one's pure lineage meant loyalty to the faith.[12] As Spaniards tried to re-create their society in the Americas, they began to view colored blood as a contamination of white blood, not only ignoring the violence of rape perpetuated against Indigenous and African women but also setting a model of pigmentocracy for the Dutch, French, and English empires that would come after. By the eighteenth century, "casta paintings" illustrated the unions between people of different castes, with special attention given to the skin color of their offspring. With up to sixteen panels, the captions betrayed which unions were approved and

---

9. Jennings, *The Christian Imagination*, 70.
10. Michael Prior, *The Bible and Colonialism: A Moral Critique* (Sheffield Academic Press, 1997), 65.
11. Jennings, *The Christian Imagination*, 78.
12. María Elena Martínez, *Genealogical Fictions: Limpieza de Sangre, Religion, and Gender in Colonial Mexico* (Stanford University, 2008), 8, 28.

which were not through the use of pejoratives.[13] For Sylvia Wynter, any earlier goal of securing eternal salvation for lost souls was replaced by the need to secure "above all else the good of the state in competitive rivalry with all other European states—all non-Christian peoples and cultures became perceivable only in terms of their usefulness to European states securing their this-worldly goal of power and wealth."[14]

The this-worldly goal attained through the consumption of human flesh is also a significant theme in Isabel Wilkerson's book *Caste: The Origins of Our Discontent*. She argues that well "before there was a United States of America, there was a caste system, born in colonial Virginia."[15] In August 1619, a year before the pilgrims landed at Plymouth Rock, a Dutch man-of-war brought "merchandise" that the English settlers had not been expecting—about twenty enslaved persons whom the governor would then purchase.[16] From 1619 to 1865, or the first 246 years of what would become this country, the majority of African Americans lived under the terror of those who dominated their bodies and their every breath without consequence. Enslavement so distorted human relationships in the Western hemisphere that it normalized the degradation of the lowest castes.

To be fully accepted in this country as immigrants, many who arrived often neutral and innocent to the American racial caste system were forced to ensure their survival by "entering a silent unspoken pact" to distance themselves from the lowest caste by learning how to be white—or as proximate to white as possible. *Whiteness* is a category of American invention. "No one," James Baldwin once noted, "was white before he/she came to America."[17] The ancestors of most Americans today entered as new immigrants within a

> preexisting hierarchy, bipolar in construction, arising from slavery and pitting the extremes in human pigmentation at opposite ends. Each new

---

13. Martínez, *Genealogical Fictions*, 5, 227–38.

14. Sylvia Wynter, "1492: A New Worldview," in *Race, Discourse, and the Origin of the Americas: A New World View*, ed. Vera Lawrence Hyatt and Rex Nettleford (Smithsonian Institution Press, 1995), 17.

15. Isabel Wilkerson, *Caste: The Origins of Our Discontents* (Random House, 2020), 19.

16. Wilkerson, *Caste*, 40.

17. James Baldwin, "On Being 'White'. . . And Other Lies," in *Black on White: Black Writers on What It Means to Be White*, ed. David R. Roediger (Schocken, 2010), 178.

immigrant had to figure out how and where to position themselves in the hierarchy of their adopted new land. Oppressed people from around the world, particularly from Europe, passed through Ellis Island, shed their old selves, and often their old names to gain admittance to the powerful dominant majority. . . . It was in becoming American that they became white . . . fused together, on the basis not of a shared ethnic culture, or language or faith or national origin but solely on the basis of what they looked like in order to strengthen the dominant caste of hierarchy.[18]

Following the Civil War (1861–65), America's original sin of direct enslavement reconfigured itself into the color line of segregation. In 1881, Frederick Douglass reflected on how he hoped that the abolition of slavery with the passing of the Thirteenth Amendment would allow the dehumanizing spirit of slavery to die. Instead, he noted how "out of the depths of slavery has come this prejudice and this color line. . . . Slavery is indeed gone, but its shadow still lingers over the country and poisons more or less the moral atmosphere of all sections of the republic. The money motive for assailing the Negro which slavery represented is indeed absent, but the love of power and dominion, strengthened by two centuries of irresponsible power, still remains."[19] Those who stepped across the line or were deemed out of line were met with the terror of lynching, keeping both whites, blacks, and everyone in between in their caste-defined place well into the middle of the twentieth century.

In the Western hemisphere, the slow deteriorating effects of racist colonialism on Christian understandings of what it means to be saved contributed to a vision of the church that reduced unity to mere abstract European uniformity. There is no mutually transformative relationship at the heart of this unity, only exterior imitation. The catholicity of the church thus also loses its qualitative dimension for communion and discipleship because it is replaced with a quantitative understanding of geographic expansion. It is not until such colonial logics of blood purity found their way back to European soil through the rise of Nazi fascism that Catholic theologians begin to rethink soteriology through a return to Scripture and the experiences of the early church.

---

18. Wilkerson, *Caste*, 49.
19. Frederick Douglass, "The Color Line," *The North American Review* 132, no. 295 (1881): 573.

Rethinking Soteriology in the Face of Fascism

Wilkerson notes that Hitler had studied America and praised the country's near-genocide of Indigenous people and the system of reservations that exiled remaining survivors. He was also familiar with the American custom of lynching and marveled at America's capacity to maintain a sense of innocence in the wake of mass death. In June 1934, a committee of Nazi bureaucrats gathered to discuss the future of their Aryan cause, two months before Hitler seized control as the *Führer*. The Nazis studied how US law separated its population into different schools for white children and colored children, required that race be stated on birth certificates, licenses, and death certificates, and mandated segregated facilities in waiting rooms, train cars, street cars, buses, steamboats, prisons, and jails.

Of all the American laws, however, the Nazis were most fascinated by the blood-purity laws governing marriage. Americans had gone so far as to make interracial marriage a crime punishable by as many as ten years in prison in some jurisdictions.[20] Americans even continued the habit of Iberian imperialism by assigning humans to categories according to perceived ancestry, with even one drop of African blood designating them as black. While the "one-drop rule" was too harsh for the Nazis,[21] they announced the Law for the Protection of German Blood and German Honor during a Nuremberg rally in September 1935. Eventually known as the Blood Laws, this legislation distinguished Jews from the rest of the German population.

As the Nazis put into practice what they had learned by reviving old medieval resentments, enacting dehumanizing legislation, and building concentration camps, French Jesuit Henri de Lubac was working on his first book, *Catholicism*. Published in 1938, his work presented one theological attempt at disrupting the idolatry of blood and race. He recognized that both fascism and Marxism promised a response to one of the "deepest yearnings of our age," namely how to create human unity. Yet both ideologies failed, in de Lubac's estimation, because both dissolved the human individual into the social order.[22] Seeking alternatives, de Lubac returned

---

20. Wilkerson, *Caste*, 84.
21. Wilkerson, *Caste*, 88.
22. Henri de Lubac, *Catholicism: Christ and the Common Destiny of Man*, trans. Lancelot C. Sheppard and Sister Elizabeth Englund, OCD (Ignatius Press, 1988), 353.

to the early church to retrieve a vision of Christianity that was inherently social, while also preserving the dignity of the person. "Catholicism," he argued, "is essentially social. It is social in the deepest sense of the word: not merely in its applications to the field of natural institutions but first and foremost in itself, in the heart of its mystery, in the essence of its dogma."[23]

De Lubac began his text with the insight that the early church focused not so much on the formation of an individual person in the garden of Eden but rather concentrated on the creation and redemption of humanity as a whole. Every person created, from the first to the last, forms a single image of God. In this sense, the original sin is not pride but fragmentation. The original unity within humans, between humans, with the cosmos, and with God is shattered. From the perspective of the early church, the work of salvation is not limited to the recovery of supernatural unity between humanity and God but also includes the natural and spiritual unity between human persons. De Lubac recognized the ecclesial mark of catholicity in the early church's insistence that the work of redemption involves the reconciliation of all peoples. The early church fathers emphasized that horizontal redemption between people is both the condition and result of the vertical redemption between God and humanity.[24] Salvation is inherently social. The fundamental paradox for de Lubac, however, was that while salvation is worked out in the historical plane of existence, especially through the sacraments of the church, it is always incomplete and yearning for full completion in the transcendent.[25]

Given the serious fundamental theological crisis explored in section one, this profound soteriological retrieval and reorientation to the social has obvious implications for the redemptive work of healing required in the aftermath of racialized colonialism. While not explicitly anticolonial in the 1930s, de Lubac still recognized what he calls the "barbarous blindness" of European colonization. He claimed that "we can beat our breasts now at the pride in our machines and in our arms that has made us so unjust toward other races, at the narrowness of an education which, claiming to furnish us with a unique human culture, has shut us off from understanding the beautiful things that man had made in other parts of

---

23. De Lubac, *Catholicism*, 15.
24. De Lubac, *Catholicism*, 33–34.
25. Joseph Flipper, "Henri de Lubac and Political Theology," in *T&T Clark Companion to Henri de Lubac*, ed. Jordan Hillebert (T&T Clark, 2017), 421.

the world."²⁶ While he did not pursue the dehumanization of racist colonial logics in further detail, de Lubac's renewed soteriological vision of human unity was put to the test with the Nazi occupation of France from 1940 to 1944.²⁷

In her book, *Soldiers for God in a Secular World*, Sarah Shortall reveals how several theologians who would go on to become council fathers wielded theology as a powerful political tool in spiritual resistance to Nazi racism.²⁸ In a two-part lecture given in January 1941 entitled "The Theological Foundation of the Missions," de Lubac elaborated on a theological basis for antiracism in his contemporary context. With a sense of urgency, he insisted that there "is no work more necessary or greater than to work, through all the chaos and all the heartbreak of this world, to construct this" human unity that is constituted by a supernatural destiny that begins in time with God's call to the people of Israel. Joseph Flipper notes that the second part of this two-part lecture was censored and unpublished until 1946, because it was a more provocative critique of Nazi ideology. Racism, de Lubac argued, was a contemporary heresy that fundamentally opposed the common unity and common destiny of humanity.²⁹ Racism presents an idolatrous worship of power and blood that contradicts Christian soteriology at its very core.

In 1953, another future council father, Yves Congar, drew from de Lubac's soteriological retrieval to write a pamphlet for the United Nations entitled *The Catholic Church and the Race Question*. Having just emerged from the traumas of the Second World War and the Shoah, he defined racism as "a theoretical rationalization and so-called justification of racial prejudice" that "takes practical shape in certain more or less violent forms of discrimination."³⁰ Such views and practices are incompatible with the principles espoused by the Christian faith. Agreeing with de Lubac, Congar insists that what unites different peoples is their common origins and their common destiny. They share a common dignity that cannot be stratified by a system that determines who is more human or less human through

---

26. De Lubac, *Catholicism*, 293.
27. Flipper, "Henri de Lubac," 421.
28. Sarah Shortall, *Soldiers of God in a Secular World: Catholic Theology and Twentieth-Century French Politics* (Harvard University Press, 2021), 4.
29. Flipper, "Henri de Lubac," 423.
30. Yves M.-J. Congar, OP, *The Catholic Church and the Race Question* (UNESCO, 1953), 10.

the distorted logics of blood purity. If there is any "community of blood," he continues, such a community is not formed by one race over against another but "in the heritage of Redemption purchased by the blood of Christ."[31] Racism, therefore, attacks the heart of Christianity. Congar further notes that racial prejudice emerged during the sixteenth century with European colonialism and expansionism. For him, "there seems to be no doubt that racial prejudice is linked, in origin and development, with colonial imperialism."[32] Such "paternalistic condescension . . . cannot embody the full ideal of catholicity."[33]

Decades after the Second Vatican Council, Cardinal Joseph Ratzinger also drew from de Lubac's *Catholicism* when he stated that

> the essence of redemption is the mending of the shattered image of God, the union of the human race through and in the One who stands for all and in whom, as Paul says (Gal 3:28), all are one: Jesus Christ. . . . Union is redemption, for it is the realization of our likeness to God, the Three-in-One. But union with him is, accordingly, inseparable from and a consequence of our own unity. . . . Only when we see this clearly can we rightly understand the purpose of Vatican Council II, which, in all of its comments about the Church, was moving precisely in the direction of de Lubac's thought.[34]

John O'Malley likewise notes that while Gerard Philips was the principal author, it was "de Lubac's theological vision" that was "reflected in the form and substance of the key document of the council, *Lumen Gentium*."[35] His renewed soteriology is especially present in the paradigmatic statement of the opening paragraph of this Dogmatic Constitution on the Church: "The church, in Christ, is a sacrament—a sign and instrument, that is, of communion with God and of the unity of the entire human race."[36] *Gaudium et Spes*, the Pastoral Constitution on the Church in the Modern World, also states that "the council . . . can find no more

---

31. Congar, *The Catholic Church*, 21.
32. Congar, *The Catholic Church*, 35.
33. Congar, *The Catholic Church*, 40.
34. Cardinal Joseph Ratzinger, *Principles of Catholic Theology: Building Stones for a Fundamental Theology*, trans. Sr. Mary Frances McCarthy (Ignatius Press, 1987), 49–50.
35. John W. O'Malley, *What Happened at Vatican II* (Belknap Press, 2008), 119.
36. Second Vatican Council, Dogmatic Constitution on the Church *Lumen Gentium*, November 21, 1964, no. 1. All quotations of Vatican II documents are from Austin

eloquent expression of this people's [referring to the church, 'all of God's people, gathered together by Christ'] solidarity, respect and love for the whole human family, of which it forms a part, than to enter into dialogue with it in conversation about all these various problems, throwing the light of the Gospel on them and supplying humanity with the saving resources which the church has received from its founder under the promptings of the holy Spirit. It is the human person that is to be saved, human society which must be renewed."[37]

The idea of the church as sacrament is rooted in de Lubac's insight from *Catholicism* that "if Christ is the sacrament of God, the Church is for us the sacrament of Christ; she represents him, in the full and ancient meaning of the term: she really makes him present."[38] For Ratzinger, it is the sacramental nature of the church that allows it to become an instrument of unity, because it is only through the eucharistic communing of God with humanity that human beings are able to commune with one another. He believes that humanity needs "a communion that goes beyond that of the collective; a unity that reaches deep into the heart . . . and endures even in death. . . . A *communio* that offers less offers too little."[39] He critiques the generation that emerged after the council for transforming de Lubac's theology of catholicity into a political theology that only sought this worldly unity without deeper conversion. He repeats this sentiment in his foreword to the fiftieth-anniversary edition of *Catholicism*, where he argues that the narrow individualism that characterized Catholicism in the early part of the twentieth century had now been replaced not by de Lubac's social vision of the faith but by mere sociology.[40] Ratzinger argues that "without conversion, without a radical inner change in our thinking and being, we cannot draw closer to one another."[41]

Flannery, ed., *Vatican Council II: Constitutions, Decrees, Declarations; A Completely Revised Translation in Inclusive Language* (Liturgical Press, 2014).

37. Second Vatican Council, Pastoral Constitution on the Church in the Modern World *Gaudium et Spes*, December 7, 1965, no. 3 (hereafter, GS).

38. De Lubac, *Catholicism*, 76.

39. Ratzinger, *Principles*, 53.

40. Joseph Cardinal Ratzinger, "Foreword," in de Lubac, *Catholicism*, 12.

41. Ratzinger, *Principles*, 52.

Francis Sullivan offers a different interpretation on the conciliar passages mentioned above by recognizing a *double unity* by which the church is a "sacrament of *integral* salvation."[42] He further explains that the council's articulation of the salvation of the human person and the renewal of society reveals that "the church's saving mission is not limited to the eternal salvation of 'souls'" but has bearing on how we relate to one another rightly in this life.[43] In their discernment of the signs of the times, the council fathers considered five areas of human existence in need of redemption: family life, culture, economic and social life, politics, and the international order.[44] For Sullivan, on this side of the eschaton, the church must help people "achieve a truly human life" (GS 74). As a sacrament of integral salvation, as a sacrament of a fully human life, "the church is called upon to be a sign to the world of what a truly just society would be, and to work, with all the resources proper to it, to overcome the causes of injustice and to promote justice in the world."[45]

One important legacy of the council's renewed soteriology, which overcame the theological distortions that contributed to the Shoah, includes reversing centuries of supersessionism through the promulgation of *Nostra Aetate*. Like the theologians of *nouvelle théologie*, the council stressed the Jewish roots of Christianity and emphasized that both Jesus and the first disciples were Jews. The council underscored how the arrival of Christ did not revoke God's covenant with the Jewish people. This meant that Jewish people "should not be spoken of as rejected or accursed" by God, as traditional racist anti-Semitism maintained, since "the Jews remain very dear to God, for the sake of the patriarchs."[46] This led some commentators to hail the document as a "Copernican revolution in Catholic thinking about the Jewish religion and people."[47]

---

42. Francis A. Sullivan, *The Church We Believe In: One, Holy, Catholic, and Apostolic* (Paulist Press, 1988), 133.

43. Sullivan, *The Church We Believe In*, 135.

44. Ormond Rush, *The Vision of Vatican II* (Liturgical Press, 2019), 107.

45. Sullivan, *The Church We Believe In*, 133.

46. Second Vatican Council, Declaration on the Relation of the Church to Non-Christian Religions, *Nostra Aetate*, October 28, 1965, no. 4.

47. John Connelly, *From Enemy to Brother: The Revolution in Catholic Teaching on the Jews, 1933–1965* (Harvard University Press, 2012), 267.

Is a similar Copernican revolution in Catholic thinking, rooted in the insights of the early church, possible regarding the generational traumas of racist colonialism that result from distorted understandings of salvation? Is there a way to hold together *both* a sacramental understanding of de Lubac's theology of catholicity that ensures interior conversion *and* an understanding of integral salvation that seeks to redeem the relationships of the descendants of both the colonizers and the colonized around the same eucharistic table?

Catholic Antiracism as a Necessary Expression of Renewed Soteriology

In his 2020 encyclical, *Fratelli Tutti*, Pope Francis reminds us that "racism is a virus that quickly mutates and, instead of disappearing, goes into hiding, and lurks in waiting."[48] In fact, as recently as December 2023, a prominent US politician revived a blood-purity logic when he said that immigrants from Asia, Latin America, and Africa were poisoning the blood of the nation. Addressing the initial strains of this mutation as early as 2017, Joseph Flipper wrote an important article in *Commonweal* entitled "The Gods of Nation and Blood," which came in response to the "Unite the Right" rally in Charlottesville, North Carolina. He drew explicit parallels between de Lubac's spiritual resistance to Nazi racism and the urgent need for Catholics to resist rising sentiments of ethno-fascism. In 2020, after the tragic murder of George Floyd, Flipper further drew on de Lubac's work to emphasize not only that racism is America's original sin but that whiteness is an ecclesiological heresy.[49] The following paragraphs will first examine what is meant by "whiteness" and how this orientation to reality distorts ecclesial belonging. This section will then explore how the renewed soteriological framework of the Second Vatican Council necessitates conversion toward Catholic antiracism.

---

48. Pope Francis, Encyclical Letter *Fratelli Tutti*, October 3, 2020, no. 97, http://www.vatican.va/content/francesco/en/encyclicals/documents/papa-francesco_20201003_enciclica-fratelli-tutti.html (hereafter, FT).

49. Joseph S. Flipper, "Whiteness as an Ecclesiological Heresy," *Church Life Journal*, September 2, 2020, https://churchlifejournal.nd.edu/articles/whiteness-as-an-ecclesiological-heresy.

In his more recent book, *After Whiteness: An Education in Belonging*, Jennings argues that the anthropology of "white self-sufficient masculinity" that emerged from centuries of colonial blood-purity logics does not refer specifically to "people of European descent but to a way of being in the world and seeing the world that forms cognitive and affective structures able to seduce people into its habitation and its meaning making."[50] Whereas Johann Baptist Metz argued that the problem was bourgeois Christianity and Ratzinger initially claimed it was narrow-minded individualism, the historical underside of racist colonialism names whiteness as the dominating, controlling, anthropological distortion of the intimate possibility of *communio*. Whiteness—or access to whiteness—not Christ, becomes one's source of belonging. In this sense, whiteness "functions as an idol in precisely the way theologians describe idolatry: a finite reality is inflated to take the place of the unnamable, uncontrollable Ultimate within which truly 'we live and move and have our being.'"[51]

As an example of this heresy present in the historical record from enslavement to the present, M. Shawn Copeland elaborates on how the Catholic Church in the United States was racially formed, through national parishes of German, Irish, Italian, and Polish heritage, into the false stability of white supremacy that defined the dominant American culture.

> [The] hierarchy held (and holds) the interpretative and judicial power to justify geographic and spatial sequestering or segregation of black flesh and bodies. Their accommodation to anti-Black logics included the establishment of segregated parishes, schools, and, in some cases, cemeteries; the denial, exclusion, and prohibition of black bodies from religious vows and from priesthood; and the proscription of black religious expression, culture, and spirituality. Their accommodation to anti-Black logics not only contested Catholic teaching regarding the *imago dei*, that all human beings participate in the divine likeness, not only defied the effect of Baptism, but interrupted the power of Eucharist to collapse barriers of space and relation.[52]

---

50. Willie James Jennings, *After Whiteness: An Education in Belonging* (Eerdmans, 2020), 9.

51. Jon Nilson, "James Baldwin's Challenge to Catholic Theologians and the Church," *Theological Studies* 43 (2013): 890.

52. M. Shawn Copeland, "White Supremacy and the Anti-Black Logics in the Making of U.S. Catholicism," in *Anti-Blackness and Christian Ethics*, ed. Vincent Lloyd and Andrew Prevot (Orbis Books, 2017), 68–69.

Just as Congar had argued in 1953 that "such paternalistic condescension . . . cannot embody the full ideal of catholicity,"⁵³ he likewise stated decades later that racial segregation in the US church is a specific example of the contradiction between the church's renewed soteriology and its concrete practice. He argued that while there may be communion in terms of faith and liturgy, there is no trace of "sociological communion—what I would call an effective and concrete human communion."⁵⁴ Even if black and white Catholics receive Communion from the same altar, he argued, they often return to their separate pews without any recognition of the other.

Just as the council irreversibly changed Catholic teaching on relationships with the Jewish community, in such a way that it condemned all forms of racist anti-Semitism, Catholic teaching must likewise emphasize antiracist and decolonial principles as inherent to its way of life. This emphasis is not only a matter of ethical concern but part of the redemptive work of healing the fragmentation caused by distorted soteriologies that profoundly wound the possibility of lived *communio* within the Body of Christ. While de Lubac does not make this turn in his writing, Andrew Prevot argues that a critical and constructive reading of his work contributes toward an antiracist and decolonial understanding of the mystical Body of Christ.

Prevot foregrounds both *anthropological* and *cruciform* interpretations that contribute to living in right relationship in the aftermath of colonial trauma. First, he argues that the incarnation is a foundational event for human nature and therefore influences *every* human body.⁵⁵ While de Lubac locates this divine-human union in the church through the celebration of the Eucharist, he does not forget the more Athanasian view of the Christ-event by which God becomes human so that humanity may be drawn back to God. Prevot insists on locating the Eucharist within the larger event of the incarnation to prevent any temptation of treating non-Christians who do not have direct access to the Eucharist as less

---

53. Congar, *The Catholic Church*, 40.

54. Yves Congar, *I Believe in the Holy Spirit*, vol. 2, trans. David Smith (Herder & Herder, 1997), 21.

55. Andrew Prevot, "Mystical Bodies of Christ: Human, Crucified, and Beloved," in *Beyond the Doctrine of Man: Decolonial Visions of the Human,* ed. Joseph Drexler-Dreis and Kristien Justaert (Fordham University Press, 2020), 140.

human or less than human. He further draws on de Lubac's "groundbreaking reflections on the natural and the supernatural" to highlight how the "'supernatural' is not just a philosophical hypothesis but rather a shorthand way to speak about a free choice that God already reveals to humans in history—namely, a choice to love and adopt them in Christ."[56] The possibility of supernatural grace is not restricted to Christians alone but is a universal given.

However, because this stance remains too vague, Prevot proceeds in his argument from the anthropological to the cruciform by reflecting on crucified bodies and crucified peoples. Unlike the soteriological distortions espoused by the colonizers, the "doctrine that Christ takes into himself and radically identifies with each and every wounded body . . . enables Christian theology today to rediscover the true meaning of the gospel and rescue it from such violent distortion."[57] Ignacio Ellacuría, James Cone, and M. Shawn Copeland elaborate on this insight in antiracist and decolonial directions that contribute toward the healing of our fragmented relationships. Copeland, in particular, recognizes that while Christians often forget the victims of history, "there is one who does not forget—Jesus of Nazareth, who is the Christ of God. He does not forget the poor, dark, and despised bodies. For these, for all, for us, he gave his body in fidelity to the *basileia tou theou*, the reign of God, which opposes the reign of sin. Jesus of Nazareth is the paradigm of enfleshing freedom: he is freedom enfleshed."[58] Prevot makes clear that because the crucifixion itself is an evil, it is love and not suffering that redeems. God's love is "so great that Christ forever enters solidaristically into their suffering."[59] It is this insight that Jennings argues remains implicit within Zurara's tears at the dawn of European colonization but which gets lost in the distorted soteriologies that falsely justified the empire-building and death-dealing consumption of human blood, sweat, and tears. Eucharistic solidarity, Copeland argues, recognizes the real presence of Christ as the source from which his disciples can stand against the powers and

---

56. Prevot, "Mystical Bodies of Christ," 141, 142.
57. Prevot, "Mystical Bodies of Christ," 146.
58. M. Shawn Copeland, *Enfleshing Freedom, Body, Race, and Being* (Fortress Press, 2009), 53.
59. Prevot, "Mystical Bodies of Christ," 151.

principalities of this world—a world that continues to worship the idols of blood and nation.

I want to conclude by offering two biblical models that can help both the descendants of the colonized and the colonizers enter into eucharistic solidarity so that the church, as the Body of Christ who incorporates both for the sake of redeemed relationality, may live more fully into its vocation as a sign and instrument of unity with God and unity of the human race. First, in 2001, the National Black Catholic Clergy Caucus issued a statement to mark the five hundredth anniversary of the arrival of the first African slave to the new world in 1501. In this statement, they argue for a hemispheric rather than a national view of the racist colonial wound that harms our intimacy and communion as church. The Joseph of the Hebrew Scriptures was sold into slavery by his brothers. Brother turned against brother, the statement notes. However, because of Joseph's deep interiority and conviction in a saving God who can bring good out of evil, he is able to resist the temptation of revenge and instead forgive his brothers. It is Joseph—the one rejected and sold into slavery—who has the capacity to heal the family by pointing to a new way of belonging.[60]

Yet, to participate in this new belonging, the brothers who have committed wrong must also undergo their own arduous conversion. Steven J. Battin argues that the Damascus Christophany offers one such model. In the question "Saul, Saul, why do you persecute me?" (Acts 9:4), we have "the only event recorded for posterity that explicitly links intergroup reality, salvation, and the risen Christ in a specifically ecclesiologically significant way during the Christian community's formative years."[61] Through this narrative, one who has been caught up in cycles of violence against innocent victims encounters the resurrected Lord and comes to see that the ones whom he wished to stone, behead, and imprison were his own. It is because of this profound conversion experience that "Paul could speak of God reconciling the world in Christ."[62]

---

60. The National Black Catholic Clergy Caucus, "The National Black Catholic Clergy Caucus Statement on Racism: A Sankofa Observance of the 500th anniversary of the First Enslaved African to Enter the Western Hemisphere (1501–2001)" (2001), http://www.inaword.com/assets/sankofa.pdf.

61. Steven J. Battin, *Intercommunal Ecclesiology: The Church, Salvation, and Intergroup Conflict* (Cascade Books, 2022), 174.

62. Battin, *Intercommunal Ecclesiology,* 177.

Nearly two thousand years later, amidst the dehumanizing logics of Nazi racism, de Lubac would reflect on Paul's conversion in relation to "that tragic enmity, symbolic of so many others, between Jew and Gentile. Christ came to bring them unity and peace. He is himself this peace in person: *Pax* nostra. . . . It is by his blood that 'those who some time were afar off are made nigh'; it is his blood that will join together the two parts. . . . While his grace restores unity in each one of us, at the same time it reunites us all together."[63] While the Second Vatican Council did not explicitly acknowledge how the fragmenting logics of racist colonialism continue to harm the possibility of true belonging among different peoples, the renewed soteriology that informs the council promises the possibility that through the arduous work of conversion, descendants of the colonized and the colonizer may experience a lived "communion that goes beyond that of the collective; a unity that reaches deep into the heart . . . and endures even in death. . . . A *communio* that offers less offers too little."[64]

---

63. De Lubac, *Catholicism,* 42–43.
64. Ratzinger, *Principles,* 53.

Chapter 12

Conciliar, Postconciliar, and Postcolonial

Vatican II, Paul VI, and the Church in South Vietnam

Tuan Hoang

The intersections of the Second Vatican Council and the Vietnamese church have been a curious lacuna in the historical scholarship about both modern Vietnam and the council itself. One reason has been the focus on the Vietnam War in the scholarship about Catholics in the Republic of Vietnam. The council (1962–65) coincided with two turning points in the Vietnam War: the assassination of President Ngô Đình Diệm in 1963 and direct US military intervention in 1965. In historical accounts, political events have completely overshadowed ecclesial matters. An additional reason is the long-standing focus on the impact of Vatican II on Europe, North America, and, to a lesser extent, Latin America. Conciliar and postconciliar impact on Catholics in Asia and Africa has received much less attention.[1]

---

1. Reflecting the paucity of scholarship, Vatican II appears in none of major histories of Vietnam: e.g., Christopher Goscha, *Vietnam: A New History* (Basic Books, 2016). Important accounts of global Catholicism or global Christianity may include small portions about Vietnamese Catholics during colonialism or postwar Catholics in the diaspora, but they have virtually nothing on Catholics in South Vietnam: e.g., John T. McGreevy, *Catholicism: A Global Revolution from the French Revolution to Pope Francis* (Norton,

This lacuna is regrettable because studies of Vatican II's impact on a postcolonial country like Vietnam, where Catholics have been in the minority, may reveal important and surprising insights about the multiplicity of conciliar outcomes and the plurality of Catholic voices shaping those outcomes. More importantly, such an exploration might help illuminate the postcolonial foundation that has contributed to the rise of the global South as the center of Catholicism. European missionaries first arrived in Vietnam in the sixteenth century, and the church grew in spurts while suffering periodic waves of persecution over the next three centuries. After the last persecution in the 1880s, the church entered an era of consolidation and expansion. The first Vietnamese bishop was consecrated in 1933, marking the beginning of the end of Vietnam as a missionary church. After a successful anticolonial war against France, Vietnam was divided in 1954 into a communist north and an anticommunist south. The partition was intended to last for two years, but it went on for another nineteen years. In 1960, the Vatican established a national church in Vietnam. The northern church, however, lost a critical mass of laity and clergy moving south in 1954, and thereafter also endured severe restrictions imposed by the government. Its bishops were not allowed to travel outside of the country and could not attend any sessions of Vatican II.

In contrast, not only were the bishops from the south able to participate in the council, but the southern church as a whole rapidly became indigenized while remaining tightly connected to the global networks of Catholicism. A result was a steady growth of membership and institutions even during brutal warfare in the 1960s. Warfare usually hinders growth; in this case, however, the Catholic population grew from 1.45 million in 1963 to 1.8 million by the end of 1973. In the same period, the numbers of diocesan priests grew from 1,302 to 1,605 and religious priests from 383 to 425. Among professed religious, the numbers grew from 4,714 to 6,571 women and 973 to 1,309 men. In the sphere of education, the southern church ran 1,130 primary schools in 1973 that enrolled nearly 427,000 students and 270 secondary schools with over 205,000 students.[2]

2022); Thomas P. Rausch, SJ, *Global Catholicism: Profiles and Polarities* (Orbis Books, 2021); and Philip Jenkins, *The Next Christendom: The Coming of Global Christianity* (Oxford University Press, 2002).

2. These numbers come from *Annuarium Statisticum Ecclesiae/Statistical Yearbook of the Church/Annuaire Statistique de L'Eglise 1973* (Typis Polyglottis Vaticanis, 1975), 38,

Though incomplete, statistics indicate there was a steady growth in membership and institutions. The growth was generated by the enthusiasm among Vietnamese Catholics who sought to control their own destiny while partaking in the activities and institutions of the global church.

It is in this postcolonial context, disrupted by national division and warfare, that I interpret the reception of Vatican II among Catholics in South Vietnam. A short chapter cannot do justice to this topic. Therefore, I modestly seek to illustrate the positive reception of the conciliar and postconciliar spirit by examining two very different Catholic magazines in South Vietnam: a devotional monthly with a more conservative bent and a weekly with a more progressive outlook. I choose these magazines because their differences represent the diversity of the Catholic experience in South Vietnam but also because many more Catholics read them than, say, periodicals published specifically for the clergy or religious. Below, I provide the background about these magazines and their contributors, and explain their political orientation and their reception of the council. Lastly, I explain their interpretations of documents and statements issued by Pope Paul VI regarding war and peace on the one hand and, on the other hand, regarding justice and economic development in the third world.

This comparison shows that the magazines were considerably different in orientation and emphasis. Nonetheless, both warmly welcomed Vatican II and embraced its postconciliar call for renewal through a postcolonial and post-missionary prism. The comparison illustrates that Vatican II provided another venue for Vietnamese Catholics to engage in the construction of their postcolonial destiny, even when they disagreed among themselves about the specifics of that destiny. It shows, too, the closeness that Vietnamese Catholics felt toward the council and the pope, especially his pronouncements on war and peace. This is not to say that Vatican II and Paul VI gave answers to all their concerns and struggles. There were many areas where the council did not speak to the needs of the community, including a lack of statements about colonialism and racism. Yet these limits did not deter Catholics in South Vietnam from interpreting the conciliar spirit to match their postcolonial aspirations toward growth and expansion. Already empowered by the creation of the national church

---

100, 101, 167, and 151; and *Việt Nam Công Giáo Niên Giám 1964* [Catholic Vietnam Yearbook 1964] (Sacerdos, 1963), 505.

in 1960, they were further motivated by the conciliar and postconciliar calls for ecclesial renewal. With added vigor, they kept doing the work they had already begun before Vatican II and expanded the national church while dealing with warfare.

The Monthly *Our Lady's Immaculate Heart*

No periodical in the Catholic press of South Vietnam was more dedicated to promoting beliefs about Marian apparitions and miracles than the monthly *Our Lady's Immaculate Heart* (*Trái Tim Đức Mẹ*). The journal was initially published in the late 1940s in Hanoi by a Dominican missionary who, at the invitation of lay Vietnamese, began the Movement for the Reparation of the Immaculate Heart of Mary. Publication ceased during the First Indochina War but resumed as a monthly in 1960 under the auspices of the Congregation of Mother Co-Redemptrix (CMC). The CMC was one of few religious orders of men, and certainly the largest, founded by Vietnamese. Originating in a northern vicariate, the order's mission was to spread the devotion to Our Lady of Fatima. It received the local bishop's approval in 1948 and the Vatican's approval in 1953. It moved south the following year and resettled in suburban Saigon. Several years later, it received permission from the Dominican missionary to restart both the journal and the movement. Unlike established congregations with resources like the Dominicans and the Lasallians, the CMC was modest in institutions, activities, and education of its members. By promoting the Movement for the Reparation, however, it carved out a well-timed position in the southern church, which had already seen a vibrant associational culture mainly organized around Catholic Action and that included many Marian sodalities.[3]

For its entire run, *Our Lady's Immaculate Heart* was edited by a CMC priest who also headed the Movement for the Reparation. True to its mission, a typical issue included articles related to the Fatima apparitions and, more generally, Marian devotionalism in the history of the church. It serialized the testimonies of Sr. Lucia and reflections by others about the appari-

---

3. On Vietnamese Marianism, see Tuan Hoang, "'Our Lady's Immaculate Heart Will Prevail': Vietnamese Marianism and Anticommunism, 1940–1975," *Journal of Vietnamese Studies* 17, nos. 2–3 (2022): 126–57.

tions. There were features on Marian sites such as Fatima and Lourdes and news about pilgrimages and Marian associations in Vietnam and across the globe. Some issues included poems, songs, and short stories with Marian themes. The magazine published many petitions, thanksgivings, and testimonies of miracles attributed to the Blessed Virgin's intervening power. The focus on the miraculous, indeed, helped to draw mass appeal to the magazine and sustained its longevity from 1960 until the fall of Saigon fifteen years later. Responding to the growing popularity of Sacred Heart and eucharistic devotionalism at the time, the magazine also published articles about the history and practices of the Sacred Heart and the Eucharist, as well as news and features about national and global eucharistic congresses. Another dimension of its mission was to publish or summarize ecclesial documents, especially those with Marian content. There were articles, sometimes serialized, of more complex doctrinal and theological content, Marian and otherwise. Since the CMC was smaller than other major men's orders and did not have the financial resources to send its members to Europe or North America, the monthly invited clergy from outside of the order, especially Dominicans such as Hoàng Văn Đoàn, bishop of the Diocese of Qui Nhơn, who had been educated in Hong Kong and Paris, to write articles on church doctrines and ecclesial documents.

Given this background, it was entirely expected that the monthly seized upon conciliar statements about the Virgin Mary to support its belief and mission. It went so far as to call Vatican II a "Council of Our Lady."[4] All the same, the magazine proudly announced John XXIII's formal invitation to the Vietnamese bishops in 1962 to attend the first session of the council. Pope John was a hero to Vietnamese Catholics because he had formally established their national church two years before, a point

---

4. *Trái Tim Đức Mẹ* [Our Lady's Immaculate Heart], October 1965, 68. Like other South Vietnamese Catholic periodicals aimed primarily at the laity, *Our Lady's Immaculate Heart* published many articles in each issue but did not always show the names of the authors. This issue, for example, includes fourteen articles but only eight with an author's name. The other six articles, including one starting on p. 68, are unsigned. They were presumably written by the editors and staff. Authorial names appeared even less frequently on the pages of *Living the Faith*. The first issue (August 14, 1966), for instance, includes five articles with an author's name, three short articles and editorials with an indication of the journal's collective authorship, and eight unsigned articles. For this reason, citations of these periodicals include only the page number(s).

reinforced by the fact that the article about this invitation included a half-page portrait of the pope.[5] For the Vietnamese, the invitation was merely the latest manifestation of the Vatican's support for their national church, which went back to the turn of the century. The staff and readers were pleased by the fact that their native bishops were going to attend a global event while carrying the same status as bishops from ancestral lands of Catholicism. The journal celebrated the bishops by providing much coverage of their participation. For example, in the journal's initial report of the council's first session, the magazine highlighted the names of three bishops from South Vietnam who rose to speak at three different meetings. While readers likely did not know that bishops from Europe and North America did most of the speaking at the council, it probably would not have mattered, because the right of their native leaders to speak was much more important.[6]

Over the next several years, *Our Lady's Immaculate Heart* frequently reported and commented on the council's preparation and proceedings regarding Mary. Before the first session, an article quoted a French bishop who rhetorically asked, "Will Our Lady be absent at the council?" It offered the bishop's proactive response that invoked both the doctrines of the immaculate conception and Mary's ascension to heaven, as well as miracles at Lourdes, Fatima, and other modern sites of apparitions. More than once, it pointed out that the opening date of the council was the Feast of the Maternity of the Blessed Virgin. The journal argued that there could be no doubt about Mary's importance at the council. This claim was supported by a letter from Rome written by Bishop Hoàng Văn Đoàn, who reported that John XXIII announced Mary as protector of the council as well as supporter of the bishops and laity.[7]

Most notable was the monthly's coverage of the third session, which culminated in the promulgation of *Lumen Gentium*, the Dogmatic Constitution on the Church. The magazine expressed relief that Paul VI signaled a pro-Marian position after pre-session rumors about a potential contentious debate on Mary. Following the promulgation of *Lumen Gentium*, it published a summary of the pontiff's homily at the closing Mass

---

5. *Trái Tim Đức Mẹ*, April 1962, 258–59.

6. *Trái Tim Đức Mẹ*, December 1962/January 1963, 187–90. Generally, many bishops from Latin America were also quiet in the general congregations at Vatican II.

7. *Trái Tim Đức Mẹ*, July 1962, 354–56; and December 1962/January 1963, 161.

and praised him for having ensured that the document devoted a full chapter about Mary's place in the church. Six months after the promulgation, it published a translation of the entire chapter.[8] The following year, it began a series called "Learning about Chapter Eight of *Lumen gentium*." Interestingly, the magazine only occasionally referenced this conciliar document outside of this feature. It was already heavily publishing on Marianism, and it took *Lumen Gentium* to be another piece of armor, albeit a significant piece, in the landscape of devotionalism. It conveniently ignored, for example, the fact that the theologically ambiguous concept "co-redemptrix," which served as part of the CMC's name, received no mention whatsoever in conciliar documents.[9] Instead, the magazine focused on Pope Paul's postconciliar homilies and speeches about the Virgin Mary and cited them in many places.

Our Lady's Immaculate Heart showed its esteem for the conciliar leader as much as it did the council. As it had honored John XXIII, it called Paul VI the "Pope of *caritas*" upon his ascension to the papacy. Reflecting the experience of being a minority religion in a non-Christian country, the monthly was highly positive about his ecumenical outlook. Consistent with its belief in reparation, the monthly went out of its way to invite its readers to follow Paul's "urgent call" to pray, fast, and do "acts of reparation" for the success of the council.[10] Notably, the magazine widely reported on Paul VI's statements and prayers for peace in Vietnam. When it introduced a papal letter to the Vietnamese bishops about peace, the magazine prefaced it with another papal message from two days earlier about world peace. Even when Paul VI did not specifically name Vietnam, the magazine often took his statements about peace, such as one made upon papal blessing of yellow roses to be sent to Fatima, to have "implied the painful situation of the Vietnamese people" at the time.[11] Shortly after the pope issued the encyclical *Christi Matri*, calling the faithful to pray the rosary for peace, especially in Vietnam, the monthly and its Movement for the

---

8. *Trái Tim Đức Mẹ*, November 1964, 112; January–February 1965, 162–64; and May 1965, 296–306.

9. The concept grew further from mainstream theological discourse following the end of the council. In 2017, the Vatican successfully requested that the CMC change its name to the Congregation of the Mother of the Redeemer (CMR).

10. *Trái Tim Đức Mẹ*, August 1963, 6–8; August 1963, 21–24; and December 1963, 131.

11. *Trái Tim Đức Mẹ*, April 1965, 259–61; and May 1965, 289.

Reparation joined six other Marian organizations, including the Legion of Mary and the Blue Army of Fatima, in a retreat about the encyclical. The retreat was led by an auxiliary bishop of Saigon and the national director of Catholic Action. It resulted in a resolution of five parts, including "a complete appreciation for the Holy Father Paul VI" and a determination to "sanctify individuals, families, and society according to the Gospels and the directions of the Second Vatican Council."[12] Not all of *Our Lady's Immaculate Heart*'s publications about Paul VI had to do with Mary, but it customarily referenced the Blessed Mother to papal documents on peace in order to reinforce its core mission.

The postconciliar emphasis on war and peace, however, should not be seen apart from the postcolonial vision of *Our Lady's Immaculate Heart*, the Movement for the Reparation, the CMC, and similar organizations. For them, the Virgin Mary as patroness of Vietnam symbolized the belief that one could be both Catholic *and* Vietnamese, which was a counter-proposition to allegations by anti-Catholic Vietnamese that their only allegiance was to the Roman pontiff. Equally important, they believed that a truly independent Vietnam must be free of Vietnamese communists because communism was the real antithesis to nationalism. Although they were not undisturbed by aspects of the American military presence, they considered it to be a temporary measure in the fight against Vietnamese communism, which was against organized religion and, specifically, Christianity. Some of this postcolonial conviction was rooted in the long history of anti-Christian persecution by Vietnamese authorities, and some was grounded in the recent history of the communist revolution following World War II that led to brutal warfare. Although their affection for the papacy and, especially, Paul VI was strong and consistent, they never took ecclesial documents and papal speeches or homilies about peace to mean yielding to the communists. If anything, they saw Pope Paul's documents about peace and documents about Mary to be of one piece. They engaged in selective reading of those documents and statements, including his blessings on the Movement for the Reparation, as reinforcements of their Fatima-inspired belief about Russia and interna-

---

12. *Trái Tim Đức Mẹ*, November 1966, 105. This encyclical was issued on September 15, 1966, in anticipation of the traditional practice of praying the rosary during October. Its references to "parts of eastern Asia where a bloody and hard-fought war is raging" left no doubt that Paul VI meant the Vietnam War.

tional communism.[13] For the most part, they might report on Paul VI's friendly gestures toward accommodation, but they never stopped interpreting his pronouncements on the Virgin Mary as being in opposition to atheism and communism. For the CMC and their popular monthly, the Pope's desire for peace in Vietnam reflected the desire of Vietnamese Catholics. But the magazine's consistent advocacy against communism also meant that peace could only come after North Vietnam and the communist insurgents in the south stopped waging war.

The Weekly *Living the Faith*

In the fall of 1966, *Our Lady's Immaculate Heart* published a brief notice that the weekly *Living the Faith* (*Sống Đạo*) had recently resumed publication. The devotional magazine called the staff and writers at the weekly a group of Catholics "knowledgeable of important issues of the Church and the present" and having "the aspiration of *living the faith in society*." The notice ended by wishing the staff at the weekly to "be LIVING well in the FAITH."[14]

The good wish sounds remarkable in retrospect, because the orientation of *Living the Faith* was on the opposite side of the ecclesial/theological spectrum from *Our Lady's Immaculate Heart*. The weekly was not critical of devotionalism, but its contents were decidedly short on promoting devotions, Our Lady of Fatima or otherwise. It opposed communism, but it also opposed capitalism while being open to dialogue between Catholics and communists. The more accommodating orientation was among the reasons that the weekly, which had first published between June 1962 and January 1964 and then resumed publication in August 1966, encountered censorship by the government. Its second run continued until early 1968, when it permanently closed after the Tet Offensive. *Living the Faith* had carefully avoided confrontational tones and contents during its first run by sticking closely to theological matters. But its second run, which is examined here, was sharp in tone and diverse in content, especially regarding political issues. It was quickly deemed controversial by government authorities as well as the national Catholic community.

---

13. *Trái Tim Đức Mẹ*, July 1965, 374.
14. *Trái Tim Đức Mẹ*, October 1966, 95. Both emphases are in the original.

The weekly was not unfriendly to *Our Lady's Immaculate Heart*. In an article about Vietnamese Catholics, *Living the Faith* singled out the devotional monthly as one of two popular Catholic journals that promoted Marian devotionalism while "raising contemporary issues."[15] The weekly, however, was primarily focused on contemporary issues. It frequently criticized US military intervention that kept South Vietnam dependent on a foreign power. It wanted to shift from the discourse regarding communism supported by northern Catholics who had moved south in 1954, including the CMC. By the weekly's second run, Vatican II had been completed and its documents were already translated and studied by contributors. As a result, writers of the second run of *Living the Faith* made many references to the council. "We were formed," declared the journal, "by laborers of body and laborers of intellect . . . to help usher in the strong wind of the Pentecost and the reforming spirit of Vatican II."[16]

The staff and contributors to *Living the Faith*, both clergy and laity, came from educated segments of the Vietnamese church. Many had studied abroad and received degrees in economics, engineering, law, medicine, political science, philosophy, and theology.[17] Many directly participated in a second wave of Catholics traveling to Europe for university and graduate education. The first wave began in 1919 with a small number of priests and seminarians. It had the support of the Vatican's policies of turning missionary lands into national churches. The second wave took place during the 1940s and 1950s, when a growing number of the clergy and laity, including contributors to *Living the Faith*, studied at Rome, Paris, Louvain, and institutions in the United States and Canada.[18] In addition, some contributors were also members of the Vietnamese chapter of Pax Romana, an international lay organization consisting of two movements

---

15. *Sống Đạo* [Living the Faith], November 15, 1966, 7. The other journal, Đức Mẹ Hằng Cứu Giúp [Our Lady of Perpetual Help], was published by the Redemptorists.

16. *Sống Đạo*, September 3, 1966, 7.

17. Ngô Quốc Đông, "Hoạt Động Chính Trị của Nhóm Trí Thức Công Giáo Cấp Tiến tại Miền Nam trước Năm 1975" [Political Activities of Progressive Catholic Intellectuals in South Vietnam before 1975], *Nghiên Cứu Tôn Giáo* [Religious Studies] 8, no. 224 (2022): 33–35.

18. Clare Thi Liên Trân, "The Role of Education Mobilities and Transnational Networks in the Building of a Modern Vietnamese Catholic Elite (1920s–1950s)," *Sojourn: Journal of Social Issues in Southeast Asia* 35, no. 2 (2020): 243–70.

of university and graduate students. As part of Catholic Action, the Pax Romana chapter in South Vietnam was small but energetic. In 1962 and 1963, for example, it organized two week-long retreats among Catholic intellectuals with the Archdiocese of Saigon's blessing. The first retreat took the theme of Catholics and their faith; the second, Catholic conscience and social justice.[19] It also sent delegations to international gatherings such as the Pax Romana conference in 1966 in Belfast on the theme of "freedom and responsibility of the laity after the council." Upon returning to South Vietnam, the lead delegate met with Catholic student groups for Mass and sharing the experience and ideas of the conference.[20]

This background helps to explain *Living the Faith*'s orientation. The weekly, however, was neither a Pax Romana mouthpiece nor an intellectual periodical. Its physical format of an eight-page (later four-page) newspaper-size spread resembled a daily newspaper, and it addressed political, economic, and social issues rather than theology. Yet it insisted on a theological perspective or motivation for its coverage rooted in the conciliar spirit of change and openness. The last two sessions of Vatican II took place when the weekly was out of circulation, and its resumption of publication was emboldened by an official call at the highest level of the council for engagement with the world. Signaling this spirit, the front page of the first issue in 1966 shows the globe with faces from different continents above three large headlines: "Catholicism and Communism in Yugoslavia," "A Catholic Church in a Buddhist Neighborhood," and "Divorce from Madame Censor." If the last line poked fun at governmental censorship, the others reflected conciliar concerns on atheism and interreligious relations.[21]

The topic of Catholic-communist relations was indeed among the periodical's priorities. On the one hand, *Living the Faith* published a number of reports, usually pulled from longer publications elsewhere,

---

19. Selected presentations at those retreats were published in *Người Công Giáo trước Vấn Đề Đức Tin* [Catholics in Regard to the Issue of Faith] (Đạo và Đời, 1962); and *Lương Tâm Công Giáo và Công Bằng Xã Hội* [Catholic Conscience and Social Justice] (Nam Sơn, 1963).

20. *Sống Đạo*, August 14, 1966, 4.

21. *Sống Đạo*, August 14, 1966, 1; August 21, 1966, 4; and August 28, 1966, 5. Although Vatican II decided to leave out the term *communism* in conciliar documents, *Gaudium et Spes* includes three chapters on atheism, with chapter 20 the closest in naming communism.

about discrimination and oppression directed at "the silent church" in North Vietnam. In some localities, for example, lay Catholics, were forced to attend "reeducation" sessions and encouraged to denounce priests for having committed counterrevolutionary crimes or even for having come from families of landlords. While the faithful suffered the most in rural areas, urban Catholics also faced discrimination as the government confiscated many church properties. The weekly also published articles about the persecution of Catholics outside of Vietnam, in places like China and Eastern Europe. It offered favorable pieces about new diplomatic agreements reached between Tito and the Holy See. It argued that the Soviet Union had been "oppressive" against religion after the Bolshevik Revolution but had sought better relations with the church since John XXIII's pontificate.[22] The weekly endorsed the Vatican's *ostpolitik* as an appropriate strategy in the postconciliar era.

Related to Catholic-communist relations were the issues of war and peace. Like *Our Lady's Immaculate Heart*, the weekly found support in Paul VI's letters, speeches, and other statements about the Vietnam War. Its interpretation, however, diverged from the Marian monthly's. *Living the Faith* believed that the destructiveness of warfare absolutely demanded the need for peace talks. At the end of 1966, the weekly reprinted a declaration by eleven progressive priests, including several of its contributors, that began by evoking Pope Paul's urgent call for peace. The authors declared their "dissatisfaction" with the conflict that pitched Vietnamese against one another while "deepening dependence on foreign countries." They called on "the superpowers to respect the self-determination of Vietnamese" and for "the governments of the North and the South to shake hands and talk about peace." The following year, *Living the Faith* commented on Francis Spellman, archbishop of New York and apostolic vicar of the US military, who had stated during a visit to South Vietnam that a victory over the communists would be the "only resolution" of the war. The weekly argued that Spellman's position was "not on par with the Holy See" and "contrary to the Pope's directives on peace." Two months later, it adopted the position of the eleven priests in a "declaration of the *Living the Faith* group."[23]

---

22. *Sống Đạo*, September 18, 1966, 5; October 15, 1967, 1; and August 21, 1966, 7.
23. *Sống Đạo*, December 4, 1966, 3; January 4, 1967, 1; and March 3, 1967, 1, 4.

The weekly's declaration came out of its conviction that a postcolonial Vietnam could not depend on American military presence in South Vietnam, or armed support to North Vietnam from China and the Soviet Union. This conviction led it to counter the dominant anticommunist view of Our Lady of Fatima with a rare article "written by a priest" without revealing his name. The article argued that the "Mother of the Savior not only denounces sin but also loves sinners" and accused pro-war devotees of Fatima of an inability to make a distinction about sin and sinners. The article agreed with the dominant interpretation that the Fatima message required the faithful to pray for Russia and the communists. But it argued that the message was also a call for conversion of "immoralities" among individuals and within society, especially economic and social injustice that had led to the appeal of communism in the first place.[24] This reasoning was unlikely to persuade devotees of Our Lady of Fatima, but it was an articulation of *Living the Faith*'s view on social justice. A similar point could be made about the weekly's perspective on war. The weekly typically evoked Paul VI rather than conciliar documents for theological justification. At the same time, it frequently called upon the conciliar "spirit" when arguing about economic, political, and social matters. This orientation could be spotted even in a report about the encyclical *Christi Matrii*. Even though both encyclical and report focused on the Vietnam War, the report noted that the pope also wrote about "developing countries and difficulties among oppressed and divided nations."[25]

The weekly took Latin America as an inspiration, maybe even a model, for the Vietnamese church. It was "not communism but Christianity," declares a headline, that served as "the hope of Latin America."[26] The spark for *Living the Faith*'s interest in Latin America was the bishops who spoke up for the poor and marginalized. It reported, for example, on the Latin American and Caribbean Episcopal Conference's advocacy for land reform. It singled out the Brazilian clergy, especially bishops in the impoverished northeast and Dominican friars, for having openly opposed the ruling military dictatorship's economic and political policies that harmed poor people. It quoted a Dominican superior in São Paulo for declaring that "we are not in politics but until death we oppose the injustices of the

---

24. *Sống Đạo*, February 5, 1967, 4.
25. *Sống Đạo*, September 25, 1966, 5.
26. *Sống Đạo*, November 6, 1966, 7.

Brazilian government."[27] The weekly was notably enthralled by Hélder Câmara, archbishop of Olinda and Recife, praising him for protesting economic policies on behalf of laborers and peasants. It quoted him arguing that the church must "awaken" the consciousness of the poor toward learning and action.[28] *Living the Faith* also went beyond Latin Americans, citing, for example, Stefan Wyszyński, the primate of Poland known for his confrontational attitude toward communist authorities, that communism continued to exist because of endemic poverty.[29]

The advocacy for economic justice grew deeper after the promulgation of Paul VI's encyclical *Populorum Progressio* in March 1967.[30] The magazine published articles on the document in almost all its weekly issues between April and July. The issues in April, for instance, introduced the encyclical, published excerpts, provided a two-part commentary on the front page, and reported on its reception among major Western media.[31] A two-day conference on the encyclical took place in Saigon during the first week of June, and the weekly reported that about three hundred people attended, mostly Catholics but also some Buddhist monks, intellectuals, and university students.[32] It later serialized the opening lecture given by Fr. Chân Tín, a leading progressive Redemptorist in the southern church. The speaker fleshed out different sections in the encyclical, pointed out its continuity with earlier social teachings of the church, and argued that the document shifted from an emphasis on the individual to an emphasis on the national. Its conclusion included a quotation from Archbishop Câmara attacking "capitalist groups" that perpetuated the accumulation of wealth and materialism.[33] Such an emphasis prioritized anticapitalist critique over anticommunism, especially the aggressive anticommunism of conservative voices such as *Our Lady's Immaculate Heart*.

---

27. *Sống Đạo*, August 2, 1967, 4; August 21, 1966, 4.

28. *Sống Đạo*, September 18, 1966, 7; and December 4, 1966, 3.

29. *Sống Đạo*, August 21, 1966, 5.

30. An analysis of the encyclical's background and initial reception is Mari Rapela Heidt, "Development, Nations, and 'The Signs of the Times': The Historical Context of *Populorum Progressio*," *Journal of Moral Theology* 6, no. 1 (2017): 1–20.

31. *Sống Đạo*, April 16, 1967, 1; and April 23, 1967, 1. Most were liberal periodicals expressing a positive opinion. The report singled out the "capitalist" *Wall Street Journal* for an expected judgment of the encyclical to be "Marxist in a religious form."

32. *Sống Đạo*, June 11, 1967, 1, 4.

33. *Sống Đạo*, July 16, 1967, 3.

Conclusion

The comparison above focuses on several differences between two popular magazines because I seek to demonstrate the diversity of perspectives among Vietnamese Catholics. The differences, however, should not obscure important affinities between them. The fact that Christianity remained a minority religion in Vietnam led different Catholic groups to voice support for one another and maintain a relatively civil tone. On conciliar and postconciliar matters, both magazines seized upon Vatican II's emphatic call for an integral involvement of the laity in the daily life of the church. This common response came out of their energetic experience of Catholic Action that flourished since its beginning in the 1930s. Still, another example is the universal appreciation for conciliar documents regarding the use of the vernacular in the liturgy. In particular, Vatican II took place during the golden age of Vietnamese liturgical music that saw a proliferation of new hymns and masses. The laity and the clergy, including staff and writers at both magazines, welcomed the employment of their native language in all major aspects of ecclesial life. Such commonalities could be discerned in many other Catholic periodicals in the southern church, both popular and specialized.

The most significant commonality, perhaps, was the fact that different groups *positively* responded to the council and its aftermath. *Very* positively at that. This development diverged from the responses in western Europe and North America, where Catholics were divided over conciliar and postconciliar outcomes. It was not only a division between traditionalists, conservatives, and liberals, but there was further division within each group.[34] In comparison, the postcolonial Vietnamese church was far less contentious, even if it was not always free of internal complications and disagreements. It was also united in pursuing strategies of growth. Vietnamese bishops and superiors, for example, took advantage of ecclesial global educational networks and sent a number of seminarians and religious to study in Belgium, France, Switzerland, Canada, and the US. A further example is the way Catholic Action organizations worked closely with priests and bishops and organized pilgrimages in order to further internal cohesion. To these ongoing postcolonial dynamics, Vatican II became a major window for Vietnamese Catholics to integrate

---

34. See McGreevy, *Catholicism*, 327–51; and Stephen Bullivant, *Mass Exodus: Catholic Disaffiliation in Britain and America Since Vatican II* (Oxford University Press, 2019).

themselves further into the global church. They might have emphasized different matters, but their reactions to the council were highly and consistently positive. They found the conciliar spirit to be a powerful justification for growing their church during a new era of their history.

From this perspective, two related points may emerge from the analysis of *Our Lady's Immaculate Heart* and *Living the Faith*. First, the comparison should alert us to the importance of studying internal debates among postcolonial churches, even among those with a relatively small population of Catholics like South Vietnam. A close reading of these magazines confirms that postcolonial Catholics often diverged on political priorities, especially when politics involved the intervention of a superpower like the United States. One group's sense of what the church should do might very well differ from the sense of another group. Such divergences, however, did not hinder or preclude institutional growth. Indeed, they might have been necessary for overall institutional growth, because these divergences motivated different groups of Catholics to pursue a multiplicity of goals rather than the same ones. An emphasis on social justice was certainly different from an emphasis on anticommunist devotionalism. Yet for the postcolonial church in South Vietnam, both could coexist— and did. It may be too far to assume that the coexistence of different agendas and programs led directly to the growth of schools, priests, religious, and seminarians as noted at the beginning of this chapter. But the growth was real, and it might very well have benefitted from a diversity of opinions and orientations among Catholics in South Vietnam.

Secondly, while the African and Asian bishops were quiet at Vatican II, it was the engagement of their flocks following the council that played a central role in the *longue durée* of demographic shift and the explosive growth of Catholics at the same time that the church in Europe and North America went into a decline. Nonetheless, lay engagement might have happened differently had it not been for the presence of native African and Asian bishops, quiet though they were, at the council. As seen from the reports published in *Our Lady's Immaculate Heart*, the fact that the bishops sat among European and American ones lent substantial encouragement and support to different Catholic groups partaking in the construction of a postcolonial church. Postcolonial Vietnamese Catholics might have had disagreements about the priorities that their national church should take at a given moment, but they were united in appreciating the presence of their native bishops at the council. Representation mattered—and it mattered most at a postcolonial moment that empowered Vietnamese Catholics into further action regarding evangelization and institutional expansion. Keenly aware that they had a lot to do to "catch up" with the larger and older European church, postcolonial Vietnamese used all the motivation that they could find. The participation of many of their bishops at Vatican II provided massive motivation for further action, not only during the Vietnam War but also among Vietnamese refugees in the diaspora since 1975.

In the end, it behooves scholars to be more attentive to the historical relationship between Vatican II and the making of modern Catholicism in the global South. Decolonization has been cited and studied as a major reason for this shift.[35] Less conceptualized are the intersections between Vatican II and newly independent countries, and how the intersections might have contributed to the growth in subsequent decades.[36] The evidence presented in this chapter indicates a similar trajectory about the Vietnamese bishops and their flocks, who took Vatican II as the central landmark on their postcolonial roadmap and as the justification for the expansion of their church. Ten years after the council, of course, the Vietnam War itself ended and led to a long period of severe restriction and discrimination under a totalitarian regime. So strong, however, was their postconciliar engagement that during the last twenty years, the church, now under an authoritarian government, has entered a new phase of growth. In addition, tens of thousands of Catholics became refugees after the war and resettled in the United States. They have since integrated into ecclesial life in their new country while supporting the church in Vietnam, which, in turn, has begun to send its seminarians, priests, and religious to study and work in the US.[37] The limits of Vatican II were many, including an absence of pronouncements on racism and colonialism. Yet the

---

35. A recent example is Elizabeth A. Foster and Udi Greenberg, eds., *Decolonization and the Remaking of Christianity* (University of Pennsylvania Press, 2023).

36. For a recent example about such a connection, see Agbonkhianmeghe E. Orobator, SJ, "The Impact, Reception, and Implementation of Vatican II in Africa," in *The Oxford Handbook of Vatican II*, ed. Catherine E. Clifford and Massimo Faggioli (Oxford University Press, 2023), 657–75. See also Elizabeth A. Foster, *African Catholic: Decolonization and the Transformation of the Church* (Harvard University Press, 2019), 257–72.

37. See Tuan Hoang, "Ultramontanism, Nationalism, and the Fall of Saigon: Historicizing the Vietnamese American Catholic Experience," *American Catholic Studies* 130, no. 1 (2019): 1–36.

council also offered an enormous opportunity for Catholics in South Vietnam to engage themselves and the global church, and furthered a momentum toward expansion even during destructive warfare.

Chapter 13

Vatican II and Caste in Postcolonial India

Brahminization of the Catholic Church or Catholicization of Brahminical Power?

Evgeniia Muzychenko

This paper examines the reception of the reforms of the Second Vatican Council in Catholic dioceses in postindependence India. Vatican II aimed to foster a dialogue between the church and humanity, striving to meet the needs of Catholic communities within their unique cultural, social, and political contexts. In India, this call led the church to champion social justice, including the fight against caste oppression. Despite the official condemnation of caste discrimination by the Catholic Church in India, the reforms of Vatican II frequently failed to adequately tackle caste oppression, primarily due to shortcomings in the inculturation of the liturgy. An elite Catholic priesthood adapted the liturgy along the lines of Brahminical, high-caste culture, disregarding the fact that many of those cultural forms were alienating to the Catholics from unprivileged castes. By observing cases in a number of diocesan churches in India, this paper will argue that Vatican II reforms overlooked caste disparities and the cultural differences that reinforced caste. While Vatican II promoted the adaptation of liturgical practices to the cultural context of different peoples, it did not account for how certain cultural forms would result in marginalization rather than inclusion of the laity in the church. The lack of clear guidelines on inculturation allowed high-caste Catholic priests to use liturgical reforms to marginalize non-elite members of the laity. Manipulating the reforms, high-caste priests appropriated discourses that reinforced their elite status as well as their religious authority. This paper looks at two such discourses. The first, on Brahminization, describes the way priests affirmed their own superiority based on Indian caste and gender norms. The second, on Catholicization, refers to the reliance of Indian priests on the authority of the Vatican.

After a brief discussion of the terms *Brahminization* and *Catholicization*, the paper will explain the relationship between the inculturation reforms in post-Vatican II churches and the caste system in India. It then explores two case studies of post-Vatican II Roman Catholic communities in India. The first case examines the priestly condemnation of accounts of female Marian possession in Tamil Nadu, described in Kristin Bloomer's *Possessed by the Virgin: Hinduism, Roman Catholicism, and Marian Possession in South India*. The second case explores language reforms led by Catholic elites in Goa, with the help of Jason Keith Fernandes's study, *Citizenship in a Caste Polity: Religion, Language and Belonging in Goa*. Focusing on the two case studies—one in Tamil Nadu, one in Goa—the paper illustrates how the teaching of Vatican II, despite clashing with the heteropatriarchal norms and caste-based discourses of Indian secular modernity, was nonetheless employed by Catholic priests in India to maintain their privileged status.

Terminology: Brahminization and Catholicization

Brahminization derives from *brahmin*—the term designating a person from the highest caste in India. From the standpoint of textual tradition, caste[38] is rooted in the concept of *dharma*, the Hindu principle of cosmic

---

38. While the term *caste* (*casta*) was introduced by the Portuguese colonizers in the fifteenth century to identify traditional social hierarchy in India, in the Hindu scriptures, the name for the fourfold division of Indian society is known as "chatur-varna" (four-varnas) and includes Brahmins (the most elite varna), Kshatriyas, Vaishyas, and Shudras (the most unprivileged) varna. It also indicates a category of those outside any varna—the untouchables, also known under the modern term *Dalits*. To avoid the exclusion of Dalits using the term *varna*, contemporary scholarship uses the term *caste* to speak of the traditional social hierarchy in India.

harmony that assigns to each being a certain place and duty to perform. Codified in ancient Hindu Brahminical[39] scriptures, *dharma* served to produce and regulate the moral order in society. In practice, the moral order is maintained through what has been called the caste system. The caste structure is hierarchical; it is reinforced through the notions of ritual purity and pollution as well as through gender norms. Since caste is also denoted by professional division, its boundaries, especially in postindependence India, are socially controlled by secular bodies such as governmental, cultural, and educational institutions.[40] As a social unit, caste permeates boundaries of religion, including the non-Indic religions such as Christianity and Islam. Religious norms and practices, promoted in institutions such as the Catholic Church, also act as a tool of reinforcing caste. In post-Vatican II churches, the priesthood of high-caste origin Brahminized the liturgy through the adoption of Sanskritic semiotic forms that included the readings from Vedas, rituals, garments, and postures.

Along with Brahminizing the liturgy, priests used Catholicized rhetoric to condemn the popular religion practiced by the laity from the unprivileged castes. Catholicization discourse involved an appeal by the priests to the authority of the Vatican (including the Vatican II reforms), as its standard for doctrine and practice, in order to justify their exclusive priestly power. Indian Catholic priests capitalized on their role as Vatican representatives, condemning "unauthorized" popular practices such as healing or female spirit possessions, and other vernacular forms of worship, widely practiced among the Catholics from lower-caste backgrounds.

Inculturation and Caste after Vatican II

Before the Second Vatican Council, the practices that reinforced caste divisions (such as separate seating arrangements for lower- and higher-caste laity, denying Communion to unprivileged groups) were a frequent

---

39. By *Hindu Brahminical*, I indicate the institutional form of Hinduism that primarily emphasizes the teachings of the Vedas, the classical texts of the Hindu tradition. I contrast it to popular Hinduism. This binary is explained below in detail.

40. On reinforcement of caste in church and secular institutions, see Sonja Thomas, *Privileged Minorities: Syrian Christianity, Gender, and Minority Rights in Postcolonial India* (University of Washington Press, 2018); Jason Keith Fernandes, *Citizenship in a Caste Polity: Religion, Language and Belonging in Goa* (Orient BlackSwan/New India Foundation, 2020).

practice in many Catholic churches in India. Vatican II's centering of human dignity and explicit condemnation of all forms of discrimination provided a platform for a potential shift in discriminatory caste practices in the church. Suhas Pereira notes that since Vatican II, the Indian Catholic Church "has committed itself anew to the social cause in India."[41] The Pastoral Constitution on the Church in the Modern World, *Gaudium et Spes*, stressed respect for human dignity and human rights as the foundation for building a just society.[42] For the Indian church, one of the major challenges in moving toward justice has been the oppressive structure of the caste system. Shortly after the council, in 1969, the Catholic Bishops' Conference of India (CBCI) gathered to discuss the question of caste oppression. The CBCI statement expressed commitment toward establishing a new Indian society that does not tolerate discrimination: "It is not only a denial of human dignity and equality, but also against the fundamental teaching of Christ who was friend of outcasts of His time. And freely mixed with them [*sic*]. He came to tell humankind that we are brothers and sisters having God as common Father."[43] In official statements, the Indian Catholic bishops condemned caste as dehumanizing and incompatible with the Gospel message. However, in practice, caste-based discrimination continued to exist within the church.[44] Notwithstanding the prohibition of caste-based discrimination by law in India, the caste mindset continued to define social relationships.[45] While the concept of caste originated in the Hindu scriptures, caste also signified a social unit that incorporated everyone in Indian society regardless of religion. As caste relationships pervade religious boundaries, conversion to Christianity does not help those from unprivileged castes escape oppression. Quoting M. R. Arularaj, Pereira writes that "for an Indian, a Dalit is a Dalit, whether Christian or not."[46]

---

41. Suhas Pereira, *The Challenges of Vatican II for an Authentic Indian Catholic Church* (LIT, 2021), 215.

42. See Second Vatican Council, Pastoral Constitution on the Church in the Modern World *Gaudium et Spes*, December 7, 1965, no. 27.

43. Catholic Bishops' Conference of India, *Final Statements of the General Body Meeting of CBCI 1962–2002* (CBCI Centre, 2003), 99–100, quoted in Pereira, *The Challenges of Vatican II*, 203.

44. Pereira, *The Challenges of Vatican II*, 192.

45. Pereira, *The Challenges of Vatican II*, 189.

46. Pereira, *The Challenges of Vatican II*, 189.

One of the reasons that caste oppression persists in the church is that caste can manifest itself subtly through culture. While Vatican II recognized the importance of liturgical inculturation, the postconciliar reforms brought a range of questions regarding the relationship between faith, religious institutions, and culture.[47] The Constitution on the Sacred Liturgy, *Sacrosanctum Concilium*, issues a general call to make the liturgy accessible to the faithful, acknowledging the diversity of cultures: "Even in the liturgy the Church does not wish to impose a rigid uniformity in matters which do not involve the faith or the good of the whole community."[48] Later, the document specifically mentions former "mission lands" and recognizes the need for applying local culture and traditions to the liturgy (SC 119). Indian bishops at the council, stressing the urgency of inculturation for the Indian church, spoke of the importance of preparing priests and the need for a shift in seminarian education.[49] Less attention, however, was paid to the role of inculturation for the Catholic laity. During the council's first session, Indian archbishop Eugene D'Souza raised concerns about the relevance of the Catholic rite of marriage for people living in rural areas. D'Souza was concerned that following the church ceremony, some couples would perform their local marriage custom, which suggested the need for adapting the existing liturgical life to the spiritual needs of the locals.[50] However, D'Souza's remark was a singular instance of problematizing the social heterogeneity of the Catholic laity in India.

Following Vatican II, the bishops of India met to discuss ways in which the church could be renewed by bringing the liturgy "close to the Indian culture and religious traditions."[51] Given that the determination of what defines the Indian style of worship rested with the Catholic elites, the

---

47. Xavier Gravend-Tirole, "From Christian Ashrams to Dalit Theology—or Beyond? An Examination of the Indigenisation/Inculturation Trend within the Indian Catholic Church," in *Constructing Indian Christianities: Culture, Conversion, and Caste*, ed. Chad M. Bauman and Richard Fox Young (Routledge India, 2014), 115.

48. Second Vatican Council, Constitution on the Liturgy *Sacrosanctum Concilium*, December 4, 1963, no. 37 (hereafter, SC). All quotations of Vatican II documents are from Austin Flannery, ed., *Vatican Council II: Constitutions, Decrees, Declarations; A Completely Revised Translation in Inclusive Language* (Liturgical Press, 2014).

49. Paul Pulikkan, *Indian Church at Vatican II: A Historico-Theological Study of the Indian Participation in the Second Vatican Council* (Maryamatha Publications, 2001), 243.

50. Pulikkan, *Indian Church at Vatican II*, 241.

51. Pereira, *The Challenges of Vatican II*, 225.

process of inculturation in India led to the incorporation of liturgical elements rooted in high-caste Brahminical traditions, neglecting to consider the broader community participating in the liturgical celebrations.[52] Paul Collins provides examples of reforms, such as the use of phraseology from sacred Hindu texts such as the Vedas and the Upanishads in the anaphora of the Mass.[53] Since the majority of Catholic laity were unfamiliar with the Vedas or Upanishads, the enhancement of the rite with cultural references from Brahminical Hinduism, especially from the texts in Sanskrit, did not bear any meaning for them.[54] In addition, the Indian Catholic Mass adopted the practices, symbols, and objects that were "typical of Indian religious tradition."[55] One example of this adaptation was the greeting of the presiding priest with a tray of flowers and a small lighted lamp, a ritual used in *puja* (worship) at Hindu temples. Another notable change was the offering of *aarti* (a form of worship involving light or incense) in front of the Communion table. Other modifications included the style of prayer, with some hymns and prayers being performed in the style of Indian devotional singing (*bhajan*) accompanied by instruments such as drums and cymbals.[56] In Pereira's view, those changes affected only the outer image of worship, which rendered inculturation peripheral and superficial. Commenting on the cultural reforms of the Indian liturgy, Paul Pulikkan notes that "the [lay] Christians often failed to respond to the true meaning of the Eucharist" since "religious practice often failed to touch [Indian Christians'] social, economic and professional life."[57]

While the liturgy underwent a number of changes, those cultural shifts did not always carry deep theological meaning for the laity. Since the reforms were introduced by the elite priesthood of Brahmin origin, their vision of what could provide for a meaningful form of worship did not

---

52. Pereira, *The Challenges of Vatican II*, 227.

53. Paul M. Collins, "Culture, Worship, and Power: A Case Study for South India," in *Church and Religious "Other,"* ed. Gerard Mannion, Ecclesiological Investigations (T&T Clark, 2011), 64.

54. Pereira notes that the Catholic Church in India has 25 million members, of which 70 percent are Dalits (the most unprivileged caste) and only 30 percent are from higher castes. Pereira, *The Challenges of Vatican II*, 189.

55. Pereira, *The Challenges of Vatican II*, 227.

56. Collins, "Culture, Worship, and Power," 65.

57. Pulikkan, *Indian Church at Vatican II*, 443.

always align with the worldview and practices of the laity from the unprivileged castes. The extent to which the priests were cognizant or ignorant of this cultural gap remains outside the purview of this paper. However, integral to the discussion is that the priests intentionally discouraged the laity from practicing popular, non-Brahminical forms of worship. In many post-Vatican II diocesan churches, the priests actively critiqued and sometimes even condemned popular forms of devotion that were meaningful to the congregation. For non-elite lay Christians, the popular forms of devotion are relevant since they are rooted in local, non-Sanskritic forms of worship,[58] some of which are different from the institutional, or Brahminical, forms of worship.[59] The Brahminical culture relies on Sanskritic semiotic forms and emphasizes priests as indispensable mediators of religious experience. The popular culture of less privileged castes, on the other hand, emphasizes unmediated interaction with the divine, the miracle-working power of divinities, and practices such as healing and exorcism. Following Vatican II's call for inculturation, the Catholic churches in India were authorized to adapt the liturgy to the cultural context of India. However, instead of engaging with the cultural forms that were important for the Catholics from non-elite castes (which constituted the overwhelming majority within congregations), local Catholic leaders opted for Brahminical forms that they deemed appropriate for the liturgy. David Mosse, studying popular Catholicism in postcolonial Tamil Nadu, draws attention to the way in which Dalit theologians repudiate the postconciliar "Indianization" of the church, on the grounds that the adoption of Sanskritic semiotic forms (postures, rituals, dress, readings of Hindu scriptures) represents an act of "Brahminic cultural domination."[60] The problem is not merely the imposition of certain high-caste practices (Brahminization) but also the priestly discouragement of

---

58. Kristin Bloomer warns against viewing non-Brahminical and Brahminical Hinduisms in binary terms. Kristin C. Boomer, *Possessed by the Virgin: Hinduism, Roman Catholicism, and Marian Possession in South India* (Oxford University Press, 2018), 256n78.

59. Mosse notes that "what the orientalists codified as the Hindu religion, included the 'authentic' Brahminical scriptural tradition and the 'inauthentic' popular tradition, in its 'imperfect' relationship to the scriptural tradition." David Mosse, *The Saint in the Banyan Tree: Christianity and Caste Society in India*, The Anthropology of Christianity 14 (University of California Press, 2012), 9.

60. Mosse, *The Saint in the Banyan Tree*, 24.

popular preconciliar forms of worship (Catholicization). Examining Catholicism in rural Tamil Nadu in the 1980s, where the vast majority of Catholic priests were upper caste,[61] Mosse observes that parish priests deemphasized popular devotion practices, suppressing exorcism cults they deemed as "backward, uncouth, and superstitious."[62]

Brahminization of Liturgical Language in Goa

As Vatican II advocated for contextual forms of worship, it promoted inculturation not merely along the lines of ritual but also along the lines of language: "A suitable place may be allotted to the vernacular in Masses which are celebrated with the people, especially in the readings and 'the common prayer,' and also, as local conditions may warrant, in those parts which pertain to the people" (SC 54). While Vatican II envisioned the turn to the vernacular to be "of very great help to the people" (SC 63), in a number of Catholic churches in India, the language of worship became a site of caste oppression. In his book *Citizenship in a Caste Polity: Religion, Language and Belonging in Goa*, Jason Fernandes describes how high-caste Catholic priests in Goa manipulated the postconciliar liturgical reform to impose Antruzi—a Brahminical dialect of Konkani—as the exclusive liturgical language in Catholic churches.

About 25 percent of the Goan population are Christians—a number explained by the fact that, for more than four hundred years, Goa was a Portuguese colony. In Portuguese Goa, the Catholic Church had played an official role in the state mechanism, but when Goa became part of independent India in 1961, the postcolonial political establishment began to view the Catholic hierarchy with suspicion.[63] The new Indian government modeled itself as a secular, modern country, challenging the special privilege accorded to Catholic elites. However, the vernacular reforms of Vatican II provided the context for the priests' "legitimization."

While Catholic priests, due to their Brahminical origin, enjoyed high privilege in society and had access to power in Goa, their status was still ambivalent, since they were Christians and not Hindus. In independent

---

61. Mosse, *The Saint in the Banyan Tree*, 126.
62. Mosse, *The Saint in the Banyan Tree*, 91.
63. Fernandes, *Citizenship in a Caste Polity*, 155.

India, a high-caste Hindu male embodied the ideal image of a citizen. This image was related to the Indian secular-nationalist notion of Aryanness, which aligned national allegiances to one's ability to embody Aryan Sanskritic culture—not merely in terms of being a Hindu but also in terms of speaking the "properly" Indian language. Ideally, that language was Hindi, although other Indo-Aryan languages also fulfilled that function. Catholic Brahmins of Goa capitalized on this notion to promote their Brahminical heritage through their ties to Konkani, an Indo-Aryan language that socially codified the Catholic elites as modern (read "Sanskritic") citizens.[64]

The liturgical vernacularization reforms took place in the context of a broader language movement led by Catholic elites in the state of Goa. In the 1960s, Catholic Brahmins launched a movement to make Konkani the official language of Goa. They wanted to implement Konkani in a particular form, recognizing it in the Nigari script and, associated with it, the Antruzi dialect as the official form of the language. The Nagari script made Konkani nearer to the standards of Indian modernity and politically legitimized Catholic elites as "Sanskritic." However, officializing this dialect over other forms of Konkani spoken in Goa marginalized those who spoke in other dialects of Konkani and used the Roman script instead of the Nagari script. This form of marginalization through language reform was also evident in the church. From the 1960s through the 1980s, the desire to modernize facilitated the shift from Latin to Konkani as the liturgical language in the Catholic Churches in Goa. This change was enabled by the reforms of Vatican II. As Fernandes notes, the new concept of inculturation in the church proclaimed that "gospel values" had to be incarnated in local cultures.[65] The problem with the shift to Konkani was that the priests "purified" the liturgical Konkani from the Portuguese accretions that had become ingrained in everyday speech over generations.[66] For the proponents of Indian secular modernity, as elite Catholic priests were, Portuguese words, as well as the Roman script, were a legacy of a colonial past that was now considered an "impure" and "uncivilized" form of the language.[67] For non-elite Catholics, to whom the use of Portuguese words was authentic, implementations of such liturgical reform were twofold. First, the reform denied

---

64. Fernandes, *Citizenship in a Caste Polity*, 118.
65. Fernandes, *Citizenship in a Caste Polity*, 155.
66. Fernandes, *Citizenship in a Caste Polity*, 155.
67. Fernandes, *Citizenship in a Caste Polity*, 97.

Portuguese as a cultural form that may be meaningful and authentic to non-elite Catholics. Second, Sanskrit was not spoken or understood by non-elite Catholic laity, and therefore, this way of vernacularizing liturgy was not facilitating the needs of the majority in the church. Implementing a "purified" form of Konkani in liturgy added to the marginalization of non-elite Catholics that was underway through the movement of standardizing Konkani in Antruzi form and Nagari script. When Antruzi Konkani became the official language of Goa in 1987 (largely due to the effort of the elite Catholic priests), non-elite Catholics were denied agency not only as believers but also as citizens: Konkani in the Roman script was not accepted and did not receive governmental support in education, professional institutions, or cultural production. By legitimizing a particular way of worship, Catholic priests furthered the marginalization of non-elite laity both within the church and beyond its walls.

Priestly Critique of Female Marian Possession

The church's concerns for social inequality inevitably raised the issue of women's rights. The Indian bishops emphasized women's emancipation and actively supported charitable activities that protected women's rights and aided women's empowerment. However, despite governmental policy and the church's efforts, gender oppression remained a steadfast issue in Indian society. Persisting heteropatriarchal gender norms continued to define the status of women as subordinate. The exclusion of women from ordination in the Catholic Church was only one of many ways that perpetuated this subordination. Reflecting on the Indian Catholic Church's role in supporting women, Pereira notes that "the Church needs to reflect on getting rid of patriarchal attitudes in order to create free space for women to come ahead and come up in the Church."[68] Regina Heyder, commenting on the conciliar texts as well as John XXIII's 1963 encyclical, *Pacem in Terris*, notes that while Vatican II contributed to promoting women's emancipation in society, it did not account for doing the same for lay women's participation in the church.[69]

---

68. Pereira, *The Challenges of Vatican II*, 216.
69. Regina Heyder, "Women and the Council: Catholic Women's Organizations and Women Theologians Prior to and During Vatican II," in *The Oxford Handbook of Vatican II*, ed. Catherine E. Clifford and Massimo Faggioli (Oxford University Press, 2023), 327.

Intersecting with caste, the conciliar stance on women made the church a site of lower-caste women's oppression by Catholic clergy. Kristin Bloomer, writing about women's experiences of Marian possession in charismatic churches in Tamil Nadu, observes a pattern of priestly condemnation of female religious agency. In her book *Possessed by the Virgin*, Bloomer features the experiences of the three Tamil women from charismatic Catholic churches—Nancy, Rosalind, and Dhanam—who claimed to be possessed by the Virgin Mary. In the Tamil culture, spirit possessions are commonly understood as a source of power, since possessed individuals are frequently known for their healing ability. As Bloomer reports, middle- and lower-caste Christians and Hindus sought out healing and blessing from these possessed women, who were empowered in a radical way by this possession. Experiencing their bodies controlled not by heteropatriarchal gender norms but by the spirit of the Virgin Mary, they embraced a new social role in a space other than their household. Those women gained spiritual authority among lay people within their communities, but the particular way in which they claimed that authority prompted severe critique from local priests.

Local Catholic priests from the diocesan churches, appealing to the authority of the Vatican, to Scripture, and to canon law, condemned these female experiences of possession experiences. These possessed women not only broke from the dominant Catholic tradition of male-exclusive spiritual authority but also challenged heteropatriarchal gender norms. Bloomer describes the reaction of Rev. Fr. Ambrose, parish priest of Our Lady of Fatima Church in Kodambakkam, Chennai (Tamil Nadu), to the experience of possession by Nancy, a woman from Our Lady Jecintho Prayer House (located in Muthamizh Nagar, another part of Chennai): "People believe, and they go for the favors, but the Church doesn't approve. Church authorities in general teach us not to encourage such beliefs. This genuinity [sic] of Our Lady [i.e., Mary] coming into a human person is a question. Even the Holy Spirit is not so easy."[70] In his critique, Fr. Ambrose attacked the idea that Mary's spirit would enter into a human—much less a human *woman*: "Mary is so great, she can't be so cheap as to come onto a human woman."[71] For the pastor, Nancy's possession experience was unauthorized by church authorities and thus was

---

70. Bloomer, *Possessed by the Virgin*, 104.
71. Bloomer, *Possessed by the Virgin*, 105.

unacceptable. He also denied that the Virgin Mary could use a female body as a medium.

Another priest, Fr. Thomas, criticized the same woman: "I personally don't believe that Mother Mary can come in such a way, and take possession of a lady like this. . . . The first thing Mary gives is a message to the bishop, or a priest." Fr. Thomas then listed the signs that Mary had given to church authorities at Marian shrines throughout the world: Lourdes, Guadalupe, Fatima, Velankanni. He continued, "My strongest conviction is that Mother Mary will not go into the church against the priest or against the bishop. . . . The mere fact that they are ready to disobey, they are ready to go against the church, in spite of instruction—it is not Mary's work."[72]

It is important to emphasize that these critiques were not solely rooted in heteropatriarchal attitudes but also involved the rejection of practices influenced by Tamil popular culture. Bloomer describes an instance in which Fr. Thomas demanded an end to the sacred chariot processions that were held at an annual festival of the Virgin Mary's birth. Those chariot festivals were modeled on eighteen-century chariot processions led by Catholic Paravas[73]—the communities from the most marginalized caste group. These processions had important significance for Catholic Paravas, as the practice served the function of asserting their social power, which was essential given their disadvantaged background. Bloomer notes that the present chariot processions, too, were about social power.[74] The Marian chariot processions usually involved the celebration of Mass on the street, which was contrary to the Catholic convention of celebrating the Mass inside a church building. Fr. Thomas prohibited the Mass at the Marian festival, claiming that the only Mass that could be celebrated was the one inside the parish church.[75] After the festival Mass was celebrated, despite his prohibition, Fr. Thomas reported the priest who celebrated the Mass to the bishop's commission, which led to the reassignment of that priest to a different community. Still, a celebration occurred, but due to the orders of their archbishop, the sermons were offered in the context of the Eucharist, the church's central liturgical celebration. As Bloomer

---

72. Bloomer, *Possessed by the Virgin*, 113.
73. Catholic Paravas, in turn, took the tradition of chariot procession from a Tamil Hindu practice, so chariot processions were a popular practice shared by Hindus and Catholics.
74. Bloomer, *Possessed by the Virgin*, 110.
75. Bloomer, *Possessed by the Virgin*, 112.

notes, according to the priestly logic, the absence of the eucharistic liturgy rendered sermons, "in Vatican-speak, simply messages."[76]

Attempting to secure their exclusive authority, some diocesan priests employed the rhetoric of obedience. Bloomer interviewed another Catholic priest, Fr. Chinnappa, who saw claims of Marian possessions as an act of disobedience to the church. The priest referred to the authority of the Bible to underline the importance of many kinds of obedience: "Obedience to the parents. Obedience to the teacher. Obedience to the statutes of any institution. . . . Obedience to the ministers of the head of the College of Minister. . . . Obedience in the religious community, to the superior, and the institutions of the congregation. So you cannot do away with obedience. When we obey God, He blesses us."[77]

Such instances of priestly rhetoric should not be read purely in terms of priests' reliance on Vatican authority in matters of religion. The priests' continued references to the tradition, Scripture, and hierarchical order become an instrument of securing their role as the single and unchallenged source of authority. Catholicization of caste discourse became another priestly instrument for reinforcing caste divisions. It was a more subtle form of oppression, allowing high-caste clergy to avoid the language of caste, substituting it with the terms from Catholic Christianity. It was their Catholic position of priestly power, as well as the prestige of their caste, that allowed high-caste priests to manipulate Catholic theology in a way that turned the church into a source of oppression rather than liberation.

Concluding Observations

While the council addressed justice and inculturation, it overlooked the contexts in which culture and injustice intersect. Exploring the discourses and practices of Catholic priests in postindependence India demonstrates the complex reception of Vatican II's call for inculturation. The Indian Catholic bishops' official commitment to fighting caste oppression did not prevent subtle forms of oppression perpetuated by the application of heteropatriarchal attitudes to liturgical reforms that reinscribed the

76. Bloomer, *Possessed by the Virgin*, 114.
77. Bloomer, *Possessed by the Virgin*, 120.

privileges of high-caste priests. As an elite priesthood took charge of postconciliar adaptation, the liturgy in many Catholic churches took the form of Brahminical, elite worship, which was alienating to the majority of lay Catholics. The incorporation of texts and semiotic forms from Sanskrit was not relevant to the laity coming from unprivileged backgrounds and unprivileged castes. Catholic priests, relying on both their high-caste status and their church authority, reinforced caste boundaries between themselves and the lay Catholics they were called to serve.

In many Catholic churches in India, Brahminization of the liturgy contributed to consolidating caste boundaries between the priesthood and laity. Reform of liturgical Konkani, as in the case with the Goan priests, also demonstrated how the discourse of secular modernity pushed the Catholic priests to "Brahminize" the transition to the vernacular, adopting an elite form of the local language not spoken by lower caste groups. The priestly discourses and practices were marked not only by coloring the liturgy with Brahminical cultural elements, but also by "Catholicizing" the existing caste and gender divisions. Clerical critique of Marian possessions demonstrates that priests were concerned not merely with guarding the spiritual realm but also with gatekeeping their power and authority, as caste and heteropatriarchal norms prescribe. The priests' appeal to the Vatican served as a reaffirmation of what was already present in Indian society, namely, caste and gender norms that circumscribe power and authority to the elite, male minority. In doctrinal terms, the authority of the Vatican takes on the role of *dharma*—the guiding moral principle that maintains the limits and potential of human agency.

One question to ask is whether the Catholic Church in India, as an institution, is "Catholicizing" the existing caste hierarchy, giving to the Brahminical authority an extra tool to maintain its domination over the unprivileged castes, or whether Catholic priests are "Brahminizing" their power, relying on caste and gender norms that have historically defined social relationships in Indian society. The cases discussed above demonstrate that the "Catholicizing" of high-caste power and the "Brahminizing" of the Catholic priesthood in postcolonial India are two cross-pollinating processes that sustain each other. These intertwined processes create a feedback loop, where religious and broader social authority reinforce each other, making it difficult to distinguish between them. This reciprocal reinforcement not only consolidates the power of high-caste priests but also perpetuates the exclusion of marginalized groups from both religious and social participation. Understanding this dynamic is crucial for any efforts aimed at genuine reform and inclusivity within the church.

Chapter 14

Vatican II and the African Catholic Church

A Decolonial Critique

William I. Orbih

Introduction

Vatican II took place during the most important decade in modern African history. While there were thirty-three independent countries in Africa at the start of the council on October 11, 1962, by 1965, that number had increased to thirty-eight. By the end of the decade, only sixteen of the presently fifty-four independent African countries remained under colonial rule. The presence of native bishops from these newly independent countries of Africa (and Asia), even though their numbers were relatively small, contributed to making Vatican II, in the words of Karl Rahner, "the Church's first official self-actualization *as* a world Church."[1] For the first time, Guiseppe Ruggieri explains, "the main actor at the Council was a body of bishops drawn from the whole world and not just a group of European bishops exported round the world in the form of European missionary bishops."[2] Not only is Vatican II the most global and ecumenical of the twenty-one councils in the history of the Catholic

---

1. Karl Rahner, "Towards a Fundamental Theological Interpretation of Vatican II," *Theological Studies* 40, no. 4 (1979): 717.
2. Guiseppe Ruggieri, "Vatican II as Church Enacted," *Concilium* 3 (2012): 36.

Church, but it is also the first council that was open to observers from other Christian denominations and even to the curious world press.

Although Vatican II, like all previous councils, was overwhelmingly dominated by the European church, the participation of these newly evangelized churches, represented by both European missionaries and native bishops, was quite significant.[3] However, far more significant than the influence of non-European bishops on the council's deliberations and outcomes is the impact the council has had on the non-European Catholic world since its closing.[4] From an African perspective, Clement Majawa describes Vatican II as "the greatest moment of meaningful re-discovery, re-defining, experiencing permanent conversion, renewal and seeking for true African-Christian identity, deeper evangelization, quality progress and universal commissioning of the Church in Africa."[5] Like most African theologians who have spoken about Vatican II, Majawa believes the African Catholic Church benefited immensely from the council. "Conflicting perspectives aside," insists Agbonkhianmeghe E. Orobator, "the positive impulse released by Vatican II for the Church in Africa is beyond dispute."[6] According to him, "it laid the foundation for the emergence and existence of a truly local African Church and continues to inspire contextualized theological production."[7] In an earlier article, Orobator celebrates how "since Vatican II, the church in Africa has discovered its public role, vocation, and mission in the socio-economic and political arena."[8]

---

3. A 2019 article by Chris Stackaruk explores ways non-Western participants at Vatican II shaped *Nostra Aetate*, which he describes as the council's "benchmark document." See Stackaruk, "The Impact of Non-Western Participants at Vatican II," *Toronto Journal of Theology* 35, no. 1 (2019): 40–49.

4. See Edward H. Peters, ed., *De Ecclesia: The Constitution of the Church of Vatican II* (Deus Books, 1965), 14. Writing as early as 1965, Butler notes that one crucial accomplishment of Vatican II that has made it as influential as it has been for the global church is its transformation of the church into "a Church with great elasticity and adaptability."

5. Clement Majawa, "African Christianity in the Post-Vatican II Era," in *Routledge Companion to Christianity in Africa*, ed. Elias Kifon Bongmba (Routledge, 2015), 214.

6. Agbonkhianmeghe E. Orobator, "The Impact, Reception and Implementation of Vatican II in Africa," in *The Oxford Handbook of Vatican II*, ed. Catherine E. Clifford and Massimo Faggioli (Oxford University Press, 2023), 668.

7. Orobator, "The Impact," 674.

8. Agbonkhianmeghe E. Orobator, "Looking Back to the Future: Transformative Impulses of Vatican II for African Catholicism," *Concilium* 3 (2012): 98.

Acknowledging the undeniable impact of Vatican II on the African church does not preclude the urgent need for a decolonial critique of Vatican II as a historical event, the African church's participation at the council, and the growth of the African church since the council's conclusion. One aim of this study is to critically evaluate the growth of the Catholic Church in Africa over the past sixty years, moving beyond what Stan Chu Ilo bemoans as a "triumphalist picture of African Catholicism" that equates population growth with "authentic and prophetic witness."[9] If the desire is for an African Catholic Church that is both authentically Catholic and prophetically active in the politics of modern Africa, in keeping with the "spirit" of Vatican II, then it is essential to subject both the council and the continent's participation to a decolonial critique.[10] The goal is, firstly, to expose and firmly repudiate any lingering manifestations of colonial hegemony within the African church and, secondly, to identify seeds of resistance already present in the African church before and during Vatican II and to analyze how watering these seeds can contribute to the emergence of a truly African church.

In other words, while African theologians are right to commend Vatican II for inspiring the remarkable growth of the church in Africa over the past six decades, it is also crucial to recognize that the African Catholic Church, in many respects, still reflects the ecclesial structure of its colonial past.[11] For the African church to truly become an agent of social transformation on the continent, it must urgently disentangle itself from what scholars decry as the colonial power matrix.[12] Only by doing

---

9. See Stan Chu Ilo, "General Introduction," in *Handbook of African Catholicism*, ed. Stan Chu Ilo (Orbis Books, 2022), xxii–xxiii.

10. Since Vatican II, the 1994 and 2009 synods of African bishops remain the two events of the highest significance in relation to the church in Africa. The apostolic exhortations *Ecclesia in Africa* and *Africae Munus* that emerged from these synods emphasized the need for greater inculturation, with the telos being a church in Africa that is authentically African and truly Catholic.

11. See Elochukwu E. Uzukwu, *A Listening Church: Autonomy and Communion in African Churches* (Orbis Books, 1996), 59. According to Uzukwu, "politically speaking," the Catholic Church in Africa is "clearly under colonial administration."

12. See Sabelo J. Ndlovu-Gatsheni, *Coloniality of Power in Postcolonial Africa: Myths of Decolonization* (Council for the Development of Social Science Research in Africa, 2013), 4–7. Ndlovu-Gatsheni defines the colonial matrix of power as "a complete package with social, economic, cultural, ideological, aesthetic and epistemological contours that

so, Emmanuel Katongole argues, will the African church begin to contribute meaningfully to "the search for a new future in Africa" and cease to mimic, mirror, perform, and perpetuate dominant patterns of its colonial history.[13]

An African Catholic Church on the Eve of Vatican II

St. Peter Catholic Church in Ferdinand Oyono's novel *Houseboy*, set in colonial Cameroon, is segregated.[14] The whites sit in comfortable velvet-covered cane armchairs in the transept beside the altar, while the black natives sit on tree trunks instead of benches in the nave.[15] Whereas in the European section, men and women sit shoulder to shoulder, the central aisle separates men from women in the African section. The natives and the Europeans also receive Communion separately, with the latter, who sit closest to the altar, going first. After Mass, the Europeans leave first, through the sacristy. The Africans are detained for a while as a sermon is preached to them in the vernacular.[16]

Oyono's account of the fictional St. Peter's Catholic Church captures truths that nonfictional accounts of the history of the Catholic Church in colonial Africa neglect or ignore. In Oyono's novel, Father Vandermayer, the European pastor of the Catholic Church, was an active member of the European Club of Dangan. Membership in the club is reserved only for the white community in Dangan, which includes missionaries from different Christian denominations, colonial administrators and actors, and their families.[17] Often in the club, the subject of discussion by the white-only members is the morality and cognitive ability of native Africans.[18] In addition to verbal abuse, physical violence against black

---

combined to reduce, silence, dominate, oppress, exploit and overshadow the non-Western world."

13. Emmanuel Katongole, *The Sacrifice of Africa: A Political Theology for Africa* (Eerdmans, 2009), 47–48.

14. Ferdinand Oyono, *Houseboy*, trans. John Reed (Waveland Press, 2012 [1956]).

15. Oyono, *Houseboy*, 33–34.

16. Oyono, *Houseboy*, 14.

17. Oyono, *Houseboy*, 48.

18. Oyono, *Houseboy*, 52.

bodies is a constant feature in the novel. Witnessing this brutality both within the church and in the larger society throws Toundi Ondoua, the narrative voice in the novel, into a crisis of faith: "Is the white man's neighbor only other white men? Who can go on believing the stuff we are served up in the churches when things happen like I saw today . . ."[19]

This scandalous violence that threatens Ondoua's nascent and naïve faith was a manifestation of the power of the Catholic Church in Dangan, wielded chiefly by its white members, and which in turn was derived from its close association with the colonial state. The European missionaries embodied or, at the very least, actively collaborated with the civilizing agenda of the colonial administrator and the wider European society to which they belonged. Jesse K. N. Mugambi argues that "Generally, the ideological position of missionary society was pro-empire since they were imperial instruments for the civilization of the natives."[20] Their mission theory and practice were shaped by soteriological fervor for the souls of black folks and the sociological assumption of the superiority of Europe's culture and civilization.

A recent study by Mark Shaw and Wanjiru M. Gitau highlights how missionaries were often very critical of colonialism's abuses and brutalities and far more respectful of African culture, religions, and autonomy than the colonial administrators. It also notes that the missionaries supported and empowered African leadership and, to a large extent, were responsible for planting the seeds of freedom from colonialism in Africa.[21] Shaw and Gitau nonetheless concede that missionaries and colonial administrators cooperated with one overall colonial agenda.[22] From the colonial administrators' perspective, the most attractive aspect of the missionary schools was their Western-oriented curriculum, which, sadly, "had little relevance to African culture or needs."[23] Instead, as depicted in Oyono's novel, one

---

19. Oyono, *Houseboy*, 76.

20. Jesse N. K. Mugambi, "From Reconstruction to Reaffirmation: African Christian Theology in an Era of Hot Peace," *Routledge Handbook of African Theology*, ed. Elias Kifon Bongmba (Routledge, 2020), 155.

21. Mark Shaw and Wanjiru M. Gitau, *The Kingdom of God in Africa: A History of African Christianity* (Langham Publishing, 2020), 237–75.

22. Shaw and Gitau, *The Kingdom of God in Africa*, 250.

23. Shaw and Gitau, *The Kingdom of God in Africa*, 257.

of the primary goals of colonial education was to ensure that African natives would not question or challenge their colonial subjugation.[24]

Placed strategically at the forefront of the colonization process, the mission schools became the primary vehicles for converting native Africans.[25] "Many children," says Nigerian prelate John Cardinal Onaiyekan, whose father was among the first converts in his hometown and a lay church leader until his death, "were converted through the missionary school."[26] The conversion of Africans was essentially abolishing African beliefs and replacing them with European Christianity. This is because the missionaries were always deeply committed to the ideals of colonialism, including the expansion of civilization, the spread of Christianity, and the promotion of progress. They served with equal zeal as agents of political empire, representatives of European civilization, and envoys of God.[27]

In summary, as Katongole aptly observes, the schools and churches were "the brains and hands of the colonial state."[28] The pervasive Eurocentrism of the colonial era inevitably influenced the missionaries who ran these institutions. It shaped their mission strategies, practices, and even their attitudes toward the natives. Fictional portraits such as Oyono's novel help us understand how deeply Eurocentrism permeated the African church, which is evident in how most European church leaders and colonial administrators regarded the native population. In the next section, we will note that this same Eurocentrism was present at Vatican II, significantly shaping both the council's proceedings and the involvement of the African Catholic Church.

---

24. This is illustrated in a scene where M. Salvain, the headmaster of the school, is accused of being a traitor by his fellow colonialists: "Ever since you came into this country you have behaved in a way unworthy of a Frenchman. You're stirring the natives up against us. You keep telling them that they are as good as we are—as if they hadn't got a high enough opinion of themselves already." Oyono, *Houseboy*, 51.

25. See Uzukwu, *A Listening Church*, 29. As Uzukwu puts it, "The machine for the realization of the colonial ideology was both technical (colonial military superiority) and religious (Christianity)."

26. John Cardinal Onaiyekan, "Synodality in the African Church Avant la Lettre," *Church Life Journal*, October 20, 2023, https://churchlifejournal.nd.edu/articles/synodality-in-the-african-church/.

27. See V. Y. Mudimbe, *The Invention of Africa: Gnosis, Philosophy, and the Order of Knowledge* (Indiana University Press, 1988), 47.

28. Katongole, *The Sacrifice of Africa*, 47.

The Eurocentric Context of Vatican II: An African Church Perspective

The 1960s might have been the great decade of Africa's independence after almost a century of different levels of European colonization of the continent. Yet independence, which marked the official end of European rule in Africa, did not mark the end of European hegemony. To presume that independence and the ongoing process of decolonization inaugurated around the time of "official" independence marked the end of European hegemony is to be oblivious to what Sabelo J. Ndlovu-Gatsheni calls "colonial continuum."[29] He argues, "What Africans celebrated as Independence was a myth taken for reality as invisible snares of coloniality of power were ignored, thereby denying the birth of a truly postcolonial African world."[30] This insightful distinction between colonialism and coloniality can serve as a critical hermeneutic lens for evaluating Vatican II from an African perspective.

While Vatican II has been accurately celebrated as the most "global" council in the church's history, those who have called Vatican II a "European" council are equally spot on. The reason lies not only in the dominance of European bishops and theologians during the council's discussions but more fundamentally in the fact that in the early 1960s, the church, if not the whole world, was still thoroughly Eurocentric. Political and ecclesial trends in Europe dictated the "global" issues raised and discussed at the council. Martin Maier explains that, while Vatican II, in many real ways, marked a transition from a Western-Eurocentric to a polycentric, universal Catholic Church, the Eurocentrism of the council cannot be overemphasized.[31] European prelates and, more specifically, theologians dominated the discussions and debates of the council.[32] The council focused mainly on developments within the Eurocentric church.[33] In the

---

29. Ndlovu-Gatsheni, *Coloniality of Power*, 12.
30. Ndlovu-Gatsheni, *Coloniality of Power*, 14.
31. Martin Maier, "Vatican II: Inspiration and Encouragement for the Church in Europe," *Concilium* 3 (2012): 122.
32. See Gerd-Rainer Horn, *The Spirit of Vatican II: Western European Progressive Catholicism in the Long Sixties* (Oxford University Press, 2015), 5–59.
33. Vincent J. O' Malley, "A Brief History of the Catholic Church in Africa," in Ilo, *Handbook of African Catholicism*, 12.

same vein, although independence and decolonization dominated the 1960s air, Eurocentrism was still the dominant political disposition.

According to Wintle, Eurocentrism, which initially meant a "harmless" concentration on Europe or viewing the rest of the world from a European perspective, with an implied belief in the superiority of Europe, historically metamorphosed into a pervasiveness whose peak was during European civilization of Africa in the nineteenth and early twentieth centuries.[34] Also central to Wintle's historical account of Eurocentrism is that while it peaked during European rule over Africa, it was forced to take on a new shape toward the end of official colonialism. He explains that whereas the First World War and its aftermath was a massive attack on Europe's prestige, the Second World War destroyed what remained of Europe's credibility in claiming cultural and anthropological superiority. The drive for decolonization, which followed soon after World War II, reflected Europe's drastic fall from grace. Although this historical embarrassment and the disaster of the twentieth century shook Europe's self-confidence, he insists, it did not put an end to Eurocentrism. Instead, it marked a change in Europe's conception of its urgent responsibility to the rest of the (third) world, a new phase of the Eurocentric ideology that ensured its longevity.[35]

From an African perspective, this means that while the continent struggled to decolonize itself from Europe's grip in the years between the end of the Second World War and the 1960s, Europe worked twice as hard to reassert itself politically and economically on the African continent. These hegemonic efforts had a particularly significant impact on Africa, not only because up until the beginning of the 1960s, much of the continent was still under European colonial rule but also because, as Wintle points out, in response to the humiliation of the two world wars, Europe sought to reassert its superiority as well as restore the belief that Europe and the West were not only superior but "obliged to assist the rest of the world in following Western ways."[36] Wintle adds, "In 1957, the European statesmen of the day were lining up to tell each other and the

---

34. See Michael Wintle, *Eurocentrism: History, Identity, White Man's Burden* (Routledge, 2020), 28–48.
35. Wintle, *Eurocentrism*, 47.
36. Wintle, *Eurocentrism*, 204.

world that, despite the unfortunate events of recent years, European culture was still the best on the planet and that Europe should rebuild itself in order to continue its essential task of educating the rest of the world in the best ways—the European ways—of organizing public life and everything else."[37]

Europe's assertion that its culture was the best inherently implied that African culture was not just inferior but the absolute worst. As Mudimbe explains, "Africa was the mediation through which Europe created its own idea of its Otherness," an Otherness that experienced its peak during the colonization of Africa. This mindset is vivid in Oyono's novel, where a character identified as the doctor's wife laments the total lack of morals in Dangan. Her remark is followed by others at the European club, sharing their "little African stories" to "demonstrate that the African is a child or a fool," each expressing the dominant colonial assumptions and biases that remained active in the 1960s. Although European colonialists had either left or were preparing to leave the continent, a popular opinion among many European scholars in the 1960s was that Africa was unready for self-rule and was better off remaining colonized.

Clearly, this dominant Eurocentrism was not absent at Vatican II. Rahner, who famously praised Vatican II as the moment the church self-actualized as a "world church," insists, in the same article, that the church's Eurocentric posturing remained visible long after the conclusion of the council and must never be ignored. Rahner compared the church in relation to the world outside Europe to "an export firm which exported a European religion as a commodity it did not really want to change but sent throughout the world with the rest of the culture and civilization it considered superior."[38] Vatican II was thus an opportune forum for the European church, still dominated by the Eurocentric ideology of the larger European society, to assert its dominance over the church worldwide, and since Africa was still under significant European control both politically and ecclesiastically, it bore the brunt of this continued dominance. Possible evidence of this is the omission of African religion, which was still the dominant religion in Africa at that time, as a distinct category

---

37. Wintle, *Eurocentrism*, 204.
38. Rahner, "Towards a Fundamental Theological Interpretation," 717.

in *Nostra Aetate*, a document that acknowledges the two other Abrahamic faiths as well as Hinduism and Buddhism—describing these last two as religions of advanced human civilizations.[39] While it is not the only religion omitted in the document, the omission of African religion might have been motivated by, among other things, the European missionaries' general demeaning view of African religious and cultural practices. In John Mbiti's words, European missionaries generally "despised, mocked and dismissed" African religion as "primitive and underdeveloped."[40] The African church's inability to resist the Eurocentrism perpetuated by Vatican II can be primarily attributed to the insufficient representation of native Africans combined with the Eurocentric bias of European bishops, theologians, and missionaries.

In the next section, the participation of the African church in the council will be examined within the broader context of African resistance to European colonial rule, which reached its height in the years following World War II. While it is crucial to acknowledge the pervasive Eurocentrism that characterized the council, it is equally important to recognize the resistance to Eurocentrism by African participants. Adrian Hastings points out that the hope for the emergence of independent African states naturally resonated with the council's desire to rejuvenate the church.[41]

The African Church at Vatican II

Orobator's recent evaluation of the African church's participation in Vatican II oscillates between the numerical disadvantage of African participants and the dominant Eurocentrism of the era. He identifies three factors chiefly responsible for the relative absence of the African voice at the council. Firstly, he emphasizes the numerical disadvantage of the

---

39. See Second Vatican Council, Declaration on the Relation of the Church to Non-Christian Religions *Nostra Aetate*, October 28, 1965, no. 2 (hereafter, NA). All quotations from this document are from Austin Flannery, ed., *Vatican Council II: Constitutions, Decrees, Declarations; A Completely Revised Translation in Inclusive Language* (Liturgical Press, 2014).

40. John S. Mbiti, *African Religions and Philosophy* (Anchor Books, 1969), 13.

41. Adrian Hastings, "The Council Came to Africa," in *Vatican II: By Those Who Were There*, ed. Alberic Stacpoole (Geoffrey Chapman, 1986), 315–16.

African bishops at the council. Next, he highlights that the African church before and during the council can best be described as "a native outpost of a Eurocentric ecclesial organization."[42] Thirdly, Orobator points out that, unlike the bishops representing the European church, the African bishops lacked theologians and other experts to support their effective participation at the council.[43]

Like all previous scholarly reflections on the African church's participation, Orobator's critical appraisal is far from exhaustive. Influenced by the dominant image of Africa as a continent of "passive" people, it ignores the reality of Africa's consistent resistance to European colonialism and how this resistance played into the council. Modern Africa's history, Ngũgĩ wa Thiong'o argues, is a long narrative of perpetual struggle against slavery, colonialism, and neocolonialism.[44] Although it devastated many things in the continent, imperialism, in its colonial form, he insists, was not able to destroy the African culture of resistance.[45] Africans sustained their anticolonial protests through writings, demonstrations, and, in a few cases, armed struggles until the very end of official colonialism.[46]

However, while Ngũgĩ and numerous others who emphasize Africa's sustained resistance against foreign domination before, during, and after colonialism provide a more accurate and balanced portrait of colonial Africa, to this day, the dominant image of Africa in the Western imagination is a vast continent of "passive" and "helpless" people who need foreign assistance, a people unable to resist awful social conditions (whether natural or product of human construction) or, even worse, a people without self-confidence and thus unwilling to take their destiny in their hands to move their continent forward, according, of course, to the Western notion of progress.[47] This dominant image of "passive" Africa,

---

42. Orobator, "The Impact," 662.

43. Orobator, "The Impact," 662–63.

44. Ngũgĩ wa Thiong'o, *Moving the Centre: The Struggle for Cultural Freedoms* (James Currey, 1993), 54.

45. Ngũgĩ, *Moving the Centre*, 45.

46. See John Parker and Richard Rathbone, *African History: A Very Short Introduction* (Oxford University Press, 2007), 93–100.

47. For an example of this sentiment, see the famous *Economist* cover story, which featured the title "The Hopeless Continent" across the cover and the uncredited editorial

baked in the furnace of Eurocentrism, shaped if not how Africans were able to participate at the council then many of the historical commentaries describing their participation and why their voices were not more present. When historians do not highlight the relative absence of the African voice at the council, they often focus on how the few native Africans among the fathers of the council who tried to make their voices heard were often largely unsuccessful.[48] Even when scholarly narrations of Africa's participation at the council highlight the organizational superiority of the African bishops, this is done only in passing. What usually follows is an emphasis on how, although organized, the African bishops at the council, overwhelmingly outnumbered and inadequately prepared, were reduced to relative silence. This narrative is incomplete.

Historical evidence of organizational superiority among African episcopal conferences contradicts the dominant narrative of unpreparedness and, by extension, the image of passivity. Elizabeth A. Foster emphasizes that, conscious of their numerical disadvantage, the African participants realized they would have to cooperate if they wanted their voices to be heard. She adds that the solidarity and poise of the African delegates received massive commendations from the other participants.[49] It is also important to emphasize that the native representatives of newly independent African countries were, as citizens and Christians, at this point, actively grappling with the reality of self-rule while engaged in a very intense search for national identity in reaction to the externally imposed identity of the outgoing colonial administrators and missionaries.

Granted that these new nations mostly related to their erstwhile colonizers with care, this must not cloud the decolonization fervor that domi-

---

introduction inside titled "Hopeless Africa." *The Economist,* May 13–20, 2000, 23–24, https://www.economist.com/leaders/2000/05/11/hopeless-africa.

48. See Étienne Fouilloux, "The Church's New Self-Understanding: Lay Movement, Episcopacy, and the Churches," in *History of Vatican II,* vol. 4: *Church as Communion, Third Period, and Intersession, September 1964–September 1965,* ed. Guiseppe Alberigo, trans. Joseph Komonchak (Orbis Books, 2003), 195–97. Fouilloux highlights the famous speech by Tanzanian prelate Cardinal Laurean Rugambwa as a key moment where an African perspective was brought to the council. He, however, emphasized that the impact of Rugambwa and the other African bishops was limited compared to other regions.

49. Elizabeth A. Foster, *African Catholic: Decolonization and Transformation of the Church* (Harvard University Press, 2019), 266.

nated this period. According to Foster, the stunning wave of decolonization on the African continent and beyond influenced Pope John XXIII's thinking about the church's role in the world as he prepared for the council.[50] Foster cites the pope's radio message to the faithful "of all the world," where he emphasized the participation of council fathers from all nations, asserted the fundamental equality of all peoples, and condemned both racism and European colonial domination.[51] However, just as Eurocentrism and African resistance coexisted at the council, these two realities remain visible in the post-Vatican II African Catholic Church, as reflected in Chimamanda Ngozi Adichie's 2003 novel, *Purple Hibiscus*. While Eurocentric influences persist, the enduring spirit of resistance against hegemony drives the church's ongoing efforts toward greater autonomy and a future African church that is both authentically Catholic and deeply engaged with the continent's political realities.

The African Church in the Post-Vatican II Era

The post-Vatican II African church, to use a phrase popularized by Adichie, is not "a single story." *Purple Hibiscus*, her first novel, told from the perspective of the teenage protagonist, Kambili, presents at least two portraits of the post-Vatican II church in Africa. Through the characters in the novel, Adichie expounds, in a theologically valuable way, on the diverse ways African Catholics have received two of Vatican II's important innovations: liturgical inculturation of *Sacrosanctum Concilium* and interreligious relations of *Nostra Aetate*. On the one hand, there are those who wholeheartedly hold on to the religion and culture of the European missionaries and discard, as much as humanly possible, their African culture and identity. On the other hand, there are those who do not perceive an intrinsic incompatibility between African culture and the Catholic faith. While the latter have wholeheartedly embraced Christianity, they maintain a respectful relationship even with "religious" elements of their African roots.

50. Foster, *African Catholic*, 260.
51. Foster, *African Catholic*, 261.

Eugene Achike, Kambili's father, belongs to the first group. Not only is he pious to the point of scrupulosity, but his preference for everything European over anything African is evident throughout the story. First, he would rather speak English with a British accent than speak Igbo, and he always preferred that people talk to him in English.[52] Like Father Benedict, the white parish priest of St. Agnes, he detests "native" Igbo songs during Mass, preferring that the Credo and Kyrie be recited only in Latin.[53] While he constantly refers to non-Catholic Christian denominations derogatorily as "mushroom" churches, he will have absolutely nothing to do with his father, Papa-Nnukwu, who refused to convert to Christianity. As far as Eugene is concerned, his father was a hopeless pagan destined for hell.[54] Despite his son's repeated appeals, including by buying him a car and building him a house, Papa-Nnukwu remained an adherent of the religion of his ancestors until his death, resisting, as Musa W. Dube describes it, his son's attempt to use "material power to coerce him to Christian conversion."[55] While Eugene prayed for his father's conversion earnestly, he avoided as much as possible any relationship or even any contact with him.

In direct contrast to Eugene is Aunty Ifeoma, his younger sister. Aunty Ifeoma (as Kambili and her brother Jaja call her), who often described her older brother as a "colonial product," is also a pious Catholic.[56] She recites the rosary daily in the morning and evening with her three children. She is, however, very tolerant of non-Catholic denominations, allowing them to pluck the flowers in her compound, and often sings Igbo songs, epitomizing, as Dube again puts it, "indigenized Christianity," while resisting her brother's use of material power to force upon her his version of Catholicism.[57] What is even more significant is her tolerance toward her non-Christian dad and his cultural and religious practices. Aunty Ifeoma had a deferential way of describing Papa-Nnukwu's religious affiliation.

---

52. Chimamanda Ngozi Adichie, *Purple Hibiscus* (Anchor Books, 2003), 48, 60.
53. Adichie, *Purple Hibiscus*, 4.
54. Adichie, *Purple Hibiscus*, 61–70.
55. Musa W. Dube, "*Purple Hibiscus*: A Postcolonial Feminist Reading," *Missionalia* 46, no. 2 (2018): 223.
56. Adichie, *Purple Hibiscus*, 13.
57. Dube, "*Purple Hibiscus*," 223.

"Your Papa-Nnukwu is not a pagan," she frequently says to Kambili, "he is a traditionalist."[58] Kambili notices that, unlike her father, Aunty Ifeoma does not pray for the conversion of Papa-Nnukwu or that God will save him from the raging fires of hell. Instead, she prays for his healing. When Papa-Nnukwu dies, Eugene is only concerned that he died without becoming a Christian. "He has gone to face judgment," he declares matter-of-factly.[59] Aunty Ifeoma, on the other hand, ensures their father is "properly" buried, that is, according to the custom of his ancestors, just as he had desired while alive.[60] Aunty Ifeoma's special care to grant her father's lifelong wish to be properly buried also reveals her generally positive attitude toward his cultural and non-Christian religious beliefs. Not only does she not condemn him to an eternity in hell just for his "heathen ways," Aunty Ifeoma obviously acknowledges the possibility and presence of elements that are "true and holy" (NA 2) in her father's religious practice.[61]

Adichie's primary interest might not have been ecclesiological. Yet a Catholic theological imagination pervades the entire novel, which has made it a treasure mine for African Catholic theologians. A religious timeframe encapsulates the narration, and the characters, mostly Catholics, are frequently in church for Mass. They pray regularly and often engage in theological arguments about liturgical and moral issues. The Catholic churches are also very clearly post-Vatican II. For example, Father Benedict, as I have already noted, is said to have reversed changes in the parish, such as reducing Igbo songs to a bare minimum, insisting that the Credo and Kyrie must be recited only in Latin, discouraging clapping or dancing, lest the solemnity of the Mass be compromised.[62] The changes that Father Benedict and Eugene reacted against and which caused them so much discomfort are part of the liturgical inculturation that Vatican II inspired. Since the council, they have become a very visible feature of the liturgy in sub-Saharan Africa.

58. Adichie, *Purple Hibiscus*, 81.
59. Adichie, *Purple Hibiscus*, 190.
60. Adichie, *Purple Hibiscus*, 189.
61. In one interesting scene, Aunty Ifeoma wakes Kambili and asks her to observe her grandfather at prayer. Kambili is amazed at, among other things, the visible peaceful calm on Papa-Nnukwu's face as he performs his religious ritual. Adichie, *Purple Hibiscus*, 166–69.
62. Adichie, *Purple Hibiscus*, 4.

It is essential to point out that *Purple Hibiscus*'s portraits of the church in Africa do not by any means exhaust the diversity of the church in Nigeria, much less Africa, and neither are these models outdated. In contemporary Africa, many people still embody a Eurocentric mindset, like Eugene, longing to return to the pre-Vatican II mode of worship. However, it is likely that there are far more people like Aunty Ifeoma who embrace the liturgical inculturation that Vatican II has inspired. *Purple Hibiscus* thus contributes at least two crucial ideas to the study of the history of the Catholic Church in Africa. The first is that the contemporary theological imagination cannot be studied without reference to a relatively recent colonial past. The second is that colonial structures remain very much alive and active and continue to portend an obstacle to the ongoing reception of the "revolutionary" teachings of Vatican II by the African church.

Discussing contemporary Africa without acknowledging its colonial past is, according to Katongole, tantamount to "a prescriptive haste."[63] Unfortunately, the African church has often succumbed to the temptation of seeking quick solutions to its challenges, as well as those of the broader society, without adequately addressing the colonial roots of many of these struggles. For instance, in the post-synodal apostolic exhortation *Africae Munus* (2011), following the synod of African bishops in 2009, Pope Benedict XVI calls for inculturation, grounding this appeal in Africa's rich intellectual, cultural, and religious heritage, which he describes as a "source of hope" for a continent facing an anthropological crisis—like the rest of the world.[64] Toward the end of the exhortation, he praises the heroism and generosity of European missionaries for building churches, schools, and dispensaries, shaping the face of today's African cultures, and, above all, freeing numerous traditional cultures from ancestral fears and unclean spirits (AM 113). However, despite acknowledging the painful scars left by the slave trade and colonialism early in the document, as well as the continent's ongoing struggles with new forms of enslavement and colonization, the pope's unqualified commendation of the missionary enterprise is problematic (see AM 9). Even more striking is the complete

---

63. Katongole, *The Sacrifice of Africa*, 31–32.

64. Pope Benedict XVI, Post-Synodal Apostolic Exhortation *Africae Munus*, November 19, 2011, nos. 10–11, https://www.vatican.va/content/benedict-xvi/en/apost_exhortations/documents/hf_ben-xvi_exh_20111119_africae-munus.html (hereafter, AM).

absence of the word *colonialism* from both the *Instrumentum Laboris* and the final propositions made by the African bishops at the synod.[65]

In the absence of sufficient attention to the enduring impact of colonial influence, the lingering thorns of coloniality are still stifling the seed of resistance planted during the time of the council. While the African church has seen the emergence of a vibrant liturgy and other positive developments, it remains subservient to the churches in Europe and America, from which it relies heavily for financial support. Leadership remains a significant issue within both the African church and society. As Orobator laments, the renewal and reform initiated by Vatican II continue to "wax and wane" under the "clericalist and hierarchical tutelage" that still dominates the African church.[66] Despite *Lumen Gentium*'s emphasis on the essential equality and common dignity of all the baptized and *Apostolicam Actuositatem*'s call for a unified mission between the clergy and laity, the African church, evangelized during colonialism, continues to struggle to free itself from the dominant features of a colonized society.[67]

Conclusion

In recognizing the lingering effect of colonialism in virtually every aspect of contemporary Africa, the church in Africa needs to reimagine leadership and other aspects of its life away from the dominant patterns of colonial Africa.[68] Despite its limitations, the impetus for renewal that Vatican II set in motion remains a vital resource for the African church.

---

65. See Synod of Bishops, *Instrumentum Laboris*, "The Church in Africa in Service to Reconciliation, Justice, and Peace," 2009, nos. 12–13, https://www.vatican.va/roman_curia/synod/documents/rc_synod_doc_20090319_instrlabor-africa_en.html; and Synod of Bishops, *Elenchus Finalis Propositionum*, n.d., https://www.vatican.va/roman_curia/synod/documents/rc_synod_doc_20091023_elenco-prop-finali_en.html. The former refers to "outside forces" and the marginalization of Africa through globalization without critically examining the historical roots of these issues.

66. Orobator, "The Impact," 673.

67. See Second Vatican Council, Dogmatic Constitution on the Church *Lumen Gentium*, November 21, 1964, nos. 3, 32; and Second Vatican Council, Decree on the Apostolate of Lay People *Apostolicam Actuositatem*, November 18, 1965, nos. 11–12.

68. See William I. Orbih, "Clericalism and the Problem of Leadership in Africa: Reimagination as Praxis," *Exchange* 52, nos. 1–2 (2023): 100–121, https://doi.org/10.1163/1572543X-BJA10027.

Catherine Clifford praises the council "for its recovery of an understanding of authority as service," adding that the council's teachings on the dignity and equality of all members of the church, as well as the emphasis on the co-responsibility of the clergy and laity in the mission of the church, provide a revolutionary framework for rethinking ecclesial leadership, mission, and even liturgy.[69]

If the goal, as highlighted in the two synods of African bishops where "inculturation" was a central theme, is to build a church that witnesses to Gospel values through Africa's rich cultural heritage, and if Vatican II, despite its limitations, contains a vital impetus for renewal, two urgent tasks emerge for African theologians and church leaders. First, they must give greater attention to the reforms of Vatican II. These reforms must be carefully adapted to the African reality, even as the church in Africa asserts its autonomy as well as its place as part of the global church. Second, they must give sustained engagement to resisting the colonial logic and power structures that continue to shape the church and society.

Zimbabwean novelist Tsitsi Dangarembga asserts that decolonization remains an ongoing necessity in Africa, calling it "the only logic that offers hope for the future."[70] Teddy Chalwe Sakupapa proposes "decoloniality as a new paradigm for contemporary African theology," arguing that it is essential for breaking away from Eurocentric theological frameworks, engaging with the diverse expressions of African Christianity, and balancing contextualization with catholicity.[71] It is not enough that the church in Africa actively participates in the ongoing effort to decolonize the continent fully. It must also incorporate a decolonial framework into its theological and pastoral practice.

---

69. For an overview of Vatican II's teachings on church leadership, see Catherine E. Clifford, "The Exercise of Ecclesial Authority in Light of Vatican II," in *The Long Shadow of Vatican II: Living Faith and Negotiating Authority Since the Second Vatican Council*, ed. Lucas Van Rompay, Sam Miglarese, and David Morgan (University of North Carolina Press, 2015). The direct quote is on p. 59.

70. Tsitsi Dangarembga, *Black and Female: Essays* (Graywolf Press, 2022), 151.

71. Teddy Chalwe Sakupapa, "The Decolonising Content of African Theology and the Decolonisation of African Theology: Reflections on a Decolonial Future for African Theology," *Missionalia* 46, no. 3 (July 2019): 407, https://doi.org/10.7832/46-3-277.

Chapter 15

Becoming Antiracist

Post-Vatican II Catholicism and the "Sin of Racism"[1]

Matteo Caponi

Antiracism: A Contested Object

This paper analyzes how mainstream Catholic culture has contributed to antiracism, focusing primarily on how the church has confronted antiblack racism. I wish to begin by suggesting that antiracism should be historicized as a heterogeneous, plural, and even contradictory movement of opinion. In general, it can be understood as any theory or action "that seeks to address, eradicate and/or ameliorate racism."[2] In addition, it is necessary to reject two opposing clichés: the a priori assumption of Christian antiracism and the thesis of white supremacy as "a genetic imprint" of Western Christianity.[3] This polarization encourages oversimplified claims instead of a nuanced study of the past. Instead, we must ask, what kinds of antiracisms (plural) has Catholic culture expressed over time? Although it may seem dissonant to us, the drive to dismiss biologically based racism as false, wrong, and immoral has coexisted historically with

---

1. I thank Sante Lesti and Raffaella Perin for reading and discussing my text.
2. Alastair Bonnett, *Anti-Racism*, Key Ideas (Routledge, 2000), 3–4.
3. Robert P. Jones, *White Too Long: The Legacy of White Supremacy in American Christianity* (Simon & Schuster, 2020).

a range of attitudes that cannot be summed up in the clear racism/antiracism dichotomy.

When did Catholicism "become" antiracist? Was the Second Vatican Council a turning point in this regard? According to John T. McGreevy, the "spirit of the Council" allowed Catholics to fully participate in the Civil Rights Movement. The March on Washington on August 28, 1963, in which Jesuit John LaFarge Jr., Washington Archbishop Patrick O'Boyle, and a large number of Catholic lay people participated, and the Selma to Montgomery marches of 1965 can be considered the most emblematic moments of change (although the majority of US Catholics looked on desegregation with reluctance).[4] For the first time at the 1963 march, Catholic organizations and prominent figures were "significantly present at a massive public demonstration under the leadership of black civil rights leaders."[5]

The idea of innate Catholic antiracism clearly has apologetic implications. It should be remembered that leading Catholic figures and intellectuals committed to the fight against racial prejudice, until the 1960s, avoided adopting this label as representative of their views. And yet, the term *antiracist* had entered the popular lexicon as early as the 1920s–1930s, in conjunction with the first organizations to combat racism (from the French *racisme*).[6] The neologism *racism* gained currency in reference to German *völkisch* ideology and later Mendelian-style eugenics and was introduced to designate a harmful system of belief, fed by hatred. From that time on, *racism* would coexist with and then replace *racialism*, the classification of human beings into different races with distinctive (and more or less evolved) psychic/spiritual hereditary capabilities. Catholicism, too, was marked by a reductionist equation between racism and Nazism that had not only descriptive value but also a polemical and self-absolving function, which allowed many to think throughout the 1950s that "temporary" racial discrimination was not in itself racist nor could culturally codified racism be called racism. What liberal-minded Catho-

---

4. John T. McGreevy, "Racial Justice and the People of God: The Second Vatican Council, the Civil Rights Movement, and American Catholics," *Religion and American Culture* 4, no. 2 (Summer 1994): 221–54.

5. Cyprian Davis, *The History of Black Catholics in the United States* (Crossroad-Continuum, 1990), 256.

6. Emmanuel Debono, *Aux origines de l'antiracisme: La LICA, 1927–1940* (CNRS Éditions, 2012).

lics targeted was essentially racism as an aggressive doctrine implying a *fixed* and *irredeemable* hierarchy among races. Since the 1930s, Catholic activists involved in so-called "Negro welfare" referred to another notion: *interracialism*.[7]

In the United States, the history of the interracial movement is mainly linked to the name of John LaFarge Jr., although historiography has moved far beyond him. LaFarge is known as the leader of the Catholic Interracial Council of New York (CICNY), founded in 1934 to "promote, in every practicable way, relations between the races based on the Christian principles, by creating a better understanding in the public as to the situation, needs and progress of the Negro group in America."[8] Envisioned as a kind of "third way" opposed to both racism (identified with the German model) and humanist antiracism that appealed to universal rights, interracialism was accused by segregationists of being a fifth column of atheism and Communism.[9] The transnational influence of the group, which gathered around the *Interracial Review*, the mouthpiece of the CICNY, was crucial. LaFarge's *Interracial Justice* was a very influential book dealing with racial integration prior to the Second World War.[10]

The rise of an antiracist sensibility in Catholic opinion was the result of several waves between the two sides of the Atlantic. The wave of the late 1950s coincided with three factors that had a global impact: decolonization, the US Civil Rights Movement, and the birth of the anti-apartheid movement. Nevertheless, there was a gap between the fact that racism was discredited scientifically in the aftermath of World War II and the time when the antidiscrimination rationale became mainstream. It was only in the 1960s that this gap was bridged, starting from the 1965 International Convention on the Elimination of All Forms of Racial Discrimination (ICERD) and activism on the part of the United Nations and in particular

---

7. Matteo Caponi, "Antirazzismo cattolico e questione nera nell'Italia del secondo dopoguerra," *Italia Contemporanea* 53, no. 297 (supplement) (December 2021): 17–54.

8. Martin A. Zielinski, "Working for Interracial Justice: The Catholic Interracial Council of New York, 1934–1964," *U.S. Catholic Historian* 7, nos. 2–3 (1988): 236.

9. R. Bentley Anderson, *Black, White, and Catholic: New Orleans Interracialism, 1947–1956* (Vanderbilt University Press, 2005).

10. John LaFarge Jr., *Interracial Justice: A Study of the Catholic Doctrine of Race Relations* (America Press, 1937); 2nd ed.: *The Race Question and the Negro: A Study of the Catholic Doctrine on Interracial Justice* (Longmans, Green, 1943).

its United Nations Educational, Scientific and Cultural Organization (UNESCO). In the case of Catholicism, it was not until the pontificate of John XXIII and the Second Vatican Council that the international church officially rejected racial discrimination unconditionally. However, the extent to which Vatican II constituted a caesura is a matter of debate. In Europe, a mass mobilization of Catholics in large-scale institutionalized antiracist activity did not really occur until the 1980s and 1990s. In the United States, black Catholicism came to widespread fruition in the post-conciliar church at precisely the same time, following the domestication of Catholic protest and more radical groups close to Black Power.

The Holy See's first document devoted entirely to the problem of racism was dated November 3, 1988. Released by the Pontifical Commission for Justice and Peace, *The Church and Racism: Towards a More Fraternal Society*[11] characterized racism as a secular ideology rooted in the Enlightenment divorce between science and faith and reflected in the senseless Nazi program, and argued that the church had promoted "courageous resistance" against it. This position reflects a tenacious pattern: racism is presented as foreign to an inherently antiracist religion, which seems to have been practiced by ordinary Catholics acting inconsistently and in contradiction to their own faith tradition. *The Church and Racism* cited several documents in support of its claim of an imagined antiracist Catholic tradition: *Mit Brennender Sorge*, Pope Pius XI's encyclical of March 1937 against racist neo-paganism operating in the German Reich; the *Instructio de erroribus circa humanam stirpem* [Instruction on errors concerning the human race], issued in April 1938 by the Sacred Congregation for Seminaries and Universities; and *Humani Generis Unitas* [On the unity of the human race], the so-called "hidden encyclical," drafted in the summer of 1938 by LaFarge together with Jesuits Gustav Gundlach and Gustave Desbuquois to condemn nationalism, anti-Semitism, and racism, but never published.[12] It is difficult to draw from all these statements a peremptory condemnation of racism, which was given a reductive definition that resulted in Catholic opposition to nothing more than the "idolatry of race." In the late 1930s, the Roman Curia did not even question the legitimacy of a "sound" and

---

11. Pontifical Commission for Justice and Peace, *The Church and Racism: Towards a More Fraternal Society* (Vatican Polyglot Press, 1988). Available at https://www.ewtn.com/catholicism/library/church-and-racism-towards-a-more-fraternal-society-2426.

12. The text did not constitute a finished draft. See Giovanni Coco, "La parabola dell'ultima' Enciclica di Pio XI," *Quaderni di storia* 49, no. 98 (July–December 2023): 5–55.

"moderate racism," identifiable with an *aestimatio stirpis* (love for one's bloodline) compatible with natural law.[13]

We are all aware of the recent controversies related to the Black Lives Matter (BLM) protests. The response of the United States Conference of Catholic Bishops (USCCB) consisted in the creation of the Ad Hoc Committee Against Racism (2017) and the publication of the pastoral letter *Open Wide Our Hearts: The Enduring Call to Love* (2018). The latter urged the faithful to ask for forgiveness: "The truth is that the sons and daughters of the Catholic Church have been complicit in the evil of racism."[14] US bishops had declared racism a "sin" for the first time in their 1979 pastoral letter *Brothers and Sisters to Us*.[15] This trope was used again in *The Church and Racism*. Yet, the reference to the "sons and daughters of the Church" has several implications. First, the focus on individuals. The overall implication is that there have been Catholics who have been racist, or who have acted racist, despite church teaching, not because of it. Second, the cultural device of *redemptive antiracism*, calling for forgiveness, atonement, and reconciliation, implies unity under religious leadership, who alone is capable of healing the wounds of racism. Third, racial thought is made to coincide with biological determinism, which is contrary to Christian siblinghood. As Bryan Massingale has noted, the bishops' moral exhortations have failed to promote a real understanding of the underlying cultural patterns that "facilitate, generate and legitimize these racist behaviors."[16]

---

13. Raffaella Perin, "Insegnare la religione contro il razzismo: Le istruzioni della Santa Sede," in *La religione istruita nella scuola e nella cultura dell'Italia contemporanea*, ed. Luciano Caimi and Giovanni Vian (Morcelliana, 2013), 167–89; Perin, *The Popes on Air: The History of Vatican Radio from Its Origins to World War II* (Fordham University Press, 2024), 110–41; Tommaso Dell'Era, "La distinction théologique entre racisme modéré et racisme exagéré du pontificat de Pie XI à celui de Pie XII: Éléments d'analyse," *Revue d'Histoire de la Shoah* 78, no. 218 (October 2023): 49–66.

14. Todd A. Salzman and Michael G. Lawler, "The United States Conference of Catholic Bishops' 2018 Statement against Racism: A Critical Analysis," *Journal of Religion & Society*, supplement 24 (2023): 30–52.

15. "Racism is a sin: a sin that divides the human family, blots out the image of God among specific members of that family, and violates the fundamental human dignity of those called to be children of the same Father." National Conference of Catholic Bishops, *Brothers and Sisters to Us* (1979), https://www.usccb.org/committees/african-american-affairs/brothers-and-sisters-us. See also Deacon Harold Burke-Sivers, *Building a Civilization of Love: A Catholic Response to Racism* (Ignatius Press, 2023), 39–72.

16. Bryan N. Massingale, *Racial Justice and the Catholic Church* (Orbis Books, 2010), 70.

At the same time, antiracism remains a contested object. Archbishop José H. Gomez's speech, "Reflections on the Church and America's New Religions," delivered in 2021 in his capacity of president of the USCCB, attributed militant antiracism to secularism, Marxism, and de-Christianization. "Woke" movements, Gomez said, would be "dangerous substitutes for true religion," causing intolerance and social division.[17] Twenty years earlier, Cardinal Roger Etchegaray—then head of the Pontifical Council for Justice and Peace—expressed skepticism toward "a certain kind of antiracism" that, "far from weakening, causes an exacerbation of racism," as it applies the charge of racism to any kind of "unequal behavior."[18] In these positions we can read the persistence of certain frames of Catholic antiracist discourse.

Before Vatican II

In the United States, Catholic interracialism entered official teaching with the publication of the bishops' statement of November 14, 1958, *Discrimination and the Christian Conscience*. For many, its release was the "proof that interracialism equaled orthodoxy."[19] This statement, which came late in comparison to similar pronouncements by other major Christian denominations, was authored by Sulpician John F. Cronin, assistant director of the Social Action Department of the National Catholic Welfare Conference. The text associated "enforced segregation" with "oppressive conditions and the denial of basic human rights," while rejecting the "separate but equal" doctrine as "obsolete."[20]

---

17. José H. Gomez, "Reflections on the Church and America's New Religions," November 4, 2021, https://archbishopgomez.org/blog/reflections-on-the-church-and-americas-new-religions.

18. Roger Etchegaray, "Le racisme, une hydre à cent têtes," in Etchegaray, *L'homme, à quel prix?* (Éditions de la Martinière, 2012), positions 154–76, Kindle. Translation mine. The cardinal referred to Pierre-Antoine Taguieff, *La force du préjugé: Essai sur le racisme et ses doubles* (La Découverte, 1988).

19. John T. McGreevy, *Parish Boundaries: The Catholic Encounter with Race in the Twentieth-Century Urban North* (University of Chicago Press, 1996).

20. "Discrimination and the Christian Conscience," *Interracial Review* (December 1958): 217–19. The original title, in its circulated typewritten version, was "Racial Discrimination and the Christian Conscience."

As an ardent anticommunist, Cronin believed that segregation discredited America's reputation by handing communism a formidable propaganda weapon and pushing the decolonizing peoples into the arms of the Soviet bloc. In the wake of the Little Rock crisis, "racial equality" was conceived as a necessity to prevent "colored peoples" from swinging "to the Communist banner. Communism would then dominate most of mankind."[21] The link between interracial justice and anticommunism was explicitly stated in the influential report by the International Agenzia Fides (the Vatican's Propaganda Fide news agency), commissioned by LaFarge: a lukewarm attitude among Catholics was considered "food for Communist propaganda throughout the world."[22]

The bishops had not made a strong call for desegregation, having distanced themselves from both civil rights activists ("the agitator") and their opponents ("the racist"). In the end, the Brown v. Board of Education of Topeka verdict (1954) had led interracialists, a few bishops, and the Holy See to overcome their hesitation. Support for New Orleans Archbishop Joseph F. Rummel's initiatives to desegregate Catholic schools and oppose the terrorist actions of the Ku Klux Klan had grown between 1955 and 1957. In August 1958, the substitute at the Vatican Secretariat of State, Angelo Dell'Acqua, finally endorsed the Chicago meeting that led to the founding of the National Catholic Conference for Interracial Justice (NCCIJ). Commenting on incidents of racism in Louisiana, *L'Osservatore Romano* had previously spoken in terms of sin: "Racial exclusiveness is a sin against the nature of Catholicism."[23] On the other hand, the apostolic delegate in the United States, Amleto Cicognani, had advised Dell'Acqua not to draw attention to a sentence contained in Rummel's famous pastoral letter of February 1956, *The Morality of Racial Segregation*, which Cicognani deemed "imprudent and inaccurate": "Racial segregation as such is morally

21. [John F. Cronin], "Suggested Draft on Race Relations," November [before 4], 1957, in Catholic University of America Special Collections, Washington DC, United States Conference of Catholic Bishops (USCCB), Executive Department/Office of the General Secretary Records [hereafter, CUASC, USCCB], box 89, folder 13.

22. John LaFarge, "The Work of the Catholic Church Among the Negroes of the United States," *Agenzia Internazionale Fides*, January 14, 1950.

23. Mark Newman, "'Racial Discrimination Can in No Way Be Justified': The Vatican and Desegregation in the South, 1946–1968," *Journal of American Studies* 56, no. 5 (December 2022): 678.

wrong and sinful."[24] These words disavowed a tradition of moralizing segregation and discrimination and distinguishing between a licit segregation, insofar as it was temporary and charitable, and an unfair and illicit one, insofar as it was programmatic, that is, taken not as a means of progress and improvement. After all, it was "undeniable" that the "vast majority" of black people was "still far from being able to put itself on a par—in social life—with the rest of the population."[25]

In the 1950s, opposition to "immediate total integration" was shared by the Southern African Catholic Bishops' Conference, which called the theory of "separate development . . . subordinated to white supremacy" a "blasphemy." However, their condemnation did not mean establishing "perfect equality." Nothing, in fact, was more evident than the "existence of profound differences between sections of our population which make immediate total integration impossible."[26] The same perspective was suggested by French theologian Yves Congar in his pamphlet *The Catholic Church and the Race Question*, published in 1953 by the United Nations Educational, Scientific and Cultural Organization (UNESCO) as part of its series "The Race Question and Modern Thought" (a highly successful series intended to dismantle the notion of race based on a hierarchy of immutable biological differences): "The great majority of non-Europeans, and particularly the Africans, have not yet reached a stage of development that would justify their integration into a homogeneous society with the European. A sudden and violent attempt to force them into the mould of European manners and customs would be disastrous."[27]

Interracial mobilization was a step forward from the "Negro apostolate" aimed at establishing missions "procuring the salvation of blacks" after the abolition of slavery. This was thought to be necessary to distance blacks from any negative Protestant influence and to free them from their ingrained vices (e.g., childish attitudes, irrationality, and sensualism), which posed a danger to society. Only the Catholic Church, according

---

24. Amleto Cicognani to Angelo Dell'Acqua, March 2, 1956, in Archivio Apostolico Vaticano (hereafter, AAV), Segr. Stato, Anno 1950—SGG, Chiese e Clero Secolare 2776.

25. Amleto Cicognani to Angelo Dell'Acqua, October 3, 1957, in AAV, Segr. Stato, Anno 1950—SGG, Popolazioni 752, f. 2r. Translation mine.

26. Southern African Catholic Bishops' Conference, "Race Relations," July 21, 1957, in *The Catholic Mind* (March–April 1958): 187–91.

27. Yves Congar, *The Catholic Church and the Race Question* (Unesco, 1953), 43–44.

to this view, had the means to elevate them socially, as it had done with "the Hun, Goth, and Vandal."[28] Within this narrative of improvement, Jim-Crowism was considered, in theory, unjust and counterproductive but in a sense still a forced choice. Racial differences made immediate and total integration practically impossible. While it was illegitimate to keep blacks in a permanent state of oppression, the only way forward was to provide them gradually with the goods of civilization, especially Catholic education. In this plan, segregated churches and parochial schools maintained their place. Legal equality was secondary to the goal of Catholicization and conversion.

For *La Civiltà Cattolica*, the journal of the Italian Jesuits, interracialism did not exclude the existence of "peoples, with morphological, psychological, linguistic and cultural differences," some of whom were superior to others temporarily (not essentially). Whites and blacks were becoming civilized at different rates of speed. As a result, provisionally, there were measures "more suitable for these than for those" (that is, different laws and rights for white and black people). Even according to the unpublished *Humani Generis Unitas*, "harmful" racism was conceived as a "rigid separation of superior and inferior races," whereas the existence of "more or less perfect or more or less perfectly developed races" was unquestionable. This interpretation was perpetuated after 1945, when racism without adjectives was rejected but once again conceived reductively. Authoritative works such as the *Dizionario di teologia morale*, published in 1954 under the sponsorship of the Sacred Congregation of the Council (the Vatican dicastery that was responsible for the discipline of clergy at the time), explained that there were "ethnic groups with somatic, psychological and cultural qualities superior to other groups." These were not permanent differences, as races were subject to evolution and change. Hence, to think that was not to be racist.[29]

Congar's *The Catholic Church and the Race Question* reaffirmed this pattern by arguing that (1) racism was an evil, anti-Christian pseudo-religion derived from the Enlightenment; (2) Christianity acknowledged "the diversity of races and peoples" not merely as a "human and earthly

---

28. These are the words of the prominent Josephite priest and activist John Slattery, quoted in William L. Portier, "John R. Slattery's Vision for the Evangelization of American Blacks," *U.S. Catholic Historian* 5, no. 1 (1986): 26.

29. See Caponi, "Antirazzismo cattolico," 18–25. Translation mine.

value, but a Christian and providentially intended value"; (3) discrimination could be "acceptable on grounds of a situation deriving from historical fact, but never on the ground of purely racial differences"; and (4) the church was "the antithesis of racism." However, Congar recognized that "the coexistence of different human groups" did present "difficult problems, not because of any radical inequality per se between the races . . . , but because the groups as constituted are at different cultural and political and hence at different 'human' levels."[30] To quote David Southern, such an approach shows the "limits of Catholic interracialism."[31]

First, while refusing racial determinism, interracialists did not deny both the reality and alterability of racial groups, whose gradation could be in agreement with Christian doctrine. LaFarge's Catholic Interracial Program[32] adhered to Robert Park's school of race relations[33] and basically contended that racial prejudice had to "be cured" and "recognized as a sin" in order to let races cooperate. But Catholic teaching alone could offer the basis to do so.[34] While they fought racism as irrational and anti-Christian, they identified (white) European civilization as a "key metric of achievement and progress" and recast racial differentiation under a seemingly nonracial notion of development.[35]

Second, the term *interracial* was opposed to *black* or *colored* (an adjective that was then used without derogatory meanings). The model of the

30. Congar, *The Catholic Church*, 13–15, 56–58.

31. David W. Southern, *John LaFarge and the Limits of Catholic Interracialism, 1911–1963* (Louisiana State University Press, 1996).

32. John LaFarge, *A Catholic Interracial Program* (The America Press, 1939). See Catholic Historical Research Center of the Archdiocese of Philadelphia, *Catholic Historical Research Center Digital Collections*, accessed November 7, 2024, https://omeka.chrc-phila.org/items/show/8779.

33. Park advocated an assimilationist position, according to which racial minorities, once prejudices were defeated, were willing to embrace the values of American society, according to a cycle of integration characterized by four stages: contact, competition, accommodation, and finally assimilation. See Robert E. Park, *Race and Culture* (Free Press, 1950).

34. John LaFarge, "Can Prejudice Be Cured?," *Interracial Review* (August 1935): 120–22. Interracialists repeatedly referred to the "sin of racism," e.g., "Racism Is a Sin," *Los Angeles Sentinel*, May 31, 1951; Mark Newman, *Desegregating Dixie: The Catholic Church in the South and Desegregation, 1945–1992* (University Press of Mississippi, 2018), 32.

35. In terms similar to those pointed out by Sebastián Gil-Riaño, *The Remnants of Race Science: UNESCO and Economic Developments in the Global South* (Columbia University Press, 2023), 5–6.

interracial councils replaced the black separatist model pursued by the Federated Colored Catholics, an association formed in 1924 whose purpose was to promote the equality of black Catholics within the church through self-organization and the assertion of a specific religious-racial identity. In contrast, interracial and color-blind mutual cooperation was conceived as a nonconfrontational program under white clerical leadership.[36] In the interracialist view, black people were victims of unjust discrimination, but, left alone, they did not know the right "cure" for the "virus" of racism.

From Interracialism to Antiracism: The Vatican II Moment

The inertia of these cultural models was not entirely shaken by Vatican II. A first example is the posthumous publication of LaFarge's entry "Racism" in the *New Catholic Encyclopedia* (1967), which included passages taken from the unpublished *Humani Generis Unitas*, teaching that it was not racist to say that every racial group has certain defined physical qualities associated with certain psychological characteristics; it was not racist to posit the existence of "more or less perfectly developed races, if we measure them by the outward of cultural life." Such statements were accompanied by the condemnation of South African-style apartheid and the assertion that John XXIII's encyclicals *Mater et Magistra* (1961) and *Pacem in Terris* (1963), together with the declarations of Vatican Council II, expressly condemned "racist doctrines."[37] A similar stance can be seen in the postconciliar edition of the *Dizionario di teologia morale*, where the entry *Razzismo* was left unchanged, adding only that the council had "spoken out forcefully" against the "enormities" of racism (a racism that the dictionary itself continued to equate with its Nazi version) in *Gaudium et Spes*, no. 29 (see the following paragraph).[38] This passage would be quoted in John Paul II's *Catechism of the Catholic Church* (1992). The Pontifical Council for Justice and Peace's *Compendium of the Social Doctrine of the Church*

---

36. Davis, *The History of Black Catholics*, 214–29.

37. John LaFarge, "Racism," in *The New Catholic Encyclopedia*, vol. 12 (The Catholic University of America, 1967), 54–60.

38. Giuseppe Monti, "Razzismo," in *Dizionario di teologia morale*, vol. 2, ed. Francesco Roberti and Pietro Palazzini (Studium, 1968), 4th ed., 1386–88.

(2005) would later state that "any theory or form whatsoever of racism and racial discrimination is morally unacceptable."[39]

The caesura on the topic of racism brought about by the conciliar *aggiornamento* cannot be underestimated. According to *Pacem in Terris* (1963), "On the doctrinal and theoretical level, at least, no form of approval is being given to racial discrimination"; "every trace of racial discrimination" must be eliminated in relations between political communities.[40] Thus, it was not a matter of affirming a vague ideological incompatibility between Christianity and racism, but rather of calling believers and all people of good will, nationally and internationally, to binding action that, even on the side of the racial issue, would realize the aspiration for unity, solidarity, justice, and progress conveyed by the language of Vatican II.[41] The council's Pastoral Constitution on the Church in the Modern World, *Gaudium et Spes*, declared: "Any kind of social or cultural discrimination in basic personal rights on the grounds of sex, race, color, social condition, language or religion, must be curbed and eradicated as incompatible with God's design."[42] The decree *Ad Gentes* urged the faithful, "as good citizens," to reject "racial hatred or exaggerated nationalism."[43] The council documents made racial discrimination unacceptable, whereas before it had been accepted under certain conditions. The issue of racism was no longer an episodic presence on the ecclesial landscape.

However, some have challenged the centrality to Vatican II in such a shift. Karen J. Johnson has recently identified Catholic interracialism as a strand of the long Civil Rights Movement that goes back long before

---

39. Pontifical Council for Justice and Peace, *Compendium of the Social Doctrine of the Church* (Libreria Editrice Vaticana and USCCB Publishing, 2005), 187. Also at https://www.vatican.va/roman_curia/pontifical_councils/justpeace/documents/rc_pc_justpeace_doc_20060526_compendio-dott-soc_en.html.

40. Pope John XXIII, Encyclical Letter *Pacem in Terris*, April 11, 1963, nos. 44, 86, https://www.vatican.va/content/john-xxiii/en/encyclicals/documents/hf_j-xxiii_enc_11041963_pacem.html.

41. On the strength of this "new way of speaking," see the classic by John W. O'Malley, *What Happened at Vatican II* (Belknap Press, 2008).

42. Second Vatican Council, Pastoral Constitution on the Church in the Modern World *Gaudium et Spes*, December 7, 1965, no. 29. All quotations of Vatican II documents are from Austin Flannery, ed., *Vatican Council II: Constitutions, Decrees, Declarations; A Completely Revised Translation in Inclusive Language* (Liturgical Press, 2014).

43. Second Vatican Council, Decree on the Church's Missionary Activity *Ad Gentes*, December 7, 1965, no. 15.

1962–65.[44] Other scholars have pointed to the difficulty with which Catholic culture embraced the antiracist agenda and to the fact that the reception of Vatican II was a source of new conflicts.[45]

A crucial factor was the worldwide media attention to the Civil Rights Movement. After the NCCIJ's endorsement of sit-in demonstrations as "morally legitimate" if conducted peacefully,[46] 1963 was the "ecumenical" year par excellence, with Catholics joining the integrationist mobilization. The first key event, the National Conference on Religion and Race, held in Chicago in January 1963, embodied an atmosphere of interracial and interfaith union. Six hundred fifty-seven delegates—among whom were over twenty Catholic bishops, Martin Luther King Jr., and Abraham Joshua Heschel—adopted an "Appeal to the Conscience of the American People," calling racial discrimination and segregation "an insult to God" and asking for forgiveness for the lack of religious commitment to human dignity.[47] Beyond this rhetoric of repentance, the conference established the master narrative that "religiously inspired love of neighbor" was the only way to rehabilitate the victims of discrimination.[48] Progressive religious cultures were presented as promoters of the civil rights agenda, a misrepresentation that reiterated an image of churches and religions—no longer exclusively Catholicism—as natural agents of siblinghood and justice. What was missing was the fact that only a minority of white Christian and Jewish figures and communities supported the African American struggle. Moreover, in the name of this ecumenical/interfaith alignment, the role of a secular, agnostic, and oppositional tradition seemed to be marginalized. Secularism was soon associated with a "forgetfulness of God," unable to defend human dignity, under the assumption that only a "perfect union" derived from spiritual values could guarantee the goal of civil rights.[49]

---

44. Karen J. Johnson, *One in Christ: Chicago Catholics and the Quest for Interracial Justice* (Oxford University Press, 2018).

45. Massingale, *Racial Justice*; Newman, *Desegregating Dixie*; Matthew J. Cressler, *Authentically Black and Truly Catholic: The Rise of Black Catholicism in the Great Migration* (New York University Press, 2017).

46. "'Sit-In' Demonstration Defended by Moralists," *The Pilot*, March 9, 1960, 1–2.

47. "Appeal to the Conscience of the American People," in *Race: Challenge to Religion*, ed. Mathew Ahmann (Henry Regnery Company, 1963), 171–73.

48. John F. Cronin, "Religion and Race," *Extension*, April 1963.

49. "Text of Bishops' Statement on 'Bonds of Union,'" *The Southern Cross*, November 21, 1963, 2.

The second crucial event in 1963 was the March on Washington for Jobs and Freedom. For the Catholic Church, "the break-through came at the end of July, when an emergency meeting in Chicago of the Catholic interracial councils announced their participation in the march."[50] Three days before, the US bishops released a pastoral letter *On Racial Harmony* (a term embedded in the Chicago sociological view of race relations). The March on Washington incorporated Vatican II Catholicism into the Civil Rights Movement, introducing the Catholic public to the category of antiracism. In Italy, the Catholic press, such as *L'Avvenire d'Italia*, spoke of an "impressive antiracist demonstration." The missionary press, too, supported the "integrationist movement" by recalling "the antiracist principles always advocated" by the church hierarchy.[51] Only a few months after, two events enshrined Dr. King's popularity among Catholics: the audience granted to him by Paul VI in September and the Nobel Peace Prize, which he was awarded in October. Ultimately, the ecumenical moment invented a tradition, that of Catholic antiracism, which did not exist before, strictly speaking.[52] In this redemptive approach, in line with the UNESCO campaign, a dark past was waning and racism itself, seen as a relic of that past, was not a matter of structures but of fallacies and moral inclinations to be corrected.

Even though the racial question was not its primary topic, *Pacem in Terris* was interpreted as a strong stance against racism, in its promotion of the goal of human unity, the moral obligation to cooperate with the United Nations, and the imperative of respect for universal civil and political rights. Ironically, LaFarge placed these instances in continuity with Pius XI's and Pius XII's magisterium: far from being an innovator, Pope John was the interpreter for modern conditions of principles already laid down by his predecessors.[53] Cronin also wrote an article, at the request of Msgr. Pietro Pavan (the encyclical's author), to dispel any doubts about the pope's mind. The correct interpretation of the text was that racial discrimination violated natural human rights and outraged Christianity, so

---

50. Daniel Degnan, "The Washington March: August 28, 1963," *Woodstock Letters* 92 (November 1963): 370.

51. Caponi, "Antirazzismo cattolico," 45–46.

52. Caponi, "Antirazzismo cattolico," 46–54.

53. John LaFarge Jr., "Pope John on Racism," *Interracial Review* 36, no. 6 (June 1963): 110–11, 123.

it could not be justified in any way ("no form of approval is being given to racial discrimination," *Pacem in Terris*, no. 44)—not, as a first unofficial English translation said, "no longer" justified. Cronin also addressed the issue of the church's silence in the face of racial discrimination. In response, he took his cue from Pius XII's silence about the extermination of the Jews, claiming that calling for "full equality" and solemnly condemning racism in earlier times would have served no purpose; in fact, this would have impeded the movement toward desegregation.[54] Moreover, within the framework of post–Civil Rights Movement Catholic antiracism, the celebration of Martin Luther King's message of love became functional in attacking the "counter-racism" of black Muslims, Malcolm X, and black nationalists, who were characterized as extremists and demagogues.

The council did not meet the expectation for a "unequivocal condemnation" of racism as "cancerous evil."[55] In the *vota* sent during the preparatory phase, communism had received much more attention than the question of race. Racism and the issue of race were included in the conciliar agenda by a narrow minority.[56] In early 1963, Archbishop Denis E. Hurley of Durban, South Africa, explained that racism was a now global problem, because nonwhite peoples of the world felt insulted by the racial sins of American, South African, and Rhodesian whites. Thus it was urgent that the council give a clear pronouncement—"something to prove beyond argument that a Christian cannot be a racist."[57] That hope remained unanswered. We should also recall that in October 1963, Bishop Robert E. Tracy of Baton Rouge, Louisiana, spoke at the council on behalf of the American episcopate to request a statement in the schema *De Ecclesia* (the basis of *Lumen Gentium*) against racial discrimination within the church, so as to provide "a doctrinal basis for future decrees."[58] This statement was reduced to the line: "In Christ and in the church there

---

54. John F. Cronin, "Pope John on Race Relations" [article for *Our Sunday Visitor*], March 19, 1964, in CUASC, USCCB, box 89, folder 18.

55. As requested by Archbishop Patrick O'Boyle of Washington in 1964: Robert C. Doty, "U.S. Bishops Urge Attack on Racism," *The New York Times*, October 29, 1964, 1, 4.

56. Joseph A. Komonchak, "U.S. Bishops' Suggestions for Vatican II," *Cristianesimo nella Storia* 15, no. 1 (June 1994): 349–52.

57. "Racism and the Council," *America* 109, no. 18 (February 2, 1963): 507.

58. Robert E. Tracy, "No Racial Discrimination," in *Council Speeches of Vatican II*, ed. Hans Küng, Yves Congar, and Daniel O'Hanlon (Paulist Press, 1964), 262–63.

is, then, no inequality arising from race or nationality, social condition or sex."⁵⁹

However, the global media coverage of Vatican II made the difference. The coverage offered by *Ebony* of the canonization of the Uganda martyrs on October 18, 1964, was a typical expression of the emotional, powerful impact of the "ecumenical moment." According to the popular African American–focused magazine, this global event before more than two thousand bishops emphasized "the stand of the Roman Catholic Church against racial discrimination."⁶⁰ For *Ebony*'s twentieth-anniversary issue, Langston Hughes chose significantly to juxtapose two covers communicating "at a glance the new roles Negroes play in today's world": the "massed faces, Negro and white" of the crowd in the 1963 March on Washington and "Pope Paul VI canonizing the Uganda Martyrs with the assistance of African Cardinal Laurian Rugambwa."⁶¹

The Limits of Post-Vatican II Antiracist Discourse

Paul VI's *Populorum Progressio* (March 26, 1967) mentioned "nationalism and racism" (without adjectives) as "obstacles to creation of a more just social order and to the development of world solidarity."⁶² In his apostolic letter *Africae Terrarum* (October 29, 1967), Montini recalled that racism had been "clearly and repeatedly condemned by the Second Vatican Ecumenical Council, in its various forms, as offensive to human dignity, 'alien to the mind of Christ,' and 'contrary to the plan of God.' "⁶³ The fact remains that the magisterium of Pope Paul VI and other postconciliar teaching are marked by a self-absolving assumption: the refrain of racism as historically anti- or non-Christian, rather than rooted in the

---

59. Second Vatican Council, Dogmatic Constitution on the Church *Lumen Gentium*, November 21, 1964, no. 32.

60. Era Bell Thompson, "Pope Confers Sainthood on 22 African Martyrs," *Ebony*, January 1965, 30.

61. Langston Hughes, "Ebony's Nativity," *Ebony*, November 1965, 41.

62. Pope Paul VI, Encyclical Letter *Populorum Progressio*, March 26, 1967, no. 62, https://www.vatican.va/content/paul-vi/en/encyclicals/documents/hf_p-vi_enc_26031967_populorum.html.

63. Pope Paul VI, Apostolic Letter *Africae Terrarum*, October 29, 1967, no. 17, https://www.vatican.va/content/paul-vi/it/apost_letters/documents/hf_p-vi_apl_19671029_africae-terrarum.html (my translation), citing *Nostra Aetate* 5 and *Gaudium et Spes* 29.

tradition of Christian supremacy itself.[64] On his apostolic journey to Uganda in 1969, Paul VI asserted the church's role in enhancing the true development of Africa's black peoples, who were considered backward but also happily unfamiliar with Western secularism and capitalist materialism. However, the esteem of African spiritual treasures was acknowledged as being vulnerable to the danger of degenerating into a reverse "racism." Remarkably, the term *racism* was now being applied to the perceived danger of Africanist black nationalism determined to erase any cultural influence of the white man, including Western Christian tradition, and thus subject to falling "into the snares of other insidious enslavements" (first of all, Marxism).[65]

The Holy See supported the United Nations' Decade to Combat Racism and Racial Discrimination (1973–83) on the basis of the "new universalism" promoted by Montini, that is, the conviction that the church's mission is to speak as an "expert in humanity."[66] Paul VI celebrated the common effort of the UN and the Vatican to protect the dignity of "every human being or every group, without distinction of race, color, language, creed."[67] The specific rationale that informed the papal position was set forth by Roger Joseph Heckel, SJ, secretary of the Pontifical Commission for Justice and Peace, in the 1978 publication *The Struggle Against Racism: Some Contributions of the Church*.[68] Heckel's report identified several enduring themes. One of these was a concern for the "ambiguous picture" of an antiracist campaign that erased cultural differences and the "positive appreciation of the complementary diversity of peoples" by overlooking

---

64. Magda Teter, *Christian Supremacy: Reckoning With the Roots of Antisemitism and Racism* (Princeton University Press, 2023).

65. Pope Paul VI, "Address of Paul VI to the Parliament of Uganda," August 1, 1969, https://www.vatican.va/content/paul-vi/en/speeches/1969/august/documents/hf_p-vi_spe_19690801_parlamento-uganda.html.

66. Jacopo Cellini, *Universalism and Liberation: Italian Catholic Culture and the Idea of International Community (1963–1978)* (Leuven University Press, 2017).

67. Pope Paul VI, "Message of His Holiness Paul VI to the President of the 28th General Assembly of the United Nations, H.E. Leopold Benites, on the 25th Anniversary of the Universal Declaration of Human Rights," December 10, 1973, https://www.vatican.va/content/paul-vi/en/messages/pont-messages/documents/hf_p-vi_mess_19731210_diritti-uomo.html.

68. Roger Heckel, *Lutte contre le racisme: Contributions de l'Eglise* (Commission Pontificale "Iustitia et Pax," 1978).

instead other kinds of discrimination, such as violations of "the sacred right to religious liberty" or the "right to life" (abortion or euthanasia).[69] Above all, the document conveyed the notion that the Catholic Church had always been antiracist. Heckel offered some arguments that would be taken up ten years later by *The Church and Racism*. These ranged from the charitable attitude toward the Indigenous people of the Americas, "confronted with the detestable behavior of explorers," or its antislavery efforts, to Pius XI's condemnation of the "the idolatry of racism." The figure of Dominican Bartolomé de las Casas, defender of the rights of Native Americans, was portrayed as an antiracist pioneer.

The assassination of Martin Luther King fostered a stronger attachment to the dream of racial equality. Catholic opinion's fascination with King's quintessential martyrdom took shape as a transatlantic phenomenon. His nonviolence was set against a divisive Black Power agenda that incited disorder in the ghettos and undermined social cohesion. A sanitized memorialization of the Civil Rights Movement represented a gateway to "banal" Catholic antiracism.[70] Black Catholicism came to widespread fruition in postconciliar mainstream Catholicism in the 1980s. It was in those years that black theology, the trope of the black Christ, and the figure of Martin Luther King himself fully entered the mass cultural industry. Cyprian Davis's landmark book *History of Black Catholics in the United States* was published in 1990, a few years after the first pastoral letter written by the black US bishops in 1984 (*What We Have Seen and Heard*). The document called black Catholics to be both "Authentically Black" and "Truly Catholic."[71] Future bishop of Belleville, Edward K. Braxton, notably spoke of "Black Power revisited."[72] The institutionalization of civil rights–style antiracism was illustrated by John Paul II, too,

---

69. I quote from the second English edition: *Struggle Against Racism: Some Contributions of the Church; The Decade of Action to Combat Racism and Racial Discrimination (1973–1983)* (Pontifical Commission "Iustitia et Pax," 2011), 19–23.

70. Matteo Caponi, "Black Martyrs, Past and Present: Racial Violence, Christian Imagination, Secular Meanings," in *Violenza sacra*, vol. 2: *Guerra santa, sacrificio e martirio in età contemporanea*, ed. Maria Paiano (Viella, 2022), 243–98.

71. *"What We Have Seen and Heard": A Pastoral Letter on Evangelization from the Black Bishops of the United States* (St. Anthony Messenger Press, 1984), 31, https://www.usccb.org/resources/what-we-have-seen-and-heard.pdf.

72. Edward K. Braxton, "The National Black Catholic Congress: An Event of the Century," *U.S. Catholic Historian* 7, nos. 2–3 (Spring–Summer 1988): 301–6.

during his 1987 apostolic journey to the United States, where he insisted: (1) Christian liberation could not be identified with black liberation, or Black Power; (2) Martin Luther King's nonviolent apostolate was the only model for Catholics; (3) "there is no black Church, no white Church, no American Church," and "black cultural heritage *enriches* the Church," basically advancing an anti-multicultural position that implicitly recognized the primacy of European/Western tradition.[73]

The duty of antiracist engagement took on unprecedented resonance in the 1980s. Did this stem directly from the Second Vatican Council? Was the Catholicism of the 1980s a belated transposition of the demands of the 1960s? Not quite. The incorporation of the difficult legacy of black radicalism came at the cost of neutralizing its most disruptive elements. What has been lost is the harsh critique of the model of antiracism devised by white Catholicism. Much has changed in the transition from black Catholicism as a counterculturalphenomenon that challenged church authorities in the name of the spirit of the council to black Catholicism as a mainstream phenomenon accepted by the church hierarchy. In 1968, the Black Catholic Clergy Caucus had denounced the Catholic Church as a "primarily white racist institution," arguing that that "non-violence in the sense of Black non-violence hoping for concessions after White brutality is dead."[74] The 1980s version of Catholic antiracism was a filtered and pacified form of that antiracist militancy.

The optimistic narrative of 1960s modernization, which translated into the momentum for universal rights, progress, racial diversity, and globalist humanity, had fueled the consensus and expectations of Vatican II. Once this framework went into crisis, manifesting also its Eurocentric and Western-centric background, religious commitment to the antiracist utopia diminished. This, in large part, renders the postconciliar response to the problem of racism out of date. Also, the opportunity to give antiracist sensibility a firmer cultural foundation has run up against the marginalization of black theology and other contextual theologies. More than any other pope, Francis has honored Martin Luther King as a source

---

73. Pope John Paul II, "Meeting with the Black Catholic Community of New Orleans," September 12, 1987, https://www.vatican.va/content/john-paul-ii/en/speeches/1987/september/documents/hf_jp-ii_spe_19870912_cattolici-new-orleans.html. Italics mine.

74. "Statement of Black Catholic Clergy Caucus" [April 18, 1968], *Journal of the Black Catholic Theological Symposium* 11 (2018): Article 3.

of inspiration.⁷⁵ However, King's race-neutral example of "fraternal love" functioned as a normative model, not only excluding the confrontational perspective of black liberation or identity politics, but also reaffirming a reassuring vision. It is time to seriously question whether the redemptive paradigm of "sin" is suitable for deconstructing an entire mindset and whether it represents a limitation in the face of the challenges of the "new" cultural racism and systemic racism.

75. See Pope Francis, Post-Synodal Apostolic Exhortation *Amoris Laetitia*, March 19, 2016, https://www.vatican.va/content/dam/francesco/pdf/apost_exhortations/documents/papa-francesco_esortazione-ap_20160319_amoris-laetitia_en.pdf; Pope Francis, Encyclical Letter *Fratelli Tutti*, October 3, 2020, https://www.vatican.va/content/francesco/en/encyclicals/documents/papa-francesco_20201003_enciclica-fratelli-tutti.html; Pope Francis, "Letter of His Holiness Pope Francis to Bernice King on the Occasion of 'Martin Luther King Jr. Day,'" January 18, 2021, https://www.vatican.va/content/francesco/en/letters/2020/documents/papa-francesco_20201203_lettera-bernice-king.html; Pope Francis, "Visit to the Joint Session of the United States Congress," September 24, 2015, https://www.vatican.va/content/francesco/en/speeches/2015/september/documents/papa-francesco_20150924_usa-us-congress.html.

Part 3

Ecclesial Responses

Chapter 16

Discerning Disciples

Lay Agency Sixty Years After Vatican II

Edward P. Hahnenberg

On November 7, 2023, Ohio voters decisively approved Issue 1, which enshrined the right to abortion in the state constitution—making Ohio the seventh state in which voters decided to strengthen or protect access to abortion since the US Supreme Court overturned Roe v. Wade in 2022.

This was not the outcome desired by the Ohio Conference of Catholic Bishops, which had campaigned aggressively to block Issue 1. The bishops themselves invested $1.7 million in the cause—including $900,000 toward an August special election ballot measure that would have made it more difficult for voters to amend the state constitution—a move clearly designed to preempt the November abortion amendment.

The failure of these efforts was cast in familiar apocalyptic terms. Following the defeat of Issue 1, the Ohio bishops wrote, "Today is a tragic day for women, children and families in Ohio. We mourn that the dignity of human life remains concealed by the duplicity of a culture of death" and promised to "pray for the conversion of minds and hearts to the gospel of life."[1]

---

1. "Catholic Bishops of Ohio Offer Statement on Issue 1 Approval," November 8, 2023, https://www.dioceseofcleveland.org/news/2023/11/08/catholic-bishops-of-ohio-offer-statement-on-issue-1-approval.

I do not have good exit poll data on how Catholics voted on the abortion amendment, but if we extrapolate from 2022 Pew data about US Catholic attitudes on abortion, it is probably safe to say that Ohio Catholics (as a whole) did not vote that differently than did other Ohioans—certainly not enough to prevent nearly six out of ten voters from supporting Issue 1, in a state that went for Donald Trump by eight percentage points in 2020 (53–45%). Although the Ohio bishops' advocacy efforts often addressed the entire Ohio electorate, their primary audience was the Catholic faithful. The media kits, bulletin inserts, and other parish resources provided by the Ohio Conference—not to mention direct appeals from the pulpit—suggest that the bishops were as concerned about mobilizing lay Catholics as they were about converting the hearts and minds of Ohioans. Close attention to the Pew data suggests that the net effect of this mobilization strategy—decades in the making—appears to be greater and greater intensity among a smaller and smaller fraction of the Catholic community. For the majority of Catholics, according to political scientist John White, the chasm between the American bishops and the laity on this issue is "a grand canyon."[2]

In highlighting the disconnect between the bishops and the Catholic laity, I do not mean to dismiss out of hand the substance of church teaching on abortion. Rather, this example serves to shine light on a broader strategy of lay mobilization being employed by church leaders. In what follows, I will argue that this mobilization strategy (a) does not seem to be working, and (b) does not seem to be working, in part, because it fails to recognize that the real challenge of the Catholic Church in the United States today, sixty years after Vatican II, is the erosion of ecclesial agency among the lay faithful.

The narrative of Vatican II's promotion of the active participation of the laity in the life and mission of the church is so firmly etched in the Catholic psyche that it may seem odd to suggest that the postconciliar story is more one of weakening, not strengthening, lay ecclesial agency. To be clear, there has not been a decline in *lay agency*, but in *lay ecclesial agency*. This decline, I will argue, is not the fault of the council but of larger societal forces. As

---

2. Cited in Brian Fraga, "Ohio Amendment Passage Shows 'Grand Canyon' Between Lay Catholics and Bishops on Abortion," November 10, 2023, https://www.ncronline.org/news/ohio-amendment-passage-shows-grand-canyon-between-lay-catholics-and-bishops-abortion. See the 2022 study by the Pew Research Center, "America's Abortion Quandary," https://www.pewresearch.org/religion/2022/05/06/americas-abortion-quandary/.

such, any attempt to foster ecclesial agency among all of the baptized today needs to attend to these larger sociological dynamics.

The argument proceeds in four steps: (1) a discussion of differing models of lay engagement on the eve of the Second Vatican Council, (2) a brief treatment of Vatican II's approach to the laity, (3) an analysis of sociological shifts in the United States, drawing on the British sociologist Margaret Archer, and (4) three suggestions for moving forward.

I. Lay Engagement on the Eve of Vatican II

On the eve of Vatican II, everyone knew that the council had to say something about the laity. There was just too much energy and interest to ignore. At least since World War I and around the world—but intensely in Europe and North America during the Catholic revival of the 1930s and the post–World War II boom of the 1950s—lay agency burst out in a proliferation of sodalities, movements, episcopal initiatives, and papal endorsements. In 1959, Holy Cross priest Fr. Leo Ward began his book *Catholic Life, U.S.A.: Contemporary Lay Movements* with exuberance: "A shelf of books could hardly tell all that is going on—in the Legion of Mary, for example, and the Rosary Crusade, the Newman Clubs, the interracial councils, the Christian Family Movement, the Retreat movement, in crowded churches and overcrowded schools, in packed communion rails, in the liturgical worship of God, in Maryknoll and Techny, in lay missionaries and lay institutes, in works and ideas associated with Dorothy Day and Thomas Merton and Bishop Sheen and John Courtney Murray—where would we ever stop?"[3]

The American experience was just one plot line in the complex, global story of lay engagement that stretched from the late nineteenth century to the Second Vatican Council. *Catholic Action* was the term coined in Italy to describe organized groups of laity advancing the church's interests. There it emerged as a response to unification in 1870, the establishment of a secular state in Italy, and the pope's concomitant loss of temporal power in the peninsula. It was, from the beginning, part of an antiliberal, antimodern program of lay mobilization and activism that aimed to reclaim the church's influence in a world gone awry. Begun under Pius IX, Catholic Action reached its peak under Pius XI, "the pope of Catholic

---

3. Leo R. Ward, *Catholic Life, U.S.A.: Contemporary Lay Movements* (Herder, 1959), 2.

Action," who organized Catholic Action into a tightly structured, hierarchically controlled, militant mass organization movement that he sought to export to the worldwide church.[4] For Pius XI, Catholic Action was restorationist through and through, part of his larger design for rebuilding society under the aegis of "Christ the King"—a feast that he established in 1925 as an enduring liturgical reminder of the papacy's last great love affair with absolute monarchy.

However, Catholic Action was not the only form of lay engagement during this period. The Italian model grew alongside a dizzying diversity of lay movements breaking out around the world in the early decades of the twentieth century. A quite different—and quite influential—model emerged in northern Europe, where the Belgian priest Joseph Cardijn established the Young Christian Workers (*Jeunesse Ouvrière Chrétienne*, or JOC) as a lay apostolate of like-to-like. Inspired by Le Sillon ("the furrow") movement in France, Cardijn adopted a methodology quite different from the more traditional dogmatic approach of other worker groups such as the French Catholic Youth Association (*Association Catholique de la Jeunesse Française*, ACJF). The ACJF process began with prayer and then moved deductively from a study of church doctrine to its application in the contemporary world. Instead, Cardijn's Jocists (from the acronym JOC) moved inductively from the concrete social reality to reflection in light of faith to action. This "enquiry method" reversed and replaced the triad of "pray–study–action" with "see–judge–act." Though his approach was very different from Pius XI's model of Catholic Action, Cardijn artfully won the pope's endorsement. Jocist groups were folded into, but not absorbed by, the pope's mobilizing agenda as *specialized forms* of Catholic Action. Subsuming Cardijn's enquiry method under the rubric of Catholic Action both masked big differences between the Italian and French-Belgian models and, at the same time, loosened the broader category of Catholic Action itself. This loosening was particularly evident in the United States, where, after 1930, the terms *Catholic Action* and the *lay apostolate* became practically synonymous—used interchangeably to describe just about anything the laity did as Catholics in the world.

---

4. John Pollard, "Pius XI's Promotion of the Italian Model of Catholic Action in the World-Wide Church," *Journal of Ecclesiastical History* 63, no. 4 (October 2012): 758–84.

These two broad tendencies reflected two different understandings of lay agency. For Pius XI, Catholic Action was "the participation of the laity in the apostolate of the Church's hierarchy."[5] It was a way for the hierarchy to continue to influence politics and culture in places clergy could no longer go. This top-town Italian model fit comfortably with a more militant confrontation with the secular world, a battle in which the hierarchy attempted to mobilize the laity for focused political activity aimed at reclaiming church prerogatives within contemporary society. The bottom-up Jocist model of "see–judge–act" imagined lay agency along the lines found in the work of Jacques Maritain, who rejected the conservative and reactionary political movements of the interwar years. Distancing himself from the Italian model of Catholic Action, Maritain preferred to speak of "the action of Catholics." He argued that direct political action is not for the church to undertake as such—whether it be undertaken by the clergy or by lay groups tightly controlled by the clergy. Instead, political action is the responsibility of lay persons acting as citizens motivated by their faith commitments. If Catholic Action privileged mobilization, Jocism privileged discernment: look around, reflect on what you see, and then act.

These different tendencies raised theological questions that were debated on the eve of the council: To whom does "the apostolate" belong? Was it given by Christ to the twelve apostles, passed down to their successors, and only then beneficently bestowed on the laity? Did ordinary Christians share in work that properly belonged to the hierarchy? Or do the lay faithful share directly in this saving mission? Is a hierarchical mandate—key to the papal vision of Catholic Action—necessary in order for the laity to act? Or do the laity take independent initiative, collaborating with the clergy, but not reliant on them?

II. Vatican II, the Laity, and Reform

Vatican II resolved the theological question decisively: The lay apostolate, as such, is not the laity's participation in the apostolate of the hierarchy. According to the council's Decree on the Apostolate of Lay

---

5. Pius XI, "Discourse to Italian Catholic Young Women," *L'Osservatore Romano*, March 21, 1927, 14.

People, *Apostolicam Actuositatem*: "Lay people's right and duty to be apostles derives from their union with Christ their head. Inserted as they are in the mystical body of Christ by baptism and strengthened by the power of the holy Spirit in confirmation, it is by the Lord himself that they are assigned to the apostolate."[6] Catholic Action—which Pius XI had once promoted as the paradigm for all lay activism—was reduced to one mode of lay engagement among many. "Collaborating with" the hierarchy replaced "participating in" their mission. Although the Decree on the Apostolate of Lay People painstakingly parsed out the various objectives, fields, and forms of lay activity, the debates and distinctions so important on the eve of the council were already melting away in the bright light of Vatican II's larger ecclesiological vision of the church as the people of God, in which all of the faithful are called to participate in the priestly, prophetic, and royal work of Christ. The triumph of Maritain, who had a champion in his friend Montini, the cardinal of Milan and future Pope Paul VI, marked a decisive turn away from the defensive, antimodern mobilization strategy of Catholic Action—symbolizing the "turn toward the world" that would characterize Vatican II's overall arc of reform.

Near the end of his long and active life, Fr. Godfrey Diekmann, the Benedictine monk, liturgical pioneer, and council peritus, summed up the ecclesiological revolution of the Second Vatican Council by quoting Pope Leo the Great: "Christian, remember your dignity!"[7] For Diekmann, the council's call was clear: "Every baptized Christian is an active, co-responsible member of the body [of Christ] having a distinctive contribution to make." This affirmation of the baptismal dignity of the laity

---

6. Second Vatican Council, Decree on the Apostolate of Lay People *Apostolicam Actuositatem*, November 18, 1965, no. 3 (hereafter, AA). All quotations from Vatican II documents are from Austin Flannery, ed., *Vatican Council II: Constitutions, Decrees, Declarations; A Completely Revised Translation in Inclusive Language* (Liturgical Press, 2014). See also *Lumen Gentium*, no. 33: "The apostolate of the laity is a sharing in the church's saving mission. Through Baptism and Confirmation all are appointed to the apostolate by the Lord himself."

7. Godfrey Diekmann, "Christian, Remember Your Baptism," remarks made as part of a panel discussion at St. John's School of Theology, Collegeville, MN, on April 17, 1997, published in *National Catholic Reporter*, February 26, 1999, https://natcath.org/NCR_Online/archives2/1999a/022699/022699j.htm.

was, for him, the first and greatest achievement—among the many achievements—of the Second Vatican Council.[8]

Taking the long view, we might see this affirmation of baptismal dignity as the culmination of the history of ecclesiology over the second Christian millennium. If the first millennium saw the gradual construction of a "two-tiered Christianity" that found its most precise articulation in Gratian's "*Duo sunt genera christianorum*"—there are "two kinds of Christians," namely, "men of religion" and "men of the world"[9]—then the second millennium was a gradual dismantling (in theory, if not in practice) of a house in which the clergy rose above and ruled over the laity.

Throughout the late medieval and early modern period, when talk turned to reform, it was the pope who got all the press. But from the Council of Constance through the Council of Trent, church reform was always understood as "reform in head *and members.*" It was as much about reforming people as it was about reforming structures. Thus, in a certain respect, both the Protestant and the Catholic Reformations of the sixteenth century had a similar goal, namely, to Christianize the peasantry of Europe. According to John O'Malley, throughout this period, the word *reform* was code for the attempt to tighten discipline, practice, and belief.[10] It was a situation in which clerical elites—both Catholic and Reformed—tried to reign in the excesses of popular religion, with all its superstitions, heterodoxy, and thinly veiled pagan culture. This tightening often meant a constriction of lay agency, which was increasingly curtailed, censored, or channeled by clerical control. The dynamics are quite complex and cannot be reduced to an elite subjugation of the masses. However, in the efforts of church leaders to get people to believe and behave, Vincent Miller sees an "elite anxiety" uncomfortable with the imaginative agency of ordinary people. "There is a seemingly intractable tension," Miller writes, "between maintaining orthodoxy and maintaining the agency of the *populus.*"[11]

---

8. Reported in Maxwell Johnson, *The Rites of Christian Initiation: Their Evolution and Interpretation* (Liturgical Press, 1999), 386.

9. See Yves Congar, *Lay People in the Church: A Study for the Theology of Laity*, trans. Donald Attwater (Newman Press, 1965), 9.

10. John W. O'Malley, *What Happened at Vatican II* (Belknap Press, 2008), 36.

11. Vincent J. Miller, "A Genealogy of Presence: Elite Anxiety and the Excesses of the Popular Sacramental Imagination," in *Sacramental Presence in a Postmodern Context*, ed. L. Boeve and L. Leijssen (Leuven University Press, 2001), 363.

Interestingly, at Vatican II—unlike all previous councils—reform was not presented as a tightening of ecclesiastical discipline, but a loosening. As O'Malley points out, rather than curtailing deviant behavior with the anathemas of the terse canon, Vatican II extended an invitation to spiritual conversion through the exhortation of long paragraphs. The council's personalist style, its emphasis on the signs of the times, its affirmation of religious liberty, its rhetoric of dialogue, its positive portrayal of other religions, other Christians, and the world at large—all of these took the form of an appeal to the hearts and minds of readers. The very style of the council encouraged personal assent and assimilation on the part of the Catholic faithful.[12] It shifted church teaching away from the model of mass mobilization and toward that of personal discernment.

Inspired by this openness, the period of enthusiasm, experimentation, and energy that followed the council represented a new style of lay agency. In the United States, this shift in style was facilitated by profound cultural shifts. Vatican II coincided with not only the societal upheaval of the Sixties, but also the culmination of American Catholicism's slow capitulation to the forces of religious voluntarism, aided and abetted by the First Amendment, religious pluralism, and the dissolution of the American Catholic subculture.[13] Even the fault line opened up by *Humanae Vitae*, Paul VI's 1968 encyclical on birth control, which is often portrayed as a pivotal moment of lay disillusion and disengagement, served only to reinforce and accelerate a shift already underway—from a mode of membership emphasizing deference and obedience toward a type of individual agency that privileged conscience and discernment. It is interesting to note that two of the most famous members of the Papal Birth Control Commission, Pat and Patty Crowley, came out of the Christian Family Movement—an international apostolate of "like-to-like" imbued with Cardijn's enquiry method of "see–judge–act." Not surprisingly, their mode was discernment, not mobilization.

Given that Vatican II's style of reform was one of loosening rather than tightening, it is not surprising that, a decade later, the pendulum began to swing back under the leadership of the dynamic Polish pope. The legacy

---

12. John W. O'Malley, "Vatican II: Did Anything Happen?," *Theological Studies* 67 (2006): 3–33; O'Malley, *What Happened at Vatican II*, 43–52.

13. William L. Portier, "Here Come the Evangelical Catholics," *Communio* 31 (Spring 2004): 35–66.

of John Paul II is complex—and impossible to reduce to a tightening of doctrine and discipline. He displayed impressive openness toward interreligious dialogue, toward engaging political leaders, toward defending the rights of workers and the dignity of human life. His writings on the universal call to holiness and the diversity of vocations are beautiful and profound. Even his efforts to reign in dissent and to shore up orthodoxy were aimed more at elites—theologians and bishops—than at ordinary people. Yet, in his dualistic vision of the "culture of life" confronting a "culture of death" and in his attempts to build an ecclesial united front in which clergy lead and laity learn, John Paul II fostered a more sophisticated (and less overtly political) version of Pius XI's mobilization strategy. This is seen nowhere more clearly than in his special solicitude for those new ecclesial movements (Communion and Liberation, Opus Dei, Legionaries of Christ, and the like) that sought his patronage and protection.[14]

III. The Reflexive Imperative of Late Modernity

The trouble with John Paul II's strategy of mobilization, which still dominates within the US hierarchy, is that mobilization requires a more or less well-defined group with a shared identity and common concerns. But this kind of group identity has been in precipitous decline for over thirty years—not just among Catholics, but among the majority of people living in postindustrial countries like the United States. Precisely at the moment that John Paul II leaned into a strategy of mobilization, forces within society, culture, politics, economics, and technology combined to undermine the very modes of socialization that such mobilization would require.

The British sociologist Margaret Archer identified the late 1980s as a turning point in the social and cultural constitution of the developed world. The launch of the World Wide Web, combined with the expansion of multinational corporations and the deregulation of finance markets opened an era of unprecedented societal change—shifting the balance from what she calls societal morphostasis (that is, a society governed by

---

14. See Massimo Faggioli, *Sorting Out Catholicism: A Brief History of the New Ecclesial Movements*, trans. Demetrio S. Yocum (Liturgical Press, 2014); Faggioli, *The Rising Laity: Ecclesial Movements Since Vatican II* (Paulist Press, 2016).

processes that tend to stabilize and reinforce the status quo) to societal morphogenesis (that is, a society governed by processes that tend toward change).[15]

As a leading theorist of the critical realist school of social thought, Archer offered a compelling approach to the classic "structure-agency" problem that has so bedeviled sociologists. In her larger project, Archer strove to avoid the extremes of both methodological individualism, which seeks to explain society exclusively in terms of human actions, and methodological collectivism, which seeks to explain human behavior exclusively in terms of social conditioning. Archer held up *agency*, *structure*, and *culture* as three irreducibly distinct realities. In doing so, she identified *reflexivity* as the key to explaining how these three realities influence one another. Reflexivity is defined as "the regular exercise of the mental ability, shared by all normal people, to consider themselves in relation to their (social) contexts and vice versa."[16] Through what she called the "internal conversation," people determine how to act by engaging in reflexive deliberations about their concerns in light of the various restrictions, enablements, incentives, and disincentives created by their place within a particular social context. Social structures move individuals, but only *through* their freedom as agents.

This dynamic plays out over the course of human history, with particular societies marked by their own combination of morphostatic and morphogenetic processes. In highly morphostatic societies—where little changes over time, traditional roles dominate, and social mobility is low—reflexivity hums along, called upon, but not overly taxed, to select from among a limited number of possible activities and life choices. With the advent of globalization, reflexivity is kicked into high gear, creating what Archer calls the "reflexive imperative." Under this imperative, everyone has to choose, from an almost infinite number of opportunities, all of the time. "This synergy increased from the 1980s onward, multiplying the variety of alternatives available, especially in terms of work and employment. It also burdened people with exercising their personal re-

---

15. Margaret S. Archer, *The Reflexive Imperative in Late Modernity* (Cambridge University Press, 2012), 4.
16. Margaret S. Archer, *Making Our Way Through the World: Human Reflexivity and Social Mobility* (Cambridge University Press, 2007), 4; see Archer, *Structure, Agency and the Internal Conversation* (Cambridge University Press, 2003).

flexivity more intensively in order to make choices in uncharted territory. The previous guidelines, functioning in a slowly changing context, were rapidly becoming outdated. The occupational pattern of sons following their fathers or peers joining their mates was shattering. In place of such guidance, subjects were increasingly thrown back upon their own personal concerns as the only compass to guide action."[17]

These shifts in the developed world led to the decline of "communicative reflexivity," characteristic of traditional societies, in which personal concerns are deeply embedded in local and familial contexts, seek affirmation from trusted others, and tend toward social reproduction (i.e., repeating what has always been done). Alongside the decline of "communicative reflexivity" came an upsurge in "autonomous reflexivity," fueled by the multiplication of opportunities, favoring individualism and independence, with personal achievement more important than social cohesion and advancement more important that stability. Alongside these two opposing tendencies, Archer's empirical research surfaced two additional categories. "Meta-reflexives" are those most committed to moral ideals that cannot be accommodated by contemporary socioeconomic and cultural structures. They are the critics of both traditional social forms as well as modern modes of competition and consumption. The fourth group are the victims of accelerated morphogenesis. These are the "fractured reflexives," who find the imperative to choose paralyzing. "For them, the internal conversation serves only to intensify personal distress and disorientation because their reflexive deliberations go round in circles without enabling them to define any purposive courses of action to lead out of their difficulties."[18]

According to Archer, these four modes of reflexivity are practiced by all of us some of the time—on different occasions around different issues. However, most people have a dominant mode.[19] In postindustrial countries like the United States, the communicative mode has been losing ground for decades; the autonomous mode is the firmly ensconced majority; the

---

17. Margaret S. Archer, "Structural Conditioning and Personal Reflexivity: Sources of Market Complicity, Critique, and Change," 40–41, in *Distant Markets, Distant Harms: Economic Complicity and Christian Ethics*, ed. Daniel K. Finn (Oxford University Press, 2014).

18. Archer, "Structural Conditioning and Personal Reflexivity," 39.

19. Archer, *The Reflexive Imperative*, 12.

meta-reflexives and the fractured reflexives are on the rise. The bottom line of the "reflexive imperative" is that *no one* now can escape the burden of individual choice. Even the neotraditionalists, as Peter Berger argues, are caught up in it: "For them tradition is not simply given, they have *chosen* it."[20] As Archer puts it, "social reproduction becomes just as reflexive an enterprise as those that promote yet further transformations."[21]

Drawing on Archer, Ulrich Beck, and Peter Berger, Gerardo Martí sums up the challenge for religious traditions today: "The combination of diversity, unpredictability, and vast scope of options means there is less opportunity for internalization of norms because there is less that is 'normal' and less that is normatively binding. We consciously supervise our selves, selecting and correcting 'on the fly,' yet unable to draw on either set patterns or past experiences."[22] The novelty of contemporary morphogenetic society fosters "an increasingly normalized experience of idiosyncrasy," undermining "many of the certainties by which human beings used to live."[23] Individuals, Martí argues, "are being released from religious action based on a deep treasure trove of stable identity packages and secure programmatic responses."[24] Quoting Archer, "in a world of novelty, there are no apprenticeships."[25]

If Martí and Archer are right, if traditional socialization and the habituation of thought and action are more difficult today, then strategies of religious mobilization—which presume that people already belong—are destined to fail. For example, there is something very different about the US Catholicism of the 1970s and 1980s and the US Catholicism of the 2020s. The slogan "We are church!" meant something then, because there was a "we" that resonated within the personal identity of individual Catholics. Traditional processes of socialization and habituation still obtained for a majority of American Catholics in the immediate post-

---

20. Cited in Peter L. Berger, *The Many Altars of Modernity: Toward a Paradigm for Religion in a Pluralist Age* (De Gruyter, 2014), 10.

21. Margaret S. Archer, "The Trajectory of the Morphogenetic Approach: An Account in the First-Person," *Sociologia: Problemas E Praticas* 54 (2007): 44.

22. Gerardo Martí, "Religious Reflexivity: The Effect of Continual Novelty and Diversity on Individual Religiosity," *Sociology of Religion* 76, no. 1 (2015): 6.

23. Martí, "Religious Reflexivity," 5.

24. Martí, "Religious Reflexivity," 2.

25. Martí, "Religious Reflexivity," 7.

conciliar period. A half-century later, that is no longer the case. Under accelerated morphogenesis, individual agents are increasingly dependent on their individual personal concerns as their only guide to action. Indeed, for Archer, it is our constellation of concerns (the things "I care about") that defines our identity. "It is our human concerns—especially our ultimate concerns—that are pivotal because they serve to direct what we do with our agency."[26] What is it that matters to me? These are the concerns that I consolidate into projects, entailing practices, that (hopefully) establish a satisfying and sustainable *modus vivendi*. I do not merely live my life. In the words of Archer, I *shape a life*.

IV. Suggestions for Moving Forward

The great threat to the church today is not a lack of orthodoxy among the faithful but a lack of ecclesial agency. What do I mean by ecclesial agency? Vincent Miller makes a distinction that I see in my own students. My students have a good sense of themselves as active agents *of their beliefs*. They know that they get to pick. And they are quite comfortable drawing from all kinds of sources in constructing their own personal, highly individualized belief system. What they do not have is a sense of themselves as active agents *of their religious tradition*. They have no sense of ecclesial agency, no sense that, as baptized Christians, they are each "an active, co-responsible member of the body [of Christ] having a distinctive contribution to make," to quote Diekmann. Why? Because they have never felt authorized to engage meaningfully in this ecclesial project for which we are all responsible. In fact, more often than not, my students (like many of us) are actively socialized into *passivity*. Whenever they are dragged to church and find it has nothing to do with them; whenever they get a lame answer to a serious question; whenever they watch their parents roll their eyes at a boring homily; whenever they hear church leaders say mean things about their gay friends, they are being socialized into passivity. Since there is really nothing for them to do about it, there is really nothing to do. Even complaining doesn't seem worth the effort. Why bother?

To be clear: The concern I have is not whether lay Catholics will continue to exercise agency. They will. In fact, as I hope I have demonstrated,

---

26. Archer, *The Reflexive Imperative*, 22.

the imperative to do so has only intensified in recent decades. The question is not whether lay people will exercise agency but whether they will see their agency as in any way tied to a particular community and tradition—to a church.[27]

"In the past," Miller argues, "clerics concerned about the excesses of popular religion could presume its unremitting vitality. Thus they could limit their responsibility to censoring, correcting, and controlling it." That is no longer the world in which we live. In the "cultural maelstrom of advanced capitalism," we simply cannot presume the vitality of any particular religious culture. Indeed, the very survival of these cultures is what is at stake. This presents a very different challenge for church leaders. As Miller concludes, "Censoring an incorrigible culture is one task, preserving a vulnerable one is quite another."[28]

In the conviction that the Christian Gospel offers a deeply meaningful way of life, that the words and deeds of Jesus Christ, the example of the saints, the teaching of the church, the celebration of the sacraments all offer a fulfilling, integrated, and life-giving *modus vivendi*, how should the church community envision its role in a world of hyper-reflexivity? How can we foster participation, activity, and engagement? How can we promote a kind of agency among all the baptized that is deeply ecclesial, that is not only an agency of the members of the body of Christ but agency *as* members of the body of Christ?

1. Reimagine Socialization as an Active Process

This is a point developed at length by Archer and Pierpaolo Donati, in their coauthored book, *The Relational Subject*. The older view of socialization as a largely passive process of internalization of group norms no longer holds. There is simply less and less that is normal or normatively binding. Even within the home, more and more parents or caretakers send mixed messages, unable to offer consistent and coherent guidelines to their children for navigating their lives in contemporary society. And then there are their phones, which offer a constantly changing, infinite array of teachers, models, and mentors. "Given the decline of authorita-

---

27. Vincent Miller, *Consuming Religion: Christian Faith and Practice in a Consumer Culture* (Continuum, 2003), 213.

28. Miller, *Consuming Religion*, 211.

tive sources of normativity, young people are increasingly thrown back upon reflexively assessing how to realize their personal concerns in order to make their way through the world."[29]

In such a situation of "contextual incongruity," socialization has to be reconceived as an active, reflexive, and relational process.[30] Young people (and not so young people) are constantly bombarded with new experiences. But subjects are not inert targets. Each "invitation" to a new experience prompts a response from the subject (agreement, disagreement, satisfaction, dissatisfaction). For Archer, the really important response "is the subject's discovery that a previously unknown experience '*matters to me.*'"[31] For something to matter, you have to care about it. To care is to have a concern. To have a concern is a challenge to make a commitment. One's constellations of concerns lead to the commitments that build our identities, affirm a particular engagement with the world, and shape a satisfying and sustainable *modus vivendi*.

As an active, reflexive, and relational process, socialization begins with the subject selecting, from a vast menu of options, what is and what is not important and thus determining what they regard as worthwhile (at least for now). Typically, a number of things emerge as important. There are multiple things that matter to each of us. So, we must prioritize our concerns, deliberating on their relative importance, and then subordinate lesser concerns to our ultimate concern or concerns. In the past, this prioritization was done for individuals by the system. Growing up in the morphostatic society that was St. Mary's Parish and School, I knew that going to church was a priority and that my relationship with Jesus Christ was the most important thing in my life. I did not have to figure that out on my own; it was simply a given. That is not the case for most young people growing up today, who have thrust onto their shoulders the full weight and responsibility of deciding what matters most.

To avoid reducing this deliberation to a kind of cost-benefit analysis among competing or incompatible ultimate concerns, Archer relies on an intuition of the philosopher Charles Taylor: People know that a diversity of concerns needs to be balanced with the unity of a life. This effort

---

29. Margaret S. Archer, "Socialization as Relational Reflexivity," in Pierpaolo Donati and Margaret S. Archer, *The Relational Subject* (Cambridge University Press, 2015), 127.
30. Archer, "Socialization as Relational Reflexivity," 128.
31. Archer, "Socialization as Relational Reflexivity," 128.

at integrating our various concerns works through a process Archer calls "dovetailing."[32] It is not that we hold up and judge the relative worth of different ultimate concerns independently. Rather, we take these concerns—arising from new experiences—and reflect on how they fit or do not fit together in the unfolding of our lives. Taylor writes, "In the end, what we are called upon to do is not just carry out isolated acts, each one being right, but to live a life, and that means to be and become a certain kind of human being."[33] Cultivating discerning disciples, thus, is a process of helping people actively construct a sense of unity of life in which their various concerns dovetail with the Gospel call. It entails, first, exposure to the kind of experiences that lead people to the realization that "this matters to me." Second, it requires providing resources that can assist people in dovetailing this newly awakened concern with the other concerns already operative in their lives.

In a society governed by the "reflexive imperative," evangelization cannot begin with a condemnation of all that is wrong with the world (even though there is a lot that is wrong with the world), nor can it take shape as a swaggering, self-assured proclamation of truth to an ignorant or inert mass audience. Rather, it begins with a recognition that everyone today is already working hard to shape a life around what they see as important. Rather than dismiss these concerns, the evangelist will need to listen to these concerns and accompany people through a lifelong process of active socialization that explores together how faith fits, forms, reforms, and gives finality to the various concerns people bring, thus shaping a satisfactory and sustainable *modus vitae christianae*.

2. Build Up Relational Goods of the Local Church Community

According to Archer's ontology of emergence, any relation (interpersonal or otherwise) formed by a subject's concerns "has its own (*sui generis*) reality because it possesses its own properties and causal powers."[34] Healthy relations between subjects generate "relational goods" (an obvious example

---

32. Archer, "Socialization as Relational Reflexivity," 135.

33. Charles Taylor, "Leading a Life," in *Incommensurability, Incompatibility and Practical Reason*, ed. Ruth Chang (Harvard University Press, 1997), 179. Cited in Archer, "Socialization as Relational Reflexivity," 136.

34. Margaret S. Archer and Pierpaolo Donati, "The Plural Subject versus the Relational Subject," in Donati and Archer, *The Relational Subject*, 55.

being friendship) that enter into the ongoing discernment of the subjects involved, whose personal reflexivity increasingly becomes a relational reflexivity insofar as subjects orient their individual actions and understand their personal identities (at least partly) in light of the relationship.

Recognizing the importance of such relational goods, Gerardo Martí argues for the ongoing relevance of religious congregations. This is not to buttress the faith of those few believers still operating out of a stable communicative mode, but rather to respond to the real needs of the autonomous, meta-, and fractured reflexives. Under the reflexive imperative of late modernity, shaping a life involves moving one's *concerns* to *projects* that involve *practices* that, together, establish a satisfactory and sustainable way of life. Concerns need networks capable of nurturing them into commitments.[35] Thus, the work of reflexivity inevitably involves a network of relationships. Martí writes: "One reason why congregations remain salient for contemporary religion is because congregations are places that coalesce a rich coterie of social relationships involved in prioritizing, accommodating, subordinating, and excluding ideas and practices. Congregations legitimate religious principles and help individual adherents stabilize and maintain personal conviction. So while individuals have various social relations and social circles, the most organized 'package' of responses, the largest 'resource' for reflection, and the highest concentration of relational exchanges that serve religious reflexivity continue to be found in organized congregations—however flexibly 'congregations' may be defined."[36] Congregations can provide contexts, relationships, imaginative options, and resources for ongoing deliberation and lifelong socialization in an active mode.

3. Advance Structural Reform to Expand Social Positions for All of the Baptized

The key mediating mechanism between agency and structure is the "internal conversation," the process by which subjects deliberate reflexively about their personal concerns in relation to their social contexts and about their contexts in relation to their concerns. Social structures influence human agents not through any kind of social determinism but

---

35. Archer, "Structural Conditioning and Personal Reflexivity," 44.
36. Martí, "Religious Reflexivity," 9.

through the exercise of human freedom. The key is to recognize that the causal power of social structures *flows through* human relations to direct human action. To put it more precisely, it is the relationship among social *positions* (which together constitute a given social structure) that create certain restrictions, enablements, incentives, and disincentives that influence the individual agents operating within a given social structure. Agents are free, but they are always already contextualized within various social structures. These structures "cause" the individual to act in certain ways but only because the individual makes decisions in light of these incentives and disincentives. It is crucial to note that these incentives and disincentives are built into the relationships among social positions—not the relations among *people* but among *positions*. People in certain positions are empowered to do certain things, and people in certain positions are disempowered from doing certain things.

The causal power of social positions is the reason why structural reform remains an important aspect of fostering lay agency in the church. Discernment, deliberation, and dedication take place within a given context. How agents imagine ways to channel their commitments depends on the roles available to them. That is why two of the most successful examples of lay ecclesial agency in the United States since the council—lay ecclesial ministers and lay theologians—took off. Both had social positions (roles within the social structure) open up, within which and through which lay people could exercise their agency. In most cases, however, once the experience of faith awakens something in an agent, the dearth of meaningful roles in many Catholic communities encourages the believer to either cultivate their faith life apart from the church or to seek out other religious or nonreligious modes of purposeful living.

Conclusion

A sign of hope is that all three of these concerns—accompaniment, community vibrancy, and structural reform—have emerged out of the synodal process currently underway. Might the universal church be slowly turning from strategies of mass mobilization and turning instead to a kind of communal discernment that attends to the actual concerns of people today?

As we reflect on the limits and legacy of Vatican II in facing deeply entrenched difficulties around gender, race, and abuse, it is important to keep mind that those of us engaged in this conversation are people who already care. We not only care about these issues, but we also care about how the church is caught up in and called to respond to these issues. All of this matters to us. If we want it to matter to others, a first step is to attend to the demands of the present to actively cultivate lay ecclesial agency.

Chapter 17

Catholic Higher Education at Our Lord's Tomb

Toward a Pedagogy of Holy Saturday in Our Age of Contempt

Timothy Hanchin

The signature document of Vatican II, *Gaudium et Spes* (The Pastoral Constitution on the Church in the Modern World), begins with an expression of solidarity: "The joys and hopes, the grief and anguish of the people of our time, especially of those who are poor or afflicted, are the joys and hopes, the grief and anguish of the followers of Christ as well."[1] This solidarity with the people of our time is the *sine qua non* for Christian discipleship today. This solidarity led by the Holy Spirit continues the work of Christ, who came into the world not to judge but to save, not to be served but to serve. Vatican II emphasized that the church must mediate not just a doctrine but the living Christ, the kerygma.

A crisis in conversation spanning the church, academy, and public square undermines solidarity with the people of our time. The failure of communication, evidenced in polarization and contempt, is a particular

---

1. Second Vatican Council, Pastoral Constitution on the Church in the Modern World *Gaudium et Spes*, December 7, 1965, no. 1, in Austin Flannery, ed., *Vatican Council II: Constitutions, Decrees, Declarations; A Completely Revised Translation in Inclusive Language* (Liturgical Press, 2014).

threat to the university, which exists in order to foster and embody "the conversation that we are," in the words of the poet Friederich Hölderlin.[2] This crisis in conversation is more than intellectual. We cannot reason our way out of deep-seated interpersonal breakdowns in communication because they implicate us in our entirety. For this reason, Catholic higher education has a unique contribution to make. Catholic education addresses the interconnectedness of intellectual, moral, and religious development. The interlocking crises of abuse, gender discrimination, racism, colonialism, and ecology remain intractable unless the fundamental breakdown in conversation is squarely addressed.

A pedagogy of Holy Saturday is a way for Catholic higher education to respond to Vatican II's clarion call for solidarity with the people of our time formed by a culture of contempt. According to Pope John Paul II's apostolic constitution *Ex Corde Ecclesiae* (From the Heart of the Church), a Catholic University "by *institutional commitment*, brings to its task the light and inspiration of the Christian message."[3] A pedagogy of Holy Saturday, according to Swiss theologian Hans Urs von Balthasar, draws inspiration from the claim that Christ went to the dead and was truly dead in solidarity with the dead.[4] Balthasar's somewhat eccentric account of Holy Saturday provides an aesthetic inversion of our culture of contempt. A pedagogy of Holy Saturday foregrounds the aesthetic dimension of Catholic education, which invites conversion beyond merely rationalistic, sociological, and psychological appeals. A pedagogy of Holy Saturday practices silence, tarrying, and empathetic understanding. These

---

2. Friederich Hölderlin, "Celebration of Peace," in Hölderlin, *Selected Poems*, trans. David Constantine (Bloodaxe, 2018), 123–30.

3. Pope John Paul II, Apostolic Constitution *Ex Corde Ecclesiae*, August 15, 1990, no. 14, https://www.vatican.va/content/john-paul-ii/en/apost_constitutions/documents/hf_jp-ii_apc_15081990_ex-corde-ecclesiae.html (hereafter, ECE).

4. Hans Urs von Balthasar, *Mysterium Paschale: The Mystery of Easter*, trans. Aidan Nichols, OP (Ignatius, 2000), 148–88. Despite his brilliance, Balthasar (1905–88) was passed over for participation in the Second Vatican Council. Pope Paul VI added him to the International Theological Commission in 1969, and Pope John Paul II named him a cardinal in 1988. He died two days before the ceremony. Balthasar embraced the *ressourcement* movement in Catholicism over against a calcified neoscholasticism. Henri de Lubac described his friend and devotee as "perhaps the most cultivated of his time." See Henri de Lubac, SJ, "A Witness of Christ in the Church: Hans Urs von Balthasar's Life," *Communio* 2, no. 3 (Fall 1975): 320.

pedagogical practices, informed by Balthasar's Holy Saturday, promote healing and unity in our age of contempt.

The Culture of Contempt

Social scientists have studied human conflict due to "motive attribution asymmetry," the phenomenon of assuming that your ideology expresses love while your opponent's ideology stems from hate. For example, researchers studying political attitudes in the United States determined that a majority of Republicans and Democrats suffer from motive attribution asymmetry.[5] Motive attribution asymmetry invalidates empathy and understands compromise as weak-kneed surrender. A January 2017 Reuters/Ipsos poll revealed that one in six Americans had stopped talking to a close friend or family member because of the 2016 presidential election.[6] Recent widespread campus unrest over the war in Gaza signals the breakdown of communication in the academy. Online, our virtual identities exacerbate these divisions. Online publications increasingly closely monitor or eliminate comment sections because of toxic communication habits. This trend is not confined to politics or cyberspace. Pope Francis decries a "virus of polarization and animosity" permeating the church itself.[7] This sickness metaphor applied to the Body of Christ indicates the failure of people of faith to disagree with each other in charity.

The crisis in conversation is commonly labeled polarization, tribalism, or partisanship. The category of *contempt* offers a deeper diagnosis because it illuminates the all-encompassing dimension of the current crisis

---

5. Adam Waytz, Liane L. Young, and Jeremy Ginges, "Motive Attribution Asymmetry for Love vs. Hate Drives Intractable Conflict," *Proceedings of the National Academy of Sciences of the United States of America* 111, no. 44 (November 2014): 15687–92.

6. John Whitesides, "From Disputes to Breakup: Wounds Still Raw After U.S. Elections," Reuters, February 7, 2017, https://www.reuters.com/article/world/from-disputes-to-a-breakup-wounds-still-raw-after-us-election-idUSKBN15M13K/.

7. Joshua McElwee, "Creating New Cardinals, Francis Warns Against Virus of Polarization in the Church," *National Catholic Reporter*, November 16, 2016, https://www.ncronline.org/creating-new-cardinals-francis-warns-against-virus-polarization-church. See also *Polarization in the US Catholic Church: Naming the Wounds, Beginning to Heal*, ed. Mary Ellen Konieczny, Charles C. Camosy, and Tricia C. Bruce (Liturgical Press, 2016), and John L. Allen, *Catholics & Contempt: How Catholic Media Fuel Today's Fights and What to Do About It* (Word on Fire Institute, 2023).

in conversation. Unlike other emotions, contempt encompasses the whole person rather than an aspect of the person. We can deal with various negative emotions in relationships, but contempt seems to be its own category. Social psychologist John Gottman can predict with 94 percent accuracy whether a couple will divorce within three years.[8] The most significant indicator of separation is not anger but signs of contempt. The little acts of sarcasm, sneering, hostile humor, and eye-rolling communicate worthlessness to the person we promise to love beyond conditions. Gottman calls contempt "sulfuric acid for love."[9] The philosopher Arthur Schopenhauer described contempt as "the unsullied conviction of the worthlessness of another."[10]

The difference between contempt and anger further illustrates the all-encompassing nature of this emotion. Typically, contempt does not produce anger because it lacks the desire to repair the relationship. Anger is usually directed at a person for something they have done, but contempt is an adverse reaction toward the person themselves. Anger signals hope, sometimes faintly, for reconciliation through continued engagement. However, contempt regards the entire person as unworthy of communication and beneath care. In his essay "Freedom and Resentment," P. F. Strawson differentiates between *participant* and *objective* attitudes. From a participant attitude, we view others as fellow moral actors, accountable for their words and actions. From an objectivist attitude, we view others as objects to manage and overcome rather than fellow moral agents.[11] Contempt shifts others from a participant to an objective relationship. Its denial of recognition is a denial of another's dignity and membership in the human community.

Contempt is dangerous because it potentially affects our relationship with all humans, including ourselves. Contempt threatens the whole

---

8. Kim T. Buehlman, John M. Gottman, and Lynn F. Katz, "How a Couple Views Their Past Lives Predicts Their Future: Predicting Divorce from an Oral History Interview," *Journal of Family Psychology* 5, nos. 3–4 (1992): 295–318.

9. Agneta H. Fischer and Ira J. Roseman, "Beat Them or Ban Them: The Characteristics and Social Functions of Anger and Contempt," *Journal of Personality and Social Psychology* 93, no. 1 (2007): 103–15.

10. Arthur Schopenhauer, *Essays and Aphorisms*, trans. R. J. Hollingdale (Penguin Books, 2004), 170.

11. P. F. Strawson, *Freedom and Resentment and Other Essays* (Methuen, 1974), 1–25.

moral community. Karen Stohr explains contempt from a Kantian perspective: "If we think that even one rational being doesn't deserve recognition respect, we are no longer treating dignity as the basis of our decisions about treating people respectfully. Instead, we're making that distinction on the basis of their race, or their political party, or just whether we like them. . . . In a way, denying recognition respect to one rational being is effectively denying recognition respect to all rational beings."[12] Responding to contempt with contempt merely legitimizes its role in the public square. Righteous indignation can readily morph into contempt, given our propensities for self-conceit and moral superiority, often fanned by social media and the outrage industrial complex. Hope in humanity requires hope that individuals—all individuals—can contribute to moral progress.

Hans Urs von Balthasar provides an aesthetic inversion of contempt through his examination of Christ's radical solidarity with the dead embodied in his non-victorious descent into hell. Balthasar's theological aesthetics provides hope for humanity with the "dark kernel of the cross at its center." According to Jennifer Newsome Martin, the "nocturnal elements of suffering and death" are transfigured to love and glory.[13]

Balthasar's Holy Saturday

Hans Urs von Balthasar's theology of Christ's descent into hell on Holy Saturday is the heart of his theological legacy and chief innovation. While previous accounts of the descent in both East and West assumed that Christ was active in hell (which reflects 1 Peter 3:19, that Christ "also . . . went and made a proclamation to the spirits in prison"), Balthasar insists on Christ's total passivity in hell:

> Jesus was truly dead, because he really became a man as we are, a son of Adam, and therefore, despite what one can sometimes read in certain theological works, he did not use the so-called "brief" time of his death for all manner of "activities" in the world beyond. . . . In the same way

---

12. Karen Stohr, *Choosing Freedom: A Kantian Guide to Life* (Oxford University, 2022), 149.

13. Jennifer Newsome Martin, *Hans Urs von Balthasar and the Critical Appropriation of Russian Religious Thought* (University of Notre Dame Press, 2015), 72.

that, upon earth, he was in solidarity with the living, so, in the tomb, he is in solidarity with the dead. One must allow to this "solidarity" an amplitude and an ambiguity, even, which seems precisely to exclude a communication on his part as subject. Each human being lies in his own tomb. And with this condition . . . Jesus is in complete solidarity.[14]

For Balthasar, Christ's transvaluation of human death is not performative; rather, "he bores right through it to the bottom, to the chaotic formlessness of the death cry (Matt 27:50) and the wordless silence of death on Holy Saturday."[15] Christ's death demonstrates solidarity with human beings both in death and in absolute forsakenness from God. Christ's descent into hell, "which is not a glorious or triumphant descent but a sinking down in the absolute passivity of true death."[16] For Balthasar, Christ was truly dead and marked by inactivity and profound loneliness, being in contact neither with other souls nor God.[17] This condition of the dead further demonstrates Jesus' perfect surrender and transparency to the Father.

According to Balthasar, our salvation stems from Christ's encounter with the reality of human death "as a whole" that is body and soul, for that is how he overcame human death: "By allowing the horror of death to penetrate his innermost, loving heart and show that, dying, buried, and descending into the underworld, he had a longer breath than death and hell."[18] In other words, "he stood *under* death and not *above* it."[19] Balthasar criticizes the traditional, rather dualistic image of Christ's descent into hell because his soul seems "too active" or rather "too alive," as if his soul were completely separated from the dead body in the tomb. Although the traditional teachings emphasize that Christ was really dead, the traditional image of Christ's soul in hell is filled with action: He preaches to the dead,

---

14. Balthasar, *Mysterium Paschale*, 148–49. See Edward T. Oaks, "The Internal Logic of Holy Saturday in the Theology of Hans Urs von Balthasar," *International Journal of Systematic Theology* 92, no. 4 (2007): 192.

15. Hans Urs von Balthasar, *Theological Anthropology* (Wipf & Stock, 2010), 242.

16. Newsome Martin, *Hans Urs von Balthasar*, 134.

17. Hans Urs von Balthasar, *Explorations in Theology*, vol. 4, *Spirit and Institution*, trans. Edward T. Oaks (Ignatius, 1993), 407–8.

18. Hans Urs von Balthasar, *You Crown the Year with Your Goodness: Radio Sermons*, trans. Graham Harrison (Ignatius, 1982), 117.

19. Balthasar, *You Crown the Year*, 116.

he delivers the just of the Old Testament out of *Sheol*, and he even fights with the devil.[20] For Balthasar, Jesus' passivity in hell contrasts with his active self-surrender on Good Friday. Balthasar explains, "For then the solidarity with the condition of the dead would be the prior condition for the work of redemption, whose effects would be deployed and exercised in the 'realm' of the dead, though that work itself would remain fundamentally finished (*consumatum est!*) on the Cross."[21]

Holy Saturday, for Balthasar, means that there is no place or state where God is not, even the moment of absolute forsakenness of human choosing, for Christ has already willingly gone down to hell. "Anyone who tries to choose complete forsakenness—in order to prove himself absolute vis-à-vis God—finds himself confronted by the figure of someone even 'more absolutely' forsaken than himself."[22] Paradoxically, Balthasar preserves hope in the possibility of salvation of all persons because of Christ's radical solidarity with the dead in his non-victorious descent into hell. On this point, Balthasar echoes the patristic teachings of Gregory of Nyssa that Christ's light shines in the darkest darkness and Athanasius that "the Lord has touched all parts of creation . . . so that each might find the Logos everywhere, even the one who has strayed into the world of demons."[23] Christ's descent into hell on Holy Saturday "is the moment at which a proleptic light of mercy can shine redemptively."[24]

Balthasar understands the descent into hell as a trinitarian event that is both inevitable and possible because God is triune. Hell is the supreme consequence of distorted human freedom. God the Father creates the world out of love, which entails human freedom, even the freedom to reject God. The Father sends the Son not to judge the world but to save it. The Son descends into hell as "the final consequence of the redemptive mission he received from the Father."[25] The Son, a cadaver in hell, reveals both God's resolute respect for human freedom and God's all-embracing

---

20. Riyako Cecilia Hikota, *And Still We Wait: Hans Urs von Balthasar's Theology of Holy Saturday and Christian Discipleship* (Pickwick Publications, 2018), 165–66.

21. Balthasar, *Mysterium Paschale*, 150.

22. Hans Urs von Balthasar, *Theo-Drama: Theological Dramatic Theory*, vol. 5: *The Last Act*, trans. Graham Harrison (Ignatius, 1998), 312.

23. Balthasar, *Mysterium Paschale*, 167.

24. Newsome Martin, *Hans Urs von Balthasar*, 136.

25. Balthasar, *Mysterium Paschale*, 174.

love, including accompanying us in hell. The Son descends to hell to be in solidarity with sinners "out of an ultimate love." The Son "disturbs the absolute loneliness striven for by the sinner."[26] Therefore, hell is both a real possibility for the sinner and the place of the triune God's limitless love.

That God is triune makes the Son's descent possible. Balthasar describes this mystery: "God can simultaneously remain in himself and step forth from himself. And, in thus stepping forth from himself into the abyss of all that is anti-divine; God does nothing anti-divine—the sinner does—but he can experience it within his own reality."[27] The Son's descent into hell is possible because the Holy Spirit reveals the enduring immanence of the Father and the Son. The Son remains God even amid the abyss of all that is alien to God. Even when the Father and the Son seem to be most separated from each other, the Holy Spirit eternally accompanies them both. Balthasar remarks, "Because he is triune, God can overcome even what is hostile to God within his eternal relations."[28] Holy Saturday reveals the Trinity as God as love.[29]

An overriding pastoral intention motivates Balthasar's theological aesthetics, including his theology of Holy Saturday. He is concerned less with clarifying the dogmatic aspect of the mystery of Holy Saturday than enriching Christian discipleship by contemplating the profound mystery. Balthasar's theological aesthetics thus develops Vatican II's pastoral orientation in the postconciliar era. Balthasar emphasizes the "in-betweenness" of Holy Saturday as the church appreciates the strange pause between life and death. Balthasar remarks:

---

26. Hans Urs von Balthasar, *Pneuma and Institution*, in Balthasar, *The Von Balthasar Reader*, ed. Medard Kehl and Werner Löser, trans. Robert J. Daly and Fred Lawrence (T&T Clark, 1982), 153.

27. Hans Urs von Balthasar, *Theo-Drama: Theological Dramatic Theory*, vol. 3: *The Dramatis Personae: The Person in Christ*, trans. Graham Harrison (Ignatius, 1992), 530.

28. Balthasar, *Theo-Drama*, vol. 3, 530.

29. The liturgical event of the Sacred Paschal Triduum is the proper context of Balthasar's theological understanding of Holy Saturday. The Paschal Triduum celebrates the memorial of the crucified, buried, and risen Lord. In *Mysterium Paschale*, Balthasar treats Good Friday (Going to the Cross), Holy Saturday (Going to the Dead), and Easter (Going to the Father) in successive order and demonstrates their distinction, interdependence, and integration as a unified liturgical event.

What follows from all this for us? Let us leave it to the theologians to discuss the dogmatic aspects. We, however, like Mary and most Christians, cannot follow Christ on this last way. We remain awake at the grave with the other holy women; What can we do? Many things. In our lives, revive the spirit of solidarity, this power to share the burden of another, to pray with fervor—and such prayer is unfailing—so that our brothers and sisters would not be lost in the end. . . . We simply attempt to put into action the small things that are possible for us.[30]

Balthasar's account of Holy Saturday challenges us to live out the spirit of solidarity that animates *Gaudium et Spes*. Balthasar writes, "The Christian, however, must open his heart and allow himself to be most intimately affected, challenged, hurt. God in Christ went to the place of the loneliest sinner in order to communicate with him in dereliction by God. Christian community is established in the Eucharist, which presupposes the descent into hell (mine and yours). No flight into an abstract unity is permitted here."[31] Balthasar invites Christians to selflessly care for others who are most alienated and self-alienated. Balthasar has been critiqued for an inattention to God's solidarity concretely expressed in history.[32] However, liberationist Roberto Goizueta, while acknowledging valid criticism, sees a common underlying methodology in Balthasar and Latin American and US Hispanic theologies, namely the Johannine claim that "God loves us first."[33] Balthasar's Holy Saturday imperative for solidarity is the basis for a pedagogy of Holy Saturday—particularly in our age of contempt.

---

30. Hans Urs von Balthasar, "Theologie des Abstiegs zur Hölle" in *Adrienne Von Speyr and Ihre Kirchliche Sendung: Aketen D. Röm. Symposiums, 27.-29. September 1985*, ed. Hans Urs von Balthasar, Georges Chantraine, and Angelo Scola, 138–46 (Johannes Verlag, 1986), 146, cited in Hikota, *And Still We Wait*, 10.

31. Hans Urs von Balthasar, "Receiving the Tradition: Communio: A Program," *Communio* 33 (2006): 167.

32. Michelle A. Gonzalez, "Hans Urs von Balthasar and Contemporary Feminist Theology," *Theological Studies* 65 (September 2004): 566–95; and Todd Walatka, *Von Balthasar and the Option for the Poor: Theodramatics in the Light of Liberation Theology* (Catholic University of America Press, 2017).

33. Roberto S. Goizueta, *Christ Our Companion: Toward a Theological Aesthetic of Liberation* (Orbis Books, 2009), x.

A Pedagogy of Holy Saturday

The mission of Catholic education grounds its teaching activity in the person of Christ. In *Ex Corde Ecclesia*, John Paul II argues:

> A Catholic University pursues its objectives through its formation of an authentic human community animated by the spirit of Christ. . . . As a result of this inspiration the community is animated by a spirit of freedom and charity; it is characterized by mutual respect, sincere dialogue, and the protection of the rights of individuals. It assists each of its members to achieve wholeness as human persons; in turn, everyone in the community helps in promoting unity, and each one, according to his or her role and capacity, contributes towards decisions which affect the community, and also towards maintaining and strengthening the distinctive Catholic character of the Institution. (ECE 21)

Contempt's fracturing of community strikes at the heart of Catholic higher education's mission. A pedagogy of Holy Saturday enfleshes a counter vision of healing that expresses the university's distinct mission.

Three pedagogical practices transpose Balthasar's Holy Saturday for the classroom: silence, tarrying, and empathetic understanding. The practice of silence ushers in "the wordless silence of death on Holy Saturday."[34] Silence also invites educators to identify with the passivity of the Word on Holy Saturday. The practice of tarrying communicates Holy Saturday's "wordless pause" in the classroom. This pause "guards against that theological busyness and religious impatience which insist on anticipating the moment of fruiting of the eternal redemption through the temporal passion—on dragging forward that moment from Easter to Holy Saturday."[35] Balthasar writes that Christ tarried in Hades.[36] The practice of empathetic understanding welcomes Christ's solidarity with the dead as "identity in non-identity, his being-with-himself in being lost, his life in being dead."[37] Empathetic understanding leads with a hermeneutic of mercy, especially toward the alienated and self-alienated. These

---

34. Balthasar, *Theological Anthropology*, 242.
35. Balthasar, *Mysterium Paschale*, 179.
36. Balthasar, *Mysterium Paschale*, 153.
37. Balthasar, *Explorations in Theology*, 413.

pedagogical practices, enriched by Balthasar's theology of Holy Saturday, incarnate a counter vision of education for a culture of contempt.

Silence

In his *Teaching with Your Mouth Shut,* teacher-scholar Donald Finkel portrays the "Great Teacher," the cultural icon that dominates the pedagogical imagination of American higher education. The Great Teacher objectifies the unexamined assumption that teaching is fundamentally and centrally performed by talking—by telling students what they are supposed to know:

> She seemed to know everything there was to know about it, and then some. She had awe-inspiring command over her material, and in response to any question, could hold forth brilliantly for as long as she wished. She was captivating when she spoke. She made her field come alive. She got excited in explaining it, and her excitement was contagious. She was clear in her expositions. She asked probing questions and followed them with illuminating answers. When her lectures were over, her students left the classroom touched by what she said. They wished that they, too, could master this subject, or some subject. Their minds felt alive, and their souls felt virtuous. They wanted to be like their teacher. They resolved to attack their books with fresh rigor, although at the back of their minds, they realized they would never be able to achieve the godlike heights she achieved, even if they were to work at it their whole lives.[38]

Finkel argues that the best teachers practice the challenging art of decentering their voice through teaching "with their mouths shut." In a university and world wired for extroversion, silence can profoundly inform the classroom when deliberate practices are integrated into a holistic pedagogy. Moreover, strategic silence can disarm defensive dispositions calcified in a culture of contempt. While contempt constructs impregnable walls that dismiss others, silence creates a clearing for self-examination and receptivity.

When educators imagine silence in the classroom, brief meditative practices such as breathing exercises, body scans, and simple moments of silence readily come to mind. Professors who ritualize these practices

---

38. Donald L. Finkel, *Teaching with Your Mouth Shut* (Boynton/Cook Publishers, 1999), 5.

often hail their educational benefit, particularly amid the frenetic demands of university life that produce harried students and faculty by midterm each semester. Parker Palmer writes about using silence at the beginning of his classes: "It may last only a few minutes, but it gives us a chance to settle in and center down, to move a bit beyond the truth-evading distractions of our minds and emotions. I do not call this practice 'prayer,' but that is what it is—a time when we can still ourselves enough to begin to feel our natural connectedness to each other and the world."[39] It is crucial that the teacher genuinely participate in this process to create a moment of silent communion or solidarity.

The following practices of teacher silence invite creative integration throughout class time.[40] One strategy for teacher silence is to direct the whole class to write down a particularly probing question raised by one of their classmates. This direction responds to a student's question with complexity, provocation, or intrigue. At times, silent writing and reflecting on the question invites richer conversation than the teacher immediately answering the question. In general, increasing the "wait time" between (student and teacher-generated) complex questions and answers produces more fruitful conversation. When a student says something interesting, vexing, or brilliant, a strategy for teacher silence allows for meditation before continuing dialogue. The teacher halts the conversation and creates a space of silence free from further spoken dialogue. The conversation continues following a specified period for reflection. Palmer reminds educators, "We need to abandon the notion that 'nothing is happening' when it is silent, to see how much new clarity a silence often brings."[41] There are multiple benefits to the simple strategy of the teacher redirecting a student question to a fellow student to eschew the model of the teacher as the central voice in the conversation. This redirection can be a kind of skillful bridge-making when it avoids coercion.

---

39. Parker J. Palmer, *To Know as We Are Known: Education as a Spiritual Journey* (HarperCollins, 1993), 80.

40. The following silent teaching strategies are adopted from Heather Anne Trahan's "The Silent Teacher: A Performative, Mediative Model of Pedagogy," *Liminalities: A Journal of Performative Studies* 9, no. 3 (2013), http://liminalities.net/9-3/silent.pdf. In addition to a taxonomy of teacher silence, Trahan provides two teacher silence events, including the open seminar and peer-to-peer conferences.

41. Palmer, *To Know as We Are Known*, 80.

Tarrying

Hans Georg Gadamer describes tarrying or lingering (*verweilen*) as the temporal dimension bound up with art. Gadamer contrasts it with "the merely pragmatic realms of understanding." He adds, "The *Weile* [the 'while' in *Verweilen*, tarrying] has this very special temporal structure—a temporal structure of being moved, which one nevertheless cannot describe merely as duration, because duration means only further movement in a single direction. This is not what is determinative in the experience of art. In it we tarry, we remain with the art structure (*Kunstgebilde*), which as a whole then becomes ever richer and more diverse . . . we learn from the work of art to tarry."[42]

When we tarry, we forgo managing time in a calculating, possessive way. Art discloses an experience of temporality dwelling in abundant riches. "And perhaps it is the only way that is granted to us finite beings to relate to what we call eternity."[43] Tarrying, for Gadamer, invites a being present as self-forgetfulness, and "being outside of oneself is the positive possibility of being wholly with something else."[44] Ordinary time is suspended, and we are drawn into an event that leads to greater awareness of our world and ourselves. For Gadamer, understanding art is not purely subjective; instead, in understanding, we participate in the event of disclosure. Moreover, the mode of being of the work of art can assist us in revealing that contemplation, understood as a disposition of gratuitous receptivity, is a fundamental dimension of understanding.

Philosopher George Yancy theorizes "tarrying" to describe what it means to occupy a space of unease. Tarrying entails staying longer than intended, lingering, hanging around, and dwelling. Yancy urges "whites to dwell in spaces that make them deeply uncomfortable, to stay with multiple forms of agony that black people endure from them. . . . I want them to *delay* the ways in which they are complicit in the operations of white racism. I want them to *delay* the hypothetical questions, to *postpone* their reach beyond the present. Reaching too quickly for hope can elide

---

42. Richard E. Palmer, *Gadamer in Conversation: Reflections and Commentary* (Yale University, 2001), 76–77.

43. Hans Georg Gadamer, *The Relevance of the Beautiful and Other Essays*, ed. Robert Bernasconi (Cambridge University, 1998), 45.

44. Hans Georg Gadamer, *Truth and Method*, trans. Joel Weinsheimer and Donald G. Marshall (Sheed & Ward, 1993), 125–26.

the importance of exposure."[45] Yancy is concerned that the rush to action shifts attention away from the present and can block hearing. Therefore, silence and tarrying can augment each other. The desire to act can indicate an obfuscation or concealment of reality, especially when reality troubles one's tacit existential assumptions and commitments. Yancy wants whites to remain in the "unfinished present" and be uncomfortable.[46]

Mara Brecht has identified a possible tension between the see–judge–act pedagogy of Catholic social learning and Yancy's plea for tarrying echoed in antiracist pedagogy. She argues that tarrying can mitigate against impatient, unreflective action that Catholic social pedagogy may foster through its top-heavy emphasis on the goal of transformative action. Tarrying can urge students to view themselves as "sites of struggle, rather than autonomous finished products, and to tarry in that place."[47] Moreover, tarrying invites Catholic social learning to broaden its understanding of action to include seeing oneself rightly. In the eliting of American Catholic higher education, tarrying can offer moral formation in humility by taking a little wind out of the sails of a student population regularly reminded of their self-agency due to their place among "the best and the brightest" of society. Like silence, tarrying can also defuse contempt through genuine encounters that "stay with" rather than readily dismissing others with fundamentally different worldviews and life experiences. Unlike contempt, silence and tarrying refuse to impose truth on others.

Empathetic Understanding

Nel Noddings, feminist philosopher of education, develops an ethics of care and relational pedagogy that stands in stark contrast to our age of contempt.[48] Noddings argues that care is the telos of education. She

---

45. George Yancy, *Look, a White! Philosophical Essays on Whiteness* (Temple University, 2012), 157.

46. Yancy, *Look, a White!*, 158.

47. Mara Brecht, "See–Judge . . . Act? The Role of Action in the Anti-Racist Catholic Theological Classroom," *Religious Education* 114, no. 3 (2019): 202–13.

48. Relational pedagogy as a twentieth-century educational theory describes and analyzes the role of relations in education. It draws from a long philosophical tradition starting with Aristotle through modern thinkers such as Bakhtin, Dewey, Gadamer, and Heidegger. Noddings highlights the significance of Martin Buber's I-thou relationship in developing her thought. Along with feminist thinkers Jane Martin and Carol Gilligan, Noddings put relational thinking into the mainstream of American educational theory.

writes, "Our main educational aim should be to encourage the growth of competent, caring, loving, and lovable people."[49] This aim recognizes a universal desire for care, even as expressions of care vary historically and culturally.[50] An ethics of care claims moral life is the primary goal of education because it is the foundation of intellectual development and academic achievement.[51] Noddings defines care: "When we see the other's reality as a possibility for us . . . when I am in this sort of relationship with another, when the other's reality becomes a real possibility for me, I care."[52] Simone Weil describes the connection between caring and attention: "The love of our neighbor in all its fullness simply means being able to say to him: 'What are you going through?' . . . This way of looking is first of all attentive. The soul empties itself of all its contents to receive into itself the being it is looking at, just as he is, in all his truth."[53] Along with Weil, Noddings draws from Iris Murdoch's description of attention as the "just and loving gaze directed upon an individual reality."[54] Noddings uses the term *engrossment* to indicate a special form of attention that is acutely receptive and includes "feeling with" that accompanies the caring relationship. Engrossment entails a motivational displacement from the self to the other.

Noddings promotes the development of empathy for education aimed at care. Typically, empathy follows engrossment. She emphasizes the cognitive and affective dimensions of empathy. Empathetic accuracy entails receptive listening, moral perception, and reflection.[55] The capacity

---

Nodding's ethics of care is a lodestar for contemporary relational pedagogy. See *No Education Without Relation*, ed. Charles Bingham and Alexander M. Sidorkin (Peter Lang, 2004), 1–4.

49. Nel Noddings, *Educating Moral People: A Caring Alternative to Character Education* (Teachers College, 2002), 94.

50. Noddings, *Educating Moral People*, 21.

51. Noddings, *Educating Moral People*, 99.

52. Nel Noddings, *Caring: A Feminine Approach to Ethics and Moral Education* (University of California Press, 1984), 14.

53. Simone Weil, *Simone Weil Reader*, ed. George A. Panichas (Moyer Bell Limited, 1977), 51.

54. Iris Murdoch, *The Sovereignty of Good* (Routledge and Kegan Paul, 1970), 34.

55. Nel Noddings, *Caring: A Relational Approach to Ethics and Moral Education*, 2nd ed. (University of California Press, 2013), 205. (For the second edition, in the subtitle, the word *Feminine* is changed to *Relational*. See n. 52 above.)

to "look lovingly," in the words of Murdoch, is a skill that develops as the cared-for learns to care for others. There is skill in asking and answering the fundamental question, "What are you going through?" Empathetic accuracy requires practice that benefits from reflection and evaluation in conversation with others.[56] An ethics of care establishes the conditions and relations that invite moral and intellectual development. That caring precedes learning is a foundational feature of Noddings's relational pedagogy. Relational pedagogy highlights that learning occurs within and through relationships. Noddings comments, "The recognition of relation, not a fixed ideal of teaching, steers the teacher's choice of methods."[57]

Paul Lakeland identifies empathy and critique as twin virtues essential to academic excellence in church-related universities.[58] Blind obedience to the hermeneutics of suspicion obfuscates the role of empathy as equally vital to critique for intellectual development. For Lakeland, the habit of empathy precludes premature critique and guards against the academic tendency to immediately catalog the object of inquiry. Empathy enables the historically conditioned academic to receive the object of inquiry on its own terms. Lakeland explains, "While eschewing sentimentality, the inquirer must in a real way *love* the object of inquiry; what is to be studied must be respected, allowed, as it were, to be itself. Only when this happens is there at least a fighting chance that critique or analysis will, in fact, reach the object of inquiry and not remain within the labyrinth of the inquirer's mental pathways. Empathy, in other words, is profoundly practical."[59]

Against caricatures of theology and religious studies as obscurantist or anti-intellectual, theologians should educate the university on the religious value of empathy as an intellectual virtue.[60] Empathy-informed teaching and scholarship demonstrate the vital role of religious tradition in the academic mission without religious tradition controlling the academy. Lakeland adds, "The church is empathic because of what it is,

---

56. Noddings, *Caring: A Relational Approach*, 205.

57. Nel Noddings, "Foreword," in *No Education without Relation*, ed. Charles Bingham and Alexander M. Sidorkin (Peter Lang, 2004), vii.

58. Paul Lakeland, "The Habit of Empathy: Postmodernity and the Future of the Church-Related College," in *Professing in the Postmodern Academy: Faculty and the Future of Church-Related Colleges*, ed. Stephen R. Haynes (Baylor University Press, 2005), 33–48.

59. Lakeland, "The Habit of Empathy," 40.

60. Lakeland, "The Habit of Empathy," 41.

the community as sacrament to/servant of the world. The academy is empathic because of what *it* is, a community devoted to the rigorous discipline of learning, whose first moment is an attention to what is to be understood so that wisdom and not merely knowledge will accrue."[61] Noddings's ethics of care and Lakeland's appeal to empathy both provide pedagogical visions that counter a culture of contempt.

Conclusion

Balthasar critiqued the modern technological ideal of knowledge as mastery, domination, and exploitation.[62] In a world without beauty, or at least a world that "can no longer see it or reckon with it," Balthasar warns, "the good also loses its attractiveness, the self-evidence of why it must be carried out."[63] Pedagogy that neglects its connection with spiritual beauty loses its ability to convince. This means that teaching should communicate "with feeling" and in images, integrating the religious and poetic elements into its mode of discourse. In his soulful article, "The Poetics of Teaching," the philosopher of education David Hansen describes the aesthetics in pedagogy: "The aesthetic aspect in teaching materializes . . . when a teacher is moved by the tapestry of human gestures, voices, strivings, and more, that come alive in any group of students. The teacher is affected by signs of grace, harmony, and beauty-in-action, as well as by indices of frustration, rupture, and breakdown. In other words, the teacher is moved by the concrete revelation of human beings."[64] Pedagogical aesthetics reminds educators that good teaching is not reducible to technique; good teaching emerges from the teacher's integrity.[65] Moreover, pedagogical aesthetics highlights that teaching is

---

61. Lakeland, "The Habit of Empathy," 47.

62. William James Jennings echoes this epistemological criticism but from a racial concern. See Willie James Jennings, *After Whiteness: A Pedagogy in Belonging* (Eerdmans, 2020).

63. Hans Urs von Balthasar, *The Glory of the Lord: A Theological Aesthetics*, vol. 1: *Seeing the Form*, 2nd ed., trans. Erasmo Leiva-Merikakis, ed. Joseph Fessio, SJ, and John Riches (Ignatius, 2009), 19.

64. David T. Hansen, "A Poetics of Teaching," *Educational Theory* 54, no. 2 (2004): 132.

65. Parker Palmer, *The Courage to Teach: Exploring the Inner Landscape of a Teacher's Life* (Jossey-Bass, 1998), 10.

about responding to learners as much as it concerns invention.[66] In an age of contempt, a pedagogy of Holy Saturday refuses to impose truth because Christ refused to impose truth.[67] A pedagogy of Holy Saturday enacts an aesthetic inversion of contempt because Christ practiced radical solidarity with those who rejected him—all the way to being really dead with the dead in hell.

The call to solidarity with the people of our time that inaugurates *Gaudium et Spes* challenges Catholic higher education to counter the culture of contempt with hope from the living Christ. Hans Urs von Balthasar's theological aesthetics provides a theological foundation for a pedagogy of Holy Saturday animating Catholic education. Balthasar's account of Holy Saturday illuminates that no one is ever beyond God's care; even in the depths of hell, God remains in solidarity with those who have rejected God. The non-victorious descent into hell is a hopeful act of mercy seeking the ultimate redemption of all. A pedagogy of Holy Saturday transposes Balthasar's aesthetic inversion through the practice of silence, tarrying, and empathetic understanding. Parker Palmer recognizes that "the shape of knowledge becomes the shape of our living; the relation the knower to the known becomes the relation of the living self to the world."[68] A pedagogy of Holy Saturday appropriates Vatican II's pastoral intention through healing conversations in a world mired in ruptured communication. A pedagogy of Holy Saturday challenges Catholic higher education to invite redemption into our dehumanizing world.

---

66. Carol R. Rodgers, "Seeing Student Learning: Teacher Change and the Role of Reflection," *Harvard Educational Review* 72, no. 2 (2002): 232.

67. Goizueta, *Christ Our Companion*, 25–43.

68. Palmer, *To Know as We Are Known*, 21.

About the Authors

Matteo Caponi, PhD, is associate professor of history of Christianity at the University of Genoa (Italy) and a founding member of CENTRA (Center for the History of Racism and Anti-Racism in Modern Italy). His research interests focus on the cultural history of Roman Catholicism in the nineteenth and twentieth centuries, with particular attention to its relationship with nationalism, war culture, racism, and antiracism. Among his publications: *Una Chiesa in guerra: Sacrificio e mobilitazione nella diocesi di Firenze, 1911–1928* (Viella, 2018).

Catherine E. Clifford, PhD, is professor of systematic and historical theology at Saint Paul University (Ottawa, Canada). Her teaching, research, and publications focus in the areas of ecclesiology, ecumenism, and the history of the Second Vatican Council. She is presently vice president of the Catholic Theological Society of America and served as a North American delegate to the XVI General Assembly of the Synod on Synodality. Among her recent publications are *The Oxford Handbook on Vatican II* (2023), coedited with Massimo Faggioli, and *Vatican II at 60: Re-Energizing the Renewal* (Orbis Books, 2024).

Kristin M. Colberg, PhD, is an associate professor of theology at Saint John's University and School of Theology and the College of Saint Benedict. Her research and writing focus on questions related to ecclesiology, Vatican I, Vatican II, and ecumenism. She has been appointed by the Vatican as a member of the Anglican-Roman Catholic International Commission (ARCIC) and the theological commission supporting the Synod on Synodality. With Liturgical Press, she published *Vatican I and Vatican II: Councils in the Living Tradition* (2016).

Agnès Desmazières, PhD, STD, is a French historian who earned doctorates in history and in theology. Her research on the history of sexual violence in the Catholic Church has recently been published by Payot Publishers, with the book *Sans loi ni foi: Prêtres et violences sexuelles: Au cœur du système catholique* (Paris, 2024).

Massimo Faggioli, PhD, is professor in the department of theology and religious studies at Villanova University (Pennsylvania, USA). He is a member of the editorial board of the journal *Concilium* and steering committee member of the project "Vatican II: Event and Mandate" for a multivolume intercontinental commentary of the council. Among his publications with Liturgical Press are *True Reform: Liturgy and Ecclesiology in* Sacrosanctum Concilium (2012) and *Sorting Out Catholicism: A Brief History of the New Ecclesial Movements* (2014).

Theresa Gardner holds an MA in theology and religious studies from Villanova University. During her graduate studies, she presented papers at several conferences on feminist theology, ecclesiology, Vatican II, and digital humanity and spirituality. Theresa is currently the director of Christian service at Loyola School (New York, NY), where she coordinates service immersion trips around the world and teaches classes related to Catholic social teaching and social justice.

Edward P. Hahnenberg, PhD, is the Breen Chair in Catholic Theology and chair of the Department of Theology & Religious Studies at John Carroll University (Cleveland, USA). He is the author or coeditor of seven books—including, from Liturgical Press, *Theodore Hesburgh, CSC: Bridge Builder* (2020); *Theology for Ministry: An Introduction for Lay Ministers* (2014); and *Awakening Vocation: A Theology of Christian Call* (2010). Dr. Hahnenberg is a past delegate to the US Lutheran-Catholic Dialogue and former theological consultant to the US Bishops' Subcommittee on Lay Ministry.

Timothy Hanchin, PhD, is associate professor and director of the Heart of Teaching in the Department of Theology and Religious Studies at Villanova University. The Heart of Teaching integrates pedagogical formation into graduate theological education and faculty development. His scholarship addresses the philosophy of Catholic education, theological pedagogy, and trinitarian theology.

Tuan Hoang, PhD, is Blanche E. Seaver Professor of Humanities and Teacher Education and associate professor of Great Books at Pepperdine University. He teaches in the Great Books, humanities, and history programs. His current research focuses on Catholics in South Vietnam and the postwar history of Vietnamese refugees in the United States.

Mary Kate Holman, PhD, is assistant professor of religious studies at Fairfield University (Connecticut, USA). She is the author of *Marie-Dominique Chenu: Catholic Theology for a Changing World* (University of Notre Dame Press, 2025).

Jaisy A. Joseph, PhD, is an assistant professor of theology and religious studies at Villanova University (Pennsylvania, USA). With interests primarily in ecclesiology and theological anthropology, her main areas of research involve understandings of unity and difference in the Catholic Church, how these definitions have shifted over the centuries, and how erroneous expressions have wounded the bonds of communion between different peoples.

Florian Klug, STD, is senior lecturer in Catholic dogmatics at the University of Vienna (Austria). His expertise includes ecclesiology and aesthetics. He was a visiting scholar at Villanova University (USA), St. Patrick's College (Ireland), and Durham University (UK). He is also a permanent deacon of the Diocese of Fulda (Germany). With Liturgical Press he published *Beyond the Visible Church: The Motif of the* ecclesia ab Abel *from Augustine to James Alison* (2024).

William G. Kuncken holds an MA in theology from Villanova University, where he is pursuing is PhD in Catholic theology. He is also a full-time faculty member in the religious studies department at St. Joseph's Preparatory School in Philadelphia, where he coordinates the school's environmental justice week.

Josephine Laffin, PhD, is a senior lecturer in the faculty of theology and philosophy at Australian Catholic University. Based in Adelaide, she teaches Christian history and is researching the impact of the Second Vatican Council on Catholicism in Australia for a forthcoming book.

Martin Madar, PhD, is an associate professor of systematic theology at Xavier University (Cincinnati, USA). He specializes in ecclesiology and theology of Vatican II. He is the author of *The Church of God and Its Human Face: The Contribution of Joseph A. Komonchak to Ecclesiology* (Pickwick, 2019).

Evgeniia Muzychenko (she/her) received her master's in theological studies from Villanova University and is a doctoral student in historical studies in theology and religion at Emory University (Atlanta, USA). Evgeniia's research interests include mission history, interfaith dialogue, and the history of Christianity in India.

William I. Orbih, PhD, is an assistant professor of theology and rector of the Seminary at the Saint John's University School of Theology and Seminary in Collegeville (Minnesota, USA). His research focuses on intercultural and comparative theology, the history and mission of the church in Africa, African literature and political thought, and decolonial theory and praxis.

Bernard G. Prusak, PhD, holds the Raymond & Eleanor Smiley Chair in Business Ethics at John Carroll University (Cleveland, USA). His books include *Catholic Moral Philosophy in Practice and Theory* (Paulist Press, 2016), and his criticism and public scholarship appear frequently in *Commonweal*, *America*, and the *National Catholic Reporter*.

Daniel A. Rober, PhD, is associate professor of Catholic studies at Sacred Heart University. His research interests include the relationship of theology to phenomenology, Vatican II, Catholic involvement in political life, and secularization. He is the author of *Recognizing the Gift: Toward a Renewed Theology of Nature and Grace* (Fortress Press, 2016).

Index of Names

Page numbers in **bold** indicate an author's chapter in this volume.

Adichie, Chimamanda Ngozi, 247–50
Ahmann, Mathew, 265n47
Alberigo, Giuseppe, 24n10, 93n1, 116n23, 246n48
Alfrink, Bernard, 102
Allen, John L., 297n7
Allitt, Patrick, 38nn2–3
Alvarez-Icaza, Luz-Marie, 147–48, 155–57, 165n4, 166
Anderson, R. Bentley, 255n9
Antoniutti, Ildebrando, 153–54
Araujo, Robert J., 33n33
Archer, Margaret, 283–87, 288–90, 291n35
Aristotle, 308n48
Arnold, Matthew, 130
Arularaj, M. R., 222
Athanasius, 301
Augustine of Hippo, 55, 62–67, 69n52

Baars, Conrad, 124
Bakhtin, Mikhail, 308n48
Baldwin, James, 186
Balthasar, Hans Urs von, 296–97, 299–305, 311–12
Barron, Robert, 46
Basil of Caesarea, 85n30

Battaly, Heather, 139n38
Battin, Steven J., 198
Bauman, M., 223n47
Baxter, Michael, 47
Beck, Ulrich, 286
Becquart, Nathalie, 169, 171
Bellarmine, Robert, 59–60, 66, 69n52, 70
Benedict XVI, Pope (Joseph Ratzinger), 22n3, 26, 30–33, 47, 54n4, 107n27, 113n13, 114, 134, 167, 191, 192, 195, 250
Berger, Peter, 286
Berrigan, Daniel, 38
Berrigan, Philip, 38
Berry, Jason, 123n52
Berry, Thomas, 84n27
Bingham, Charles, 308n48, 310n57
Bloomer, Kristin, 220, 225n58, 229–31
Boeve, Lieven, 281n11
Bonaventure, 58n15, 66, 67n47
Bongmba, Elias Kifon, 236n5, 239n20
Bonnett, Alastair, 253n2
Boylen, Dan, 124
Boyne, John, 132n7, 140n42

Bozell, L. Brent, Jr., 38–39, 42, 50
Braxton, Edward K., 270
Brecht, Mara, 308
Brennan, Frank, 174–75, 176
Brolly, Mark, 114n16
Browne, Michael, 156
Bruce, Tricia C., 297n7
Buber, Martin, 308n48
Buchanan, Patrick J., 39
Buehlman, Kim T., 298n8
Bullivant, Stephen, 215n34
Burke-Sivers, Harold, 257n15
Butler, Basil Christopher, 236n4

Cafardi, Nicholas, 48n50, 49n52
Caimi, Luciano, 257n13
Câmara, Hélder, 158–59, 214
Cameron, Michael, 63n33
Camosy, Charles C., 297n7
Caponi, Matteo, **253–72**, 255n7, 266nn51–52, 270n70
Cardijn, Joseph, 278, 282
Carpenter, Anne, 182
Carroll, Francis, 122
Casas, Bartolomé de las, 270
Casey, Paul, 122n47, 123n51
Cassam, Quassim, 139n38
Cellini, Jacopo, 269n66
Chang, Ruth, 290n33
Chân Tín. See Tín, Chân
Chantraine, Georges, 303n30
Chappel, James, 41nn14–15
Childs, James M., 75n9, 76n12
Cicognani, Amleto, 259–60
Clifford, Catherine E., **ix–xiii**, **3–19**, 15n19, 28, 29nn25–26, 43n21, 150n8, 164n2, 170, 217n36, 228n69, 236n6, 252
Coblentz, Jessica, 147n1
Coco, Giovanni, 256n12
Colberg, Kristin M., **ix–xiii**

Collins, Paul, 224
Cone, James, 197
Congar, Yves, 43, 44, 61, 66n46, 106, 116, 153, 190–91, 196, 260, 261–62, 267n58, 281n9
Connelly, John, 44n27, 193n47
Connors, Peter, 112, 119
Cooperman, Alan, 94n2
Copeland, M. Shawn, 171, 195, 197
Corley, Jeremy, 70n55
Cox, Kathy Lilla, 147n1
Cranney, Stephen, 127n67
Crenshaw, Sharon L., 139n41
Cressler, Matthew J., 265n45
Cronin, John F., 258–59, 265n48, 266–67
Crowley, Pat and Patty, 282
Crowley, Paul, 39n5
Curso, Carmen, 94
Cyprian of Carthage, 57

Dallavalle, Nancy A., 48–49
Dangarembga, Tsitsi, 252
Davis, Cyprian, 254n5, 263n36, 270
Day, Dorothy, 38, 277
Day, John, 110, 115
Debono, Emmanuel, 254n6
Degnan, Daniel, 266n50
Dell'Acqua, Angelo, 259
Dell'Era, Tommaso, 257n13
De Mey, Peter, 25n11
Deneen, Patrick, 38, 39–42, 49
Desbuquois, Gustave, 256
Desmazières, Agnès, **93–108**, 106n25, 114, 134
Devoy, Frank, 122n47, 123n51
Dewey, John, 308n48
DeYoung, Rebecca Konyndyk, 143n63
Diekmann, Godfrey, 280, 287
Diệm, Ngô Đình, 201

Đoàn, Hoàng Văn, 205, 206
Domezi, Maria Cecilia, 159n30
Donaghue, Mary Pat, 171
Donati, Pierpaolo, 288, 290n34
Doty, Robert C., 267n55
Douglass, Frederick, 187
Doyle, Thomas, 118–19
Dreuzy, Agnes de, 43n24
Drexler-Dreis, Joseph, 196n55
D'Souza, Eugene, 223
Dube, Musa W., 171, 248
Dupont, Anthony, 62n32, 64n38
Dwyer, Vincent, 123

Ebner, Martin, 58n12
Edwards, Denis, 114n15
Ellacuría, Ignacio, 197
Etchegaray, Roger, 258

Faggioli, Massimo, **ix–xiii**, 29n25, 31n29, 33, 34n37, 43n21, 48n49, 127, 141n53, 150n8, 164n2, 217n36, 228n69, 236n6, 283n14
Feder, Julia, 147n1
Felici, Pericle, 155
Fernandes, Jason Keith, 220, 221n40, 226–27
Finke, Roger, 46
Finkel, Donald, 305
Finn, Daniel K., 285n17
Fischer, Agneta H., 298n9
Fleischner, Eva, 150–51
Fleming, Daniel J., 133n10
Fletcher, Hill, 183
Flipper, Joseph, 189n25, 190, 194
Floyd, George, 194
Flynn, Gabriel, 54n2
Fogal, Daniel, 139n37
Forell, George W., 75n9
Foster, Elizabeth A., 217n35, 246, 247
Fouilloux, Étienne, 246n48

Fraga, Brian, 170n13, 276n2
Francis, Pope, ix, xi, 5–6, 8–10, 12, 13, 15, 16, 21, 22, 26, 29, 35, 52, 70n55, 71n57, 82n23, 107n27, 127, 168, 169, 171, 177, 194, 271–72, 297
Franco, Francisco, 50
François, Wim, 62n32
Franklin, James, 124n56
Freitas, Donna, 147n1
Fricker, Miranda, 139, 140, 143n60
Frings, Josef, 102

Gadamer, Hans Georg, 307, 308n48
Gaillardetz, Richard R., 26, 27n18, 35n39, 54n2, 126n64
Ganzer, Klaus, 59n17
Gardner, Theresa, **163–78**
Garhammer, Erich, 54n4
Gauthier, Paul, 157–59
Gauvreau, Michael, 51n60
George-Tvrtkovic, Rita, 147n1
Geraghty, Christopher, 113n14, 115–16
Gilbert, Margaret, 137–39
Gilligan, Carol, 308n48
Gil-Riaño, Sebastián, 262n35
Ginges, Jeremy, 297n5
Gitau, Wanjiru M., 239
Gleeson, James, 122
Goizueta, Roberto, 303, 312n67
Goldie, Rosemary, 153, 165n4, 166
Gomes, Sebastian, 169n11
Gomez, José H., 258
Gonzalez, Michelle A., 303n32
Goscha, Christopher, 201n1
Gottman, John, 298
Granfield, Patrick, 60n24
Gravend-Tirole, Xavier, 223n47
Greenberg, Udi, 217n35
Gregory of Nyssa, 301
Gregory the Great, 55n5, 66

Grey, Carmody, 85n29
Grimes, Katie Walker, 182n3
Groome, Thomas H., 126n64
Gründer, Karlfried, 65n43
Guardini, Romano, 53, 61
Gundlach, Gustav, 256

Hadro, Catherine, 177n28
Hahnenberg, Edward P., **ix–xiii**, 130n5, **275–93**
Hakim, George, 158, 159
Hanchin, Timothy, **295–312**
Hansen, David, 311
Hanycz, Colleen, 170
Harris, Daniel W., 139n37
Harvey, John Francis, 120
Hastings, Adrian, 244
Haught, John F., 83n24
Haynes, Stephen R., 310n58
Healy, Nicholas J., Jr., 43n23
Heckel, Roger Joseph, 269–70
Heft, James L., 21n1
Heidegger, Martin, 308n48
Heidt, Mari Rapela, 214n30
Henold, Mary J., 161n33
Henry the Navigator, 181, 183
Heschel, Abraham Joshua, 265
Heyder, Regina, 29n25, 150n8, 152n12, 164, 165nn3–4, 228
Hikota, Riyako Cecilia, 301n20
Hilberath, Bernd Jochen, 60n25
Hillebert, Jordan, 189n25
Hoang, Tuan, **201–18**, 204n3, 217n37
Hoàng Van Đoàn. *See* Đoàn, Hoàng Van
Hodgens, Eric, 114n17
Hölderlin, Friedrich, 296
Hollenbach, David, 48, 49, 51
Holman, Mary Kate, **147–62**, 158n26
Hoover, Jesse A., 64n36
Horn, Gerd-Rainer, 241n32

Howard, Thomas Albert, 130
Hoysted, Peter, 111n6
Hudock, Barry, 37n1
Hughes, Edward, 135
Hughes, Langston, 268
Hünermann, Peter, 60n25, 116
Hurley, Denis E., 267
Hus, Jan, 66
Hyatt, Vera Lawrence, 186n14

Icaza, José, 155–57, 165n4
Ignatius of Loyola, 143n61
Ilo, Stan Chu, 237
Imesch, Joseph, 167
Imperatori-Lee, Natalia, 150
Irene (empress), 151
Ivereigh, Austen, 70n55

Jedin, Hubert, 59n17
Jenkins, Philip, 201n1
Jennings, Willie James, 181–82, 184, 195, 197, 311n62
Joachim of Fiore, 47
John Damascene, 55n5
John Paul II, Pope, xi, 21, 22n3, 31–33, 47, 51, 134, 167, 263, 270–71, 282–83, 296, 304
Johnson, Karen J., 264–65
Johnson, Maxwell, 281n8
John XXIII, Pope, 74, 75–77, 86, 98, 99, 104, 113, 127, 205–6, 207, 212, 228, 247, 256, 263–64, 266
Jones, Robert P., 253n3
Joseph, Jaisy A., **181–99**
Jossua, Jean-Pierre, 24n10
Julian of Eclanum, 64
Justaert, Kristien, 196n55

Kampe, Walter, 150
Kasper, Walter, 59n17, 68n51, 77n16, 78n17

Index of Names   321

Katongole, Emmanuel, 238, 240, 250
Katz, Lynn F., 298n8
Kaveny, M. Cathleen, 21n1, 144n64
Keefe, Thomas M., 96n4
Keenan, James F., 113n14, 133n10, 142n57
Keenan, Marie, 113n14, 132, 133n11, 134, 136n26, 141, 143
Kehl, Medard, 302n26
Kellert, Stephen R., 74n4
Kelley, Theresa, 51n59
Kerr, Nicholas, 122n49
Kidd, Ian James, 139n38
King, Martin Luther, Jr., 265, 266, 267, 270, 271–72
Klug, Florian, **53–71**, 58nn13–14, 60n22, 61n28
Komonchak, Joseph A., 24, 40, 43n22, 160, 267n56
Konieczy, Mary Ellen, 297n7
Kuncken, William G., **73–87**
Küng, Hans, 267n58

Lacaze, Marie-Thérèse, 157–59
LaFarge, John, Jr., 254, 255, 256, 259, 262, 263n37, 266
Laffin, Josephine, **109–28**
Lakeland, Paul, 310–11
Lamb, Christopher, 175
Lamb, George, 44n28
Langton, Rae, 139n37
Lasch, Ken, 133, 140–41
Latini, Giuseppe, 96n3
Lawler, Michael G., 257n14
Lee, James K., 65n42, 66n45
Leemans, Johan, 62n32
Lefebvre, Charles, 100
Léger, Paul-Émile, 102, 104
Leijssen, L., 281n11
Lennan, Richard, 126n64
Leo the Great, Pope, 280

Leo XIII, Pope, 45, 77
Lesti, Sante, 253n1
Levering, Matthew, 22n3
Liedl, Jonathan, 176n27
Little, Francis (Frank), 112, 113–14, 115, 118–20, 123, 125–26, 127–28
Lloyd, Vincent, 195n52
Löser, Werner, 302n26
Lubac, Henri de, 44, 47, 61, 158, 182, 188–90, 192, 194, 196–97, 199, 296n4
Luciani, Rafael, 26n13
Luther, Martin, 66

MacDonald, Sarah, 166n5
Madar, Martin, **21–35**, 21n2
Maier, Martin, 241
Majawa, Clement, 236
Malcolm X, 267
Manent, Pierre, 40
Mannion, Gerard, 224n53
Manns, Cynthia Bailey, 169–70
Marcion of Sinope, 58
Maritain, Jacques, 43, 44, 279, 280
Maritain, Raïssa, 151
Marmion, Declan, 25n12, 106n25
Martí, Gerardo, 286, 291
Martin, Jane, 308n48
Martínez, María Elena, 185
Massingale, Bryan, 257, 265n45
Maximos IV Saigh of Antioch, 102, 103
Mbiti, John, 244
McAlister, Shannon, 147n1
McCarrick, Theodore, 134–37, 140, 143
McCunnie, Bill, 119
McElwee, Joshua, 297n7
McElwee, Kate, 169, 171
McEnroy, Carmel, 151n9, 152, 154nn16–17, 155–56, 166

McFadden, Thomas L., Jr., 39n4
McGreevy, John, 129, 130, 132n8, 201n1, 215n34, 254, 258n19
McHugh, James, 136, 140, 143
McKinnon, John, 125nn59–60
McLeod, Hugh, 70n56
Méndez Arceo, Sergio, 156
Merry Del Val, Rafael, 105n22
Merton, Thomas, 277
Messori, Vittorio, 31n30
Metz, Johann Baptist, 195
Meyer, Albert, 103
Micara, Clemente, 102, 103
Michel, Florian, 44n31
Miglarese, Sam, 252n69
Miller, Vincent J., 48, 281, 287, 288
Millies, Steven P., 49n53
Molony, John, 115, 119
Monti, Giuseppe, 263n38
Morello, Gustavo, 51n58
Morgan, David, 252n69
Morozzo della Rocca, Roberto, 97n5
Moss, Matt, 139n37
Mosse, David, 225–26
Moyn, Samuel, 43n26
Mudimbe, V. Y., 240n27, 243
Mugambi, Jesse K. N., 239
Mulkearns, Ronald, 110–14, 115, 119–23, 125–26, 127–28
Münch, Josefa, 150
Mundelein, George, 96
Murdoch, Iris, 309, 310
Murray, John Courtney, 37, 43, 44, 45, 48, 277
Muzychenko, Evgeniia, **219–33**

Ndlovu-Gatsheni, Sabelo J., 237n12, 241
Nestor, John, 113n13
Nettleford, Rex, 186n14

Newman, Mark, 259n23, 262n34, 265n45
Newsome Martin, Jennifer, 299, 300n16, 301n24
Ngô Đình Diệm. *See* Diệm, Ngô Đình
Ngũgĩ wa Thiong'o, 245
Nicholas V, Pope, 181
Nilson, Jon, 195n51
Noble, Theresa Aletheia, 143n62
Noceti, Serena, 152n12, 161n34
Noddings, Nel, 308–11
Novak, Mary, 171
Novak, Michael, 45–46

O'Boyle, Patrick, 254, 267n55
O'Collins, James, 119
O'Connor, John, 135
O'Grady, Desmond, 158
O'Hanlon, Daniel, 267n58
O'Laughlin, Michael J., 170n12
O'Malley, John W., 24, 106n24, 116n24, 129, 151, 152, 191, 264n41, 281, 282
O'Malley, Vincent J., 241n33
Onaiyekan, John, 240
Orbih, William I., **235–52**, 251n68
Ormerod, Neil, 110n4, 126
Orobator, Agbonkhianmeghe E., 217n36, 236, 244–45, 251n66
Orphanopoulos, Carolina Montero, 133n10
Ottaviani, Alfredo, 101
Oyono, Ferdinand, 238–40, 243

Paiano, Maria, 270n70
Palazzini, Pietro, 263n38
Palencia Gomez, Maria de los Dolores, 176
Palmer, Parker, 306, 311n65, 312
Palmer, Richard E., 307n42

Index of Names

Papesh, Michael L., 140n44, 141n52
Park, Robert, 262
Parker, John, 245n46
Paul VI, Pope, x, xi, 10, 16n20, 101, 103, 110, 113, 117, 147–48, 149, 160, 165n4, 203, 206–9, 212, 213, 214, 266, 268–69, 280, 282, 296n4
Pavan, Pietro, 266
Pecknold, C. C., 62n31
Pell, George, 112, 126
Peoples, Kevin, 113n14
Perdomo, Ismael, 105n22
Pereira, Suhas, 222, 223n51, 224, 228
Perin, Raffaella, 253n1, 257n13
Pesch, Otto Hermann, 24
Peters, Edward H., 236n4
Philips, Gerard, 191
Pink, Thomas, 50
Pius IX, Pope, 277
Pius XI, Pope, 96n3, 113, 256, 266, 270, 277–79, 280, 283
Pius XII, Pope, 43, 129, 266, 267
Pollard, John, 278n4
Portier, William L., 261n28, 282n13
Pottmeyer, Hermann, 24, 25
Prejean, Helen, 132n6, 171
Prevot, Andrew, 195n52, 196–97
Primavesi, Oliver, 65n43
Prior, Michael, 185
Prusak, Bernard G., **129–44**, 134n15
Pulikkan, Paul, 223nn49–50, 224

Radcliffe, Timothy, 7, 10–11
Radner, Ephraim, 78n19
Rahner, Karl, 25n12, 235, 243
Ramsey, Boniface, 135
Rathbone, Richard, 245n46
Ratzinger, Joseph. *See* Benedict XVI, Pope (Joseph Ratzinger)
Rausch, Thomas P., 201n1

Reding, Marcel, 61n29
Regan, Hilary, 113n14
Regatillo, Eduardo, 100n13
Regnerus, Mark, 127n67
Reynolds, Susan Bigelow, 148, 172n18, 173
Riccardi, Andrea, 97n5
Rice, Jill, 171n14
Richaud, Paul, 101–2, 103
Ridsdale, Gerard, 120–21, 123–24
Ritter, Joachim, 65n43
Ritter, Joseph, 103, 105
Rober, Daniel A., **37–52**
Roberti, Francesco, 263n38
Robinson, Geoffrey, 113n14
Rodgers, Carol R., 312n66
Roediger, David R., 186n17
Root, Michael, 62n31
Roseman, Ira J., 298n9
Routhier, Gilles, 32n31
Rowland, Tracey, 31n29, 47
Ruether, Rosemary Radford, 149, 160, 167
Rugambwa, Laurean, 246n48, 268
Ruggieri, Guiseppe, 235
Rummel, Joseph F., 259
Rush, Ormond, 23n4, 24, 27, 193n44
Russell, Jesse, 45n33
Ryan, John E., 113n14, 124–25
Ryan, Paul David, 120, 121, 123
Ryan, Salvador, 106n25

Sakupapa, Teddy Chalwe, 252
Salisbury, Joyce E., 57n10
Salzman, Todd A., 257n14
Sanneh, Lamin, 78n18
Santamarina, Mónica, 177
Scatena, Silvia, 43n21, 43n25
Schindler, David L., 43n23, 46–48, 49
Schloesser, Stephen, 39n5

Schmitt, Carl, 37, 41
Schmitt, Frederick F., 137n31
Schopenhauer, Arthur, 298
Schulte, Karl, 96n3
Schultheis, Dominik, 56nn6–7
Schüssler Fiorenza, Elisabeth, 171
Scola, Angelo, 303n30
Searson, Peter, 118
Shaw, Mark, 239
Shea, Daniel J., 94
Sheen, Fulton, 277
Sheils, W. J., 70n56
Shortall, Sarah, 190
Sidorkin, Alexander M., 308n48, 310n57
Sittler, Joseph, 86n31
Slater, Jennifer, 127n66
Slattery, John, 261n28
Smith, Meg Stapleton, 147n1
Southern, David, 262
Spadaro, Antonio, 5–6
Spellman, Francis, 212
Stackaruk, Chris, 236n3
Stacpoole, Alberic, 244n41
Stark, Rodney, 46
Steinfels, Peter, 133
Stohr, Karen, 299
Strawson, P. F., 298
Suárez, Francisco, 66
Suenens, Leo Jozef, 163
Sullivan, Francis A., 193
Superson, Anita M., 139n41
Sweeney, Fergal, 136n26

Taguieff, Pierre-Antoine, 258n18
Tanner, Kathryn, 171
Tapsell, Kieran, 112–13
Taylor, Charles, 288–89
Teilhard de Chardin, Pierre, 73n2, 80n20, 81n21, 83n25, 84n28, 86n34

Teter, Magda, 269n64
Tetlow, Tania, 170
Thomas, Rachel, 177n28
Thomas, Sonja, 221n40
Thomas Aquinas, 66
Thompson, Era Bell, 268n60
Tilley, Maureen A., 63n35
Tín, Chân, 214
Tito (Josip Broz), 212
Tobin, Mary Luke, 147, 148, 152–54, 157, 162, 165n4, 166, 167
Toom, Tarmo, 62n31
Tracy, Robert E., 267
Trahan, Heather Anne, 306n40
Trân, Clare Thi Liên, 210n18
Trump, Donald, 276
Tück, Jan-Heiner, 68n51
Turpin, Hugh, 51n61

Uzukwu, Elochukwu E., 237n11, 240n25

Valerio, Adriana, 156n24
Van Rompay, Lucas, 252n69
Vermeule, Adrian, 38, 40–42, 49
Vermurlen, Brad, 127n67
Vessey, Mark, 63n33
Vian, Giovanni, 257n13
Vicini, Andrea, 48n49

Wallace, Ruth A., 167n9
Ward, Leo, 277
Waytz, Adam, 297n5
Weigel, George, 22n3, 45–46, 48, 49
Weil, Simone, 309
Wheeler, Rachel, 147n1
White, John, 276
Whitesides, John, 297n6
Wilkerson, Isabel, 186–87, 188
Wilson, Edward O., 74n4
Wilson, Philip, 113n13

Winters, Michael Sean, 26n15
Wintle, Michael, 242–43
Wolf, Hubert, 59n18, 60n23, 68n48
Wood, Diana, 70n56
Wood, Susan K., 126n64
Woods, Alan, 50nn55–57
Wynter, Sylvia, 186
Wyszyński, Stefan, 214

Yamada, Nozomu, 65n41

Yancy, George, 307–8
Young, Guilford, 117–18
Young, Liane L., 297n5

Zagano, Phyllis, 169, 172–73, 174
Zielinski, Martin A., 255n8
Zollner, Hans, 133n10
Zurara, Gomes Eanes de, 183–84, 197
Zwartz, Barney, 114nn16–17, 119n35

www.ingramcontent.com/pod-product-compliance
Ingram Content Group UK Ltd.
Pitfield, Milton Keynes, MK11 3LW, UK
UKHW042344020625
459219UK00006B/234